Gendered Domains

Gendered Domains

Rethinking Public and Private in Women's History

EDITED BY

DOROTHY O. HELLY

AND

SUSAN M. REVERBY

ESSAYS FROM THE
SEVENTH BERKSHIRE CONFERENCE
ON THE HISTORY OF WOMEN

Cornell University Press

ITHACA AND LONDON

For information, address Cornell University Press, 124 Roberts Place, Ithaca, New York 14850.

First published 1992 by Cornell University Press.

International Standard Book Number 0-8014-2444-5 (cloth)
International Standard Book Number 0-8014-9702-7 (paper)
Library of Congress Catalog Card Number 91-55561
Printed in the United States of America
Librarians: Library of Congress cataloging information appears on the last page of the book.

♾ The paper in this book meets the minimum requirements of the American National Standard for Information Sciences—Permanence of Paper for Printed Library Materials, ANSI Z39.48-1984.

Contents

Illustrations

Preface

Nannerl O. Keohane

The Berkshire Conference at Wellesley College in June 1987 was the seventh in an illustrious series that has grown in size and scholarly accomplishment over the years. The conferences provide opportunities for the exchanges of ideas and creative stimulation which are the lifeblood of scholarship in any field. They are also an eagerly awaited opportunity for the renewal of friendships and professional ties.

Scholarship in the history of women, like scholarship about women in every field, was not easily accepted by the established gatekeepers of the discipline. The Berkshire conferences have helped solidify the place of historical inquiry centering on women's experiences. Participants in earlier conferences shared the sense of being a small, beleaguered band; in recent years this feeling has been supplanted by an awareness of increasing power and influence as a rapidly growing number of scholars take women's history as a major focus of their work.

Wellesley College was proud to welcome the Seventh Berkshire Conference, seeing a happy consonance between its purposes and the college's ideals. The dedication to scholarship by, for, and about women has been central in Wellesley's history, reaching back to the ardently feminist ideals of the founders of the college. Our burgeoning women's studies program, our strong offerings in women's history, and the varied work of our Center for Research on Women provided an auspicious setting for welcoming more than two thousand kindred spirits to our campus.

For all those who have taught and done research in any aspect of scholarship on women, the theme of the Seventh "Berks" was especially auspicious, too. In every field of the social sciences, the dichotomy of "public/private" has long dominated scholarly discourse. We have tended to take for granted in our scholarly work, as we have in ordinary conversation, a separation of our lives into two distinct categories, clearly marked as "public" or "private." When we try to probe into what we actually *mean* by these terms, however, we discover complexity. As with many common binary concepts, the apparent clarity of the distinction dissolves under analysis.

Which aspects of our lives are private, and which are public? Among the examples that come to mind, voting is a public act, walking along an isolated beach is private. Yet we speak of entering "the privacy of the voting booth" to cast our ballots; and isolated beaches are accessible only in states where the laws consider beaches public rather than private land. Running for political office is public; making love in one's own bedroom, private. Yet the private lives of political candidates these days are very much a topic for public scrutiny, and lovemaking is recurrently subject to public regulation about the appropriate choice of partners, contraception or abortion, and the control of AIDS.

The "public" is sometimes associated with government, sometimes with aspects of life that are open and accessible rather than hidden, sometimes with aspects that pertain to everyone or large groups of people rather than to only a few. The "private" is sometimes associated with the family or the home, sometimes with solitariness or the single individual, sometimes with certain human activities such as sex or excretion. Despite these disparate meanings, we blithely and incessantly use the distinction in our ordinary discourse.

Some of the burden of responsibility for this commonplace usage must be borne by the long line of political theorists, beginning with the ancient Greeks, whose works have influenced our commonplace usages more than we often realize. These philosophers, in defining an area of government or state or common life, have organized many of their most powerful insights around some dichotomy between affairs that are common or public and those that pertain to domestic or individual affairs. Thus the distinction between recognizably public and private areas of human life has been fundamental to a good deal of the political theory written in the West, especially by liberal political thinkers concerned to protect some parts of life from government intrusion.

One significant aspect of this familiar theoretical dichotomy has been generally ignored by such thinkers until recently. "Public" and "private" have often had very different implications for the lives of women from those they have for the lives of men. By pointing out this radical asymmetry, feminist analysis has shed new light on the old dichotomy. Some of the most important insights in feminist social analysis, particularly in anthropology, have come from the recognition of this distinction across cultures and the particular association of women with "private" or domestic pursuits. According to this view, private pursuits absorb the whole or a very large part of the lives of women in most societies, whereas men spend relatively little of their time in private life and have opportunities often denied to women to exercise their skills outside the sphere of home and family.

Some feminist scholars in the 1970s built a promising theory about gender difference around our public/private dichotomy. These scholars argued that because women are almost universally associated with domestic activities such as child rearing and homemaking, they are persistently excluded from the more public areas of life such as government and war, and for that reason, women's activities are often accorded less value than those of men who engage in these public activities.

More recently, however, feminist theorists have questioned the universality and usefulness of the public/private distinction. Such theorists contend that the dichotomy mystifies or misleads us into thinking of life in two separate boxes and makes it easy to assume that each of us fits more naturally into one box or the other, according to our sex. The most familiar slogan of contemporary feminism, "the personal is political," subverts the public/private separation by denying that it operates as it is usually supposed to do. Feminists who use this slogan see that our private lives are shaped by political realities, that the same "power dynamics" operate in the home and the workplace. This form of reconstruing our ordinary domestic relationships provides the basic insight around which much of the most fruitful contemporary feminist theory has been constructed.

In the past few years, scholars from many fields have been developing these insights with increasing sophistication and with far-reaching implications for our understanding of human lives. It is against this background that the essays in this volume from the Seventh Berkshire Conference should be read. Anthropologists, students of literature, sociologists, economists, and psychologists have been deconstructing the dichotomy from several vantage points. The contribution of historians is especially important to this work. Theorists in other areas of social science have too often taken for granted that the lives of ordinary men and women across cultures and historical eras conform neatly to the familiar dichotomous categories that we use for our analyses. Our colleagues in history remind us that the lives of the men and women they study are far more complex than such a clear dichotomy would suggest. They also show that the persistent assumption that life is divided neatly into these two categories can have powerful implications for people's lives, particularly the lives of women. And they suggest that the dialectical tension between the "individual" and the "political community," "family" and "state," "private" and "public" may reflect enduring forms of human need and purpose, even though the meanings of these familiar terms change continually across diverse cultures, lives, and histories. The papers in this volume are an essential contribution to this contemporary rethinking of an ancient dichotomy.

Acknowledgments

The final task, or privilege, of cochairing a Berkshire Conference on the History of Women is the opportunity to edit a volume of papers. Once recovered from the actual event in June 1987, we considered the most appropriate way of proceeding with this work. Given the importance of the conference's theme—Beyond the Public/Private Dichotomy: Reassessing Women's Place in History—we thought it crucial that the volume distill and illustrate the multiple meanings that historians were giving to the concept of separate spheres. We wrote to all those who gave presentations at the conference and asked them to send us their papers if they were relevant to our theme. We received over two hundred submissions. The essays in this volume reflect our effort to select the papers from the Seventh Berkshire Conference that represent the widest range of contexts and complexities of historians' use of gendered separate spheres. We are grateful to all those who sent their papers, and we regret both that we were not able to publish more of them and that our criteria limited the historical range that could be included.

In completing the book, we have incurred the usual intellectual and personal debts. We appreciate the goodwill of our contributors, who responded with unusual promptness to our numerous requests. Peter Agree, our editor at Cornell University Press, was an early enthusiast of this volume. The Press's readers supplied perceptive comments to us and the contributors, while the copy editor, Trudie Calvert, production editor, Joanne Hindman, and production manager, Richard Rosenbaum, did all their work with professional timeliness.

We are particularly grateful to Helen Callaway, Harry Marks, Sonya Michel, Susan Porter, Lise Vogel, and the Press's reviewers for their comments on our introduction. Nancy Hewitt's perceptive comments and her editorial prowess helped to sharpen our concepts and our writing, even if she destroyed many of our favorite, and overused, metaphors.

Both Hunter College and Wellesley College gave us released time in the year preceding the conference. The Women's Studies secretaries, Marilynn Madzar and Margaret Centamore at Wellesley, Ayna Soskin at Hunter, and numerous work-study students, including Jamie Lehman, Cathy Roberts-Gersh, Paige Gerling, and Ann Rowland, did much to make the conference happen. Our local arrangements director, Jean Proctor, remained calm and in control in the face of numerous difficulties and was a model of administrative finesse. The Bunting Institute at Radcliffe College provided Susan Reverby with a haven in the year following the conference. Wellesley College Faculty Research Awards supported a professional indexer.

We appreciate the opportunity the Berkshire Conference of Women Historians gave us to show that a planned intellectual partnership can prove fruitful. To our long-suffering but always caring families, who wondered when we were ever going to finish this volume—Walter Helly, Randi Helly, Tim Sieber, Mariah Sieber, and Micah Sieber—we publicly acknowledge our private debt. We are acutely aware that the boundaries between public and private are more than semipermeable. We dedicate this volume to the upcoming generation of historians in the hope that they will better understand some of the debates that framed the use of the concept of gendered spheres and will join with us in continuing to build upon a rich historical legacy for a more meaningful past.

DOROTHY O. HELLY
New York, New York

SUSAN M. REVERBY
Wellesley, Massachusetts

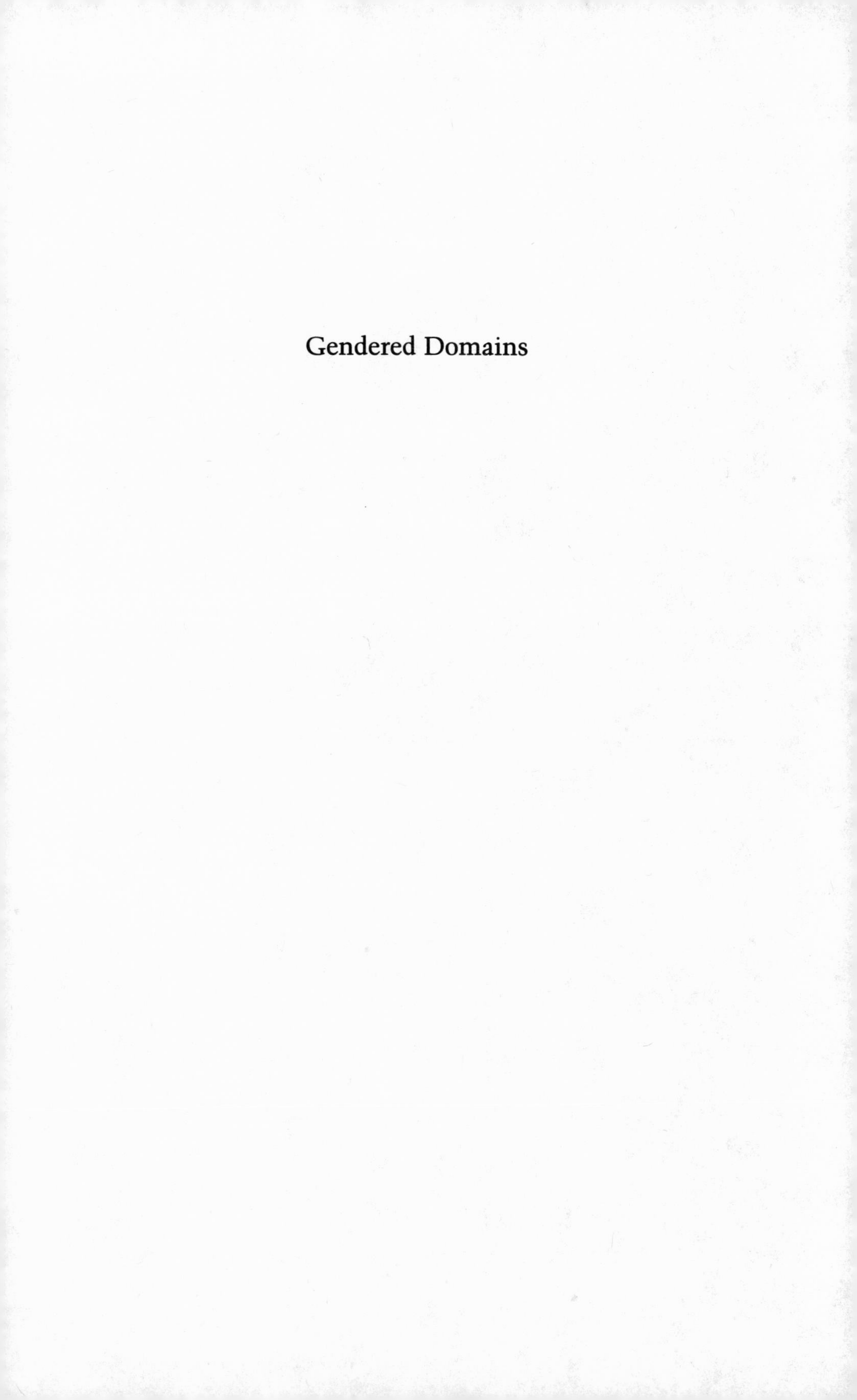

Gendered Domains

INTRODUCTION

Converging on History

Susan M. Reverby and Dorothy O. Helly

In the contemporary search for meanings and contexts, history matters. How it matters and how universal its explanations are remain problematized.[1] As recently as 1989, one feminist historian argued that "neither feminist activists nor feminist scholars in other disciplines are paying much attention to history." In the last decade, she charged, the lead history once took in feminist scholarship has been lost to literary criticism.[2] Although fashions change in academic circles, we are convinced that women's history has not become the scholar's version of an old-fashioned pillbox hat and white gloves. We do agree that historians of women who identify themselves as feminists run the danger of focusing on the struggles that institutionalization in the academy requires, consequently losing sight of their role as educated critics of the forces leading to women's oppression.[3] This book, a selection of essays from the Seventh Berkshire Conference on the History of Women, serves as a guide to the varying ways the oppression of women has been encoded or disguised by our employment of the concept of divided spheres. Our introduction examines

[1] For a pertinent discussion for women's history, see "Forum: Beyond Dichotomies," esp. Tani Barlow, "Asian Perspective," *Gender and History* 1 (Autumn 1989): 291–329.

[2] Judith M. Bennett, "Feminism and History," *Gender and History* 1 (Autumn 1989): 255–56. See a similar argument by Alice Kessler-Harris in her keynote address for the Seventh Berkshire Conference in this volume.

[3] Bennett, "Feminism and History," p. 256. Just as Bennett reminds us that not all women's historians are feminist historians, Sharon Sievers argues that not all women's history is the history of feminism. See "Dialogue: Six (or more) Feminists in Search of a Historian," *Journal of Women's History* 1 (Fall 1989): 134–46; see also Karen Offen, "Defining Feminism: A Comparative Historical Approach," *Signs* 14 (Autumn 1988): 119–57.

some of the scholarly debates surrounding a gendered public/private dichotomy as an idea and an ideology, suggesting the ways a convergence on history is central to understanding these debates.

It seems fitting that the editors for a book that questions the historical meanings and relevance of the boundaries between public and private were originally strangers to each other, matched under the carved lintel of a dignified Smith College doorway. Our partnership came about because, while attending the Sixth Berkshire Conference on the History of Women at Smith College in 1984, we were asked to cochair the Seventh "Berks" at Wellesley College in 1987. All we knew about each other was that we were both directors of women's studies programs. Our similar intellectual interests proved vital to our developing relationship. Playing with ideas for the theme of the seventh conference, we readily agreed that one of the key questions in the field was whether the "separate spheres" framework advanced by feminist anthropologists in the early 1970s remained useful. According to this theory, women's place everywhere was in part determined by the division of societies into public and private spheres and the cultural assignment of women to the private, men to the public.

In December 1984 we talked about ideas for the call for papers for the Seventh Berkshire Conference and agreed on the importance of pushing beyond the theory of a public/private framework. Aware that the idea of a separate women's culture had gained currency in the 1970s, we also knew that there were serious questions about its use as a universal analytical framework for women's history.[4] It seemed a good time to think more about those instances when a public/private framework might be imposing a structure on history that obscured rather than revealed the past. Was it possible that the theory we believed had led us into such useful paths of inquiry the decade before might itself be creating barriers to understanding the past? We talked about the relevance of Michelle Rosaldo's work, particularly her article in *Signs* that questioned the separate spheres dichotomy she had helped to create, and our sense of personal loss at her death, although neither of us had actually met her.[5] We laughed at our self-

[4] Although there was much interest in separate women's cultures, this view of writing women's history was never completely hegemonic. See, for example, Ellen DuBois et al., "Symposium: Politic and Culture in Women's History," *Feminist Studies* 6 (Winter 1980): 26–64; Gerda Lerner, "Reconceptualizing Differences among Women," *Journal of Women's History* 1 (Winter 1990): 106–22; Lise Vogel, "Telling Tales: Historians of Our Own Lives," *Journal of Women's History* 2 (Winter 1991): 89–101. As Vogel noted, there has been a tendency to produce a "triumphalist narrative" that assumes that ideas of women's culture and women's sphere overwhelmed all other historical points of view in the writing of women's history by the 1970s, while evidence of the diversity that did exist has been less well remembered.

[5] Michelle Rosaldo, "The Use and Abuse of Anthropology: Reflections on Feminism and Cross-Cultural Understanding." *Signs* 5 (Spring 1980): 389–417.

consciousness at needing to translate the women's studies language of our conversation into the more traditionally historical idiom. In the process, *spheres* became *realms* and *separateness* switched to *dichotomy.*

We wanted to frame a call for papers that would encourage historians of women to raise questions about both the existence and the permeability of boundaries between "the public" and "the private." We drew on our understanding of differences that came from our studies, teaching, and political work around issues of class, ethnicity, sexuality, and race as well as gender. We knew that the language of separate spheres set up a binary framework that would need to be broken by rethinking some of the assumptions of the last decade. We needed to remember one of the earliest insights from the second wave of American feminism and women's history: that gender was never the only relevant identity or analytic category.[6]

Out of our exchange came the wording of the call for papers for the Seventh Berkshire Conference on Women's History and the title of the conference, "Beyond the Public/Private Dichotomy: Reassessing Women's Place in History." The call explicitly encouraged "sessions that explore how women's consciousness and political activities reflect the links between the public and private realms." Aware that issues focusing on difference had helped to stimulate this reevaluation of theory, we encouraged "panels that compare the experience of women in different countries, and of different races, classes, ages, ethnicities, and sexual identities."

We were exposing the undercurrent of critique which had emerged alongside the spheres argument. We were trying to use the setting of the Berkshire Conference to establish the critical importance of history, and thus contextualized meanings, in the swirling debates on this issue within women's studies and to move forward the analysis within women's history as well. In rethinking the intellectual history of separate spheres, we have to remember just how provocative historians and scholars in women's studies found that original conceptualization in the mid-1970s. If the second wave of the American women's movement has started a fire by declaring that "the personal was political," the academic conflagration was set off by two anthologies, edited by

[6] Because of the media and political power of liberal feminism, it is often forgotten that issues of race, ethnicity, class, and sexual preference differences were discussed early in the women's movement. See, for examples, *Sisterhood Is Powerful,* ed. Robin Morgan (New York, 1970), and *Liberation Now!* ed. Madeline Belkin and Deborah Babcox (New York, 1970). On the more academic side, see *America's Working Women: A Documentary History* ed. Rosalyn Baxandall, Linda Gordon, and Susan Reverby (New York, 1976), and *Black Women in White America: A Documentary History,* ed. Gerda Lerner (New York, 1972). For an overview see Vogel, "Telling Tales."

feminist anthropologists. In *Woman, Culture, and Society* (1974), Michelle Rosaldo proposed that

> an opposition between "domestic" and "public" provides the basis of a structural framework necessary to identify and explore the place of male and female in psychological, cultural, social, and economic aspects of human life. . . . Though this opposition will be more or less salient in different social and ideological systems, it does provide a universal framework for conceptualizing the activities of the sexes. The opposition does not determine cultural stereotypes or asymmetries in the evaluations of the sexes, but rather underlies them, to support a very general (and, for women, often demeaning) identification of women with domestic life and of men with public life.[7]

Rosaldo concluded that "women seem to be oppressed or lacking in value and status to the extent that they are confined to domestic activities, cut off from other women and from the social world of men."[8]

The excitement stirred by this volume was long-lasting. It contained the first formulations of important theoretical work by, among others, Nancy Chodorow, Jane Collier, Louise Lamphere, Sherry Ortner, Karen Sacks, Peggy Sanday, and Nancy Tanner. Their essays raised new issues about family structure and the formulation of a "feminine personality," the ideological identification of women and nature, and how women as social actors affected male politics. Some authors demonstrated that the domestic world had a power structure, focusing readers on the nature of "matrifocality" and on the circumstances that surrounded female status in the public domain.[9] One of the most provocative articles was by Sherry Ortner: "Is Female to Male as Nature Is to Culture?"[10] In contemplating the universal devaluation of women, despite great variation in their social roles across cultures, Ortner posited that the linkage of women (and their child-caring role) to domestic pursuits and men to "higher level, integrative, universalistic sorts of concerns" led to identification of all women with "natural" nurturing efforts and all men with "finer and higher aspects of human thought," that is, with created culture.[11] The spheres argument introduced by Rosaldo was thus meshed with the nature/culture analysis by Ortner to form a powerful grid by which feminist scholars reinspected the world and its past.

[7] Michelle Rosaldo, "A Theoretical Overview," in *Woman, Culture, and Society,* ed. Michelle Rosaldo and Louise Lamphere (Stanford, 1974), pp. 23–24.

[8] Ibid., p. 41.

[9] The volume also contained major feminist reexaminations of Marxist theory and nineteenth-century reconstructions of the myths of matriarchy.

[10] Sherry Ortner, "Is Female to Male as Nature Is to Culture?" in *Woman, Culture, and Society,* ed. Rosaldo and Lamphere, pp. 67–87.

[11] See Linda Nicholson, *Gender and History: The Limits of Social Theory in the Age of the Family* (New York, 1986), pp. 73–75.

Rayna Reiter [Rapp], in the introduction to her edited collection, *Toward an Anthropology of Women* (1975), focused on the implications of this analysis. Feminist anthropologists, in contrast to their predecessors, she declared, were not content to argue from biology to culture but wanted to know why various societies had used women's role in reproduction to rationalize the earliest forms of the division of labor that bolstered male supremacy.[12] Thus, she argued, if separate spheres existed, they were socially constructed and susceptible to change.

The volume contained the now classic essay by Gayle Rubin, "The Traffic in Women: Notes on the 'Political Economy' of Sex." Rubin demonstrated that theories about incest, gift exchanges, psychosexual development, and an inevitable gender division of labor were all based on the explanatory power of viewing the sexes as dichotomous and their spheres as "naturally" different. Her critique of these theories pointed the way to rethinking both the nature of these arguments and the issue of essential difference, not only in terms of the bipolarity of the spheres assigned to women and men but also of the cultural construction of gender. Introducing the term *sex/gender system,* Rubin provided a new way to describe both the socially constructed and biologically functional nature of the bipolarities identified as "women" and "men." Using this concept, her essay demonstrated how theories central to modern social science depended on the assumption that the sexes were "fundamentally" different. From this it followed that "public" men were agents subject to historical changes over time, while "private" women were not change agents, but tokens (Lévi-Strauss), symbolic others (Freud), property (Marx), or gifts (Mauss) exchanged by men in search of autonomy, selfhood, power, and status.

In her essay "Men and Women in the South of France: Public and Private Domains," Reiter supplied an analysis of the contradictions between apparent separate spheres and actual social and economic connectedness. In modern industrial capitalist states, she declared, although the privatized kinship realm was defined as women's work,

> the domestic realm produces and sustains the one resource most necessary to all extractive classes: people. Kin groups can be seen as the first colonized structures within emergent states, for their goods and personnel are expropriated by a public authority over which they have little control. It is women's labor that underwrites the capacities of families to produce these resources. Yet this labor is socially unrecognized or accorded a subordinate status while power and prestige are vested in the public domain, which is increasingly controlled by a class of men.[13]

[12] *Toward an Anthropology of Women,* ed. Rayna Reiter [Rapp] (New York, 1975), pp. 11–12.

[13] Ibid., pp. 280–82.

If history had taught us, as Leonore Davidoff has argued, to see "rational man at the center and embodied woman at the periphery," feminist anthropologists were decentering the male experience and historicizing what had appeared as women's merely biological and unchanging worlds.[14] For the acceptance of spheres gave intellectual permission to explore women's lives in the so-called private sphere, validating the difference from the male experience without rendering it lesser. Furthermore, it allowed historians to explore the realms of women's experiences without seeming to accept a biologically essentialist or culturally determinist model.

While the anthropologists appeared to be creating universal theory, American historians of women, stimulated by the same political atmosphere, began to focus much of their work on what came to be called "women's culture." A pathbreaking array of studies, focused primarily on white middle- and working-class women, examined women's emotional bonds, work cultures, visiting patterns, and reform activities.[15]

However dazzling the model appeared, scholars almost immediately begin to query its power and universality. Many noted that the idea of separate public or private domains hardly existed in other societies, foreshadowing historians' later argument that the very notion of a division between public and private was historically created.[16] Similarly, the emptiness of public and private as categories became an important refrain among those concerned with illuminating the specificities of gender, culture, class, race, ethnicity, sexuality, and historical time. As evidence mounted that the public/private dichotomy could obscure as well as reveal how women and men actually lived their lives, the voices proclaiming the role of this dichotomy as ideology became more insistent.[17] Historians of the lives of white working-class women and

[14] Leonore Davidoff, "Beyond the Public/Private: Thoughts on Feminist History in the 1990s," paper delivered at Harvard University, Center for European Studies, November 27, 1990.

[15] The list of these studies is extremely long and includes such critical works as Carroll Smith-Rosenberg, "The Female World of Love and Ritual," *Signs* 1 (Autumn 1975): 1–30, and Nancy Cott, *The Bonds of Womanhood: "Woman's Sphere" in New England, 1790–1835* (New Haven, 1977). For an overview of these studies see Linda Kerber, "Separate Spheres, Female Worlds, Woman's Place: The Rhetoric of Women's History," *Journal of American History* 75 (June 1988): 9–39.

[16] The earliest formulation of this argument predated the appearance of the anthologies and was articulated most clearly by Eleanor Leacock in her Introduction to *Origin of the Family, Private Property and the State* by Friedrich Engels (New York, 1972). See also Leacock, *Myths of Male Dominance* (New York, 1981).

[17] This section is a partial summary of the arguments in the Introduction to *Beyond the Public/Domestic Dichotomy: Contemporary Perspectives on Women's Public Lives*, ed. Janet Sharistanian (Westport, Conn., 1986), and *Gender, Ideology, and Action: Historical Perspectives on Women's Public Lives*, ed. Sharistanian (Westport, Conn., 1987). Sharistanian provides excellent bibliographies. See also Sharon W. Tiffany,

African-American women in particular began to query the relevance of a seemingly middle and "middling class" formulation for all women.[18]

By 1980, in one of her last, and perhaps ultimately best-known, pieces, and in the face of widespread debate over the concept of public and private, Rosaldo rethought her own powerful and suggestive position. Reminding her readers of the dangers in the search for universal meanings, she claimed:

> It now appears to me that woman's place in human social life is not in any direct sense a product of the things she does (or even less a function of what, biologically, she is) but of the meaning her activities acquire through concrete social interactions. And the significances women assign to the activities of their lives are things that we can only grasp through an analysis of the relationships that women forge, the social contexts they (along with men) create—and within which they are defined.[19]

Rosaldo's last warning—echoed in the writings of other feminist scholars—cautioned us about the necessity to historicize our notions of public and private and to link them to other hierarchies of power and social relations.[20] In summarizing what we had learned from the critiques of Rosaldo's and Ortner's earlier work, philosopher Linda Nicholson noted succinctly:

> We need to think about gender and female devaluation historically. There has been a tendency among feminist theorists to employ a causal model of analyzing the origins of such devaluation. By translating questions of origins into questions of causes, the tendency has been to search for cross-cultural factors generating a supposedly cross-cultural phenomenon. But as female devaluation is not one fact but many, interlinked with specificities of culture, so also should we abandon the search for one cross-cultural cause.[21]

"Woman, Power and the Anthropology of Politics: A Review," *International Journal of Women's Studies* 2 (September–October 1979): 430–42; Susan Carol Rogers, "Woman's Place: A Critical Review of Anthropological Theory," *Comparative Studies in Society and History* 20 (January 1978): 123–62; Louise A. Tilly, "The Social Sciences and the Study of Women," ibid., 163–80; Rosette C. Lamont et al., eds., "Women: The Dialectic of Public and Private Spaces," special issue of *Centerpoint: A Journal of Interdisciplinary Studies* 3 (Fall–Spring 1980); *Women United, Women Divided,* ed. Patricia Caplan and Janet M. Bujra (London, 1978).

[18] For an overview of these studies, see Lerner, "Reconceptualizing Differences among Women," pp. 106–22, and Elizabeth Fox-Genovese, "Socialist-Feminist American Women's History," *Journal of Women's History* 1 (Winter 1990): 181–210.

[19] Rosaldo, "The Use and Abuse of Anthropology," p. 400.

[20] For a similar reading of Rosaldo, see Carole Pateman, "Feminist Critiques of the Public/Private Dichotomy," in *Feminism and Equality,* ed. Anne Phillips (New York, 1987), p. 112.

[21] Nicholson, *Gender and History,* p. 102.

In rethinking her position, Rosaldo also argued that the assumption that societies could be analyzed in terms of gendered public and private spheres paralleled time-honored frameworks within Western political and social science theory.[22] Other feminist political theorists, philosophers, and historians of political thought, she noted, were providing detailed arguments to explain the existence and consequences of this theoretical embeddedness. The realization that our own best analytic model for critique—the concept of gendered and divided spheres—might merely be a reflection of long-standing categories within the minds of our intellectual oppressors served as an ironic and disturbing comment on the entire feminist scholarly enterprise.[23]

The need to understand how the categories had been created and used historically in political theory and social practice became clearer, even as critiques (coming mainly from political theorists and philosophers) illuminated divided allegiances within the feminist camp. Susan Moller Okin's *Women in Western Political Thought* (1979), for example, reexamined Plato, Aristotle, Rousseau, and Mill to understand how their conceptions of women revealed their beliefs about the naturalness of the family and its separation from the *polis.* Okin's analysis compelled us to recognize that adding women back into the polity would require a rethinking of the basic political categories and, perforce, the dissolving of the false barrier between public and private.[24] Forces had been set in motion to "deconstruct" (in the general sense of this word) the traditional theorists as well as to reconstruct feminist conceptualizations.[25]

Some of this work was done by scholars focusing on historical critiques of the public/private dichotomy in modern liberal and Marxist theory.[26] As Carole Pateman and Zillah Eisenstein argued, liberal theorists needed to posit the separation between public and private

[22] Rosaldo, "The Use and Abuse of Anthropology," pp. 401–2.

[23] For an overview of the public and private in social theory, see *Public and Private in Social Life,* ed. S. I. Benn and G. F. Gaus (London, 1983).

[24] Susan Moller Okin, *Women in Western Political Thought* (Princeton, 1979). In *Public Man, Private Woman: Women in Social and Political Thought* (Princeton, 1981), Jean Bethke Elshtain sought to reveal, with a broader brushstroke and a different political focus than Okin, the public and private images in Western political theory and to connect them to a reconstructed feminist politics. For Elshtain, however, the argument became a thinly veiled attack on the liberal welfare state and a reconstituted separation of the public and the private realms in the guise of feminizing the state. See Judith Stacey, "The New Conservative Feminism," *Feminist Studies* 9 (Fall 1983): 559–84.

[25] *Discovering Reality: Feminist Perspectives on Epistemology, Metaphysics, Methodology, and Philosophy of Science,* ed. Sandra Harding and Merrill B. Hintikka (Boston, 1983), quoted in Seyla Benhabib and Drucilla Cornell, "Beyond the Politics of Gender," in *Feminism as Critique,* ed. Benhabib and Cornell, (Minneapolis, 1987), p. 1.

[26] This is not to suggest that the public/private dichotomy is an idea born with the Western liberal or Marxist theory; see Nannerl O. Keohane's preface in this volume.

realms to focus on the rights that men had as individuals.[27] In creating the notion of the separation of public and private, liberal theorists naturalized paternal power in the household, labeling it different from political power in the social or public realm. In doing so, they "forgot," as Pateman put it politely if ironically, to discuss domestic life and saw the division of public and private as merely aspects of civil society.[28] The "distorting effects," as Nannerl Keohane has labeled them, of such forgetting have been to limit political theorists' abilities to explain the world.[29] Feminist scholarship has focused therefore on examining the very creation of this dichotomy and the role gender plays in concealing the permeability of the boundaries.

Thus it was that many contemporary feminist theorists turned to historical evidence to make the case against forgetting and for placing the division between public and private in the realm of culture and politics, not nature. To buttress her argument about the political problems that the belief in gendered spheres created for liberalism, Carole Pateman used Ellen DuBois's analysis of the nineteenth-century American suffrage movement. She pointed especially to the risks for political stability inherent in the suffrage demand for a citizenship that bypassed women's place in the family. Similarly, Linda Nicholson argued that the emergence of both liberalism and Marxism—with their particular ideas about how to divide the public and the private—had to be understood historically against the changing relationships among the family, kinship systems, and the emerging state. In *Women and the Public Sphere in the Age of the French Revolution,* political scientist Joan Landes, building on the theoretical work by Jürgen Habermas, sought to understand the extent to which the emergence of bourgeois political life out of absolutism in eighteenth-century France depended upon the renaming of public space as male. "The structures of modern republican politics," she claimed, "can be construed as part

[27] Pateman, "Feminist Critiques," p. 105; Zillah Eisenstein, *The Radical Future of Liberal Feminism* (New York, 1981), p. 223. See also Anna Yeatman, "Gender and the Differentiation of Social Life into Public and Domestic Domains," *Social Analysis,* Special Issue Series, "Gender and Social Life," no. 15 (August 1984): 32–50; Catherine A. MacKinnon, "Privacy v. Equality: Beyond Roe v. Wade," in her *Feminism Unmodified: Discourses on Life and Law* (Cambridge, Mass., 1987), pp. 93–102.

[28] Pateman, "Feminist Critiques," p. 107. See also a discussion of this point in Nancy Fraser, "The French Derrideans: Politizicing Deconstruction or Deconstructing the Political?" in her *Unruly Practices: Power, Discourse and Gender in Contemporary Social Theory* (Minneapolis, 1989), pp. 69–92.

[29] Nannerl Keohane, "Speaking from Silence: Women and the Science of Politics," *Soundings: An Interdisciplinary Journal* 44 (Winter 1981): 432. It was indeed this forgetting that Mary Astell and Mary Wollstonecraft so deeply railed against when they argued for the personhood of women and was the reason Wollstonecraft argued for the necessity of transforming the private realm to make good on liberalism's promise in the public realm.

of an elaborate defense against women's power and public presence."[30]

The feminist critique of the public/private was particularly central to the debates among socialist feminists, who sought to move beyond what appeared to be the traditional Marxist answer to "the Woman Question," namely the entrance of women into the paid labor force. They tried to "marry" theories of sexuality, reproduction, and patriarchy from radical feminism to theories explaining class and production from Marxism.[31] The ensuing debates moved from placing what was labeled "domestic labor" into a theory of social reproduction, to theories on the division of labor. Various kinds of historical evidence were used and abused to make the case for monocausality.[32]

Efforts to explain women's oppression in more sophisticated and dialectical ways led to the problem of "dual systems theory," the mechanical linking of what sociologist Lise Vogel has labeled the "ahistorical and psychologistic origins" of the radical feminist concept of patriarchy and the "economic reductionism and functionalism" of Marxism. As philosopher Iris Young argued, dual systems theories

[30] Pateman, "Feminist Critiques," p. 114; Ellen DuBois, "The Radicalism of the Woman Suffrage Movement," *Feminist Studies* 3 (Fall 1975): 63–71; Nicholson, *Gender and History,* passim, esp. pp. 201–8; Joan Landes, *Women and the Public Sphere in the Age of the French Revolution* (Ithaca, 1988), p. 203; see also her "Women and the Public Sphere: A Modern Perspective," *Social Analysis,* Special Issue Series "Gender and Social Life," no. 15 (August 1984): 20–31. For an explanation, in English, of Habermas's idea of the public sphere see Peter Uwe Hohendahl, *The Institution of Criticism* (Ithaca, 1982), pp. 242–80; and Geoff Eley, "Nations, Publics, and Political Cultures: Placing Habermas in the 19th Century," paper presented at the Conference on Habermas and the Public Sphere, Program in Social Theory and Cross-Cultural Studies, University of North Carolina, September 1989. See also Jürgen Habermas, *The Structural Transformation of the Public Sphere* (Cambridge, Mass., 1989).

One historian critic of Landes's work has charged that the change Landes notes is more the "emergence of a new *construction* of gender," rationalized by the emerging social sciences, rather than the emergence of gender itself as a relevant category. See Karen Offen, "The Use and Abuse of History," *Women's Review of Books* 6 (April 1989): 15–16. Offen's review also examines a philosopher's use of historical evidence from nineteenth-century British suffrage efforts, see ibid. and Denise Riley, *"Am I That Name?" Feminism and the Category of "Women" in History* (Minneapolis, 1988). Eley gives a more positive reading of Landes's work in his "Nations, Publics, and Political Cultures," pp. 11–14.

[31] There is an enormous literature on this topic. See, as a beginning, Eli Zaretsky, *Capitalism, the Family, and Personal Life* (New York, 1976); Lise Vogel, *Marxism and the Oppression of Women* (New Brunswick, 1983; Heidi Hartmann, "The Unhappy Marriage of Marxism and Feminism: Towards a More Progressive Union," *Capital and Class* 8 (Summer 1979): 1–33; *Women and Revolution: A Discussion of the Unhappy Marriage of Marxism and Feminism,* ed. Lydia Sargent (Boston, 1981); *Capitalist Patriarchy and the Case for Socialist Feminism,* ed. Zillah Eisenstein (New York, 1979); and Fraser, *Unruly Practices.*

[32] As a guide to these debates with an excellent bibliography we have relied on Lise Vogel, "Feminist Scholarship: The Impact of Marxism," in *The Left Academy,* vol. 3, ed. Bertell Ollman and Edward Vernoff (New York, 1986), pp. 1–34; see also Alison Jaggar, *Feminist Politics and Human Nature* (Totowa, N.J., 1983); and Fox-Genovese, "Socialist-Feminist American Women's History," pp. 181–210.

tended once again to locate women in the realm of the private and men in the realm of the economic/public.[33] The concern to be more synthetic and to theorize the family and its relationship to the wage and political system in more sophisticated ways often faltered in abstract disagreements over how to conceptualize the family. Surveying these debates, Vogel concluded, "The controversy cannot be settled in the abstract, however, for the issue is largely historical."[34] Nicholson agreed, echoing Rosaldo's final warning: only by historicizing the concepts of separate spheres could we learn how "connections . . . occurred in the very process of their separation" within Western liberalism and Marxist theory.[35]

Historicizing these concepts, of course, is not a simple task. As historian Karen Offen so bluntly put it, we run the danger of forgetting that "the historical record, however incomplete, is not a mere convenience store where one can drop by, day or night, to shop casually for facts that seem to illustrate an abstract line of reasoning." Nor, as Tani Barlow has written from the perspective of a historian of China, can we construct theories from a Eurocentric model and then look to area studies to prove their universality.[36]

The work of feminist historians informed, and was formed by, this larger interdisciplinary discussion. For example, both a reading of feminist anthropologists and an analysis of the material underpinnings of structural difference were central to Joan Kelly's thinking in her *Signs* article "The Social Relation of the Sexes: Methodological Implications of Women's History." Looking for a universal explanation, Kelly, following Friedrich Engels, saw the development of private property as the origin of women's loss of control over "property, products, and themselves as surplus increases." She concluded that the attachment of women to domestic work and the forms this took constituted one of the central problems confronting feminist anthropology and history, and she saw in property relations the basic determinant of the gender division of labor.[37]

33 Vogel, "Feminist Scholarship," p. 9, Iris Young; "Beyond the Unhappy Marriage: A Critique of Dual Systems Theory," in *Women and Revolution*, ed. Sargent, p. 49.

34 Vogel, "Feminist Scholarship," p. 14. By *historical*, Vogel is referring here to the actual impact of the family wage. But Linda Nicholson also notes that Marxist categories themselves are a function of theory development at a particular point in history: see *Gender and History*, p. 199.

35 Linda Nicholson, "Feminist Theory: The Private and the Public," in *Beyond Domination: New Perspectives on Women and Philosophy*, ed. Carol Gould (Totowa, N.J., 1984), p. 223.

36 Offen, "The Use and Abuse of History," p. 16; Barlow, "Asian Perspective," pp. 319–20.

37 Joan Kelly [-Gadol], "The Social Relation of the Sexes: Methodological Implications of Women's History," *Signs* 1 (Summer 1976): 809–23. Kelly first gave this paper at the Barnard College Conference on the Scholar and the Feminist II, April 1975.

If other historians did not always share Kelly's reliance on private property relations as the sine qua non determining the development of spheres, they nevertheless were equally drawn to the concept. According to Linda Kerber, the idea of separate spheres became "the figure of speech, the trope on which historians came to rely when they described women's part in American culture."[38] Indeed, it is not hyperbolic to suggest that it would have been difficult to read almost anything in American and European women's history for a decade and a half after the late 1960s without constantly finding the idea of separate spheres. Yet whether using or challenging the concept of spheres, historians were redefining the very nature of what counted as history.[39]

As with many overdetermined ideas, the implications of an argument based on separate spheres were seemingly endless and often undefined. Kerber has suggested that American historians applied this trope in a series of stages, first specifying the spheres themselves, then identifying them to understand "women's culture." Later, historians explored how a women's sphere was "constructed both for and by women," moving into seeing how " 'separate spheres' was a metaphor for complex power relations in social and economic contexts." In more recent analysis, Kerber concluded, historians have treated the spheres as literal physical spaces within which men and women operate differently. As Kerber so eloquently argued, however, "The language of separate spheres was vulnerable to sloppy use . . . [and] historians referred, often interchangeably, to an ideology *imposed on* women, a culture *created by* women, a set of boundaries *expected to be observed* by women."[40]

[38] Kerber, "Separate Spheres," p. 10 (see n. 15 above). This article serves as an excellent summary of the role of the spheres argument in the historiography of writing about American women's history.

[39] See Joan Wallach Scott, "Women's History" and "Gender: A Useful Category of Historical Analysis," in her *Gender and the Politics of History* (New York, 1988), pp. 15–52; Judith Allen, "Evidence and Silence: Feminism and the Limits of History," in *Feminist Challenges: Social and Political Theory,* ed. Carole Pateman and Elizabeth Gross (Sydney, 1966), pp. 173–89; Carroll Smith-Rosenberg, "Hearing Women's Words: A Feminist Reconstruction of History," in her *Disorderly Conduct* (New York, 1985), pp. 11–52.

For examples in European history see Patricia H. LaBalme, *Beyond Their Sex: Learned Women of the European Past* (New York, 1980); Bonnie G. Smith, *Ladies of the Leisure Class: The Bourgeoises of Northern France in the Nineteenth Century* (Princeton, 1981); Barbara Taylor, *Eve and the New Jerusalem: Socialism and Feminism in the Nineteenth Century* (London, 1983); and *When Biology Was Destiny: Women in Weimar and Nazi Germany,* ed. Renate Bridenthal, Atina Grossman, and Marion Kaplan (New York, 1984).

[40] Kerber, "Separate Spheres," pp. 9–39, quotation on p. 17. Further, as Kerber noted, the idea of separate spheres was primarily applied only to white and middling or middle-class women.

By the 1980s, feminist historians of European women refined and deepened our conceptualizing of separate spheres by examining its function as an ideology. At the 1981 Berkshire Conference, for example, Hilda Smith contended that the concept of citizenship in early modern England was tied to agency in the public sphere and qualities labeled "masculine virtues" by contemporary society.[41] Men's need to exclude women from a self-consciously constructed public arena, many historians began to argue, flowed conceptually in part from women's active role in that realm.[42] Other work on twentieth-century European women has examined the gendered notions of public space and its different use by women and men.[43]

The historical origins of the ideology of separate spheres in the English case were presented forcefully by Leonore Davidoff and Catherine Hall in *Family Fortunes: Men and Women of the English Middle Class, 1780–1850*.[44] These authors challenged the traditional accounts of class formation by examining the gendered patterns of class life. They looked for the ways "family" constituted "class," as well as vice versa, thus accounting for the importance of paternalism in the nineteenth-century language of class. They exposed the changing structures of social arrangements in the family and in networks of community associations. The results were new definitions of "manliness" and "womanliness," part of the developing ideology of separate spheres that at once prescribed appropriate gender behavior and claimed for it a "naturalness" that presumed inevitability. This ideol-

[41] Hilda Smith, "Masculinity as a Political Concept in English thought, 1600–1850." Smith is following this up with a book-length study.

[42] See Gay Gullikson's chapter in this volume. See also Darline Gay Levy and Harriet Branson Applewhite, "Responses to the Political Activism of Women of the People in Revolutionary Paris, 1789–93," paper presented at the Fifth Berkshire Conference on the History of Women, June 1981. By this time they had published a sourcebook: Darline Gay Levy, Harriet Branson Applewhite, and Mary Durham Johnson, *Women in Revolutionary Paris, 1789–1795: Selected Documents Translated with Notes and Commentary* (Urbana 1979). More recently they have edited an anthology: *Women and Politics in the Age of the Democratic Revolution* ed. Levy and Applewhite (Ann Arbor, 1990), and will soon publish *Gender and Citizenship in Revolutionary Paris* (Durham, N.C., forthcoming.)

[43] Temma Kaplan, "Women's Collective Action and Communal Organization," paper presented to the Columbia University Seminar on Women and Society, February 16, 1981. Kaplan incorporated this perspective in "Women and Communal Strikes in the Crisis of 1917–1922," in *Becoming Visible: Women in European History*, ed. Renate Bridenthal, Claudia Koonz, and Susan Stuard, 2d ed. (Boston, 1987), pp. 429–49. See also Temma Kaplan, *Red City, Blue Period: Social Movements in Picasso's Barcelona* (Berkeley, 1992).

[44] (London, 1987). Although the book appeared in 1987, the issues it explored were discussed in a series of earlier papers; see Catherine Hall, "The Early Formation of Victorian Domestic Ideology," and Leonore Davidoff, "The Separation of Home and Work? Landladies and Lodgers in Nineteenth and Twentieth Century England," both in *Fit Work for Women*, ed. Sandra Burman (London, 1979).

ogy spread upward and downward in the social scale in the next half-century, and ultimately played a critical role in shaping the conceptualization of the new social sciences developing at the end of the century.[45]

Exposure of the social construction of the separate spheres ideology was accompanied in the 1980s by widespread concern with differences within women's studies and the intellectual undermining of universalist gender theory. At the October 1979 Second Sex Conference held at New York University to reexamine Simone de Beauvoir's contributions to feminist thought, the political limitations of a universal model of women's oppression became apparent. In the words of poet and feminist theorist Audre Lorde, there could be no "discussion of feminist theory . . . without examining our many differences, and without a significant input from poor women, black and third-world women, and lesbians." As the political debate within women's studies raged over how to understand the linkages among race, class, ethnicity, sexuality, and gender, the weakness of the separate spheres model, which had always been recognized, became more obvious. Similarly, ongoing struggles over reproductive rights made clear the need to rethink the historical analysis of the division between public and private. As psychologist Aída Hurtado stated for contemporary theory (with obvious implications for history): "The American state has intervened constantly in the private lives and domestic arrangements of the working class. Women of Color have not had the benefit of the economic conditions that underlie the public/private distinction. . . . There is no such thing as a private sphere for people of Color except that which they manage to create and protect in an otherwise hostile environment."[46]

[45] Davidoff and Hall spelled out the focus of their initial investigation in writing *Family Fortunes: Men and Women of the English Middle Class, 1780–1950* (Chicago, 1987) at a session at the Eighth Berkshire Conference at Douglass College, June 9, 1990. At the session, Mary Ryan made parallel arguments for the middle class in the United States in the nineteenth century, and Yvonne Hirdman suggested the Swedish parallels for the 1930s. See also Mary Ryan, *The Cradle of the Middle Class: The Family in Oneida County, New York, 1790–1865* (New York, 1981).

[46] Audre Lorde, "The Master's Tools Will Never Dismantle the Master's House," in *This Bridge Called My Back: Writings by Radical Women of Color*, ed. Cherríe Moraga and Gloria Anzaldúa (New York, 1981), pp. 98–99; Aída Hurtado, "Relating to Privilege: Seduction and Rejection in the Subordination of White Women and Women of Color," *Signs* 14 (Summer 1989): 849. The lack of an extensive history of women of color, reproductive rights, and the public/private dichotomy became clear when historians (Susan Reverby included) participated in the writing of a brief in the *Webster v. Reproductive Health Services* case before the Supreme Court in 1989. See also Rosalind Petchesky, *Abortion and Woman's Choice*, rev. ed. (Boston, 1990).

See also *The Afro-American Woman: Struggles and Images*, ed. Sharon Harley and Rosalyn Terborg-Penn (Port Washington, N.Y., 1978); Darlene Clark Hine, *Black Women in White: Racial Conflict and Cooperation in the Nursing Profession, 1890–1950* (Bloomington, 1989); Jacqueline Jones, *Labor of Love, Labor of Sorrow* (New York, 1985);

Women's historians concerned with African-American women and the American South have been particularly sensitive to the impossibility of using a simple gender model. As Jacqueline Dowd Hall has maintained, this work "expose[s] the figurative nature of separate spheres" and therefore questions "the dualisms that have shaped our scholarship and our lives." Deborah Gray White demonstrated both the particular meanings and the limits attached to separate spheres in her study of slave women. And Darlene Clark Hine has argued that it is impossible to understand the historical migration of African-American women out of the South without understanding the connection of public and private that took the form of their "desire to achieve personal autonomy and to escape both from sexual exploitation from inside and outside of their families and from the rape and threat of rape by white as well as Black males."[47]

Furthermore, when historians of women in Africa, Asia, the Middle East, and Latin America examined the applicability of separate spheres to their particular contexts, the historical and cultural differences from the white Eurocentric model became evident. Historians found that definitions of public, private, community, and kin, which had specific ideological meanings in the United States and Europe, were not directly relevant. Examining these historic specificities both adds to the limitations of the spheres argument in the Euroamerican context and begins to provide nuances to what actually happens in areas defined as public and private that may help us create more complex and usable models.

Historians of both Japan and China, for example, have argued that the efforts to impose European and American beliefs about womanhood were often thwarted by the differing political economies and culture systems of these societies.[48] Other historians of Latin American women's lives have suggested that the model was either of little relevance or that the difference between ideological prescription and daily behavior was vast. The attempt to recreate the framework in terms of a *marianismo,* to parallel *machismo,* soon began to break down.[49]

Dolores Janiewski, *Sisterhood Denied: Race, Gender, and Class in a New South Community* (Philadelphia, 1985); *Unequal Sisters: A Multi-cultural Reader in U.S. Women's History,* ed. Ellen DuBois and Vicki Ruiz (New York, 1990).

[47] Jaqueline Dowd Hall, "Partial Truths," *Signs* 14 (Summer 1989): 907; Deborah Gray White, *Ar'n't I a Woman?: Female Slaves in the Plantation South* (New York, 1985); Darlene Clark Hine, "Rape and the Inner Lives of Black Women in the Middle West: Preliminary Thoughts on the Culture of Dissemblance," *Signs* 14 (Summer 1989): 914.

[48] Nancy Hewitt, "Sisterhood in International Perspective: Thoughts on Teaching Comparative Women's History," *Women's Studies Quarterly* 16 (Spring–Summer 1988): 22–31. We are grateful to Nancy Hewitt for her help in formulating this section.

[49] Personal communication from Asunción Lavrin; see her "Women, the Family and Social Change in Latin America," *World Affairs* 150 (Fall 1987): 108–28.

Historians studying African women added further complexities by examining women's power within kinship networks, trade, and agricultural work, which hindered any easy assumptions about the meaning of public and private in the Eurocentric sense. These works suggest, as Nancy Hewitt has argued, how important comparative historical work is to our sophisticated understanding of the categories that inform our analysis.[50]

Poststructuralist theory also poses important challenges to the theorizing and analysis that historians continue to do. Since poststructuralist theory is at its heart a critique of the language of dualisms, it has particular implications of how we handle the question of public and private as well as the historical creation of all gendered categories. The concerns advanced by the poststructuralists have been undertaken by many feminist writers, even if the language they continue to employ remains outside the poststructuralists' lexicon. Yet there is much we can learn from the nuanced historical examination of language and the analytic categories posed by poststructural analysis. For as Joan Scott has argued, a deconstructed understanding of gender leads us to the study of kinship and the polity, the public and the private, the permeability and relational aspects of all power and life.[51]

Before all women's historians disappear into the land of gender, language, binary oppositions, and representations, we need to remain ever mindful of the necessity of grounding our analysis in the material realities of class, race, sexuality, social structure, and politics. As the hot and heavy debates that have taken place within literary criticism and anthropology over this kind of theorizing begin to threaten the historical gates, we have the chance to avoid creating a new rigid and reigning paradigm.[52] Many of the sessions at the Eighth Berkshire Conference that we attended in 1990, just as this introduction was be-

[50] Hewitt, "Sisterhood in International Perspective." For an overview, with bibliography, see *Restoring Women to History: Teaching Packets for Integrating Women's History into Courses on Africa, Asia, Latin America and the Caribbean, and the Middle East*, rev. ed., ed. I. Berger et al. (Bloomington, 1990). Contributors to this volume are Iris Berger, Cheryl Johnson-Odim, Guity Nashat, Marysa Navarro, Barbara N. Ramusack, Virginia Sánchez Korrol, Sharon Sievers, Margaret Strobel, Judith Tucker, and E. Frances White.

[51] Scott, "Gender," pp. 41–50.

[52] See Linda Alcoff, "Cultural Feminism versus Post-Structuralism: The Identity Crisis in Feminist Theory," *Signs* 13 (Spring 1988): 405–36; Barbara Christian, "The Race for Theory," *Feminist Studies* 14 (Spring 1988): 67–79; Frances E. Mascia-Lees, Patricia Sharpe, and Colleen Ballerino Cohen, "The Postmodernist Turn in Anthropology: Cautions from a Feminist Perspective," *Signs* 15 (Autumn 1989): 7–33; Fraser, *Unruly Practices*; Scott, *Gender and the Politics of History*; Claudia Koontz, "Post Scripts," *Women's Review of Books* 6 (January 1989): 19–20; Vogel, "Telling Tales"; Judith Bennett, Nancy Hewitt, Lyndal Roper, Irene Silverblatt and Deborah White, "Roundtable: What Should Women's History be Doing?" Eighth Berkshire Conference on the History of Women, Douglass College, June 9, 1990.

ing completed, give us great hope that an openness to debate and a foreclosing on premature orthodoxy in our field is possible. We agree with Jacqueline Dowd Hall, who has called "for a historical practice that turns on partiality, that is self-conscious about perspective, that releases multiple voices, rather than competing orthodoxies, and that, above all, nurtures an 'internally differing but united political community.' "[53] We offer this book and its essays as a beginning step toward that historical practice.

In this volume, multiple voices speak to the meanings and usefulness of the analytic conception of gendered separate spheres. In the first section, the essays reexamine the definition of public and private in situations that appear to be exemplars of separate spheres, only to yield a far more complex history. In the case of the cloistered nuns of northern France in the medieval period, Penelope Johnson describes enclosure in the nunnery as the physical embodiment of the nuns' private world as well as the symbolic representation of their divorce from the public sphere. Yet in this construction of meaning the private is neither familial nor domestic and the contrasting public embraces family, kin, the larger community, the structures of the institutional church, and the state. Johnson argues that the responsibility for the "temporal and spiritual welfare of their communities" and the desire for autonomy made it possible for abbesses and nuns continually to breach the walls of their enclosures. She demonstrates the significance of the difference between the acceptance of this permeability among the lay community and its condemnation by male clerics concerned with maintaining their own sexual control.

In her study of the imperial harem in the royal Ottoman Empire of the sixteenth and seventeenth centuries, Leslie Peirce takes another example of gendered seclusion to show how the power of the women of the dynastic family was exercised in public through the private means of arranged marriages and manumission of slave women. In reconceptualizing our notions of power and influence, Peirce demonstrates that the seemingly private harem was deeply embedded in the exercise of public power. The physical existence of divided spheres based on gender, she argues, did not debase the power of the women of the Ottoman ruling class.

Londa Schiebinger introduces us to Maria Winkelmann, a late seventeenth- and early eighteenth-century Prussian astronomer. Winkelmann's ability to practice her craft depended on familial connections at a time when the separation between home and workplace was not yet fully formalized in astronomy. Her assignment as a woman

[53] Hall, "Partial Truths," p. 908.

to the familial and private sphere, however, severely limited her educational attainments and her independent working life as a scientist. Schiebinger shows that the increasing professionalization of the practice of European science and the demise of the old craft traditions resulted in a hardening of the wall between the public and private spheres, thwarting Winkelmann's efforts on gendered grounds.

Barbara Sicherman analyzes the subversive and daring role reading played for the women of the Hamilton family of Indiana at the height of the self-consciousness of a separate domestic sphere for white middle- and upper-class America women in the late nineteenth century. "Women's intense engagement with books." Sicherman argues, provided them with a way "to overcome some of the confines of gender and class" and to free their imagination. Reading encouraged "new self-definitions and, ultimately, the innovative behavior associated with the Progressive generation." The very private experience of reading, in conjunction with family support, provided the springboard for the creation of a new female subjectivity and an active role in the public world.

In a study of lesbian bar culture in working-class Lynn, Massachusetts, in the 1950s and 1960, Janet Kahn and Patricia A. Gozemba show how private needs for love, sex, and friendships provided the impetus for a "public, although often hidden, space." Their analysis of the butch/femme roles in particular shows the pressures of a homophobic and class-ridden society on the private actions and social systems lesbians created. Their study provides a window into rethinking the structures of gender relationships and the definition of public space. "In a context in which the private realm of the family was not providing traditional family support," they conclude, "these women forged new families in the public space of the bar."

The essays in Part II focus on the concepts of public and private spheres as means to circumscribe women's actions and to serve as explanations for other means of social control. In her essay, Patricia Cline Cohen questions what happened when a U.S. white middle-class woman moved about on the new forms of public transport in the early nineteenth century to become a "public" woman. As changing technologies made possible differing forms of commercial travel, Cohen argues, the older forms of distancing and formality between the sexes could not be maintained and an undercurrent of sexual vulnerability surrounded the female traveler. In reading traveling women's letters and diaries, Cohen finds that "women were 'not out of place' in public, but they were not traveling on the same terms as were men." In constructing appropriate behavior for public travel, women became accountable for the private behavior of men and travel became another site for controlling women's actions in public in the name of private responsibility.

In her essay on female criminality in nineteenth-century Paris, Ann-Louise Shapiro demonstrates the public use of the unbounded female body as it appeared in medical, legal, and historical discourse. She shows how the ideology of public and private spheres rested, in part, on the description of the female body as other and the pathological embodiment of sexuality. "In exploring the private realm of female biology," Shapiro argues, "medical men participated in the gendering of the patterns of public life . . . . [and] articulated the meanings that would be given to the intimate experiences of female biology and sexuality. These processes were interactive and mutually reinforcing."

Gay Gullickson's essay seeks to understand why the horrors of the Paris Commune of 1871 are remembered in the figures of the *pétroleuses,* the petroleum-throwing women deemed responsible for the burning and fighting in Paris. The representation of these women as "hideous and fierce but sexually compelling" came to symbolize the possible overturning of the entire social and political bourgeois order, even though the evidence suggests that more men than women were involved in the burnings. Gullickson's nuanced analysis of the punishment of these women, in particular the execution of one woman on her doorstep, demonstrates the conflating of women's seeming usurpation of male public power with total social disorder.

Turning to the women active within the Universal Negro Improvement Association (UNIA), formed in 1914 under the leadership of Marcus Garvey in Jamaica and the United States, Barbara Bair examines why a gender ideology of divided spheres that tied men to the public arena and women to the home was perceived as reversing the racist double standard. When racist gender stereotypes labeled black women as masculine for their work role and attributed " 'feminine' qualities (passivity, subordination, exclusion from skilled and professional employment) to black males," UNIA gender theory sought to make black men masters of their own households and destinies and black women their "helpmates." The UNIA women demonstrated commitment to "racial solidarity and uplift" and understood why UNIA's gender ideology was an attack on racist assumptions. In addition, however, Bair finds examples of their protest against women's assignment to the domestic sphere and a struggle for greater roles in setting policy in the organization. Her essay examines the need to understand the ideology and actual practice of gendered spheres in the context of the historical specific realities of racial, class, and ethnic difference.

Dolores Janiewski draws our attention to the efforts of white missionaries, women's groups, and officials in the Bureau of Indian Affairs to impose "natural" models of family life on the Native Americans of the Inland Northwest. Her study demonstrates the integral link between assumptions about family structure in the private sphere and public policy applied to conquered peoples and the resistance differing patterns of gender economy provided. Janiewski also argues that the colonizers feared the differences in the Native American gender division of labor for they provided "subversive examples that might suggest that [the white dominant] arrangements could and should be changed."

The essays in Part III address the question of how notions of public and private spheres are both shaped and contradicted by the necessity for social welfare. In her essay on the urban working poor of early modern England, Diane Willen shows that women were objects of state intervention into their familial and personal lives and served as the work force for that social welfare intervention. Her analysis provides evidence that a simple dichotomy into public and private distorts the relationship between individual and state among the urban poor. Furthermore, Willen's essay suggests how much intervention by the early modern paternalistic state is replicated in our own era, even though the rhetoric of public/private division has changed.

In her essay on good and bad mothering in early twentieth-century London, Ellen Ross examines how working-class women saw themselves "simultaneously as child caretakers, as workers, and as members of neighborhoods and kinship groups." At the same time, the middle-class women who served as "friendly visitors" sought to valorize the meaning of motherhood in new ways. Critiquing the assumption that social welfare activities meant merely the imposing of middle-class norms of motherhood, Ross underlines the complicated meaning of good and bad mothering that underlay some of the possibilities, however problematic, for alliances among women of differing classes. Her essay illustrates how women's entrance into public policy often involves both cross-class (and cross-race in the United States context) friendships and the public articulation of seemingly private or domestic needs.

In the United States in the 1920s, the first national social welfare measure—the Sheppard-Towner Maternity and Infancy Protection Act—provided federal funds for the instruction of mothers in the care and feeding of children. In her essay on this act, Molly Ladd-Taylor shows how the women of the U.S. Children's Bureau "undermined traditional fatalism about maternal suffering and generated a broad-based movement demanding government responsibility for women's and children's health." Ladd-Taylor assesses the effectiveness of the act not merely by analyzing its defeat by the late 1920s but by studying its differential impact in various states and for individual women who both accepted and resisted the middle-class messages the Children's Bureau workers disseminated about birthing, motherhood, and health care. But, she argues, in forcing both the government and the medical profession to take maternal and infant health seriously, in the end the Sheppard-Towner Act contributed to privatization of such care for the middle class and its labeling as public charity of the poor.

If the Sheppard-Towner Act helped transform American cultural attitudes toward maternal and child suffering, in her essay Linda Gordon argues that both organized groups of feminists and victims of wife beating waged political struggles to "delegitimate" the right of men to beat women. Gordon's analysis of the records of Boston child protection agencies in the late nineteenth and early twentieth centuries reveals the various strategies, both public and private, that working-class women used to thwart the beatings and to reform the men who beat them. Battered women, she concludes, were both victims and agents, whose claims "to rights, to a claim upon the state to protect them from violence, arose precisely because of the weakening of patriarchy and the contradictions, imperfections, and dysfunctionality of the social control system." Finally, she suggests that in articulating a right "not to be beaten," working-class women built a language of political struggle that redefined their private situation into a legitimate call for public support and social change.

Jessie M. Rodrique's essay on birth control in the U.S. black community in the twentieth century shows how much racial as well as sexual politics shaped the struggle for the provision of birth control services in the African-American community. She analyzes the ways birth control was accepted and sought from within the black community, which both cooperated with and resisted white birth control advocates to obtain needed services. Aware of the often racist intent behind the public provision of such private needs, the black community, Rodrique shows, "maintained a degree of independence that allowed the organization for birth control in their communities to take a qualitatively different form."

In Part IV, the essays examine how notions of public and private spheres affected the world of paid labor. In the keynote address to the Seventh Berkshire Conference, Alice Kessler-Harris stressed that historical arguments are often used to shore up contemporary political controversies. She reminds us that seemingly private decisions are integral to changing public social processes and cultural beliefs. Using the contemporary debate about the implementation of comparable worth legislation to regulate pay equity, she sketches the history of the "just price" to illustrate how the market has always been "tempered by customary notions of justice and fairness." In critiquing the idea of an autonomous market unaffected by social relations, Kessler-Harris argues that notions of equity, justice, and the family wage are always historically contingent on and subject to political and economic struggle.

Just as Alice Kessler-Harris argues that the idea of the market and just wage are impinged upon by cultural beliefs, Ava Baron looks at the meaning of gender and particularly masculinity in the definition of work for male printers in the nineteenth- and early twentieth-century United States. Baron focuses on the introduction of the Linotype into the trade, its acceptance by the male printers "because it posed less of a threat to their class and gender positions," and the ways technological change forced the men "to redefine the source of masculinity" in their work. Baron analyzes the contradictions inherent in the male printers' arguments and shows us how seemingly private beliefs about gender have public consequences in the work world.

In a study of women in the French metalworking factories in the first third of the 20th century, Laura Lee Downs delineates how the organization of work emphasizing Taylorism and pronatalism necessitated the creation of a position for a "middle-class welfare lady." Downs argues that "by linking maternal health to productivity, welfare management effectively erased the line between public and private, as far as the woman metalworker was concerned, opening her sexuality, personal health, and domestic arrangments to the sharp scrutiny of the employer's newest intermediary." Downs shows that despite some attempts at reform and cross-class alliances, this linking of the public and private became a form of management control.

Laura Anker's study, based on the records of the Works Progress Administration (WPA) Connecticut Ethnic Survey of the 1930s, analyzes the various strategies for survival used by immigrant women. Anker's essay weaves the women's voices from the survey into a collective biography of a generation's effort to balance the demands of family and the necessity for work. She demonstrates how individual, personal decisions based on family needs affected large-scale "public" phenomenon such as patterns of immigration and work-force participation.

In the concluding essay on contemporary life in California's Silicon Valley, sociologist Judith Stacey argues that, in the context of what she labels "postfeminism," women are forging a new understanding of the relationship between work and family. Stacey suggests that "postfeminist strategies correspond to different generational and individual experiences with feminism and with postindustrial family and work conditions." Her analysis demonstrates how we need "to devise a personal politics that respects the political and personal anxieties and exhaustion of women contending with the destablized family and work conditions of the postindustrial era." As both history and this contemporary study demonstrate, our public and private lives are integrated and take their meaning from historical circumstances, cultural contexts, individual identities, and actions.

The nature of gendered domains of public and private and their relationship to power were never more clear than in the confirmation process for Judge Clarence Thomas's elevation to the U.S. Supreme Court in October 1991. In the Senate Judiciary Committee hearings on Professor Anita Hill's charges of sexual harassment by Thomas, it became clear that what was to be considered public and what was to be considered private had divided along gender lines. The male nominee from the outset defined unequivocally what he thought was private, while what should have been private for the female complainant of sexual harassment became public against her wishes. The nominee never accepted questions from his interrogators that invaded the lines of privacy he had set down, and they, all male senators, respected his demands and did not invade by question or speculation the limits he had clearly marked.

In contrast, once Hill's statements were made public in the hearing, her all-male interrogators felt no limits on their right to invade her private thoughts, her reasons for what she did and did not do in connection with her response to what she characterized as unwelcome behavior toward her. The senators felt free to speculate in public about her sanity, her fantasies, her ambitions, and her conduct toward others, inside and outside of work. They engaged in no such speculation about the actions of the nominee, following his injunction about what he viewed as private and therefore "off limits." In response to the black male nominee's emotional accusations about the racism involved in the process of examining his suitability for a lifetime appointment to the Supreme Court, the senators trod carefully. In response to the unemotional answers offered by the black female complainant about the sexual harassment she said she had experienced, the senators proceeded to speculate about what she was hiding.

Thus the meaning of privacy took on a gendered dimension that lasted through the hearing and into the subsequent Senate debate, when senators entered into the public record further private records regarding Anita Hill's earlier work record. During these events, Clarence Thomas was shown to be a powerful man both before and during his confirmation hearings, and he used his power to define his privacy at work and in the Senate hearings. Anita Hill was shown to be aware of her weaker position in relation to him before the hearing and proved to be in no better position during the hearings. The structure of power along gender lines confirmed differential rights to defining effectively what was private in their lives. Future historians of late twentieth-century American life will have to assay how much these hearings rigidified, exposed, or transformed the gendered structures of public and private.

As the debate over Thomas's nomination and the essays in this book demonstrate, however, historians can no longer employ the concept of separate spheres unself-consciously, without a full awareness of its origins, limitations, and complications. Without this self-consciousness, historians run the danger of missing the nuanced realities of lived experience and the theoretical debates that underpin the spheres concept. The history of the separate spheres concept that is sketched in these essays demonstrates the interdisciplinary nature of gender scholarship and the benefits, as well as the risks, that come from such endeavors. Taken together, the essays in this volume begin to suggest the richness of the analytical tasks that lie ahead and serve as a tribute to the ability of those engaged in the writing of women's history to continue to reinvent the field.

PART I

RETHINKING SEPARATE SPHERES

CHAPTER ONE

The Cloistering of Medieval Nuns: Release or Repression, Reality or Fantasy?

Penelope D. Johnson

In the twilight of the Roman Empire, monasticism began in the deserts of Egypt and spread to become the preeminent religious institution in western Europe by the central Middle Ages, the eleventh, twelfth, and thirteenth centuries. Devout Christians pursued spiritual perfection by withdrawing from the world to dedicate their lives to prayer and meditation. Ironically, the strength of their spiritual communities made them necessary to secular society. Thus monasteries developed into centers of learning, charity, and social order; they functioned as land banks, bed-and-breakfasts for travelers, and shelters for widows and orphans. They ran hospitals and almshouses. Their recruits came only from the upper social levels, which partly explains why monastics, nuns as well as monks, functioned to hold society together. As monasticism evolved, it took many forms, but all—until the innovation of the friars in the thirteenth century—meant to cloister both nuns and monks. Cloistering had two facets: active cloistering kept the monastic person within the monastery walls, while passive cloistering excluded all other folk from entering. In theory, if both active and passive cloistering were absolute, two distinct spheres would exist, separated by the impermeable barrier of monastery walls: a public religious life for all Christians, who were expected to adhere to church teachings while living in the world, and a private religious life for the elite, the spiritual athletes.[1]

This essay will be published in a French version in the proceedings of the Second International Conference of the Centre Européen de Richerches sur les Congrégations et Ordres Religieux. I thank the president of the society for permission to publish this version, and the University of Chicago Press for permission to publish part of chapter 4 of *Equal in Monastic Profession: Religious Women in Medieval France*, © 1991 by the University of Chicago.

From its outset, the monastic life was open to women as well as men, but the church felt anxious about its female recruits. A generalized fear of women—particularly of their sexuality—led religious authorities to want a more total seclusion for nuns than for monks. Contemporary observers recognized that being regular clergy (following a monastic rule) imposed enclosure on monks—at least in theory—just as it did on their female counterparts. But when Caesarius of Arles (ca. 470–542) instituted the first strictly cloistered rule intended just for women, he lent his authority to a growing belief that enclosure was more important for nuns than for monks.[2] Some later writers, like the monk Idung in the twelfth century, defended the inequity of this tighter cloistering of religious women. Idung rooted his case in the authority of St. Jerome (ca. 340–420), whose belief in the fundamental weakness of female nature led him to call for more stringent enclosure for women than for men.[3] Whatever the rationalizations, cloistering was not generally imposed in most male monasteries, except in extremely austere orders such as that of the Carthusians.[4]

But what transpired in the houses of medieval nuns? Were monastic women permanently sealed into their convents and everyone who was not a member of the community totally excluded? Was the public/private dichotomy rigorously observed for nuns?

The writings of many of the important male monastic legislators indicate that they clearly intended to impose rigorous seclusion on monastic women. Stephen of Obazine attracted crowds of both female and male followers in the first half of the twelfth century. When the saint regularized these people into monastic communities, he enclosed the nuns in "perpetual claustration."[5] In the same period, Abelard in his

[1] For the monastic life in general, see C. H. Lawrence, *Medieval Monasticism: Forms of Religious Life in Western Europe in the Middle Ages* (London, 1984). For medieval nuns see Michel Parisse, *Les nonnes au moyen âge* (Lepuy, 1983); Paulette L'Hermite-Leclercq, *Le monachisme féminin dans la société de son temps: Le monastère de La Celle (XIe–début du XVIe siècle)* (Paris, 1989); *Distant Echoes,* Vol. 1 of *Medieval Religious Women,* ed. John A. Nichols and Lillian Thomas Shank (Kalamazoo, Mich., 1984). For cloistering see G. Huyghe, *La clôture des moniales des origines à la fin du XIIIe siècle* (Roubaix, 1944).

[2] Donald Hochstetler, "The Meaning of Monastic Cloister for Women According to Caesarius of Arles," in *Religion, Culture, and Society in the Early Middle Ages: Studies in Honor of Richard E. Sullivan,* ed. Thomas Noble and John Contreni (Kalamazoo, Mich., 1987), p. 27.

[3] Idung, "Argumentum super quatuor questionibus," ed. R. B. C. Huygens, in *Studi medievali,* 3d ser. 13 (1972): 355–62. Jean Leclercq, "Medieval Feminine Monasticism: Reality versus Romantic Images," in *Benedictus: Studies in Honor of St. Benedict of Nursia,* vol. 8 of *Studies in Medieval Cistercian History,* ed. Rozanne Elder (Kalamazoo, Mich., 1981), p. 59, describes the case of the Abbey of Valladolid, whose monks King Juan I put under strict claustration in imitation of the cloistering of nuns.

[4] Lawrence, *Medieval Monasticism,* pp. 134–36.

[5] *Vie de St. Etienne d'Obazine,* trans. Michel Aubrun (Clermond-Ferrand, 1970), pp. 98–99.

letter of direction to Heloise for the Paraclete argued: "Solitude is indeed all the more necessary for your woman's frailty, inasmuch as for our part we are less attacked by the conflicts of carnal temptations and less likely to stray towards bodily things through the senses." He urged that all the required resources for a nunnery be encircled by its walls so that they would be "places where the sisters may carry out their daily tasks without any need for straying outside."[6] Thirteenth-century statutes for the nuns of Prémontré legislated punishments for any sister who failed to observe claustration, and Jacques de Vitry, that champion of religious women, enthusiastically described nuns as living in rigid enclosure, sealed away from all outside contacts.[7]

Passionate defense of enclosing holy women did not necessarily cloud the good sense of its supporters. The rather pragmatic precepts set out for the nuns of Fontevrault stated that nuns should never go out but acknowledged that they would sometimes have to leave their house; the rule therefore attempted to legislate seemly behavior by requiring that two men—one religious and one secular—should always accompany any nun sallying out of her cloister.[8] Abbot Peter the Venerable wrote with enthusiasm of the absolute enclosure at the Cluniac nunnery of Marcigny; yet when faced with the demands of the cellaress, his mother Raingarde, Peter acknowledged that she would sometimes have to venture out of her convent to attend to various needs.[9] Theory might have to bend to practicality, but it persisted. Some even acknowledged the difficulty, if not outright danger, of rigid cloistering; Humbert of Romans preached to nuns of the problems of enclosure which could lead them to become gloomy, hungry for gossip, and lax about both active and passive cloistering.[10]

These are all the voices of men, for it was the male clerical hierarchy which was most deeply concerned with cloistering nuns. The women's voices are mute on the subject, even in the extraordinary case of Heloise. If, however, we put aside the "documents of theory" (clerical admonitions and legislation), we can discover part, at least, of religious women's lives through the evidence that can be gleaned from the "documents of practice" (administrative records of what actually

[6] *The Letters of Abelard and Heloise,* trans. Betty Radice (Harmondsworth, 1974), p. 196.

[7] *Les statuts de Prémontré au milieu du XIIe siècle,* ed. Placidius F. Lefevre and W. M. Grauwen, in *Bibliotheca analectorum praemenstratensium* 12 (Averbode, 1978), pp. 113–15; Jacques de Vitry, *Historia occidentalis,* quoted by Parisse, *Nonnes au moyen âge,* p. 31.

[8] Rule of Fontevrault, in *Patrologiae cursus completus: Series latina,* ed. J.-P. Migne, 221 vols. (Paris, 1841–64), 162:1079 (hereafter cited as *PL*).

[9] Peter the Venerable, *PL* 189:889 D and 220 D.

[10] Humbert of Romans, "De eruditione praedicatorum," in C. Casagrande, *Prediche alle donne de secolo XIII* (Milan, 1978), pp. 142–43.

transpired). Since the sources are particularly rich, my research is based on documents generated by nunneries in northern France in the central Middle Ages.[11]

A survey of French nuns and canonesses in this period, who followed the Benedictine, Cistercian, and Augustinian rules and belonged to the whole gamut of orders, yields surprisingly constant results.[12] The documents of practice in contrast to the documents of theory reveal that neither active nor passive cloistering was absolute: religious women commonly left their houses on all sorts of errands, and non-community members entered the monastic precincts on all sorts of pretexts; much of this movement both into and out of monasteries was seen by nunnery officials as licit, but some was judged illicit by their clerical overseers and some even by the nuns themselves.

The most commonly authorized reason for a nun to be outside her convent was to secure a powerful support for her house. For instance, religious women could pursue help for their communal privileges or temporal possessions, which often entailed seeking episcopal aid. The abbess of Holy Trinity, Poitiers, went to the bishop's palace for negotiations; likewise the nuns of St. Pierre aux Nonnains, Metz, presented themselves before their bishop to request the return of purloined income.[13] A nun could leave to search for spiritual aid, as in the case of the Fontevrist nun who traveled to the archbishop of Bourges to seek support for her rigorous fasts.[14] Sometime the authority before whom a nun appeared was a secular lord. Maria, abbess of St. Sulpice, went with a considerable entourage and appeared before Jocelin, lord of Beaupré, to receive concession of rights from the monks of St. Sergius.[15]

The uncloistered nun was not always a supplicant. Often she was assertively doing business or looking out for her abbey's interests. Nuns strode around the fields walking boundaries with lay officials; nuns

[11] I am defining northern France linguistically to include that territory in which *langue d'oïl* was spoken.

[12] I have worked with a representative sample of nunneries from northern France, among them Val St. Georges, Salzinnes; ND, Bourbourg; ND, Montivilliers, Le Havre; St. Amand, Rouen; Clairruisel, Gaillefontaine; ND la Royale, Maubuisson, Pontoise; St. Georges, Rennes; St. Sulpice le Forêt, Rennes; La Barre, Château-Thierry; Pont aux Dames, Crécy-en-Brie; ND aux Nonnains, Troyes; the Paraclete, Nogent-sur-Seine; ND Basse Fontaine, Bar-sur-Aube; ND la Pommeraie, Sergines; Mont Ste. Catherine, Sens; St. Avit, Châteaudun; Les Clairets, Theil; ND Voisins, Meung-sur-Loire; Lieu ND les Romorandin, Orléans; ND la Charité, Ronceray, Angers; St. Pierre aux Nonnains, Metz; Ste. Trinité, Poitiers; ND Saintes; La Magdeleine lez Orléans, Orléans.

[13] Poitiers, Bibliothèque départementale, 2 H 2, carton 12, 2 (hereafter cited as BD); and Paris, Bibliothèque nationale, MS Latin 10027, fol. 45 r and v (hereafter cited as BN).

[14] J. D. Mansi, *Stephanus Balluzius: Miscellanea*, vol. 1 (Lucca, 1761). p. 270 (hereafter cited as Mansi).

[15] *Cartulaire de l'abbaye de Saint-Sulpice-la-Forêt, Ille-et-Vilaine*, ed. Pierre Anger (N.p., 1911), p. 417, no. 220, 1138.

traveled considerable distances on abbatial business; they went to a donor's family to receive each relative's consent to his gift.[16] When a wounded count wanted to settle his affairs, he made a donation to the nuns of Saintes, four of whom crowded into his bedroom to be among the group of witnesses.[17] When St. Aubin in Normandy was in severe financial straits, two nuns left the abbey, apparently with the approval of the abbess, to raise funds for their impoverished community.[18]

Nuns also left their enclosures intent on righting wrongs done their nunneries. The abbess of Saintes sent a legation consisting of the nun Constance and two abbey men to forbid a certain Radulf from taking monastic vows as a ploy for evading reparations to the abbey.[19] A few years later, when the nuns were locked in conflict with two brothers, they heard that one had died without having returned properties he had stolen from the convent. The nuns went in procession to the church to confront the brother, who was grieving over the body of his dead sibling; dramatically bearding the opposition, the band of religious women won their point and then graciously promised the bereaved brother commemorations for the souls of relatives. The physical presence of the nuns outside of their cloister, standing before the corpse, proved an invincible weapon in their battle to regain stolen property.[20]

Abbesses who bore responsibility for the temporal and spiritual welfare of their communities were the most visible of all uncloistered nuns. Abbess Agnes of Barbezieux, superior of Notre Dame, Saintes, traveled to the Abbey of St. Jean d'Angély so that she could plead before the bishop in a case of contested property.[21] When a plea was settled for Holy Trinity, Poitiers, Abbess Petronilla and two of her nuns were present at the bishop's residence.[22] Abbesses who made such appearances moved in state as befitted any great ecclesiastical power so that all who saw them were struck by their imposing presence outside the cloister.

Another reason that nuns ignored precepts of claustration and left their abbey's precincts was to seek refuge in time of danger. When the canonesses of La Barre in Château-Thierry received a farm, it became

[16] *Cartulaire de l'abbaye royale de Notre-Dame de Saintes de l'ordre de Saint-Benoiî*, vol. 2: Cartulaire inédits de la Saintonge, ed. Thomas Grasilier (Niort, 1871), p. 80, no. 88, dated 1150; and p. 64, no. 68, dated 1163 (hereafter cited as *CND*); Also Poitiers, Bibliothèque municipale, MS 27, p. 105, no. 109, 1161 (hereafter cited as BM).

[17] *CND*, p. 85, no. 99, 1119–23.

[18] *The Register of Eudes of Rouen*, trans. Sydney M. Brown, ed. Jeremiah F. O'Sullivan, Columbia Historical Records, Ser. 72 (New York, 1964), p. 537 (hereafter cited as *RER*).

[19] *CND*, p. 147, no. 227, dated 1100–1107.

[20] *CND*, pp. 98–99, no. 122, 1133.

[21] *CND*, pp. 73–75, no. 82, 1174.

[22] Poitiers, BD, 2 H 2, carton 12, no. 2, dated 1144.

their haven in wartime.[23] The ever-present danger of fire, which could be one of the horrors of warfare inflicted on noncombatants, was another common, threatening experience in the Middle Ages. Perhaps because of medieval people's inability to contain fire and the terror it evoked, fire occurs in didactic tales of holiness.

In medieval stories of sanctity, a pious person might avert a conflagration, as did Bishop Mellitus, who had himself borne into the path of an encroaching fire to shield the city of Canterbury with his frail body.[24] But what of a nunnery in the path of leaping flames? Since nuns were theoretically not to leave their convent, religious women could be burned alive, trapped within their monastic walls. The literary topos gets inverted in an interesting way in these tales. The holy nuns refuse all appeals to quit the cloister and seek safety as urged by their male advisers; the power of their commitment to their vows serves as holy asbestos, and they are miraculously protected.[25] Nunneries in some instances may have survived fierce fire storms, protected by stone buildings or other bulwarks. The documents of practice, however, mention convents destroyed by fires in which some of the inmates perished and other occurrences in which the only mention is of property loss.[26] The death of nuns in a fire could have been an accidental tragedy rather than a voluntary choice, although the possibility exists that some may have chosen to die rather than leave the cloister.

Not all of the comings and goings of nuns were for necessary business or in search of refuge. Nuns often left their abbeys without permission to see family or on personal or even clandestine trips. Nuns went to visit their relatives, and when illness struck, a nun could be

[23] "L'abbaye de la Barre et son recueil de chartres," ed. Alexandre-Eusèbe Poquet, *Annales de la société historique et archéologique de Château-Thierry* 58 (1884): 151, no. 31.

[24] Bede, *A History of the English Church and People,* trans. Leo Sherley-Price (Harmondsworth, 1968), pp. 111–12.

[25] This is a much repeated story. Two famous examples are the steadfastness of the nuns of St. John's, Arles, the congregation under the direction of Bishop Caesarius of Arles in the sixth century, and the Cluniac nuns of Marcigny, who refused to heed the pleas of the archbishop to flee to safety. See J.-B. Thiers, *Traité de la clôture des religieuses* (Paris, 1681), pp. 12–13, for the story and its continued hortatory use at the end of the seventeenth century; and Peter the Venerable, "De miraculis," *PL* 189:890 C and D.

[26] The year after the fire of 1188 which devastated the nunnery of Notre Dame aux Nonnains, Count Henry reconfirmed his and his family's donations to the nuns, noting that they should perpetually "hold this church and land, which I gave to them for the pressing accident to the ladies who perished miserably here in the fire of Troyes" (*Documents sur l'abbaye de Notre-Dame-aux-Nonnains de Troyes,* ed. Charles Lalore, *Mémoires de la société académique d'agriculture, des sciences, arts et belles-lettres de département de l'Aube* 11 (1874): 12, no. 7, dated 1189). St. Amand in Rouen experienced two severe fires in 1136 and 1248. Pope Innocent IV awarded the nuns an indulgence because of their need to rebuild (Rouen, BD, H 55, carton 1, no. 3).

called out of her monastery to nurse her sick relative; in fact, religious women seem to have remained closer to their families than were monks, and nuns' visits home were not uncommon.[27] In cases when nuns were censured by the official visitand for wandering, it is not always clear what they did to deserve opprobrium.[28] But sometimes the circumstantial evidence makes it clear that a nun was illicitly meeting with a lover or visiting her child.[29]

Even if religious women left their cloister precincts, was not that walled community at least off-limits to non-community members? To the contrary, religious, lordly, and hospitable responsibilities overrode the obligation to keep people out. The oblation of a noble widow at Jully and her gift to the abbey necessitated the gathering of a veritable crowd of witnesses in the chapter house.[30] The ratification of a gift Count Baldwin had made earlier brought him with twenty-eight male witnesses to the Abbey of Bourbourg to reaffirm his generosity "publicly in the church," and a few years later, a comital court heard a case at Bourbourg "in the abbess's private chamber."[31] Nunneries also had to honor their obligations to serve ritual meals to those in their *societas* or confraternity, so that Mainard, Achard, and their foresters had the right to bread and wine twice a year in the refectory of Notre Dame, Saintes.[32] Perhaps the most intrusive and disruptive entries of outsiders into convents came because of monastic obligations to offer hospitality. What must it have done to the quiet of the cloister when in 1169 the nuns of Jully hosted Count Henry of Troyes traveling on pilgrimage to Vézelay with his entire train?[33]

In addition to the lay people who entered nunnery cloisters with some particular purpose—as donors, witnesses, members of a *societas*, or travelers—there were many others who just wandered in and out. Guibert de Nogent's mother not only freely entered her neighborhood nunnery but also removed an elderly nun to be her companion.[34] The visitation records of Archbishop Eudes Rigaud for the third quarter of the thirteenth century in the province of Normandy show that out-

[27] *RER*, pp. 212, 383, 386, 680 for visits home, and p. 335 for going home to nurse a sick relative.

[28] *RER*, pp. 337, 518, 569.

[29] *RER*, pp. 560, 537.

[30] *Cartulaire du prieuré de Jully-les-Nonnains*, ed. Ernest Petit, *Bulletin de la société des sciences historiques et naturelles de l'Yonne* 34 (1880): 257, no. 3, dated 1128. The same situation occurred at La Trinité, Poitiers, when a large crowd gathered for an oblation and gift to the house (Poitiers, BM, MS 27, p. 105, no. 109, dated 1161).

[31] *Cartulaire de l'abbaye de Notre-Dame de Bourbourg*, ed. Ignace de Coussemaker, 3 vols. (Lille, 1882–91), 1:12, no. 16, dated 1112; and 1:33, no. 37, dated 1128–69.

[32] *CND*, p. 59, no. 59, dated 1107. This was a common abbatial gift to supporters; also see p. 62, no. 64, dated 1096–1107, and p. 63, no. 65, dated 1137.

[33] *Cartulaire de Jully*, p. 268, no. 34, dated 1169.

[34] *Self and Society in Medieval France: The Memoirs of Abbot Guibert of Nogent*, ed. John Benton (New York, 1970), p. 75.

siders routinely entered nunneries.[35] At least 7 percent of these inappropriate intrusions were by relatives coming to visit the nuns, to eat in the refectory, or even sleep at the nunnery. Sometimes, however, the archbishop specifies that unsavory sorts were wandering around such as the two clerics and "a certain miller, named Frongnet," who were to be kept out of St. Aubin; other times Eudes records that general procedures were lax: "The gate looking towards the fields is open too often; we ordered it closed."[36] Nuns had to be alert to specific troublemakers as well as to general security.

I have concentrated so far on religious women who in actual practice often did not live by the theory of enclosure. How did their behavior compare to that of monks? Sources for a broad comparison of cloistering by gender are not available, but it is possible to compare gender in a representative sample, using the data base I have constructed from the visitation register of Eudes Rigaud. These data allow a comparative look at cloistering in thirteenth-century Norman women's and men's houses.

Looking first at the results for passive cloistering, Eudes had occasion to censure the presence of unauthorized people on 21 percent of his visits to Norman nunneries and on 18 percent of his visitations to male houses.[37] These figures suggest that outsiders meandered into the cloisters of nuns and monks in roughly equal numbers and that the gender of monastics had no statistical significance for their ability to bar non-community members. The slightly larger proportion of censures for outsiders' entry into convents reflects the problem nunneries had in excluding people because women's houses could always be entered by clerical men, whether these individuals belonged or not. Archbishop Eudes strenuously forbade the seemingly respectable abbot of Jumièges from paying inappropriate visits to one convent because of the scandal.[38] It would have been extremely difficult for the nuns to attempt to forbid entry to such an eminent ecclesiastic. How often did outsiders force their way into nunneries either by dint of birth or by authority of office?

In contrast to the figures for passive cloistering, the numbers from my data base for active cloistering are decidedly different by gender. Nuns were censured for unauthorized exits from their houses on 26 percent of Eudes's visits to convents and monks on only 11 percent of

[35] *RER*, passim.

[36] *RER*, pp. 676, 317.

[37] Nunneries had 27 censures out of 129 visitations, and male houses had 85 censures out of 467 visitations.

[38] *RER*, p. 674.

his stops at male houses.[39] These figures suggest that nuns were either more prone to wander than monks or more apt to be found delinquent for behavior that might escape notice when done by a monk. Both were probably true. We have seen how necessary it was to the well-being of nuns to have the ability to confront enemies and to meet with friends. Indeed, those houses that had few qualms about enclosure were the same ones that were the most prosperous.[40] Institutional success was not necessarily achieved at the expense of spiritual health, for in my research, poverty—not wealth—correlates with evidence of monastic decadence.[41]

All medieval people must have been aware of the presence of houses of religious women and men scattered around the countryside, and it would have been almost impossible not to have had feelings about these ubiquitous monastics. We might posit, therefore, that lay patronage of nunneries would have dwindled noticeably in the central Middle Ages in response to the casual comings and goings of nuns if the breaking of cloister offended a convent's lay neighbors. This did not occur. Donations and oblations to nunneries kept proportional pace with those to men's houses throughout the thirteenth century. A drop is apparent in the late Middle Ages—the fourteenth and fifteenth centuries—but this shrinkage was a response to multiple shifts in society, economics, and demography, rather than to breaches of enclosure which had been occurring for centuries. Indeed, a qualitative comparison of charters from women's and men's monasteries shows a very similar pattern of donations and support, which shifts for both nuns and monks from large land grants to smaller gifts of dues and rents over the course of the central Middle Ages. Since nuns exited the cloister

[39] There were 33 unauthorized cases of "wandering" by nuns out of 129 total visits and for monks 50 out of 467.

[40] The Paraclete, Notre Dame in Saintes, and other such rich Benedictine houses were casual about cloistering and stayed prosperous and free of major scandals throughout the period. But did the freedom to tend exterior needs lead to well-being, or did wealth lead to enough power so nuns felt enclosure to be unnecessary? Both are partly true, I suspect. For example, external control leading to conventual problems hurt the Abbey of Notre Dame aux Nonnains, which gradually fell under episcopal control and experienced losses of prestige and income in the thirteenth century. See Théophile Boutiot, *Des privilèges singuliers de l'abbaye de Notre-Dame-aux-Nonnains de Troyes* (Paris, 1864); and Régis Rohmer, "L'abbaye bénédictine de Notre-Dame-aux-Nonnains de Troyes des origines à l'année 1503," in *Position des thèses de l'Ecole des Chartes* (Mâcon, 1905), pp. 123–29.

[41] Multivariable analysis of factors that might contribute to the decadence of Norman convents visited by Eudes produces poverty as the only independent variable that consistently is associated with deeply troubled houses. My research reinforces Jane Schulenberg's findings that enclosure was a control mechanism that impeded nuns' achievement of spiritual autonomy by suggesting that this holds true also for the central Middle Ages (Schulenberg, "Strict Active Enclosure and Its Effects on the Female Monastic Experience [500–1100]," in *Distant Echoes*, p. 79).

or received visitors in response to family and friends, these same lay supporters were not alienated by a loose rather than strict interpretation of enclosure. In contrast, the church hierarchy responded angrily to breaches in the cloistering of nuns. It may be that religious women's casual attitude toward enclosure helped to damn them in the eyes of their male monastic counterparts, for from the mid-twelfth century on, many male orders became increasingly hostile toward female houses and their inmates.[42]

How are we to assess casual cloistering? Would it lead to frivolity, or worse, lechery, as was feared?[43] A temperate scholarly voice reminds us that "those modern writers who interpret every violation of enclosure as evidence of a moral lapse forget that economic necessity often forced nuns to go outside their convents."[44] This argument, however, only covers business outside the nunnery walls; I would expand the defense because nuns had other legitimate and innocent needs for exiting the cloister besides the economic exigencies of their convents.

Some of the contradictions and confusions can be avoided if we separate the impact of cloistering on nunneries from its effect on the lives of individual nuns. Strict enclosure could devastate a convent. For instance, in investigating the decline she sees of women's monasticism from its early medieval heights to a low point in the mid-eleventh century, Jane Schulenberg indicts rigid enclosure for damaging the economy of nunneries and perhaps also their ability to recruit oblates.[45] My research suggests that the need continued in the central Middle Ages for nuns to be free of cloistering in the best interests of their houses. If a convent could not send a member out to tend its business, it was hamstrung; the house became dependent on the ability and honesty of its male provosts. To entrust affairs to unsupervised personnel was to invite trouble. Faced with this dilemma, female superi-

[42] The resistance to women in one male order is described in Sally Thompson, "The Problem of the Cistercian Nuns in the Twelfth and Thirteenth Centuries," in *Medieval Women*, ed. Derek Baker, Studies in Church History, Subsidia 1 (Oxford, 1978), pp. 227–52.

[43] Medieval male critics assumed the worst of uncloistered nuns, a position that is swallowed without question by Graciela S. Daichman, *Wayward Nuns in Medieval Literature* (Syracuse, 1986), pp. 19–22, who posits (with a paucity of historical evidence) that nuns who wandered physically strayed morally.

[44] Catherine Boyd, *A Cistercian Nunnery in Mediaeval Italy: The Story of Refreddo in Saluzzo, 1220–1300* (Cambridge, Mass. 1943), p. 109.

[45] Schulenberg, "Strict Active Enclosure," p. 77. John Nichols sees later English Cistercian nuns hurt by their tight enclosure ("English Cistercian Nunneries and English Bishops," in *Distant Echoes*, p. 247). Other scholars suggest that nuns were freer in the earlier period: Suzanne Wemple, *Women in Frankish Society: Marriage and the Cloister, 500 to 900* (Philadelphia, 1981), pp. 167–68, 173, views cloistering as an unattainable ideal before the eleventh century. Parisse, *Nonnes au moyen âge*, p. 184, argues that female cloistering intensified in the twelfth century. A chronological study of the ebb and flow of the theory and practice of enclosure is needed.

ors routinely left the cloister or sent delegates out on conventual business, and since the theory of enclosure forbade such behavior, monastic or episcopal overseers routinely denounced it.[46] Convent superiors felt that their members who went out on house business were not breaching the rules, but visitands did not always see nuns' absences in this same benign light. The interpretation of behavior becomes, at least in some instances, a judgment of a nunnery's autonomy. In fact, we can go even further to say that the real issue of claustration was that of social control—a control often resisted by female communities, which judging by their own lights, saw many legitimate reasons for their extracloistral activities.[47]

Although most nunneries defied cloistering because it inhibited their autonomy, enclosure could be positive for the individual nun. From a modern perspective, restrictions on one's movements sound repressive, but this was not necessarily true for medieval women. The records left about the lives of extraordinary women suggest that some of them eagerly sought the cloistered life. A young woman might so yearn for the austerities of enclosure that she would travel considerable distances to become an anchoress. Thus the twelfth-century English ascetic Eve journeyed to the Loire valley to take up the eremitical life in a cell attached to the Priory of l'Evière.[48] The probability is strong that Eve chose this life because, if it had been solely a family decision, many closer places would have been available for her enclosure. Certainly, the exceptionally pious woman might desire a life of contemplation removed from the world, and claustration created for her a quiet place for prayer. It is also possible that cloistering freed nuns from unwanted outside demands. A nun might have welcomed the news that her father needed her nursing skills at home, but perhaps her heart sank at a duty she perceived as onerous. An abbess might have relished going to court to do legal battle over abbey property, or maybe she thankfully handed the litigation to her male provost. Within the cloister a woman's first concern was her own salvation, not the care of her kin. We cannot be sure, but for some women, cloistering may have provided useful insulation from the demands of an importunate world. Finally, cloistering seems to have positively promoted communal sensibilities; separation from outside ties fostered the feeling of shared responsibility and interdependence, building the group's awareness of its own identity. Thus the irony is that although

[46] *RER*, pp. 386, 518, 537.

[47] One of the themes of monastic history is the drive of houses to win exemption from episcopal control, a goal hotly pursued by convents seeking autonomy. See the case of Montivilliers' forged exemptions in Georges Priem, "L'abbaye royale de Montivilliers," in *La Normandie bénédictine au temps de Guillaume le Conquérant (XIe siècle)* (Lille, 1967), pp. 155–57.

[48] André Wilmart, "Eve et Goscelin," *Revue bénédictine* 50 (1938): 428.

strict enclosure often worked against the institutional well-being of convents, it may have helped to create a positive spiritual environment for individual nuns.

Theoretically, claustration was meant to free nuns by protecting them from evil outside their walls and inside themselves. The positive aspect of this theory may have been sincerely believed by individuals, but enclosing nuns also represented an anxious institutionalization of pollution fears, reinvigorated in the twelfth century as a defensive clerical response to reform. Nuns were both "imprisoned" and "dead to the world."[49] Society incarcerates the antisocial and disposes of the dead; criminals and corpses damage and infect society, not the other way around. The new rhetorical intensity about nuns that developed in clerical writing in the twelfth century sprang, I believe, from the increased emphasis on virginity and the imposition of clerical celibacy on the clergy by its leaders.[50]

The latter part of the eleventh century witnessed the battle between reformers and married clergy over the issue of clerical celibacy. The reformers prevailed at Second Lateran Council in 1139, and clerical marriage was finally and irrevocably banned.[51] By midcentury the clerics, who had to minister to growing numbers of nuns, were forced into celibacy; yet priests had to hear confessions and administer sacraments to those women whom they saw as able to destroy their chastity. Therefore, the male clergy insisted on the rigid cloistering of nuns, which served two purposes: strict enclosure made these tempting women as inaccessible as possible to protect men from the pollution of arousal, and it allowed the clergy to vent their frustration by punishing nuns as the scapegoats for male sexual feelings.[52]

The clerics who judged the nun outside her cloister as being at risk saw women through the biases of the ancients, as inferior beings. Thus

[49] Peter the Venerable, *PL* 189:217 B and 350 B-C.

[50] See Anne L. Barstow, *Married Priests and the Reforming Papacy: The Eleventh-Century Debates* (New York, 1982). Jean Leclercq, "Spirituality of Medieval Feminine Monasticism," in *The Continuing Quest for God*, ed. William Skudlarek (Collegeville, Minn., 1982), p. 131, suggests that Eastern contact produced stricter enclosure. Some of the more hyperbolic statements are infamous, like that of Abbot Conrad of Marchtal: "The wickedness of women is greater than all the other wickedness of the world . . . we will on no account receive any more sisters . . . but will avoid them like poisonous animals" (quoted in R. W. Southern, *Western Society and the Church in the Middle Ages* [Harmondsworth, 1970], p. 314).

[51] Barstow, *Married Priests*, p. 1, argues that to win the battle to control the right ordering of society, the church threw its priests into the fray with the empire; priests would live chastely to show their worthiness to lead society. Clerics found their new image uncomfortable and prone to contradictions.

[52] Mary Douglas, *Purity and Danger: An Analysis of the Concepts of Pollution and Taboo* (London, 1966), pp. 149, 163–64, discusses pollution taboos as a response to social contradictions, positing that high moral goals often lead to hypocrisy and pollution taboos.

the clergy read women's nature as weak and liable to corruption. These critics also misunderstood the real needs and contributions of nunneries, seeing them as institutions that should be encapsulated from rather than integrated into society. The criticism that medieval nuns ignored cloistering is valid: they continually bent and broke the rules of enclosure. But the further accusation that this behavior inevitably led the nun astray is unfounded; some nuns broke their vows when outside the convent, but the insistence that uncloistered nuns were acting immodestly, if not immorally, was off the mark.

Charters from nunneries show a laity remarkably unconcerned with either the passive or active cloistering of nuns.[53] Nuns go out to visit their mothers; brothers come into the cloister to see their sisters; nuns deal constantly with the laity both inside and out of their convents. The laity does not protest such uncloistered activity, and secular benefactors continue eagerly to seek suffrages from religious women. If the laity who funded convents and supplied them with recruits was not threatened by the women vowed to chastity being in touch with secular life, then perhaps the often hysterical rhetoric of clerics was unfounded.

The church had established its public/private dichotomy between secular and regular people—a separation that at its beginning was not along gender lines. When, however, the church demanded cloistering of religious women but not of religious men, nuns were defined as different from monks—as those regular people whom the clergy literally wanted to wall away from society.

The nuns of northern France in the central Middle Ages generally had a strong sense of the importance of their mission, and this corporate self-confidence was confirmed and reflected by continued lay support and approval. Church authorities saw nuns in a less positive light, becoming more insistent after the reforms of the eleventh and early twelfth centuries on containing them behind the impenetrable barrier of convent walls. Nuns, however, treated their enclosures as permeable membranes, crossing over the private/public ecclesiastic barrier in search of their own and society's well-being. Thus cloistering existed in theory but was modified in practice when nuns bent rules, resisting social control to make their convents more functional for themselves and society at large.

[53] In the thousands of monastic charters I have read from the central Middle Ages, I have found no trace of lay criticism of monastics for breaking strict claustration.

CHAPTER TWO

Beyond Harem Walls: Ottoman Royal Women and the Exercise of Power

Leslie P. Peirce

For roughly one hundred years, from the mid-sixteenth to the mid-seventeenth centuries, women of the Ottoman royal family exercised so much influence on the political life of the empire that this period is often referred to, in both scholarly and popular writing, as "the sultanate of women." High-ranking dynastic women, especially the mother of the reigning sultan and his leading concubines, were considerably more active than their predecessors in the direct exercise of political power—in creating and manipulating domestic political factions, in negotiating with ambassadors of foreign powers, and in acting as regents to their sons. In addition, this period is notable for the important role acquired by dynastic women, the queen mother in particular, in the symbolics of sovereignty—the ceremonial demonstrations of imperial legitimacy and the patronage of artistic production.

The standard historical treatment of this salience of the imperial harem in Ottoman politics views it, in the framework of the Islamic polity and Islamic society, as an illegitimate exercise of power. The Ottomans, who established the longest-lived (ca. 1300 to 1923) and indisputably one of the greatest of Islamic states, were noted for their devotion to Islamic legal precepts and traditions.[1] One of the essential requirements of rulership in Islam, ideally conceived as successorship to the prophet Muhammad, is that the sovereign be male. Scholarly tradition, however, by denying the legitimacy of other channels of female political participation and influence, has taken a position with

[1] Joseph Schacht, *Introduction to Islamic Law* (Oxford, 1964), pp. 89–90.

regard to the political roles of women that would have been congenial to the most conservative elements in classical Islamic and Ottoman thinking. As an issue of public versus private and its role in the reading of gender in Islamic history, it has been assumed that the segregation of the sexes, a prevalent feature of traditional urban upper-class Muslim society, created a gender-based dichotomy between easily discernible public and private spheres. Women are identified exclusively with the harem and denied any influence beyond its physical boundaries. Conversely, the harem is seen as a woman's world, domestic, private, and parochial. Its only commerce with the world of men is fundamentally sexual. Political activity by women is "meddling" in an arena to which females have no rightful access.

Within the context of Ottoman history, it has been particularly difficult to challenge this view because the rise of the imperial harem to political prominence took place principally after the death of Suleiman the Magnificent. The reign of this celebrated sultan (1520–66) has generally been accepted as the apogee of Ottoman fortunes and the period initiated by his death one of precipitous decline from which the empire never fully recovered. The rise of the harem in the post-Suleimanic period has been attributed to the weakening in the moral fiber and institutional integrity of the society traditionally accepted as the hallmark of this period. According to the conventional etiology of Ottoman decline, the "intrigue" and "meddling" of harem women is both a symptom of collapse and a principal cause of further corruption of institutions and customary practices.

Although it is certainly true that the late sixteenth and early seventeenth centuries were a period of intense difficulty for the empire—militarily, economically, and politically—only recently has scholarly attention begun to be given to the means Ottomans devised to adapt to changing circumstances and the ways in which responses that had their genesis in times of crisis were resolved into permanent solutions.[2] Combined with the contributions of feminist studies, this recent challenge in Ottoman studies to traditional views of post-Suleimanic decline creates a climate that is hospitable for taking a new look at the imperial harem. The aim of this essay is, first, to correct certain misconceptions regarding the harem institution, and, second, to explore the networks through which royal women in this gender-segregated society exercised power in the world beyond the walls of the harem.

[2] Two notable exceptions to this view are Halil İnalcık, "Military and Fiscal Transformation in the Ottoman Empire, 1600–1700," *Archivum Ottomanicum* 6 (1980): 283–337, and İ. Metin Kunt, *The Sultan's Servants: The Transformation of Ottoman Provincial Government, 1550–1650* (New York, 1983).

The Myth of the Harem

The persistence of the view that the exercise of public power by women is illegitimate derives largely from two areas of misunderstanding of traditional Ottoman society. The first is a misunderstanding of the nature and function of the harem institution. In stark contrast to the historically persistent Western image of a group of concubines existing solely for the sexual convenience of their master, the harem of a household of means included women related to the male head of household and to each other in an often complex set of relationships, many of which did not include a sexual component. The harem of a prosperous household would include the wife or wives of the male head of the household and perhaps one or more slave concubines,[3] children of the family, perhaps the widowed mother or unmarried or divorced sisters of the head of the household, and female slaves, who might be the personal property of the women or the men of the family.

The imperial harem was similar but more extensive and its structure more highly articulated.[4] The mother of the reigning sultan was the head of the harem. The queen mother exercised authority over both family members—royal offspring, the consorts of the sultan, who might themselves acquire considerable power, and unmarried or widowed princesses—and the administrative/service hierarchy of the harem. During the last half of the sixteenth century, this latter organization grew rapidly in numbers and status.[5] High-ranking administrative officers of the harem—all of them women—received large stipends and enjoyed considerable prestige, especially the harem stewardess, chief of the administrative hierarchy. These women oversaw not only the large number of servants who performed the housekeep-

[3] Islam permits a man four wives and an unlimited number of slave concubines. For the legal and social status of slave concubines, see Shaun Marmon, "Concubinage, Islamic," *Dictionary of the Middle Ages,* and R. Brunschvig, "ʿAbd," *Encyclopedia of Islam,* 2d ed. The incidence of polygyny (the number of legal wives) varied from time to time and place to place in the Islamic world and appears to have been confined to approximately 1 to 2 percent of the Ottoman middle and upper classes in this period (Ö. L. Barkan, "Edirne Askerî Kassamī 'na Ait Tereke Defterleri (1545–1659)," *Belgeler* 3, nos. 5–6 [1966]: 13–14; Haim Gerber, "Social and Economic Position of Women in an Ottoman City, Bursa, 1600–1700," *International Journal of Middle East Studies* 12 [1980]: 232).

[4] Leslie P. Peirce, *The Imperial Harem: Women and Sovereignty in the Ottoman Empire* (New York, forthcoming), chap. 5.

[5] The size of the imperial harem was exaggerated by Western travelers and scholars: in the mid-sixteenth century it consisted of approximately 150 women and in the mid-seventeenth century approximately 400 women (Prime Ministry Archives in Istanbul: Ali Emiri Series, Register Kanuni 24; Kamil Kepeci Series, Register 7098; Maliyeden Müdevver Series, Registers 774, 1509, 1692).

ing tasks of the harem but, more important, the training of select young harem women who would wait on the sultan or his mother. With the exception of the reigns of one or two notoriously uxorious sultans, few women of the imperial household occupied the sultan's bed. Indeed, as the more astute and well-informed of Western observers commented, the imperial harem resembled a nunnery in its hierarchical organization and the enforced chastity of the great majority of its members.[6]

The word *harem* is one of a family of important words in the vocabulary of Islam derived from the Arabic root *h-r-m*. These words partake of one or both of two general—and obviously related—meanings associated with the root: to be forbidden or unlawful and to declare sacred, inviolable, or taboo.[7] A harem is by definition a sanctuary or a sacred precinct and by implication a space in which certain individuals or certain modes of behavior are forbidden. Mecca and Medina, the two holiest cities of Islam, are commonly referred to as "the two noble harems" (*haremeyn-i sherifeyn*), and in Ottoman usage the interior of a mosque is known as its harem. Because Islamic law limits open contact between the sexes to a specified degree of kinship, the private quarters of a house and by extension the female members of the household are its harem. The word *harem* is a term of respect, redolent of religious purity and honor. With the exception of its reference to the women of a family, it is not gender-specific. Indeed, the residence of the Ottoman sultan contained not one but two harems: the other, the innermost courtyard of the palace, populated exclusively by males and containing private quarters for the sultan as well as the famed school that trained youths for government service, was known as "the imperial harem" or "the honored harem" (*harem-i hümayun, harem-i muhterem*) by virtue of the presence of the sultan, "God's shadow on earth."

A second misunderstanding of the nature of Ottoman society is the erroneous assumption that the seclusion of women precluded their exercising any influence beyond the walls of the harem, that women were meant to play only a narrow role within the family, subordinate to its male members. The segregation of the sexes created for women a society that developed its own hierarchy of authority. The larger the

[6] Robert Withers, "The Grand Signiors Serraglio," in S. Purchas, *His Pilgrimes*, vol. 9 (Glasgow, 1905), p. 339 (translation of Ottaviano Bon, *Descrizione del Serraglio del Gran Signore*, in *Le relazioni degli stati Europei*, Ser. 5, Turchia, ed. Nicolò Barozzi and Guglielmo Berchet [Venice, 1871], 1:59–124); Michel Baudier, *Histoire généralle de Serrail, et de la cour de Grand Seigneur, empereur des Turcs* (Paris, 1631), p. 19; J[ean] B[aptiste] Tavernier, *Nouvelle relation de l'interieur du Serrail de Grand Seigneur* (Paris, 1681), p. 541.

[7] For an excellent discussion of the concept *harem* see Shaun Marmon, "Eunuchs of the Prophet: Space, Time, and Gender in Islamic Society" Ph.D. diss., Princeton University, 1990, pp. 6–26.

household, the more articulated was the power structure of its harem. Women of superior status in this female society, the matriarchal elders, had considerable authority not only over other women but also over younger males in the family, for the harem was also the setting for the private life of men.[8] Furthermore, female networks sustained through formal visiting rituals provided women with information and sources of power useful to their male relatives.[9] In both its sources and its effects, the authority enjoyed by female elders transcended the bounds of the individual family. In a polity such as that of the Ottomans, in which the empire was considered the personal domain of the dynastic family and the empire's subjects the servants or slaves of the dynasty, it was natural that important women within the dynastic household—in particular, the mother of the reigning sultan—would assume legitimate roles of authority in the public sphere.

A further source of women's influence beyond the family was their ownership and exploitation of property. A woman's economic independence was derived from her rights under Islamic law to the dowry provided by her husband and to specified shares of the estates of deceased kin.[10] As property owners and litigants in property, inheritance, divorce, and other legal suits, women—or at least women of means—had access to economic and social power;[11] it must be admitted, however, that at present we lack the historical evidence to determine the extent to which women of different social levels were able to exploit these theoretical rights to their advantage. That prominent women often used their wealth to the advantage of other women is suggested by contemporary histories and testamentary documents, which show well-to-do individuals making provision not only for female family members and retainers but also for less fortunate women—orphans, paupers, prisoners, and prostitutes.[12] Through their practice of the charity incumbent on Muslims, women asserted the prerogative of claiming and organizing a sector of public life for their own welfare.

[8] On the Turkish family see Alan Duben, "Turkish Families and Households in Historical Perspective," *Journal of Family History* 10 (Spring 1985): 75–97. On the influence that Turkic tribal women today derive from their separate social organization see Nancy Tapper, "Matrons and Mistresses: Women and Boundaries in Two Middle Eastern Tribal Societies," *Archives Européennes de Sociologie* 21 (1980): 59–79.

[9] On the subject of visiting among the female Ottoman elite, see Lady Mary Wortley Montagu, *The Complete Letters of Lady Mary Wortley Montagu*, ed. Robert Halsband (Oxford, 1965), 1:347–52, 380–87; Fanny Davis, *The Ottoman Lady: A Social History from 1718–1918* (Westport, Connecticut, 1986), pp. 131–56.

[10] For a brief exposition of the legal position of women see John Esposito, *Women in Muslim Family Law* (Syracuse, 1982), pp. 13–48.

[11] See Gerber, "Social and Economic Position of Women"; Ronald C. Jennings, "Women in Early 17th Century Ottoman Judicial Records—the Sharia Court of Anatolian Kayseri," *Journal of the Economic and Social History of the Orient* 18 (Part 1): 53–114.

[12] Peirce, *The Imperial Harem*, chap. 7.

Thus in the Ottoman case, conventional notions of public and private are not congruent with gender. In fact, an examination of the structure of male society and the interaction of male and female networks shows that, at the highest reaches of society at least, notions of public and private tend to lose meaning altogether. In many ways, male society observed the same criteria of status and propriety as did female society. The degree of seclusion from the common gaze served as an index of the status of the man as well as the woman of means. No Ottoman male of rank appeared on the streets without a retinue, just as a woman of standing could maintain her reputation for virtue only if she appeared in public with a cordon of attendants.[13] Poor men and poor women mingled in the city streets and bazaars, their cramped households and lack of servants preventing them from emulating the deportment of the well-to-do. At the highest levels of government, there were no public buildings set aside for the conduct of the state's or the people's affairs; instead, the household compound served as the locus of government. Ottoman society was thus dichotomized into spheres characterized not by notions of public/commonweal/male and private/domestic/female but rather by distinctions between the privileged and the common, the sacred or honorable and the profane—distinctions that cut across the dichotomy of gender.[14]

Sources of Harem Power

These observations will facilitate an examination of the reasons why dynastic women acquired a substantially increased role in the exercise of political power in the sixteenth century. There were two principal features that distinguished the careers of women during the reigns of Suleiman and his successors from the careers of their predecessors: greater physical proximity to the sultan and greater status within the royal family. Both resulted from a profound change in dynastic politics, a transformation from a decentralized to a centralized style of government. In this transformation, women of the dynastic family—the sultan's mother, his principal concubines, and occasionally his sisters—gained power as princes lost it.

According to custom that had prevailed for nearly a century before Suleiman's accession in 1520, if not longer, princes, princesses, and

[13] See the responses to queries on points of Islamic law (*fetva*) of the late sixteenth-century Ottoman chief mufti Ebu Suud, in M. Ertugrul Düzdağ, *Şehyülislâm Ebussuûd Efendi Fetvaları* (Istanbul, 1976), p. 55.

[14] For discussion of the importance of the division between privileged and common (*khass* and *'amm*), see Roy P. Mottahedeh, *Loyalty and Leadership in an Early Islamic Community* (Princeton, 1980), pp. 115–29, 154–55; Bernard Lewis, *The Political Language of Islam* (Chicago, 1988). p. 67.

their mothers lived apart from the sultan. The royal offspring and their mothers (by the end of the fifteenth century virtually all slave concubines)[15] were housed in a palace separate from that of the sultan. When they reached puberty, the sultan's daughters were married to provincial governors and his sons dispatched with great ceremony to their own provincial governorates. Although the independence of princes was carefully circumscribed by the sultan, they were prominent political figures who functioned as the most visible and important representatives of the power and charisma of the dynasty after their father. The system of succession that prevailed in this period—all princes were considered eligible for the throne, and the heir was the one who could eliminate all other claimants—inevitably rendered them rival foci of political factions. Each prince was accompanied to his provincial post by his mother, who was expected to support her son's efforts to win the throne. The practice of fratricide (whereby, in the interests of security, a new sultan executed his defeated brothers and their sons) meant that both a prince and his mother had as their highest priority his political survival. Only the mother of a victorious prince would return to the imperial capital, as queen mother to the new sultan. The fate of a royal wife or concubine thus depended almost entirely on that of her son.

The sixteenth century witnessed a reversal of this policy of dynastic decentralization, as the royal family was gradually centralized in the capital and lodged in the harem quarters of the sultan's palace. This process began with two innovations introduced by Suleiman. In a reversal later political commentators were to lament as impolitic, he married his sisters, daughters, and granddaughters to top-ranking statesmen, whenever possible to his grand viziers.[16] Since the duties of such statesmen required them to remain in proximity to the sultan, their wives lived in the capital rather than in the provinces. Suleiman also abandoned the practice of serial concubinage, regarded as binding tradition; this practice appears to have been aimed at ensuring that the mother of a prince would have no more than one son so that no prince would be disadvantaged in the contest for succession. Suleiman raised one of his concubines, Hurrem, to an extraordinarily privileged position: he had five sons and a daughter by her, contracted a legal marriage to her, and established in his palace a permanent residence for her where she remained when her sons were dispatched to the provinces.

[15] It was common for Islamic dynasties to reproduce themselves by means of slave concubinage, either exclusively or in combination with formal marriage. On the Ottoman transition from interdynastic marriage to slave concubinage, see Peirce, *The Imperial Harem*, chap. 2.

[16] Koçu Bey, *Risale*, ed. Ali Kemali Aksüt (Istanbul, 1939), p. 61.

The last support in the edifice of dynastic decentralization—the princely governorate—was dismantled by Suleiman's son and grandson. With the demise of their political role, princes became faceless individuals, strictly confined to the palace, where they were kept in a perpetual state of preadulthood, denied the right to marry or to father children by concubines. By the end of the sixteenth century, no members of the royal family except the sultan left the capital. Indeed, the only members of the family to leave the palace residence were married princesses. As a consequence, the imperial harem expanded greatly in size as it absorbed the suites of mothers and sons and acquired the requisite administrative structure.

More important, women of considerable status and political influence now pursued their careers and promoted those of their sons in close proximity to one another. The rise of the harem as the central arena of dynastic politics endowed royal women with considerably greater political leverage than they had previously enjoyed and more opportunities to exert it. Furthermore, women began to fill the vital role of publicly demonstrating the dynasty's legitimacy and magnificence, a role left empty by the departure of princes from the stage of royal politics. Where once princes' weddings were ceremonial occasions, the marriages of princesses were now lavishly celebrated. The sultan's mother, featured in numerous royal progresses in the capital and in surrounding provinces, became the most celebrated public figure after her son.

It is beyond the scope of this essay to do more than briefly list the factors underlying the transformation of dynastic politics outlined above. Suleiman's privileging of women has generally been seen as "indulgence," a personal weakness that opened the Pandora's box of female "lust for power" and "greed for wealth" that future generations were unable to shut. I suggest instead that his creation and exploitation of family-based networks is more properly viewed as a political strategy. This strategy was useful in building a personal base for the sultan's authority and creating a political force to oppose increasingly entrenched interests, for example the Janissary corps, that might resist the sovereign.[17] The political roles made possible for women during the reigns of Suleiman and his successors were reinforced by a series of dynastic accidents in the first half of the seventeenth century. The six sultans who came to the throne in this period were either minors or mentally incapable of governing, and it became customary in such circumstances for the sultan's mother to act as regent. The enormous prestige enjoyed by two of these regent queen mothers, Kösem Sultan

[17] I am indebted to Roy P. Mottahedeh for suggesting a parallel in the exploitation of family-based political networks between Suleiman and the famed Abbasid caliph, Hârûn al-Rashîd.

and her daughter-in-law Turhan Sultan, had the effect of transforming the queen mother's relationship with her son from an essentially private one into one that encompassed the entire empire. Evidence of this broader relationship can be seen in the attribution to the queen mother of the honorific "mother of the Muslim believers" (*umm al-mu'minîn*), a Qur'anic title bestowed on the wives of the prophet Muhammad.

Perhaps the most broadly influential factor in the transformation of dynastic politics was the coming to an end around the mid-sixteenth century of the great age of Ottoman conquest and expansion. Suleiman continued to campaign until the end of his reign, but his successors found it more politic to downplay the martial role heretofore, a sine qua non of sovereignty. The wisdom of a peace policy was, however, not always recognized by the sultan's subjects, who began to wonder if the sedentariness of their sultans was responsible for the problems plaguing the empire toward the end of the century. In these circumstances, it was wiser to remove princes, potential candidates for a forcible change of rulership, from the field. A further advantage to the abandonment of the princely governorate was freedom from the ravaging civil wars that had occurred among rival princes; the confinement of princes to the capital was soon followed by a change in the succession system to the principle of seniority (the succession henceforth went to the eldest male member of the dynasty, be he the brother, cousin, or son of the former sultan). The move from an expansionist policy to one based principally on maintaining the frontiers of the empire influenced the conduct of dynastic politics in another way: in promoting its claim to legitimate sovereignty, the dynasty now began to deemphasize the role of warrior for the Muslim faith and to stress instead its propagation of the faith through piety and munificent support of the community of believers. Women were easily incorporated into public expressions of this latter policy.[18]

Networks of Power

Despite their often considerable influence, women of the imperial harem were inescapably confined to the palace. They left the royal residence only under the tight surveillance of the black eunuch guards of the harem. Only the queen mother appears to have had mobility outside the confines of the harem: in public ceremonials she might make

[18] For a striking parallel in the incorporation of women into dynastic propaganda during a "sedentarizing" stage, see Kenneth Holum, *Theodosian Empresses: Women and Imperial Dominion in Late Antiquity* (Berkeley, 1982). I am grateful to Peter R. Brown for drawing this work to my attention.

herself visible from within her carriage or palanquin as she cast coins to onlookers or acknowledged their obeisances. She might also meet with high-ranking government officials in private conference if she were carefully veiled, but even she had no routine, face-to-face contact with men. Thus it was essential that harem women develop links with individuals or groups in the outside world. There was no lack of parties eager to cooperate, for as the harem came to enjoy a greater share of imperial authority, not only did its residents seek outside channels through which they might accomplish their political goals, but outsiders were anxious to form ties with potential patrons within the palace.

Like the sultans during this period, harem women built much of their networking on family-based relationships. It is crucial to recognize that the family was not limited to blood relationships but included the entire household, the vast majority of which, in the case of the dynastic family, was composed of slaves. Like other Muslim states before them, the Ottomans based their authority on a military slave elite, which was recruited from outside the empire, converted to Islam and carefully trained, and instilled with loyalty to the dynasty. From the second half of the fifteenth century on, this slave elite came to dominate the ruling class, taking over administrative positions from the native Turkish elite, with the exception of the scribal bureaucracy and the religious hierarchy. What has gone unnoticed is the remarkable parallel between the growing influence of male and female slaves in the ruling class: the dynasty began to rely exclusively on slave concubines for its reproduction at the same time that the highest offices of the state began to be awarded to male slaves.[19] By the reign of Suleiman (possibly by the reign of his father, Selim), the only free Muslim women in the imperial harem were the sultan's sisters, daughters, aunts, and mother (originally a slave concubine, the latter, by virtue of having borne a child to her master, was freed according to Islamic law upon his death). Toward the end of the sixteenth century, the male "harem" in the imperial palace—the third courtyard, where select young slaves were trained for the offices that would eventually be granted them—began slowly to be penetrated by native Muslims,[20] but the female harem appears to have maintained its exclusively slave nature.

For the members of the dynastic family, the harem served as residence. For female slave members of the sultan's household, it might best be described as a training institution, where the education given to young women had as its goal not only the provision of concubines for the sultan but also the provision of wives for men near the top of

[19] This parallel has been briefly noted by Halil İnalcık, *The Ottoman Empire: The Classical Age, 1300–1600*, trans. C. Imber and N. Itzkowitz (New York, 1973), p. 85.

[20] Kunt, *Sultan's Servants*, p. 96.

military/administrative hierarchies (the highest-ranking officials would marry Ottoman princesses). Just as the third-courtyard school prepared men through personal service to the sultan within his palace for service to the dynasty outside the palace, the harem prepared women through personal service to the sultan and his mother to take up their roles in the outer world. Manumitted and frequently married to graduates of the palace school, these women, together with their husbands, would form households modeled on that of the palace. For both men and women, the palace system of training had as one of its fundamental goals the inculcation of loyalty to the ruling house. But because women as well as men sustained the ties that bound the empire's elite, the focus of the latter's loyalty was not only the sultan himself but the women of his family as well.

Within the imperial harem, the sultan's mother and favorite concubine or concubines were best positioned to build for themselves and/or for their sons factional support bridging the palace and the outer world. They were mothers not only of the sultan or potential sultans but of princesses as well. Moreover, their status and wealth permitted them to control the careers of a large number of personal attendants and to influence the careers of the harem's administrative officials. It was a meritorious act for a Muslim, male or female, to educate and manumit a slave. The manumission of a slave also worked practically to the benefit of the former owner, who enjoyed the loyalty of the former slave in a clientage relationship. The seventeenth-century historian Mustafa Naima praised the generosity of the queen mother, Kösem Sultan, who appears to have taken pains to cultivate close ties of patronage with her freed slaves:

> She would free her slave women after two or three years of service, and would arrange marriages with retired officers of the court or suitable persons from outside, giving the women dowries and jewels and several purses of money according to their talents and station, and ensuring that their husbands had suitable positions. She looked after these former slaves by giving them an annual stipend, and on the religious festivals and holy days she would give them purses of money.[21]

Manumitted slaves might act as agents for their former mistresses, just as princess daughters, when married, could help their mothers, who remained within the imperial compound. Both princess daughters and manumitted slaves might be counted on to influence their husbands to act as advocates; for this reason, harem women strove to exert as much control as possible over the choice of husbands for their daughters or slaves.

[21] Mustafa Naima, *Tarih-i Naima*, 6 vols. (Istanbul, 1280/1863–64), 5:113.

Several incidents related in contemporary histories demonstrate the extent to which members of a harem woman's suite acted as allies within the palace and might go on to become agents outside. The mother of Mahmud, the eldest son of Mehmed III (r. 1595–1603), was not sufficiently circumspect in her efforts to look after her son's interests. Mahmud and his mother were executed when the queen mother, Safiye Sultan, intercepted a message sent into the palace to the prince's mother by a religious seer whom she had consulted about her son's future. The message indicated that Mahmud would succeed his father within six months. The sultan, who had grown so fat and physically unfit that his doctors warned him against campaigning, was particularly threatened by this augury because of Mahmud's popularity with the powerful Janissary troops and his pleas to be allowed to take up arms against Anatolian rebels challenging his father's authority. A substantial number of harem women were implicated in the affair and suffered the same fate as the prince's mother. Their death by drowning at sea—a form of exemplary execution whose use for women can probably be attributed to its upholding the principle of gender segregation by preserving the female corpse from the public gaze—was reported by Henry Lello, the English ambassador to the Ottoman court: "That nighte [the mother was] wth 30. more of her followers wch they supposed to be interessed in the busines shutt up alyve into sacks & so throwne into the sea."[22] This affair vividly illustrates the clash of two royal mothers trying to protect the interests of their sons.

Perhaps the most dramatic example of the transfer of loyalty from the palace to the outside world is the career of Meleki Hatun, originally a member of the suite of the queen mother Kösem Sultan. In 1648 Kösem's second sultan son was deposed for mental incompetency, an event that should have brought her twenty-five-year career as queen mother to an end. Instead of retiring and thus permitting the succeeding sultan's mother to assume the position of queen mother, however, she was asked by leading statesmen to stay on as regent to the new sultan, her seven-year-old grandson, because of the youth of his mother, Turhan. When Turhan began to assert what she saw as her rightful authority, Kösem reportedly planned to depose the young sultan and replace him with another prince, whose mother she believed to be more tractable. At this point, Meleki deserted Kösem and betrayed her plans to Turhan, thus enabling the latter to eliminate her mother-in-law (Kösem was murdered in a palace coup led by Turhan's chief black eunuch). Meleki became the new queen mother's loyal and favored retainer and was eventually manumitted and married to Shaban Halife, a former page in the palace training school. As a team,

[22] Henry Lello, *The Report of Lello, Third English Ambassador to the Sublime Porte*, ed. O. Burian (Ankara, 1952), pp. 14–15, 57–58.

Meleki and Shaban were ideally suited to act as channels of information and intercessors on behalf of individuals with petitions for the palace: Shaban received male petitioners, Meleki female petitioners; Shaban exploited contacts he had presumably formed while serving within the palace, and Meleki exploited her relationship with Turhan Sultan. The political influence of the couple became so great that they lost their lives in 1656, when the troops in Istanbul rebelled against alleged abuses in government.[23]

High-ranking harem officers might establish important links outside the palace through family connections. Particularly valuable were the connections of the sultan's former wet nurse and the harem stewardess; in the stipends they received and in their ceremonial prestige, these two were the highest-ranking women in the harem after the royal family. A harem woman who lacked daughters might turn to one of these women to form a political bridge to the outside world, as did the mother of Mustafa I (r. 1617–18, 1622–23). No one had expected that Mustafa, who suffered from severe emotional problems, would become sultan. Within the imperial harem, his mother (whose name is lost to history) did not enjoy a position of much status: on the eve of her son's accession in 1617, her daily stipend was only one hundred silver pieces, while the newly deceased sultan's favorite concubine (the future queen mother Kösem) received one thousand and the former queen mother Safiye, now in retirement, two thousand.[24] When Mustafa was suddenly catapulted to the throne, one of the few political alliances that his mother was able to forge was with her son's sword-bearer, a high-ranking inner palace officer, who was brought out of the palace and awarded the prestigious and strategically vital post of governor of Egypt on condition that he marry the sultan's wet nurse.[25] Within a few months the pasha was brought back to Istanbul as grand vizier.

Probably the most important links with centers of power outside the palace were forged by harem women through the marriages of their daughters, the princesses of the dynasty, to leading statesmen. To become a royal son-in-law was a mark of high honor, conferred generally on the highest-ranking government officers or on promising younger officers. These weddings were lavishly celebrated state occasions, serving in the sixteenth and seventeenth centuries to demonstrate imperial magnificence and munificence, as the weddings of princes, now shut up in the palace and forbidden to marry, had done in the fourteenth and fifteenth centuries. The royal son-in-law, known as *damad*, would be given an elegant palace and was likely to become grand vi-

[23] For the career of Meleki Hatun, see Naima, *Tarih-i Naima*, vols. 5 and 6, passim.
[24] Prime Ministry Archives, Maliyeden Müdevver Series, Register 397.
[25] Naima, *Tarih-i Naima*, 2:159.

zier at some point in his career. Although he was not immune to dismissal or execution, he could get away with more than the non-*damad* statesman could.

The dynasty had always used the marriages of princesses for political ends; what stands out in this period is the frequency with which they occurred. By the seventeenth century, serial marriages of princesses were common. The most extreme example of this practice was two daughters of Kösem Sultan and Ahmed I, Ayshe and Fatma, who were married six and seven times respectively; Ayshe was approximately fifty and Fatma sixty-one at their final betrothals.[26] Serial marriage was possible because princesses might first be married at the age of two or three; by the time a princess reached puberty she could be in her third or fourth marriage because her husbands encountered many risks in high office, including death in battle or execution. These unions could be very happy: a sixteenth-century princess, Shah Sultan, and her second husband were said to be so compatible that they fell fatally ill simultaneously, lay side by side in their deathbeds, and expired at the very same moment.

Linking important statesmen to the royal family clearly worked to the advantage of the sovereign. With the greater seclusion of the sultan in the post-Suleimanic period, the strong personal bonds that had earlier existed between the sultan and his leading subjects, fighting together and sitting in the imperial council together, were no longer possible. Providing the hand of a princess functioned to seal the loyalty of statesmen to their sovereign. Bringing a pasha into the royal family as *damad* sometimes even served to control sedition, as in the case of rebel vizier Ibshir Mustafa Pasha, who became the final husband of the six-times-married Ayshe. The importance of princess-statesman marital alliances—and the consequent strategic interest in princesses as political contacts—is seen in the care taken by foreign ambassadors to keep track of who was married to whom[27] and in the lavish gifts they bestowed on these politically key members of the dynasty.

Obviously, not only sultans but queen mothers as well benefited immensely from this practice. Married princesses enjoyed relatively easy access to the imperial harem, their parental home, and could serve as informants, couriers, and political strategists. Because the interests of princesses and their mothers in the harem were harmonious—the goals of the former being to prolong the political careers, indeed the lives, of their husbands, and of the latter to secure loyal allies on the outside, the networks formed by the marriages of princesses were vital. It is surely no coincidence that the most powerful queen

[26] Çagatay Uluçay, *Padişahların Kadınları ve Kızları* (Ankara, 1980), pp. 50–52.

[27] Eugenio Alberi, *Relazioni degli Ambasciatori veneti al Senato*, Ser. 3, 3 vols. (Florence, 1840–55), 1:117. 404–7; 2:354–58; 3:239–42, 288–93, 366–74.

mothers were those with several daughters: Nurbanu (queen mother from 1574 to 1583) had three, Safiye (1595–1603) had two, and Kösem (1623–52) had at least three. Indeed, it was largely the efforts of queen mothers that resulted in the frequency of princess-statesman alliances in this period. The queen mother arranged the marriages not only of her own daughters but of the daughters of her son and his concubines as well. The Venetian ambassador reported in 1583 that Nurbanu planned to marry her son Murad III's second daughter to the head of the palace guards.[28] Kösem's long career gave her considerable opportunity to forge such alliances. In 1626 or thereabout she wrote to the grand vizier proposing marriage to one of her daughters: "Whenever you're ready, let me know and I'll act accordingly. We'll take care of you right away. I have a princess ready. I'll do just as I did when I sent out my Fatma."[29] In the early 1640s, Kösem emerged victorious from a conflict with a concubine of her recently deceased son Murad IV over the marital fortunes of thirteen-year-old Kaya, daughter of the concubine and grand-daughter of Kösem. The concubine was anxious for Kaya to marry one of her own political allies, the former sultan's sword-bearer, but Kösem's candidate, a pasha in his forties, won out.[30]

By creating and exploiting the variety of networks described above, a queen mother or a powerful concubine could work different sectors of public government. Through the marriages of princesses or the imperial wet nurse, alliances could be formed with the most powerful of statesmen and with the representatives of foreign powers. Through clientage ties with former slaves, contacts could be created with a wide range of middle-level public officials. It is important to recognize that this establishment of a constellation of contacts outside the palace was by no means surreptitious. Nor was it a uniquely "female" or "harem" paradigm for the organization of political patronage and the creation of political influence. The governing class of the Ottoman Empire in this period operated not so much on the basis of institutionally or functionally ascribed authority as through a complex of personal bonds and family and household connections. Functionally ascribed authority—authority devolving from one's office—certainly existed, but more important was the web of individual relations—of patronage and clientage, of teacher and student, of kinship and marriage—that brought one to that office and that one used in the exercise of one's official power. Men as well as women sustained their careers by means of such

[28] Ibid., 3:243.
[29] Topkapı Palace Archives, Evrak 2457/2.
[30] *Le relazioni degli stati Europei*, ed. Barozzi and Berchet, 1:370; Sieur du Loir, *Les voyage du Sieur du Loir* (Paris, 1654), pp. 124–26; Uluçay, *Padişahların*, pp. 54–55.

networks, and men and women played significant roles in the formation of each other's networks.

Only when the paradigm of rigidly separate public/male and private/female spheres is discarded can we begin to appreciate the ways in which the structure of the Ottoman ruling class enabled women to participate in the political life of the empire. Conversely, by understanding how women were able to acquire and exercise power, we obtain a clearer picture of the structure of Ottoman politics and society. For example, it is widely recognized that the household was the fundamental unit of Ottoman political organization in this period, but the role of women in the construction and maintenance of the household system has been ignored. Future research will demonstrate whether or not the essential role played by women in the Ottoman dynastic household was reflected in the organization and operation of households of lesser status.

CHAPTER THREE

Maria Winkelmann at the Berlin Academy: The Clash between Craft Traditions and Professional Science

Londa Schiebinger

European science was in many ways a new enterprise in the seventeenth and eighteenth centuries, which, at least ideologically, welcomed broad participation. The major European academies of science—important spurs to the scientific revolution—were founded in the seventeenth century. Women, however, were not to become regular members of these academies for three centuries. The Royal Society in London elected its first women members, Marjory Stephenson and Kathleen Lonsdale, in 1945. The prestigious Académie des Sciences in Paris first admitted a woman, Yvonne Choquet-Bruhat, in 1979. (Even Marie Curie, the first person ever to win two Nobel prizes, was denied membership.) At the Berlin Academy of Sciences the first woman scientist was awarded membership in 1949.

Support for this research was provided by the National Endowment for the Humanities, the Rockefeller Foundation, and the Deutscher Akademischer Austauschdienst. My thanks to Christa Kirsten, Director, Zentrales Akademie-Archiv der Akademie der Wissenschaften der DDR; Gerda Utermöhlen of the Leibniz Archiv, Niedersächsische Landesbibliothek, Hannover; and the staff of the Observatoire de Paris for their kind assistance with materials for this essay. My thanks also to Robert Proctor, Richard Kremer, Margaret Rossiter, Roger Hahn, Merry Wiesner, Robert Westman, and Lyndal Roper for their comments. This essay was first published in *Isis, Journal of the History of Science Society* 78 (1987): 174–200. Another version appears in *Current Issues in Women's History*, ed. Arina Angerman et al. (London, 1989).

I have used Winkelmann's maiden name throughout because this is the name she used for her publications. The use of the maiden name is also consistent with the practice of the day. Astronomer Maria Cunitz, for example, published under her maiden name; midwives listed in Prussian address lexicons also used their maiden names (their married names were given in parentheses). Winkelmann also referred to herself as "Kirchin" (the feminine form of Kirch) in correspondence with Leibniz and academy of-

It would be a mistake to think that women were excluded because none were qualified as scientists when these academies first opened their doors. There were, in fact, a significant number of women trained and ready to take their place among men of science. Between the years 1650 and 1720, for example, more than 14 percent of German astronomers were women.[1] The exclusion of women from these academies was not a foregone conclusion but resulted from a process of extended negotiation between these women and the academy officials.[2]

The case of Maria Winkelmann at the Royal Academy of Sciences in Berlin was decisive and pivotal. In 1712 Maria Winkelmann lost her battle to become academy astronomer. Already a seasoned astronomer when her husband and academy astronomer, Gottfried Kirch, died, Winkelmann asked to be appointed in her husband's stead. The story of Maria Winkelmann's rejection by the academy is compelling. More importantly, it illustrates patterns in women's participation in early modern science. Craft traditions fostered women's participation in astronomy. Through apprenticeships, women gained access to the secrets and tools of a trade, whether illustrating manuscripts or using telescopes. Winkelmann's petition to become academy astronomer drew legitimacy from guild traditions that recognized the right of a widow to carry on the family business. Craft traditions, however, were counterbalanced by other trends, both old and new. For centuries, women had been excluded from universities, as they were to be excluded from the new scientific academies. In many ways, the new trend of professionalization served to reaffirm the traditional exclusion of women from intellectual culture. Indeed, there were those at the Berlin Academy who judged it improper for a woman to practice the art of astronomy and suggested that Winkelmann return to her "distaff" and "spindle."[3]

---

ficials, playing (I assume) on her husband's reputation in her quest for employment. Academy officials referred to her as "Kirchin" or "widow Kirch."

[1] This number is drawn from Joachim von Sandrart, *Teutsche Academie der Edlen Bau-, Bild- und Mahlerey-Künste* (Frankfurt, 1675); Friedrich Luce, *Fürsten Kron* (Frankfurt am Main, 1685); Friedrich Weidler, *Historia astronomiae* (Wittenberg, 1741); and Christian Jöcher, *Allgemeines Gelehrten-Lexicon, darinne die Gelehrten aller Stände sowohl männ- als weiblichen Geschlechts* (Leipzig, 1760). In reference to the astronomers Maria Winkelmann and Maria Cunitz, Alphonse des Vignoles, Vice President of the Berlin Academy, wrote, "If one considers the reputations of Madame Kirch [Maria Winkelmann] and Mlle Cunitz, one must admit that there is no branch of science . . . in which women are not capable of achievement, and that in astronomy, in particular, Germany takes the prize above all other states in Europe" (Alphonse des Vignoles, "Eloge de Madame Kirch à l'occasion de laquelle on parle de quelques autres femmes & d'un paison astronomes," *Bibliothèque germanique* 3 [1721]: 182–83).

[2] See also Londa Schiebinger, *The Mind Has No Sex? Women in the Origins of Modern Science* (Cambridge, Mass., 1989), pp. 10–36.

[3] Vignoles, "Eloge de Madame Kirch," pp. 115–83, esp. p. 181.

Craft Traditions in Astronomy

Edgar Zilsel was among the first to point to the importance of craft skills for the development of modern science in the West.[4] Zilsel located the origin of modern science in the fusion of three traditions: that of letters exemplified by the literary humanists; that of logic and mathematics exemplified by the Aristotelian scholastics; and that of practical experiment and application exemplified by the empirical artist-engineers. Astronomy drew from each of these traditions.[5] The craft aspects of astronomy, however, were especially important in the sixteenth and seventeenth centuries. The astronomer was both theoretician and technician; he or she was versed not just in Copernican theory and mathematics but also in the arts of glass-grinding, instrument making, calculating, and observing. These were skills of the artisan, not the scholar. Astronomers of the seventeenth century thus bore a close resemblance to guild masters and apprentices, though they were never officially organized into guilds.

Of the various institutional homes of astronomy, only the artisanal workshop welcomed women. Women were not newcomers to workshops: it was here that the fifteenth-century writer Christine de Pizan had located women's greatest innovations in the arts and sciences—the spinning of wool, silk, and linen and "creating the general means of civilized existence."[6] Women's position in guilds and household production remained especially strong in Germany: of the thirty-eight guilds in Cologne (a city where women's economic position was especially strong), women were full members of more than twenty.[7]

[4] See Edgar Zilsel, "The Sociological Roots of Modern Science," *American Journal of Sociology* 47 (1942): 544–62, esp. pp. 545–46.

[5] Astronomers served at universities, royal courts, or as lords of their own fiefs. Noble patrons themselves became avid amateurs. See Robert Westman, "The Astronomer's Role in the Sixteenth Century: A Preliminary Study," *History of Science* 18 (1980): 105–47; see also Ernst Zinner, *Die Geschichte der Sternkunde von den ersten Anfängen bis zu Gegenwart* (Berlin, 1931), pp. 587–90.

[6] Christine de Pizan, *The Book of the City of Ladies* (1405), trans. Earl Jeffrey Richards (New York, 1982), pp. 70–80.

[7] Margret Wensky, *Die Stellung der Frau in der stadtkölnischen Wirtschaft im Spätmittelalter* (Cologne, 1981), pp. 318–19. Jean Quataert has warned against conflating important distinctions between guilds and households ("The Shaping of Women's Work in Manufacturing: Guilds, Households, and the State in Central Europe, 1648–1870," *American Historical Review* 90 [1985]: 1122–48, esp. p. 1134). For the case of astronomy, however, the larger danger has been to ignore almost entirely both of these forms of production. Here I use the term *craft* to refer to household production and *guild* to refer to regulated crafts. For women's role in production in Germany see also Peter Ketsch, *Frauen im Mittelalter: Quellen und Materialien*, 2 vols. (Düsseldorf, 1983), 1:141–224; Merry E. Wiesner, *Working Women in Renaissance Germany* (New Brunswick, 1986), esp. chap. 5; and Martha Howell, *Women, Production, and Patriarchy in Late Medieval Cities* (New Brunswick, 1986).

The craft aspects of astronomy in this period, then, provide the key to understanding Maria Winkelmann's active participation in German science. Maria Margaretha Winkelmann was born in 1670 at Panitzsch (near Leipzig), the daughter of a Lutheran minister. She was educated privately by her father and, after his death, by her uncle. From an early age she served as an unofficial apprentice to the farmer and self-taught astronomer Christoph Arnold, learning the art of astronomy through hands-on experience in observation and calculation.

Women in this period trained as apprentices but not as journeymen. A journeyman might travel over the course of several years from master to master, but a young woman took what training was available in her home. For a woman, the single most important factor for her future in science was her father. Winkelmann trained with Arnold, outside her home; her case was extraordinary because she was an orphan.

Had Maria Winkelmann been male, she would probably have continued her studies at the nearby universities of Leipzig or Jena. Leading male astronomers—Johannes Hevelius, Georg Eimmart, Gottfried Kirch—all held university degrees, though not in astronomy. Hevelius, for example, was by profession a beer brewer and was educated in jurisprudence.[8]

Women typically entered the crafts through apprenticeship or marriage. At Arnold's house Winkelmann met Gottfried Kirch, Germany's leading astronomer. Though her uncle wanted her to marry a young Lutheran minister, he consented to her marriage to Kirch, a man thirty years her senior. Knowing she would have little opportunity to practice astronomy as an independent woman, Winkelmann moved, in typical guild fashion, from a position as an assistant to Arnold to become an assistant to Kirch. As Kirch's second wife, Winkelmann could care for his domestic affairs, as well as serve as a much-needed astronomical assistant, helping in calculations, observations, and the making of calendars.[9]

In 1700, Kirch and Winkelmann took up residence in Berlin, the expanding cultural center of Brandenburg. This move represented an advance in social standing for both husband and wife, yet the route to Berlin was at this time very different for a man and for a woman. A university education at Jena and apprenticeship to the well-known astronomer Hevelius afforded Kirch the opportunity to move from the household of a tailor in the small town of Guben to the position of astronomer at the Societas Regia Scientiarum. Maria Winkelmann's

[8] See Johann Westphal, *Leben, Studien und Schriften des Astronomen Johann Hevelius* (Königsberg, 1820).

[9] Alphonse des Vignoles, "Lebens Umstände und Schicksale des ehemahles berühmten Gottfried Kirchs," *Dresdenische Gelehrte Anzeigen* 49 (1761): 769–77, esp. p. 775; Vignoles, "Eloge de Madame Kirch," pp. 172–73.

mobility came not through education but through marriage. Though coming via different routes, both served at the Berlin Academy—Kirch as astronomer, Winkelmann as an unofficial but recognized assistant to her husband.[10]

Though guild traditions gave women access to certain sciences, it is important not to see this in romantic terms. Women's position in astronomy was similar to their position in the guilds—valued but subordinate. Only a few women, such as the astronomer Maria Cunitz or Maria Winkelmann, directed and published their own work. More often a woman served in various support positions, editing her husband's writings or performing astronomical calculations.

Comets and Calendars: Winkelmann's Scientific Achievement

In 1710, Winkelmann petitioned the Academy of Sciences for a position as calendar maker and assistant astronomer. Was Winkelmann merely a wifely assistant engaged at the periphery in what Margaret Rossiter has defined as "women's work" in science—work typically involving tedious computation, lifelong service as an assistant, and the like?[11] Or was she a qualified astronomer capable of setting and carrying out her own researches?

Though Maria Winkelmann is little known today, she was well-known in her time.[12] Her scientific accomplishments during her first decade at the Berlin Academy were many and varied. Every evening, beginning at nine o'clock, she observed the heavens.[13] During the course of an evening's observations in 1702, she discovered a previously unknown comet—a discovery that should have secured her position in the astronomical community. (Her husband's position at the academy rested partly on his discovery of the comet of 1680.) Today there is no question about Winkelmann's priority in this discovery.[14]

[10] Erik Amburger, *Die Mitglieder der deutschen Akademie der Wissenschaft zu Berlin, 1700–1950* (Berlin, 1950), p. 173.

[11] Margaret Rossiter, "Women's Work in Science, 1880–1910," *Isis* 71 (1980): 381–98. See also her *Women Scientists in America: Struggles and Strategies to 1940* (Baltimore, 1982), pp. 51–72.

[12] For a full bibliography for Winkelmann, see Londa Schiebinger, "Maria Winkelmann at the Berlin Academy: A Turning Point for Women in Science," *Isis* 78 (1987): 174–200, esp. n. 18. See also Dietrich Wattenberg, "Zur Geschichte der Astronomie in Berlin im 16. bis 18. Jahrhundert II," *Die Sterne* 49 (1972): 104–16, and P. Aufgebauer, "Die Astronomenfamilie Kirch," *Die Sterne* 47 (1971): 241–47.

[13] Winkelmann to Leibniz, Leibniz Archiv, Niedersächsiche Landesbibliothek, Hanover, Kirch, no. 472, p. 11.

[14] F. H. Weiss, "Quellenbeiträge zur Geschichte der Preussischen Akademie der Wissenschaften," *Jahrbuch der Preussischen Akademie der Wissenschaften* (1939): 223–24. A copy of Winkelmann's report is also found at the Paris Observatory, Kirch Papers, MS A.B. 3. 7, no. 83, 41, B. All translations given are my own.

In his notes from that night, Kirch recorded that his wife found the comet while he slept: "Early in the morning (about 2:00 A.M.) the sky was clear and starry. Some nights before, I had observed a variable star, and my wife (as I slept) wanted to find and see it for herself. In so doing, she found a comet in the sky. At which time she woke me, and I found that it was indeed a comet. . . . I was surprised that I had not seen it the night before."[15]

News of the comet, the first scientific achievement of the young academy, was sent immediately to the king. The report, however, bore Kirch's name, not Winkelmann's.[16] Published accounts of the comet also bore Kirch's name, which unfortunately led many historians to attribute the discovery of the comet to him alone.

Why did Winkelmann let this happen? Certainly, she was not hesitant about publishing—she was to publish three pamphlets under her own name between the years 1709 and 1711. Her inability to claim recognition for her discovery hinged, in part, on her lack of training in Latin—the shared scientific language in early eighteenth-century Germany—which made it difficult for her to publish in the *Acta eruditorum,* then Germany's only scientific journal. Her own publications were all in German.

More important to the problem of credit for the initial sighting of the comet, however, was that Maria and Gottfried worked closely together (see Figure 3.1). The labor of husband and wife did not divide along modern lines: he was not fully professional, working in an observatory outside the home; she was not fully a housewife, confined to hearth and home. Nor were they independent professionals, each holding a chair of astronomy. Instead, they worked very much as a team and on common problems. As family friend and vice-president of the Berlin Academy Alphonse des Vignoles put it, they took turns observing so that their observations followed night after night without interruption. At other times they observed together, dividing the work (he observing to the north, she to the south) so they could make observations that a single person could not make accurately.[17]

During the years of their acquaintance, academy president Gottfried Leibniz (who generally supported women's intellectual endeavors) had expressed a high regard for Winkelmann's scientific abilities. In 1709, he presented her to the Prussian court, where Winkelmann was to explain her sighting of sunspots. In a letter of introduction Leibniz wrote:

[15] Kirch Papers, Paris Observatory, MS A.B. 3.5, no. 81 B, p. 33.

[16] Adolf Harnack, "Berichte des Secretars der brandenburgischen Societät der Wissenschaften J. Th. Jablonski an der Präsidenten G. W. Leibniz (1700–1715)," *Philosophisch-historische Abhandlungen der Königlichen Akademie der Wissenschaften zu Berlin* 3 (1897): no. 22.

[17] Vignoles, "Eloge de Madame Kirch," p. 174.

Figure 3.1. Johannes Hevelius, Gottfried Kirch's teacher, and his wife Elisabetha collaborated in astronomical work at their private observatory in Danzig much as Kirch and Winkelmann did in nearby Berlin. This illustration from Hevelius's *Machinae coelestis* shows husband and wife working together with the sextant (Danzig, 1673, facing p. 222). By permission of Houghton Library, Harvard University.

> There is [in Berlin] a most learned woman who could pass as a rarity. Her achievement is not in literature or rhetoric but in the most profound doctrines of astronomy. . . . I do not believe that this woman easily finds her equal in the science in which she excells. . . . She favors the Copernican system (the idea that the sun is at rest) like all the learned astronomers of our time. And it is a pleasure to hear her defend that system through the Holy Scripture in which she is also very learned. She observes with the best observers and knows how to handle marvelously the quadrant and the telescope *[grandes lunettes d'approche]*.[18]

He added that if only she had been sent to the Cape of Good Hope instead of astronomer Peter Kolb, the apprentice given the job, the academy would have received more reliable observations.[19]

Winkelmann also made important contributions in making calendars. Calendars—what Leibniz called "the library of the common man"—had been issued since at least the fourteenth century and drew much of their popular appeal from astrology.[20] Until 1768 there was little distinction between calendars and farmers' almanacs; each predicted the best times for haircutting, bloodletting, the conceiving of children, planting of seeds, and felling timber.

Calendar making was a project of both scientific and monetary interest for the academy. Unlike many major European courts, the Prussian court did not yet have its own calendar. In 1700, the Reichstag at Regensburg ruled that an improved calendar similar to the Gregorian calendar was to be used in German lands. Thus the production of an astronomically accurate calendar became a major project for the Academy of Sciences founded in the same year. In addition to fixing the days and months, each calendar predicted the position of the sun, moon, and planets, the phases of the moon, eclipses of the sun or moon to the hour, and the rising and setting of the sun within a quarter of an hour for each day of the year. The monopoly on the sale of calenders was one of the two granted to the academy by the king (the other was the production and sale of silk). Throughout the eighteenth century, the Berlin Academy of Sciences derived a large part of its revenues from the sale of calendars. The income from the calendar (some 2,500 talers per year in the early 1700s) made the position of astronomer particularly important in the academy.[21]

[18] Leibniz to Sophie, January 1709, in Gottfried Leibniz, *Die Werke von Leibniz,* ed. Onno Klopp, 11 vols. (Hanover, 1864–88), 9:295–96.

[19] Leibniz is referring to the attempt to get an exact measurement of the lunar parallax. See Hans Ludendorff, "Zur Frühgeschichte der Astronomie in Berlin," *Vorträge und Schriften der Preussischen Akademie der Wissenschaften* 9 (1942): 3–23, esp. p. 15.

[20] Adolf von Harnack, *Geschichte der Königlich Preussischen Akademie der Wissenschaften zu Berlin,* 3 vols. (1900; rpt. Hildesheim, 1970), 1:124.

[21] Aufgebauer, "Die Astronomenfamilie Kirch," pp. 244–46.

The Attempt to Become Academy Astronomer

Gottfried Kirch died in 1710. It fell to the executive council—President Leibniz, Secretary Johann Theodor Jablonski, his brother and court pastor, D. E. Jablonski, and the librarian—to appoint a new astronomer. The council needed to make the appointment quickly, but apart from one in-house candidate, Secretary Jablonski could think of no one qualified for the position. Though there were few candidates, Maria Winkelmann's name did not enter the deliberations, which is particularly surprising when one considers that her qualifications were similar to her husband's. They both had long years of experience preparing calendars (before coming to the academy, Kirch had earned his living selling Christian, Jewish, and Turkish calendars). They had both discovered comets—Kirch in 1680, Winkelmann in 1702—and made numerous observations and calculations. What Winkelmann did not have, which nearly every member of the academy did, was a university degree.

Since Winkelmann's name had not come up in discussions about the appointment, she submitted it herself, along with her credentials. In a letter to Secretary Jablonski, she asked that she and her son be appointed assistant astronomers in charge of preparing the academy calendar.[22] Her argument for her candidacy was twofold. First, she pointed out that she was well qualified because she had been instructed in astronomical calculation and observation by her husband. Second, and more important, she had been engaged in astronomical work since her marriage, and had, de facto, been working for the academy since her husband's appointment ten years earlier. Indeed, she reported, "for some time, while my dear departed husband was weak and ill, I prepared the calendar from his calculations and published it under his name." She also reminded Jablonski that he himself had remarked on how she lent a helping hand to her husband's astronomical work—work for which she was paid a wage. For Winkelmann, a position at the Berlin Academy was not just an honor, it was a way to support herself and her four children. Her husband, she reported, had left her no means of support.

Jablonski was aware that the academy's handling of Winkelmann's case would set important precedents for the place of women in Germany's leading scientific body. In September 1710, Jablonski cautioned Leibniz: "You should be aware that this approaching decision could

[22] Maria Margaretha Kirchin to the Societät der Wissenschaften zu Berlin, August 2, 1710. Original in Kirch Papers, Akademie der Wissenschaften der DDR, I–III, 1, pp. 46–48. A copy is also found at the Leibniz Archiv, Jablonski, no. 440, Blatt 154–56.

serve as a precedent. We are tentatively of the opinion that this case must be judged not only on its present merits, but also as it could be judged for all time, for what we concede to her could serve as an example in the future." The effect on the academy's reputation of hiring a woman was a matter of concern. Again Jablonski wrote to Leibniz: "That she be kept on in an official capacity to work on the calendar or to continue with observations simply will not do. Already during her husband's lifetime the academy was burdened with ridicule because its calendar was prepared by a woman. If she were now to be kept on in such a capacity, mouths would gape even wider."[23] By rejecting Winkelmann's candidacy, the academy ensured that the stigma attached to women would not further tarnish its reputation.

Leibniz was one of the few at the academy who supported Winkelmann. In the council meeting of March 18, 1711 (one of the last meetings at which he presided before leaving Berlin), he held that the academy, considered either as a religious or academic body, should provide a widow with housing and salary for six months, as was customary. At Leibniz's urging, the academy granted Winkelmann the right to stay in its housing a while longer; the proposal that she be paid in a salary, however, was defeated. Instead, the council paid her forty talers for her husband's observation notebooks. Later that year, the academy showed some goodwill toward Winkelmann by presenting her with a medal.[24]

The academy never spelled out its reasons for refusing to appoint her to an official position; Winkelmann, however, traced her misfortune to her sex. In a poignant passage, she recounted her husband's assurances that God would show his grace through influential patrons. This, she wrote, does not hold true for the "female sex." Her disappointment was deep: "Now I go through a severe desert, and because . . . water is scarce . . . the taste is bitter." It was about this time that Winkelmann felt compelled to defend women's intellectual abilities in the preface to one of her scientific works. "The female sex as well as the male possesses talents of mind and spirit," she argued. With experience and diligent study a woman could become "as skilled as a man at observing and understanding the skies."[25]

[23] Harnack, "Berichte des Secretars," nos. 115, 116. Unfortunately, Leibniz's response to Jablonski has not been preserved.

[24] Protokollum Concilii, Societatis Scientiarum, December 15, 1710, Akademie der Wissenschaften der DDR, I, IV, 6, 1. Teil, p. 54, and March 18, 1711, pp. 65–66, 93. Unfortunately, the reason Winkelmann received a metal is unknown.

[25] Winkelmann to the Council of the Berlin Academy, March 3, 1711, Akademie der Wissenschaften der DDR, Kirch Papers, I, III, 1, p. 50, and Maria Winkelmann, *Vorbereitung, zur grossen Opposition, oder merckwürdige Himmels-Gestalt im 1712* (Cologne, 1711), pp. 3–4.

Although Winkelmann had been involved in preparing the calendar for ten years and knew the work well, the position of academy astronomer was awarded to Johann Heinrich Hoffmann. An undistinguished astronomer, Hoffmann is nearly forgotten today. During his tenure as academy astronomer, he was censured twice for his poor performance.[26]

Did Winkelmann have a legitimate claim to the post of assistant astronomer? Why did she think her request to continue the calendar project would be taken seriously? Winkelmann owed her position at the academy to the perpetuation of guild traditions.[27] When she petitioned the academy council to allow her to continue as assistant calendar maker, she was invoking (though not explicitly) principles well established in the organized crafts.[28] In most cases guild regulations gave the widow the right to run the family business after the death of her husband. In some guilds, the widow was allowed to serve as an independent master as long as she lived. In others she was allowed to continue the family business but only with the help of journeymen or apprentices. In still others, she filled in for one or two years to provide continuity until her eldest son came of age.[29] Within lower echelons of the academy, a widow was allowed to continue on in her husband's position. A woman whom we know only by the name of "Pont," widow of the keeper of academy mulberry trees, was allowed to complete the last four years of her husband's six-year contract.[30] Winkelmann also tried, after the death of her husband, to carry on the family business of calendar making as an independent master. Yet she found that traditions which had once secured women a (limited) role in science were not to apply in the new institutions.

Though the academy retained vestiges of an older order, it also contained the seeds of a new. The founding of the academy in 1700 represented a first step in the professionalization of astronomy in Germany. Earlier observatories—those of Hevelius in Danzig and Eimmart in Nuremberg—had been private. The academy's observatory, however, was a public ornament of the Prussian state. The astronomers were no longer owners and directors of their own observatories but employees

[26] Harnack, "Berichte des Secretars," nos. 143, 144.

[27] Wolfram Fischer, *Handwerksrecht und Handwerkswirtschaft um 1800* (Berlin, 1955), p. 18. W. V. Farrar, "Science and the German University System: 1790–1850," in *The Emergence of Science in Western Europe*, ed. Maurice Crosland (London, 1975), p. 181. See also Anthony Black, *Guilds and Civil Society in European Political Thought from the Twelfth Century to the Present* (Ithaca, 1984).

[28] See also Merry Wiesner, "Women's Defense of Their Public Role," in *Women in the Middle Ages and the Renaissance: Literary and Historical Perspectives*, ed. Mary Beth Rose (Syracuse, 1986), pp. 1–28.

[29] See Wensky, *Die Stellung der Frau in der stadtkölnischen Wirtschaft im Spätmittelalter*, pp. 58–59; Ketsch, *Frauen im Mittelalter*, 1:29, 204, 210.

[30] Protokollum Concilii, December 15, 1710, I, IV, 6, 2. Teil, 32. pp. 230–32.

of the academy, selected by a patron on the basis of public credentials rather than family tradition. This shift from a private to a public character of scientific institutions had dramatic implications for women's work in science. As astronomy moved more and more out of the private observatories and into the public world, women lost their toehold in modern science.

Although Winkelmann could not stay on at the Berlin Academy, she did continue her astronomical work. At Baron Bernhard Frederick von Krosigk's private observatory, where she and Gottfried Kirch had worked while the academy observatory was being built, Winkelmann reached the height of her career. With her husband dead and her son away at university, she enjoyed the rank of "master" astronomer. She continued her daily observations and—now the master—had two students to assist her. The published reports of their joint observations bear her name.[31]

In 1716, the Winkelmann-Kirch family received an invitation from Peter the Great of Russia to become astronomers in Moscow.[32] The family decided instead to return to Berlin when Winkelmann's son Christfried (along with J. W. Wagner) was appointed observer for the academy. Thus Winkelmann returned once again to the work of observation and calendar making, this time as assistant to her son.[33]

But all was not well. The opinion was still afoot that women should not do astronomy, at least not in a public capacity.[34] Winkelmann was soon reprimanded by the academy council for talking too much to visitors at the observatory. The council cautioned her to "retire to the background and leave the talking to Wagner and her son." A month later, the academy again reported that "Frau Kirch meddles too much with society matters and is too visible at the observatory when strangers visit." Again the council warned Winkelmann "to let herself be seen at the observatory as little as possible, especially on *public* occasions."[35] Maria Winkelmann was forced to make a choice. She could either continue to badger the academy for a position of her own, or, in the interest of her son's reputation, she could retire, as the academy requested, to the background. Vignoles reports that Winkelmann chose the latter option. Academy records show, however, that the choice was not hers. On October 21, 1717, the academy resolved to remove Winkelmann—who apparently had paid little heed to its warnings—from the academy grounds. She was forced to leave her house

[31] Christfried Kirch, *Teutsche Ephemeris* (Nuremberg, 1715), pp. 78–80, 82–84.

[32] Vignoles, "Eloge de Madame Kirch," p. 180.

[33] Protokollum Concilii, October 8, 1716, and April 6, 1718, I, IV, 6, 2. Teil, p. 236.

[34] Vignoles, "Eloge de Madame Kirch," p. 181.

[35] Protokollum Concilii, August 18, 1717, I, IV, 6, 2. Teil, pp. 269, 272–73, emphasis added.

and the observatory. The academy did not, however, want her to abandon her duties as mother; academy officials expressed their hope that Winkelmann "could find a house nearby so that Herr Kirch could continue to eat at her table."[36]

In 1717, Winkelmann quit the academy's observatory and continued her observations only at home, as was thought appropriate, "behind closed doors"—a move Vignoles judged detrimental to the progress she might have made in astronomy. With few scientific instruments at her disposal, she was forced to quit astronomical science. Maria Winkelmann died of fever in 1720. In Vignoles's opinion "she merited a fate better than the one she received."[37]

Winkelmann's daughter Christine Kirch continued to prepare the academy calendar—silently and behind the scenes—from 1720 until her death in 1782. This is not surprising; by the 1740s calendar making was no longer part of mainstream astronomy but merely tedious and time-consuming work. During the course of the eighteenth century, the Berlin Academy elected three high-ranking women (among them, Catherine the Great) to honorary membership; the election of a woman purely on scientific merit had to wait until 1949, when the physicist Lise Meitner was elected—but only as a corresponding member.[38] The first woman to be awarded full membership was the historian Liselotte Welskopf in 1964. Since the founding of the Academy of Sciences in Berlin in 1700, only fourteen of its twenty-nine hundred members have been women. Of those fourteen, only four have enjoyed full membership. As of 1983, no woman had ever served in any leadership role as academy president, vice-president, general secretary, or head of any of the various scientific sections.

The Consequences for Women's Participation in Science

As the case of Maria Winkelmann illustrates, the poor representation of women in the Berlin Academy cannot be traced to an absence of women qualified in science but to policies consciously implemented at a decisive moment in the academy's history. The academy did not, however, make its decisions in a vacuum. Larger developments in both science and society set parameters within which it maneuvered. The professionalization of the sciences (a gradual process that took place

[36] Vignoles, "Eloge de Madame Kirch," pp. 181, 275–76.

[37] Ibid., pp. 181–82.

[38] The Berlin Academy, unlike its fraternal counterparts in London and Paris, awarded honorary membership to a few women of high standing—Catherine the Great (elected 1767), Duchess Juliane Giovane (1749), and Maria Wentzel (1900).

over the span of two centuries) weakened craft traditions within the sciences and, in turn, weakened women's position in those sciences. With the gradual professionalization of astronomy, astronomers ceased working in family attics that doubled as observatories. In 1704, before moving to the royal observatory, Gottfried Kirch recorded in his diary: "July 4, [The sky is] light early. But I was unable to use the floor [to make observations through windows in the ceiling] since the washing from two households was hanging there. It was a pity, because I missed the conjunction of Jupiter and Venus."[39] Kirch's complaint reveals a striking juxtaposition of science and private life that began to disappear in the course of the eighteenth century. With the increasing polarization of public and private spheres in the eighteenth and nineteenth centuries, the family moved into the private sphere of hearth and home, while science migrated to the public sphere of university and industry.

With the privatization of the family, husbands and wives ceased to be partners in family businesses, and women became increasingly confined to the domestic role of wives and mothers. A wife such as Maria Winkelmann-Kirch could no longer become assistant astronomer to a scientific academy through marriage. Positions such as these became reserved for those with public certification of their qualifications.

With the changes in the social structure of science, women's participation in science changed. Some women attempted to follow the course of public instruction and certification through the universities, like their male counterparts. These attempts, however, were not successful until nearly two centuries later, at the turn of the twentieth century.[40] A second option open to women was to continue to participate within the (now private) family sphere as increasingly invisible assistants to a scientific husband or brother.

Changes in both the structure of science and the structure of the family served to distance wifely assistants from the professional world of science. Whereas Gottfried Kirch acknowledged his wife's work in scientific publications, Hermann von Helmholtz in the mid-nineteenth century praised his wife for her help in his experiments only privately and never publicly acknowledged her help either in his books or his papers.[41]

In eighteenth-century Germany, modern science was a new enterprise forging new institutions and norms. With respect to the problem of women, science (and society) at this time may be seen as standing at

[39] Wattenberg, "Zur Geschichte der Astronomie," p. 166.

[40] Laetitia Böhm, "Von dem Anfängen des akademischen Frauenstudiums in Deutschland," *Historisches Jahrbuch* 77 (1958): 2298–2327.

[41] I thank Richard Kremer for information on Helmholtz.

a fork in the road: it could either affirm and broaden practices inherited from craft traditions and welcome women as full participants, or it could reaffirm university traditions and continue to exclude them. As the case of Maria Winkelmann demonstrates, the Berlin Academy of Sciences chose to follow the latter path.

CHAPTER FOUR

Sense and Sensibility: A Case Study of Women's Reading in Late Victorian America

Barbara Sicherman

The influence of the printed word may well have been at its peak in late Victorian America, a time of rapidly expanding education and literacy, book and magazine production, and opportunities for self-improvement. Women were integral to the culture of reading. Besides participating in self-study programs like the Society to Encourage Studies at Home, they established reading clubs and literary societies in hundreds of communities across the nation. Taking their cultural mission seriously, club women and other community leaders gave high priority to establishing libraries; indeed, one source estimates that women founded 75 percent of all American public libraries.[1]

As yet we know little about the import of these activities or how women decoded what they read. Scholars who have examined the domestic novels of American antebellum women writers have variously

This essay appeared originally in *Reading in America: Literature and Social History*, ed. Cathy N. Davidson (Baltimore, 1989), pp. 201–25. Permission from the Johns Hopkins University Press to reprint it is gratefully acknowledged. The text has been cut slightly, the notes drastically. The original version should be consulted by anyone wishing to follow up sources or do further research.

I want to thank Cathy Davidson, Marlene Fisher, Martin Green, David D. Hall, Mary Kelley, and especially my fellow Berkshire Conference panelists Joan Jacobs Brumberg, Janice Radway, and Martha Vicinus for their helpful comments; Ann Brown, Tammy J. Banks-Spooner, and Elizabeth Young for research assistance; W. Rush G. Hamilton for permission to quote from the Hamilton Family Papers, Schlesinger Library, Radcliffe College, Cambridge, Mass.; and Marybelle Burch for providing materials from the A. Holman Hamilton Papers, Indiana State Library, Indianapolis.

[1] Anne Firor Scott, "Women and Libraries," *Journal of Library History* 21 (Spring 1986): 400–405. See also Karen J. Blair, *The Clubwoman as Feminist: True Womanhood Redefined, 1868–1914* (New York, 1980), esp. pp. 57–71, and Theodora Penny Martin, *The Sound of Our Own Voices: Women's Study Clubs, 1860–1940* (Boston, 1987).

found in them feminist messages of subversion or conservative reinforcement of the cult of domesticity.[2] Though interesting as exegesis, these studies rarely consider actual reading experiences, which included the work of English as well as male writers; nor do they tell us how contemporary readers engaged with texts.[3] Moreover, as Janice Radway demonstrated in her study of twentieth-century romance reading, critics have been too quick to impose their own views on texts and to assume they have a universal and controlling power over readers.[4]

A study of a late Victorian upper-middle-class, mainly female family permits us to explore how reading functioned as a cultural style and how it affected women's sense of self (subjectivity) in the past. Historians have noted the puzzling aspects of the Progressive generation of women, in particular their ability—despite growing up at the height of Victorianism, when images of "true womanhood" and the sanctity of the home still dominated popular culture—to move out into the world in daring ways. A study of women's intense engagement with books suggests that many found in reading a way of apprehending the world that enabled them to overcome some of the confines of gender and class. Reading provided space—physical, temporal, and psychological—that permitted women to exempt themselves from traditional gender expectations, whether imposed by formal society or by family obligation. The freedom of imagination women found in books encouraged new self-definitions and, ultimately, the innovative behavior associated with the Progressive generation.

This essay has been influenced by reader-response criticism, an approach that changes the locus of literary study from texts to readers and that emphasizes readers' ability to find their own meanings in texts.[5] Applied to historical subjects, this approach enables us to reconstruct the situational aspects of reading (the what, where, when, and how), while also casting light on individual "stories of reading"

[2] See Ann Douglas, *The Feminization of American Culture* (New York, 1977); Nina Baym, *Woman's Fiction: A Guide to Novels by and about Women in America, 1820–1870* (Ithaca, 1978); and Mary Kelley, *Private Woman, Public Stage: Literary Domesticity in Nineteenth-Century America* (New York, 1984). See also Linda K. Kerber, *Women of the Republic: Intellect and Ideology in Revolutionary America* (Chapel Hill, 1980), pp. 233–64; and Dee Garrison, *Apostles of Culture: The Public Librarian and American Society, 1876–1920* (New York, 1979), pp. 67–101.

[3] An exception is Nina Baym, *Novels, Readers, and Reviewers: Responses to Fiction in Antebellum America* (Ithaca, 1984).

[4] Janice A. Radway, *Reading the Romance: Women, Patriarchy, and Popular Literature* (Chapel Hill, 1984). Cathy N. Davidson, *Revolution and the Word: The Rise of the Novel in America* (New York, 1986), has also pioneered in developing a reader-centered approach.

[5] *The Reader in the Text: Essays on Audience and Interpretation*, ed. Susan R. Suleiman and Inge Crosman (Princeton, 1980), and *Reader-Response Criticism: From Formalism to Post-Structuralism*, ed. Jane P. Tompkins (Baltimore, 1980), are useful introductions to reader-response theory.

and reading as a social system. In this particular case, the Hamilton family constituted an "interpretive community," one that privileged certain texts and interpreted them according to its own codes. Within this common framework, individuals singled out books to which they attached special importance and meaning. In this essay, I have attempted to identify the varied uses of reading in a highly cultured family and to suggest ways in which evidence about reading can be used not only in writing individual and family biography but also in understanding shared generational values and changing female subjectivity. The study suggests the need to modify assessments of how women read fictional texts. It also casts doubt on current generalizations about late-nineteenth-century reading and suggests that women's reading behavior may have diverged from that of men.

I

The Hamiltons of Fort Wayne, Indiana, were an intensely and self-consciously literary family. The fortune acquired by the patriarch, a Scots-Irish immigrant who came to the city in 1823, provided his five surviving children and eighteen grandchildren with the accoutrements of the good life, including education, books, and travel. As one of the city's most prominent families, Hamiltons of three generations were distinguished by their literary interests. The oldest members of the third generation, seven women and one man, all born between 1862 and 1873, belonged to three nuclear families; in childhood the cousins were each others' only playmates. Two of them attained international renown: Edith Hamilton as a popular interpreter of classical civilizations, her younger sister Alice Hamilton as a pioneer in industrial medicine and Harvard's first woman professor. All had serious aspirations. Margaret and Norah had careers in education and art, respectively. Their cousin Agnes, who hoped at first to become an architect, later entered settlement work, while as young women her older sisters Katherine and Jessie studied languages and art. Allen Hamilton Williams became a physician.[6]

The family's literary tradition descended from their paternal grandmother, Emerine Holman Hamilton, a member of a prominent Indiana political family and a supporter of temperance and woman suffrage. Alice remembered her chiefly as a woman who "lost herself" in books:

[6] On the family, see Alice Hamilton, *Exploring the Dangerous Trades* (Boston, 1943), hereafter cited as *EDT*; Barbara Sicherman, *Alice Hamilton: A Life in Letters* (Cambridge, Mass., 1984), esp. pp. 11–32 and genealogy; and Mina J. Carson, "Agnes Hamilton of Fort Wayne: The Education of a Christian Settlement Worker," *Indiana Magazine of History* 80 (March 1984): 1–34.

"She loved reading passionately. I can remember often seeing her in the library of the Old House, crouched over the fireplace where the soft-coal fire had gone out without her knowing it, so deep had she been in her book." Emerine "enthralled" her grandchildren with Sir Walter Scott's poems, which she rendered mainly in prose, sometimes dropping into poetry.[7] With her three daughters Emerine established a Free Reading Room for Women in 1887; after her death in 1889, the reading room was renamed for her and became a circulating library. In 1896, after the founding of a public library, the collection, then numbering more than four thousand volumes, went to the Young Women's Christian Association, headed by Emerine's granddaughter Agnes.[8] It is significant that although everyone in this family read passionately, it was the women who extended reading from a private pleasure to an occasion for community service. Emerine's two sons ensconced themselves in their libraries, which were well stocked with port and cigars as well as books. The collection of Edith and Alice's uncle was, at six thousand or more volumes, the largest in Fort Wayne.

Edith once exclaimed that she wished "people did not think us quite so terribly bookish."[9] It is difficult to see how it could have been otherwise. The cousins were inducted into the family's literary culture at an early age, their lives and happiness closely bound up with books. When the Hamiltons thought of each other, they thought of each other reading. Edith away at school wished she could fly home and watch her closest cousin Jessie reading (Sunday books on Sunday), while Jessie later recalled Edith at thirteen reading a book in Greek while combing her hair.[10] The young women had access to their fathers' ample libraries—except for a few "forbidden" books, of which Alice later recalled only *The Decameron*, the *Heptaméron* of Marguerite of Navarre, and Eugène Sue's *Wandering Jew*.[11] Bookstores constituted a central focus of interest on shopping sprees in New York City with their unmarried aunt Margaret Vance Hamilton.

Reading constituted the core of the Hamiltons' education, indeed was barely distinguished from it. Edith, Alice, and their younger sisters were educated entirely at home until age sixteen or seventeen, when they went to Miss Porter's School in Farmington, Connecticut (as did the cousins and the aunts). They received formal instruction

[7] *EDT*, pp. 23–24.

[8] Robert S. Robertson, *History of the Maumee River Basin* (Allen County, Ind., 1905), pp. 2, 337–40; and library file in the Indiana Collection, Vertical File, Allen County Public Library, Fort Wayne, Ind.

[9] Edith Hamilton to Jessie Hamilton, August 3, 1892, Hamilton Family Papers, Schlesinger Library, Radcliffe College, Cambridge, Mass. All references to archival sources not otherwise identified are from this collection.

[10] Doris Fielding Reid, *Edith Hamilton: An Intimate Portrait* (New York, 1967), p. 30.

[11] *EDT*, pp. 18–19.

only in languages, and even these were largely self-taught. Otherwise their father had them read his favorites and assigned them research tasks in his ample reference library. He had Edith and Alice memorize all of *The Lady of the Lake;* and, in their early teens, he gave them a page of *The Spectator* to read over three times and then write out from memory. They also learned the Bible, which Alice claimed she knew better than any other book. Religion was a serious matter in this household, at least for the women, who attended the First Presbyterian Church and taught Sabbath school. But Montgomery Hamilton, more interested in theology than devotional practice, taught religious texts like any others: he had Edith and Alice do research in the Bible and memorize the Westminster Catechism.[12]

Both the method of learning—reading, memorizing, and reciting—and the subject matter formed an important substrate of the Hamilton women's mental landscape. Exposure to the classic works of male writers connected them to an important tradition of historical writing. In his fiction and poetry, Scott opened up the imaginative possibilities of the past, while Joseph Addison explicitly sought to bring philosophical discourse to the "tea-tables," that is, to women. Edith responded to *The Spectator* exercise by humorously announcing a literary vocation to Jessie: "I flatter myself my style is getting quite Addisonian. I hope you keep all my letters; some day, you know, they will be all treasured up as the works of 'Miss Hamilton, the American Addison, Scott & Shakespeare'!"[13] Alice perceived the gender symbolism of this education, contrasting her parents' reading tastes along with differences in their temperaments and religions as markers of character. Her father, who had a passion for "clarity and definiteness," favored Thomas Babington Macaulay, Addison, and Alexander Pope, while her mother, Gertrude Pond Hamilton, preferred *The Mill on the Floss, Adam Bede,* and Thomas Gray's *Elegy.* Noting that her father's hatred of sentimentality sometimes included his wife's "generous enthusiasms," Alice concluded that his attitude was "probably a wholesome factor in a household of women."[14]

The young Hamiltons read widely in books the Victorians designated "the best." These included numerous works of history and biography—Charles Knight's as well as Macaulay's history of England, but evidently not the American historians George Bancroft and Richard Hildreth. Fiction, which had only recently become approved intellectual fare, played a major part in their upbringing. The Hamiltons were familiar with the full range of English middle-class fiction, not only George Eliot, Charles Dickens, and William Makepeace

[12] *EDT,* pp. 27–31.
[13] Edith Hamilton to Jessie Hamilton, Tuesday evening [early 1882?].
[14] *EDT,* pp. 30–32.

Thackeray, but those they considered "old novelish," like Maria Edgeworth.[15] Scott was a favorite with three generations—Emerine and her second son, Montgomery, as well as Edith and Jessie. Two points about the Hamiltons' reading preferences deserve special mention: their bypassing of the New England literary tradition so important to many intellectual families and their penchant for British fiction; although British fiction dominated the American literary scene until the 1890s, the Hamiltons probably represent an extreme. They were, however, avid readers of the magazines of Gilded-Age America, of which *Harper's* seems to have been a special favorite.

In addition to the books one expects serious Victorians to have read, a wide range of works, popular in their day but no longer in the canon, were central to the Hamiltons. These included books read in childhood and adolescence, including the Katy books by "Susan Coolidge" (which they preferred to Louisa May Alcott's) and the works of Mrs. (Juliana) Ewing and Charlotte Yonge.[16] Religious novels also absorbed them, as did the devotional literature that constituted suitable Sunday reading in this very Presbyterian family. There was also an array of now-forgotten books read mainly for diversion, some verging on "trash," a designation that probably included excessively romantic or sentimental as well as lurid works. The Hamiltons accepted the category without always agreeing on its boundaries: one person's trash was evidently another's sensibility. Thus Edith noted of a book her younger sister's college friends considered trashy: "It seems to me an earnest, thoughtful book, with a high tone through it all. I do like it very much."[17]

II

There was, then, considerable freedom in the Hamiltons' choice of reading and in the range of books that mattered. There was also greater diversity in reading behavior than has been assumed. The conventional wisdom among historians of the book is that by the late nineteenth century reading had become a private rather than public activity (one that promoted individualism and isolated individuals from one another) and that there had been a shift from a pattern of intensive reading of a few books to one of extensive and presumably

[15] Agnes Hamilton to Jessie Hamilton, July 14, 1894.

[16] *EDT,* p. 19. Susan Coolidge was the pen name of Sarah Chauncy Woolsey.

[17] Edith Hamilton to Jessie Hamilton, July 14 [1889]. The book was *The Silence of Dean Maitland* (n.d.) by Mary Gleed Tuttiett, using the pseudonym Maxwell Gray. See also Edith Hamilton to Jessie Hamilton, September 14 [1889].

more passive reading.[18] Yet the reading customs of the Hamilton family suggest that these interpretations have been too monolithic in general and that reading had a different context, and therefore meaning, for women. Chief among these practices was reading aloud, which for the Hamiltons was a pleasurable and a lifelong habit.[19] Most such occasions were informal and structured by circumstance. There might be two participants or several; texts as well as readers might alternate. At times reading aloud was a duty as well as a pleasure: parents read to children, older siblings to younger ones, adult daughters to their mothers, women to invalids. Above all, reading aloud was social.

Hamiltons of two generations for a time constituted themselves into "a sort of a reading club."[20] In richly detailed letters, Jessie described the group and other reading occasions to her younger sister Agnes, away at school between 1886 and 1888. Daily at half past four, the Hamilton cousins "went over to Gibbon" (also known as "Gibbon-hour") at their Aunt Mary Williams's:

> You don't know what fun it is to go into her rooms where the dark red curtains are pulled across the windows and the lamps and wax candles are lit and spend an hour reading. Gibbon is becoming quite interesting[,] it is no longer an effort to listen. After dinner at seven we went to Aunt Marg's room to read Carlyle's French Revolution, it is splendidly written and wonderfully powerful when you can tell exactly what he is driving at. Of course the mind was not the only part refreshed, the fruit, oranges, bananas, green, purple and pink grapes made a lovely picture in a straw basket. And what do you think we did there, something that seemed to make one of my dreams suddenly to become substance—we hemmed the dish towels for the Farmington House.[21]

When someone had to be absent, the group switched to *A Bachelor's Blunder*, of which Jessie observed: "I read parts of it aloud to mamma

[18] Burton J. Bledstein, *The Culture of Professionalism: The Middle Class and the Development of Higher Education in America* (New York, 1976), pp. 77–78, emphasizes the isolating nature of Victorian reading. In "The World of Print and Collective Mentality in Seventeenth-Century New England," in *New Directions in American Intellectual History*, ed. John Higham and Paul K. Conkin (Baltimore, 1979), pp. 171–72, and "Introduction: The Uses of Literacy in New England, 1600–1850," in *Printing and Society in Early America*, ed. William L. Joyce et al. (Worcester, 1983), pp. 1–47, David D. Hall accepts the intensive-extensive dichotomy. Davidson, *Revolution and the Word*, pp. 72–73, and Robert Darnton, *The Great Cat Massacre and Other Episodes in French Cultural History* (New York, 1984), pp. 249–52, criticize the claim that the intensity of reading diminished.

[19] Reading aloud was also a ritual at Miss Porter's. Even in their nineties Alice and Margaret Hamilton belonged to a reading club.

[20] Agnes Hamilton Diary, April 25 [1885].

[21] Jessie Hamilton to Agnes Hamilton, January 9, 1887. See also Jessie Hamilton to Agnes Hamilton, January 19, 23, 1887; and Allen Hamilton Williams to Agnes Hamilton, June 1, 1887.

and though it is not anything you care about as you do Thackeray or George Eliot still it is very interesting." On another occasion, *A Bachelor's Blunder* followed *King Lear.*[22] Carlyle was resumed the following winter, but on at least one occasion Jessie reported that "somehow it did not work and we rambled off to other things."[23]

The letters suggest that for Jessie, an aspiring artist, the sensuous and social aspects of the reading sessions were central to her enjoyment—the physical accompaniments, the food, the alluring rooms with their beauty and hint of mystery. A range of family business was transacted at the sessions, including sewing (in this case for the cottage in Farmington that Margaret Vance Hamilton was fixing up for her nieces), planning their vocational futures, and gossiping about absent members. Altogether there is a fluidity about this reading circle: several books are kept going at the same time, there is no rush to finish, at times the sessions even break down. Jessie's comments further suggest a receptivity to a great variety of books and a lack of self-consciousness, even in this very proper family, about reading "light" fiction. Although differentiated from the classics, *A Bachelor's Blunder* is mentioned in the same breath with, and deemed worthy of substituting for, Carlyle or Shakespeare. Jessie's description of social reading reveals the playful side of Hamilton family life, a quality seen as well in their love of word games. Such playfulness can be afforded only by those who are both seriously committed to literature and secure in their position as members of a cultured class.

The multiple possibilities of reading are most fully revealed in the diaries and letters of Agnes Hamilton. The most morally earnest of the Hamiltons, Agnes was inclined to worry that she spent too much time reading novels, particularly the sort designated trash. She likened her "insane passion" for reading to an addiction and attributed her indulgence to a desire to escape unpleasant family situations, a trait she thought she shared with her paternal grandmother. After completing *Our Mutual Friend* and Bulwer-Lytton's *My Novel,* she wrote: "I have resolved not to read another novel for a week, at least, and consequently I feel like a reformed drunkard."[24] But Agnes's investment in books was more than a matter of escape or obsession. At twenty-one she wrote: "I live in the world of novels all the time[.] Half the time I am in Europe, half in different parts of America; I am sober and sensible, gay and frivolous, happy or sorrowful just as my present heroine

[22] Jessie Hamilton to Agnes Hamilton, January 23, 1887; see also Jessie Hamilton to Agnes Hamilton, February 11, 1887. *A Bachelor's Blunder* (1886) was a contemporary English novel by William Edward Norris.

[23] Jessie Hamilton to Agnes Hamilton, March 11, 1888. See also Jessie Hamilton to Agnes Hamilton, February 13, 1887.

[24] Agnes Hamilton Diary, July 31 [1887]. See also Agnes Hamilton to Edith Trowbridge, August 19, 1895.

happens to be or rather as the tone of the book happens to be. I never heard of a person more easily influenced. Sunday I read Stepping Heavenward. I had not read it for years and for two weeks I could not keep it out of my mind."[25] In addition to articulating the appeal of literature to fantasy and imagination, Agnes's comment suggests that reading could be an experience of considerable intensity. After completing Charles Kingsley's *Hypatia,* which she liked "almost as well as any book I ever read," she observed: "I cannot enjoy these books I am reading now as much as I ought for I hurry so from one to another. All the enjoyment is while I am in the midst of it. Usually when I read a splendid novel I don't touch another for months so that I go all over it again in my mind."[26] Thus, in contrast to the rather offhand character of the group sessions, the Hamiltons invested a great deal of themselves in certain books, some of which they undoubtedly approached expecting to be overwhelmed. Clearly, different styles of reading coexisted, dictated in part by the nature of the book, by the occasion, and by readers' expectations.

Among the books that acquired intense emotional meaning were those read in childhood and adolescence. These continued to be the stuff of Hamilton family life well into adulthood. Reading has long been recognized as a topic of absorbing interest to adolescents, especially adolescent girls.[27] For girls books have represented an important arena for shared friendship as well as a means of creating a world more satisfying than the one ordinarily inhabited, a world in which to formulate aspirations and try out different identities. The Hamiltons' continued intense preoccupation with books, including children's books, well into adulthood suggests the prolonging of behavior that would be considered adolescent today. In this family at least, such deferred maturity—what Erik Erikson has called a moratorium—prolonged the period in which the women, encouraged by one another, formulated and often reformulated their vocational plans.

For the Hamilton women, reading offered the occasion for a relatively unmediated experience, exemption from artificial social conventions, and an invitation to fantasy and imaginative play. Although they rejected society and looked down on women whose sole interest was finding a husband, they nonetheless—especially in Jessie and Agnes's family—experienced the restrictions of Victorian gentility. In a world full of social constraints, the Hamiltons associated reading with

[25] Agnes Hamilton Diary, May 7 [1890]. Agnes had a penchant for works like Elizabeth Payson Prentiss's *Stepping Heavenward* (1869), a spiritual manual in the guise of a novel. Its heroine, who is depicted as ill-tempered and selfish at the outset, emerges, after intense suffering, as a paragon of Christian womanhood.

[26] Agnes Hamilton to Jessie Hamilton, December 31, 1886.

[27] Lewis M. Terman and Margaret Lima, *Children's Reading: A Guide for Parents and Teachers,* 2d ed. (New York, 1931), esp. pp. 68–84.

freedom and possibility. Edith once observed: "Alice and I are out of humour, because at four o'clock we must get into something stiff and go down to Mrs. Brown's to meet some people and drink some tea. What I want to do, is to take *Wuthering Heights* and go and sit down on the shore below Arch Rock. I can feel how sweet and still and cool it would be there, how smooth and misty and pale blue the water would be, and how the little ripples would break at my feet with a soft splash."[28] In less poetic vein, reading gave the Hamiltons access to people and situations they would normally neither encounter nor countenance. Thus Agnes noted her eagerness to read *The Old Mam-'selle's Secret,* "utter stuff as it is, and full of the nastiest people I should not speak to in real life."[29]

Books also gave the Hamiltons a way of ordering, and understanding, their lives. They provided a common language and a medium of intellectual and social exchange that helped the women define themselves and formulate responses to the larger world. The process started early. When Jessie went off to Miss Porter's, seven younger Hamiltons ranging in age from fourteen to six wrote a joint letter addressed to "Dear boarding school girl." Agnes and Alice, thirteen and twelve respectively, elaborated: "Do you find boarding school as nice as it was in 'Gypsy's Year at the Golden Crescent', or in 'What Katy Did at School'? or are you homesick like the story Mrs. Stanton told in one of the 'Bessie's'?"[30] The symbolic code and shorthand for experience provided by books continued throughout the Hamiltons' lives. When cousins or sisters were geographically distant, a literary allusion captured experience in relatively few words. Thus Alice could describe a rector as "a delicious mixture of Trollope and Mrs. Oliphant and Miss Yonge" and expect to be understood precisely.[31] Only occasionally did literature fail. Edith had difficulty in fathoming Bonté Amos, an audacious but intriguing Englishwoman who belonged to the advanced Bertrand Russell set: "She is a kind of girl I have never even read of before."[32]

As the boarding school letter indicates, reading did not foreclose experience for the Hamiltons but offered them a range of possible responses. When Agnes began her diary shortly after her fifteenth birthday, she cited three fictional models from which to choose:

[28] Edith Hamilton to Jessie Hamilton, Thursday [late 1890s], folder 604.

[29] Agnes Hamilton to Edith Trowbridge, August 19, 1895. *The Old Mam'selle's Secret* (1868) was by the popular German romance writer E. Marlitt, the pen name of Eugenie John.

[30] To Jessie Hamilton [early 1882], folder 385. The books, by Susan Coolidge, Elizabeth Stuart Phelps (Ward), and Joanna Hooe Mathews respectively, were published in the late 1860s and early 1870s.

[31] Alice Hamilton to Agnes Hamilton [June? 1896].

[32] Edith Hamilton to Jessie Hamilton [fall 1896 and December 18? 1896]. See also Sicherman, *Alice Hamilton*, pp. 104–7.

"There are so many different ways of commencing journals that I did not know how to commence mine, whether to do as Else did and commence by telling about every member of the family or as Kate in Stepping Heavenward did and describe myself, but I think I will do as Olive Drayton and go right into the middle of it with out any commencement."[33] Such explicit formulation of the possibility of choice suggests both the open-ended quality of reading in this family and the degree to which the Hamiltons maintained control over their reading experiences.

The Hamiltons' world was peopled with fictional characters. It was not just that as readers they were "admitted into the company and present at the conversation."[34] The fictional company was very real to them. Allen Williams at twenty-one exclaimed: "I never can get over a feeling of personal injury in never having known the Abbottsmuir children; don't you think that, after Ellen Daly and Norah, they and Polly and Reginald seem to belong especially to us?"[35] To Agnes, too, characters in a favorite book "seem dear friends and I get a homesicky feeling if I cannot get hold of the book not for anything especially fine in it but just for the people."[36] Alice Hamilton in her seventies observed: "Since we saw so little of any children outside our own family, the people we met in books became real to us . . . [among them] Charlotte Yonge's May and Underwood families, who still are more vivid to me than any real people I met in those years."[37] For the Hamiltons, then, there was a reciprocal relation—a continuum—between fiction and life.[38] If fiction was a referent for people one encountered in real life, life also cast light on fiction: Alice claimed she understood William Dean Howells's women "much better" through knowing a real-life stand-in.[39] In view of the fluidity of the boundaries, it is not surprising that the Hamiltons fictionalized their own lives. After being absorbed for weeks in the story of a romance between the art teacher and a student at Miss Porter's, Edith wrote Jessie: "Don't you feel as if you had got into a story book? And with Susy Sage of all people for the heroine."[40]

The tendency to fictionalize their lives was most evident at the time of Allen Williams's engagement. His fiancée, Marian Walker, a Radcliffe student preparing for a medical career, reminded Allen not only

[33] Agnes Hamilton Diary, December 6 [1883].

[34] Benjamin Franklin quoted in Davidson, *Revolution and the Word*, p. 52.

[35] Allen Hamilton Williams to Bag [Agnes Hamilton], August 11, 1890. These characters are drawn from books read in childhood or early adolescence.

[36] Agnes Hamilton to Edith Trowbridge, August 19, 1895.

[37] *EDT*, p. 19.

[38] See Davidson, *Revolution and the Word*, esp. pp. 112–35.

[39] Alice Hamilton to Agnes Hamilton [postmarked November 9, 1896].

[40] Edith Hamilton to Jessie Hamilton, January 31 [1886].

of his closest cousins, Alice and Agnes, but also of the heroines of two novels beloved by the young Hamiltons, Nora Nixon in *Quits* (1857) by Baroness Tautphoeus, a popular English writer of the 1850s and a distant relative of the Hamiltons, and Ellen Daly in Annie Keary's *Castle Daly* (1875). As Allen informed Agnes: "[Marian] is very fond of Quits! I have told her she cannot meet any of the family until she has read Castle Daly. Can you forgive her for not having done that?" To Alice he exclaimed: "Of course she is like Nora, otherwise I could not have fallen in love. And of course *Quits* is one of her favorite books."[41] The use of such preferences as a means of establishing boundaries for group membership may strike us as quintessentially adolescent, but Allen was in his late twenties. Though professing greater maturity, Alice responded in kind:

> And it just warms my heart and fills me with gladness to have the boy turning into the sort of a man that I wanted him to be, to have him doing an impulsive, unpractical, youthful thing. . . . Why he talks like the heroes in Black's novels, like Willy Fitzgerald and George Brand and Frank King. I am so glad. . . . Agnes it mustn't pass over, it is too sweet and dear and fresh and cunning. . . . I think almost the funniest part is his account of the effect the announcement had on the two mothers. It is just like poor Traddles and his Sophie in "David Copperfield" and these poor children seem to take it just as seriously.[42]

Although Alice Hamilton cast Allen as a hero, there is no evidence, then or later, that she was interested in the marriage plot for herself. Allen called her an "unconscious hypocrite" for suggesting that Marian give up her medical career because he believed his cousin cared only for her work.[43] At forty-nine Alice still gushed about a book in words similar to those she had deployed for Allen's romance: "It is just as cunning as can be and so romantic, you can't believe any hero could be so noble."[44] But her life history, like that of the other Hamilton women, makes it clear that she preferred her heroes in the covers of a book rather than at first hand; in this one case at least, the boundaries between fiction and life remained fixed. Given their assumption that women must choose between marriage and career, for the Hamiltons and other ambitious women of the era, heroes in books were safer than men encountered in life. Indeed, there was a potent antimarriage sen-

[41] Allen Hamilton Williams to Bag [Agnes Hamilton], July 30, 1896, and to My dear girl [Alice Hamilton], August 15 [?], 1896.

[42] Alice Hamilton to Agnes Hamilton, September 12 [1896]; the letter is reprinted in its entirety in Sicherman, *Alice Hamilton*, pp. 101–4.

[43] Allen Hamilton Williams to Dear child [Alice Hamilton], September 17, 1896.

[44] Alice Hamilton to Margaret Hamilton, Sunday [July 7], 1918, Alice Hamilton Papers, Schlesinger Library.

timent in this family. Of the eleven women of the third generation, only the youngest married; a generation younger than her oldest cousins, she did so as an act of rebellion.[45]

III

The Hamiltons' experiences of reading suggest a need to reconsider traditional assumptions about how fiction works on readers. It is usually assumed that women respond to fiction principally through the mechanism of identification with heroines, especially the heroines of "romantic" plots. Among the Hamiltons, however, it was the men who seem to have been fascinated by heroines and who took them as models of womanhood. Montgomery, for example, wrote an essay on the subject for the Princeton literary magazine and, like his nephew Allen Williams thirty years later, alluded to Baroness Tautphoeus's novels during his romance with Gertrude Pond.[46] By contrast, plots of adventure and social responsibility appealed to the Hamilton women. Favorite novels—even those that end with an impending marriage—provided models of socially conscious and independent womanhood. In reading *Quits*, for example, the women probably responded more to the character of the heroine than to her fate. Nora Nixon, the unaffected and generous heroine of *Quits*, is a natural woman who loves the outdoors, orders her life rationally, and does exactly what she pleases, which happens also to be socially useful. Active, worldly, and independent, she provides a striking contrast to the stereotyped domestic and submissive "true woman." Ellen Daly, the Irish heroine of *Castle Daly*, is less able to control her surroundings than Nora, but she too is unselfconscious, generous, and independent.[47]

The heroine of Charlotte Yonge's paradigmatic *Daisy Chain* (1856) may have provided the model for real family projects as well as fantasy. In much the same manner as Jo March in *Little Women*, Ethel May is transformed from a helter-skelter tomboy and prospective bluestocking into a thoughtful and family-centered woman. In Ethel's case this is her family of origin, for she resists marriage to care for her father and siblings. But Ethel has a public as well as a private mission and succeeds in carrying out her resolve to found a church in a poor neighborhood. Her passion for Cocksmoor had its counterpart in the Hamiltons' involvement in Nebraska, a poor section of Fort Wayne where the women and some of the men taught Sabbath school. Agnes,

[45] Interview with Hildegarde Wagenhals Bowen, December 30, 1976.

[46] Montgomery Hamilton to A. Holman Hamilton, July 30, 1864.

[47] Although there is no evidence that Nora and Ellen were as important models of heroinism to the women as they were to Allen, there are numerous references to *Quits* and *Castle Daly* in their correspondence.

who later worked at a religious settlement, was instrumental in persuading her own First Presbyterian Church to establish a regular church there. Ethel May's deepest commitments—her loyalty to family and religion—were also major preoccupations of Agnes's, and it is likely that she found in Ethel a model, as she did in similarly inclined women she encountered in novels and biographies.

If the Hamiltons had a penchant for socially conscious heroines, an analysis of their reading also suggests that the traditional emphasis on identification with one character is far too restrictive an approach to an experience as complex as reading.[48] Recent work reveals the possibilities of more varied interactions between readers and texts. Norman Holland insists on the organic unity of a literary work, including plot, form, and language as well as characters, each of which can influence a reader's response. Starting from the premise that what readers bring to texts is themselves, he further suggests that the reader identifies not so much with a particular character as with the total interaction of characters. Holland's concept of "identity themes," characteristic modes of response that influence reading as well as other behaviors, is useful for historians because it provides a key to individual reading preferences that can be applied to the past.[49] Within an explicitly feminist framework, Cora Kaplan emphasizes the possibilities of multiple identifications by women readers, with heroes as well as heroines.[50]

Certainly for the Hamiltons, the continuum between fiction and reality gave considerable play to the imagination. Reading provided both the occasion for self-creation and the narrative form from which they might reconstruct themselves. The way they peopled their lives with fictional characters and the intensity of their interactions with books enabled them to read themselves into fiction or other forms of adventure without a strong identification with a particular heroine.

Alice Hamilton offers a striking example in claiming a literary inspiration for her decision to become a physician: "I meant to be a medical missionary to Teheran, having been fascinated by the description of Persia in [Edmond] O'Donovan's *The Merv Oasis.* I doubted if I could ever be good enough to be a real missionary; but if I could care for the sick, that would do instead, and it would enable me to explore far countries and meet strange people."[51] Since *The Merv Oasis* (1882)

[48] See, for example, Rachel M. Brownstein, *Becoming a Heroine: Reading about Women in Novels* (New York, 1984).

[49] Norman Holland, *The Dynamics of Literary Response* (New York, 1975), esp. pp. 262–80. One need not accept Holland's exact psychoanalytic formulation to recognize the value of his approach in illuminating individual responses to literature.

[50] Cora Kaplan, "*The Thorn Birds:* Fiction, Fantasy, Femininity," in her *Sea Changes: Feminism and Culture* (London, 1986), pp. 117–46.

[51] *EDT,* p. 26. Alice also attributes the growing consciousness of social problems she and Agnes shared to reading Charles Kingsley and Frederick Denison Maurice. Claiming

is a work of travel and adventure, over a thousand pages in length and with no discernible missionary focus, Alice clearly drew from it what she would. The message she found there is consistent with her early preferences in fiction, among them Charlotte Yonge's novels, which highlight conflicts between individual achievement and the family claim. This was a matter that deeply troubled her as a young woman, and she resolved it only when she found work that enabled her to combine science and service, thereby effecting a balance between individualism and self-sacrifice as she saw it.[52]

Edith's aspirations and literary preferences were different. There is no mention in her letters of doing good, a frequent theme of Alice's; rather there is a longing to "live" and to do great things. Often moody as a young woman, she found in reading a lifeline, a way of getting out of herself. At sixteen her favorites were Scott's *Rob Roy* (1818) and *Lorna Doone* (1869) by R. D. Blackmore.[53] The heroine of *Rob Roy*, Diana Vernon, is one of Scott's most appealing—she is an outdoorswoman, well read, outspoken, and fearless. But the characterization is unlikely to account for the novel's appeal. (Diana fades away, becoming first an obedient daughter, then, in a hastily contrived ending, a wife.) It is more likely that Edith responded to the settings and plots: her favorites were tales of derring-do in wild places (the Scottish highlands, the Devonshire moors) and historical settings. They might well have cast a spell on one who was herself "a natural storyteller" and who later captured the imagination of millions with her retellings of classic myths and her romantic vision of ancient Greece.[54]

In suggesting that for the Hamiltons reading reinforced a family culture that promoted personal aspiration and achievement, I am not claiming a direct cause-and-effect relationship between reading and behavior. The late nineteenth century was a time of expanding opportunities for women, without which the aspirations of various Hamiltons could not have been enacted in the way they were. In this context, a reading culture such as the one maintained by the Hamiltons provided a means for accustoming and encouraging women to imagine new possibilities for themselves. In a supportive environment, such possibilities had a greater chance of becoming realities.

"we knew nothing about American social evils," she ignores their work at the Sabbath mission school in Nebraska. Alice was interested in "slumming" by age eighteen, which was probably before she read the English social theorists. This seems to have been another case of literature seeming more real than life. *EDT*, pp. 26–27.

[52] On this conflict, see Sicherman, *Alice Hamilton*.

[53] Edith Hamilton to Jessie Hamilton, Thursday, July 24 [1884]. Each book contains a sympathetic Robin Hood figure, whose dubious morality is treated ambiguously.

[54] Alice called her sister "a natural storyteller" (*EDT*, p. 19).

How typical were the Hamiltons? In the intensity of their involvement with books, in the degree to which their reading activity was family-centered, and perhaps too in their bypassing of the New England literary tradition they may have been somewhat idiosyncratic. But they were at the extreme end of a continuum rather than the oddities they might at first appear to be.

Testimony to the importance of reading comes from the autobiographies of prominent women who came to maturity in the 1880s and 1890s. For many, books acquired an almost magical status, books in general as well as particular books; among the consequences attributed to specific works are religious conversion, loss of faith, choice of vocation, and the breakup of a marriage. By contrast, formal schooling received little attention, an omission that is not surprising at a time when self-study was common, when the early education of even those who attended college was often informal and erratic, and when most formal learning was by recitation. The invocation of books was no doubt a convention of a cultural elite. But its frequency is significant and contrasts with the lack of attention to peers and formal education, both staples of more recent autobiographical narratives. The diminished religiosity of educated Victorians undoubtedly contributed to this new veneration of literature as a source of cultural authority and models of selfhood.

Books were also markers of "taste" and, therefore, ultimately of class. What one read, how much, and even how one read, not to mention the size of the paternal library, were important markers of cultural style in middle- and upper-middle-class homes. But love of books was not the prerogative of the wealthy alone; indeed, for many individuals raised in a religious tradition suspicious of display, a reverence for books was a way of distancing themselves from those with merely social aspirations. For women in particular, the level of a family's intellectual aspirations was more important than its bank account or social pedigree in encouraging ambition.

Of course, a passion for books and other cultural artifacts could become the means by which the cultured classes insulated themselves from unpleasant realities. In a memorable passage in her autobiography Jane Addams warns against the dangers of self-culture, in particular the habit of her class of "lumbering our minds with literature," an epiphany that followed the intrusion of a literary reflection when she confronted extreme poverty. Yet Addams, too, fell back on the literary culture of her youth and tried to pass it on to her immigrant neighbors: one of the first public activities at Hull House was a group that read George Eliot's *Romola*, a work set in Renaissance Florence.[55] In so do-

[55] Jane Addams, *Twenty Years at Hull-House* (1910; rpt. New York, 1960), pp. 63–64.

ing, she was continuing a tradition of women's reading that had social as well as private dimensions.

Growing up in an era when the printed word was venerated, women like the Hamiltons found in books not just the messages of official purveyors of culture, though they found these, too. For some, engagement with books in childhood and adolescence permitted entry into a world of fantasy that helped them to formulate aspirations for themselves different from those traditional to women, and ultimately to act on them as well. Although many of the pejorative connotations of the old association of women and fiction had disappeared by the late nineteenth century, when "good" fiction had attained the status of a cultural icon, reading was still a gender-marked activity, no doubt because it seemed a relatively passive form of intellectual exercise and one that had no practical outcome. This essay has tried to demonstrate that reading had more practical and positive consequences for women than has been assumed. Many found in reading an occasion that, by removing them from their usual activities, permitted the formulation of future plans or, more generally, encouraged vital engagement with the world, a world many thought would be transformed by women's special sensibilities. Women's passion for reading must then be viewed as more than simple escapism, as absorption in books has often been designated.

IV

What generalizations may be drawn from a case study such as this one? In the matter of method, a contextual study of groups of real readers permits historians to adapt the approach of ethnographers to the past. If one looks at groups of readers, it becomes clear that reading was not restricted to writers of one genre, sex, or nationality and that both occasions for reading and particular texts developed complex symbolic meanings for specific reading communities. Further, by studying reading as behavior rather than as textual analysis, historians can peel back later layers of interpretation and come nearer to the contemporary meaning of a work. A study of past readings also permits a deeper understanding of aspirations and emotional preferences as distinct from ideology—what Raymond Williams calls "structures of feeling" or sensibilities.[56] These are often difficult to get at, particularly in an era when sentimentality and self-revelation were suspect, as they were in the late nineteenth century.

Substantively, a case study of this sort can cast light not only on the impact of books and the nature of reading experiences in the past but

[56] Raymond Williams, *Marxism and Literature* (Oxford, 1977), pp. 128–35.

on our understanding of these processes. The emphasis on the escapist aspects of certain kinds of fiction, indeed on the distinction between "light" and "serious" reading, seems misplaced in view of the varied and complex reading behaviors that existed in the past. Reading theorists have argued that reading is not simply a passive form of cultural consumption, that something happens to readers that becomes imperative for them to understand, and that reading stimulates desire rather than simply pacifying it. The spectator role permits readers to remove themselves temporarily from the necessity to act, enabling them to use this freedom "to *evaluate* more broadly, more amply" and thus to "modify categories according to 'the way I feel about things.' "[57] The Hamilton family engaged in different sorts of reading, but their experiences of reading, both social and individual, encouraged them to extend the range of the possible. In their interpretive community, children's books, "light" fiction, and devotional literature (fiction or nonfiction) could all play a part in the formation of one's sense of self. From this study, it is also apparent that generalizations based on assumed oppositions between modes of reading (intensive/extensive) and loci of reading (public/private) cannot be sustained.

Evidence of the sort provided by the Hamiltons makes it possible to discover how reading behavior and self-consciousness changed over time. This study suggests a link between reading and the formation of female subjectivity in a particular historical period. By so doing, I do not wish to minimize the importance of reading for women in other times and places: adolescent girls seem to have exhibited consistently greater passion for reading than their male counterparts. Nevertheless, a variety of factors seem to have contributed to the empowering nature of women's reading experiences in the late nineteenth century. Books were especially revered cultural artifacts (without serious competition from nonprint forms of entertainment) and, at a time of rapidly expanding educational opportunity, women had freer access to them than in earlier generations. The lesser importance of formal education in children's early years may have fostered a greater degree of self-invention compared with later, more routinized educational patterns. It is likely, too, that the relatively informal mode of transmitting cultural values played a part in the open and playful approach to reading exhibited by the Hamiltons.[58]

[57] James Britton, *Language and Learning* (London, 1970), pp. 97–125; quotation on pp. 109–10. See also Wolfgang Iser, "Interaction between Text and Reader," in *The Reader in the Text*, ed. Suleiman and Crosman, pp. 106–19, and Hans Robert Jauss, "Literary History as a Challenge to Literary Theory," in *New Directions in Literary History*, ed. Ralph Cohen (Baltimore, 1974), pp. 35–37.

[58] Paul Lauter, "Race and Gender in the Shaping of the American Literary Canon: A Case Study from the Twenties," *Feminist Studies* 9 (Fall 1983): 435–63, and Joan Shelley Rubin, "Self, Culture, and Self-Culture in Modern America: The Early History of the

Finally, the literature of the era was especially conducive to dreams of female heroism outside family life. The downplaying of sexuality in Victorian fiction and the lesser concentration on the marriage plot in girls' adventure stories encouraged women to fantasize about other sources of fulfillment, including those that gave women a large public role.[59] Books could not create a desire for female heroism when none existed in the reader. But in conjunction with a family culture that encouraged female aspiration and education, reading could provide the occasion for perceiving one's inmost needs and wants—desires that could later be acted upon. Like earlier critics who viewed women's reading as suspect, though for different reasons, some feminist critics have recently emphasized the dangers of reading for women.[60] In the context of late Victorian American life, however, the impact of reading was more likely to be liberating than confining.

Book-of-the-Month Club," *Journal of American History* 71 (March 1985): 782–806, discuss the standardization of cultural fare in the twentieth century.

[59] See Martha Vicinus, "What Makes a Heroine?: Nineteenth-Century Girls' Biographies," *Genre* 20 (Summer 1987): 171–88.

[60] See, for example, Patrocinio P. Schweickart, "Reading Ourselves: Toward a Feminist Theory of Reading," in *Gender and Reading: Essays on Readers, Texts, and Contexts*, ed. Elizabeth A. Flynn and Patrocinio P. Schweickart (Baltimore, 1986), pp. 31–62.

CHAPTER FIVE

In and around the Lighthouse: Working-Class Lesbian Bar Culture in the 1950s and 1960s

Janet Kahn and Patricia A. Gozemba

In *Another Mother Tongue,* Judy Grahn says of her experience of coming out in the 1950s: "We were frightened all the time. Yet still we found our world exciting and wouldn't have stopped being Gay for anything." The world Grahn refers to centered largely around gay bars, which she describes as "the only public expression of Gay culture that I would find in a closeted world." Exploring that world in an attempt to understand the creation of the culture Grahn described fascinated several of us involved in the Boston Area Lesbian and Gay History Project. The research became a recapitulation of some of our own experiences in going to bars. We could identify with Grahn when she admitted that "going to my first Gay bar certainly felt as terrifying, mystifying, and life altering as any ritual procedure could have felt."[1] Our work builds on, confirming and questioning, some of the earlier and ongoing explorations in this culture by other grass-roots history projects and lesbian and gay researchers.[2]

[1] Judy Grahn, *Another Mother Tongue: Gay Words, Gay Worlds* (Boston, 1984), p. 29.

[2] The grass-roots history projects that inspired us existed in San Francisco, Buffalo, and New York. Libby Bouvier of the Boston Project particularly assisted us in reviewing tapes and cataloging them. The work of Elizabeth Kennedy and Madeleine Davis in Buffalo (*Boots of Leather, Slippers of Gold* [London, forthcoming]) raised the initial questions we explored with the lesbians from the bar. The pioneering work of Jonathan Ned Katz in *Gay American History* (New York, 1981) and *Gay/Lesbian Alamanc* (New York, 1983) and John D'Emilio in *Sexual Politics, Sexual Communities: The Making of a Homosexual Minority in the United States, 1940–1970* (Chicago, 1984) provided a lucid background against which our questions could be raised. The ongoing work of Judith Schwarz, Deborah Edel, and Joan Nestle at Lesbian Herstory Archives has provided insights and inspiration. Joan Nestle's book *Restricted Country* (Ithaca, 1987) contains

Grahn's description of the fear, joy, and excitement of the lesbians in the Rendezvous, a big-city downtown bar, also holds true for the lesbians who created love and friendship networks, gay culture, and gay and lesbian space in the Lighthouse, a neighborhood bar in the working-class city of Lynn, Massachusetts. The evolution of the Lighthouse, later renamed Fran's Place, into a lesbian and gay bar began during World War II, when it was frequented by military personnel from bases in nearby Nahant and Salem. Their presence drew prostitutes, some of whom were lesbian, and created a climate conducive to the initiation of gay male activity. Fran Collins, whose family has owned the bar continuously since the 1940s, recalls that officers occasionally posted notices at the bases declaring the Lighthouse off-limits for military personnel because of the gay clientele. Nonetheless, the bar thrived.

Allan Berube illuminates how the war provided unprecedented opportunities for gay men and lesbians to discover one another in sex-segregated contexts on military bases and in the anonymity of big cities.[3] Many of these men and women learned that there was a name, *homosexual,* for people like themselves who had same-sex affectional and sexual preferences. Unfortunately, homosexuals had been deemed pathological by popular sexologists and thus for many in the military in particular the realization of who they were came as a negative experience. Yet many of them retained their spirit and in the midst of the oppression in the 1940s and 1950s these pioneers in the lesbian and gay movement created a semipublic community and culture through the bars which would sustain them.

Lesbian Bar Culture

This essay is based on in-depth interviews with ten women who frequented the Lighthouse in the 1950s and 1960s. These women were identified initially by their attendance at the annual bar reunion in September 1983. Many former patrons of the bar who no longer are "regulars," some of whom live out of state, return for these parties to see old friends. Although the bulk of the material from each narrator was gathered in a single evening or weekend session, we have maintained contact with all of these women since the work began in 1983. We have thus had the opportunity to return to the women for further

many important essays on our topic; of particular interest is "Butch-Femme Relationships: Sexual Courage in the 1950s."

[3] Allan Berube, "Coming Out under Fire," *Mother Jones* 8 (February–March 1983): 23–29, 45.

information and to receive their ideas on our theories and interpretations of their lives.

Gay bars are often found in the factory sections of cities. Thus, typically, the Lighthouse is located in the heart of the once thriving shoe industry in Lynn. A few blocks beyond the shoe factories are the three- and four-decker houses that were the standard working-class homes of the Boston area and the rooming houses that were built to accommodate single factory workers. It was the Lighthouse, however, more than the neighborhood, which many of our working-class narrators thought of as home. After long hours at work in sometimes deadening and boring jobs, the women found in the bar relief from the heterosexual world and the promise of friendship, romance, love, and sex. Here they created a life.

The lesbian bar culture of the 1950s and 1960s was a complex world in which violence existed side by side with sisterhood, friendship, and love, and competition and cooperation created an ongoing tension. In observing the ways in which a hostile society inflicted punishment upon them, we gain an appreciation for the creativity and resiliency that the lesbians evidenced in shaping their lives.

Over the years significant changes have occurred, and there now is a wide range of gay organizations, activities, and institutions. In the 1950s and 1960s, however, lesbians and gays were not publicly visible. Says one narrator, "I was very involved in bar culture. There was nothing else at that point. It was either the bars or you knew a few people and you socialized at someone's house." As the only public, although often hidden, space in which people acknowledged their gayness, the bar played an important role in helping women come to grips with their sexual inclinations.

All of our narrators mentioned that when they went to the bar for the first time, they experienced a thrill at seeing other women dancing together and socializing openly. In their recollections of the experience, they characterize it as liberating. The very existence of so many other women who identified themselves as lesbian made them feel that they were sane and that there was at least one place where they could congregate that would offer them an escape from the straight world. It provided relief for their social schizophrenia even though for some that dichotomy would eventually be exacerbated as they spent more time at the bar.

Many of our narrators were teenagers when they first entered the Lighthouse. As one put it, "Oh yeah, I felt great. I thought, oh well, it's not me. Thank god, finally I'm not crazy! It's not me—look at them all." Although many lesbians have felt their sanity was affirmed when they first entered a gay bar, this narrator had more reason than most to feel reassured. As a young teen she had been incarcerated in a state mental hospital for being suspected of homosexuality. Her survival there had depended in large part on denying her lesbianism. Thus she was very surprised when she was approached one day by a woman on the staff: "I was sitting right there in the hospital on the bed and she came up to me and said, 'Alice I know you're gay.' I felt I could trust her the whole time . . . but I never could understand why. . . . And she goes, 'as soon as you get out of here' and she told me where it is and she says, 'you come there, I'll be there, and you'll find all kinds of people just like you.' And I'm looking at her and I thought, oh god let me go now, please I've got my sanity now."

On the day she was released from the hospital, Alice went to the Lighthouse and quickly became a regular. As for many other lesbians in many other cities, it was in the bar, with its gift of affirmation and permission, that Alice sought and created her identity, both discovered and determined what it meant to be gay in America in the mid-1950s.

The Atmosphere

Bar life gave a certain freedom, but there also were many constraints. Our narrators were creating their identities within specific conditions, and their effects could not be avoided altogether. One of these conditions was a central fact of bar life—alcohol. A woman recalled, "We'd get a pay at the end of the week. We'd go in there on a Friday afternoon and that would be the start of everything. We'd get the ten cent beers. We used to call it swamp juice."

About drinking, one of our narrators, Barbara, said: "What else was there to do? We would go out; we'd go out and drink . . . go to different bars. . . . Once you went into a gay bar and you met the people that you met and they all wanted to hang out . . . that's when the drinking started right there and then. That's where it all starts."

Because bars were the only gay social space available, drinking became an inevitable focus of social life, yet many of the narrators feel that alcohol facilitated social interaction. According to one, "There are times I've been with people that I would never had been with if I was sober. Never. When you're sober, you think more. You're fussy. But when you're drinking, they look beautiful to you."

For many, alcohol became a controlling feature of their lives. When Barbara, a former bartender in numerous gay bars, decided she had to quit drinking, she paid a heavy price. "Once you stop drinking you lose your friends because they're still drinking." Friendships that had withstood decades of good times and hard times, love affairs and breakups, illness, and unemployment could not withstand the effect of one friend becoming sober while the others continued to drink. In this way, gay alcoholics were no different from straight alcoholics. The difference was their lack of social alternatives.

Alongside the constant presence of alcohol, and perhaps related to it, was the constant possibility and frequent reality of violence. Sometimes the violence seemed random. "I went to Jacques [a downtown Boston bar] until 1969. The last time I went in there was St. Patrick's Day 1969 and I got up to go to the ladies room and just before I got to the ladies room, I don't know where it came from or why I got it, but this guy came out with this big fist and knocked me out cold. . . . Never did figure out why the guy hit me." Other times it didn't take much figuring. Straight men would sometimes come into gay bars specifically to provoke fights with lesbians, and the assailant would state his intentions clearly: " 'You look like a man, then fight like one.' That's what we got. So many times. I had more black eyes, broken arms. . . . And we didn't say anything, we were just . . . having a good time at the bar." Another narrator recalled that an ambulance arrived at the bar every Friday and Saturday night.

Not surprisingly, violence invaded the relationships between women. According to our narrators, many fights were related to love relationships. Karen recalls, "People used to fight a lot in those days. Not that they still don't . . . but I remember lots of fights, lots of bad fights." One recalls a night in the Lighthouse, "with bottles flying across the room and chairs and tables as well."

We can only speculate about what sparked such physical violence among the women. In addition to the hostility from the outside, it is important, as Barbara attests, to realize that "most of the women learned violence and fighting in their own families." It was not an unusual experience for them. Perhaps women fought about lovers and those trying to impose themselves into love relationships because little else in their lives was as precious to them as their relationships. Women received validation about their identity in the bar, and their relationships were an important part of that identity.

A frequent consequence of the fighting was the arrival of police to haul off those who were disorderly or just happened to be standing by. One narrator reported, "Several times I was lucky; they took enough people in front of me that I escaped." Sometimes when violence occurred outside the bar, the owner would be unwilling to call the police because she did not want to draw attention to the bar. Alice talked about seeing people who were stabbed and bleeding being pushed out the door by the owner when they tried to come back into the bar after having been attacked outside.

Finally, the lives of our narrators were circumscribed by their poverty. Said one, "At the Lighthouse there were two kinds of classes—the working-class and the not-working-class, but we were all good friends." Friendship and alcohol may have taken some of the sting out of factory life for a while, but it was no long-term solution. Those who chafed under these conditions sometimes took desperate measures to escape them. Two of our narrators, for instance, had worked at a series of jobs together, including waitressing and employment in a shoe factory. When Judy, the older of the two, decided she had to find a way out, she convinced her friend Mae to push a rack filled with cartons of shoes onto her as she walked by. Her body was her only valuable asset, and she risked all she had on that well-known working-class dream, the insurance settlement. Mae explains Judy's decision:

> She didn't want to work no more. Some people don't want to work anymore. She wasn't that young . . . I think maybe she was 35 you know. Running around all those years trying to make a buck, you know, it gets to you. So she sees her out, and that was it, and you take your opportunity. And she had to take it, so she did. And she won. You know, if you see your opportunity and you don't take it, well right or wrong, you are the one who has to pay the consequences. You know "If I" or "Gee should I" or "Could I" or "Gee I wish I would have." What is all that—do it! Sometimes you have to make decisions you don't like to make.

It was, then, in bars filled with alcohol, poverty, and violence that young women—for most of our informants were young when they first came out—sought to live as lesbians. As Diane describes it, "When you went to the office all week long you led one life but come Friday night you were ready to go out and you could throw on anything and go and sit with what you felt was your own people. . . . You were uptight all week. You were pretending to be something." Mae notes, "A lot of these kids did not pretend. The kids I knew, none of them would pretend." The comments of Mae and Diane indicate the two extremes of being "out."

Another important difference between Diane and Mae is the choices each made about the social/sexual construct called butch/femme. As a femme, Diane could easily pass in straight society and thus spent her week pretending to be a heterosexual woman. Mae was a butch, and as Joan Nestle has explained, butches carried the political responsibility of being publicly identifiable as lesbians. Their dress and manner meant that everywhere they went they were out. Some women were out only to themselves and those in the bars, while others led a more integrated life, being out almost everywhere.

Butch and Femme

Our research indicates that there was a strong correlation between these two approaches to being out and the choice one had made in relation to the social construct of butch and femme. "One of the first times I was in a bar a woman came over to me and said what are YOU, butch or femme? I said butch or femme—I didn't even know what those terms mean."

Almost all of our narrators were asked some form of this question early in their introduction to gay life. In the role-defined 1950s, lesbians, like heterosexuals, sought ways to bring order and predictability to their relationships. The constructs butch and femme lent some clarity to the way they presented themselves in public situations, as well as guidelines for the treacherous waters of romantic, affectionate, and sexual relationships. There was a special term for lesbians who did not follow the rules: "Oh yeah, they used to call you kiki. If a butch was with a butch you were kiki. If a femme was with a femme, you were kiki. At the time there were two butches that I saw that went together. . . . They used to sneak it. Most of the people would sneak it, you know, like two women together that had long hair, they'd care for each other but they couldn't be with each other because of the way things were."

John D'Emilio hypothesizes that possibly "one function of butch-femme in the bar subculture was that it served as a kind of lesbian incest taboo. The prohibition of butches romantically pairing off with butches or femmes with femmes" meant that there would always be women who were off-limits and assured that permanent friendships would be maintained.[4]

For some people, choosing was not a problem; they had a strong inner sense of their identity, which they often carried painfully through their adolescent years before finding the gay world. "God, I looked like a little boy. I mean, all the girls at school used to say, 'Why couldn't you have been a boy; you're so cute. Just like Dr. Kildare.' A lot of them thought I looked like Dr. Kildare." For Alice, looking like Richard Chamberlain, the handsome star of a weekly television series, was a status symbol.

For others, choosing was not so obvious, and their hesitance to declare themselves was met with firm insistence on the part of their bar companions. "If I wasn't gonna choose then I couldn't be in a gay bar; I couldn't be with gay people. I HAD to make a choice. It was like I was a nonperson until I made a choice." But the choice was not easy. "I thought about it for a long time—a long time being like two hours. I sat there saying, 'No, I don't need to,' but obviously I did need to stay there." Finally, having hit the limits of their patience, her friends endeavored to speed up her decision-making process. "Well, they said,

[4] John D'Emilio, "Comments on the Session 'Love and Friendship in the Lesbian Bar Communities of the 1940s, 1950s, and 1960s,' " paper presented at the Berkshire Conference on the History of Women, June 19, 1987, Wellesley College, Wellesley, Mass.

'Who would you pick if you had to pick someone you wanted to be with.' And I said, 'her, right there.' And she turned out to be my first lover; and she was butch." And thus Doreen became a femme.

Butch or femme, what was the difference? When asked that question, most of our narrators responded first with physical descriptions. The femmes "wore dresses, skirts. If they wore slacks, it was very feminine looking slacks. No fly in the front; it was on the side. If it was in the winter maybe a tweed, but never anything that even slightly looked masculine." Butches usually wore pants and a shirt, a suit for a good night out, and perhaps a tux for a special affair. Whereas femme attire aided passing, butches ran some risks because of their appearance. When Alice thought of her appearance, she said:

> Well, all of my gay life, the one problem I had . . . like when I went into stores they'd say, "Yes, sir, may I help you?" I've constantly had that line. I still get that line. And I'll tell you a funny story. Back then if you had to go out for an interview, you had to wear a skirt. I didn't own any; I must have borrowed one. I had a skirt and blouse on and I'm walking around Central Square in Lynn and a couple of guys ride by and yell, "Hey, look at the fag with a skirt on." Well, I turned around, went right home, gave the skirt back to whoever I borrowed it from and said, "Well, the hell with this."

Thus ended her pursuit of an office job; she took a job pumping gas.

Being women, all lesbians had had a certain amount of training in many aspects of the femme role, however successful or unsuccessful that training had been. Some young lesbians completed their education in butchness by seeking role models in the bar. Mae remembered two classic butch role models.

> Elvis lived in Boston and she went to reform school. She wore the motorcycle jacket, the black boots. I mean she was tough. . . . Where Elvis was one type of person, now Geri Nichols was the other. Strictly class! She was older than almost all of us, but she was sharp. When she danced with a woman, you'd see her glide across the dance floor. And you're a young little punk that is just running around and you don't know too much, but you say, "Now, if I had a choice of being Elvis or her, I'd rather be Geri Nichols." You see what I mean? Elvis was too tough, too rude, too crude, too everything. But Geri was a class of her own. . . . She was a sharp lady . . . and you could talk to her. I mean, every other word wouldn't be a nasty word. . . . You could have a nice conversation with Geri Nichols.

As nicknames like "Elvis" indicate, these women also drew their role models from mainstream culture.

But what did it mean to be butch? Judy Grahn has said of the butch role:

> For all our boyish clothes and mannerisms . . . we women did not pass as men or boys. We dikes did not want to be taken for men and were insulted and shamed . . . when someone said we were "trying to be men" or when a clerk called me "Sir." . . . For our point was not to be men; our point was to be butch and get away with it. We always kept something back: a high-pitched voice, a slant of the head . . . something that was clearly labeled female. I believe our statement was "Here is another way of being a woman," not "Here is a woman trying to be taken for a man."[5]

This description generally fits the behavior of the women in our sample. We were told, for instance, "Stormy had tattoos from her arms to her stomach, you know. She had them all over. These people . . . were tough, but if you talked to them, they weren't really that tough, you know." Our narrators, did not always share Grahn's analysis. Many butches said that other butches, or butches in general, wanted to be men. They never said this about themselves, however, and sometimes they struggled for words, saying that they did not exactly want to be men, but they sort of did. The femmes seemed more consistent in their view that butches wanted the status men had and worked to acquire that status in the bar and sometimes at home.

For working-class butch lesbians in the 1950s and 1960s the world was a difficult place. Our narrators did not come from, nor were they likely to attain, the American dream of middle-class comforts, and they knew it. As women they were not respected and were vocationally constrained. As homosexuals they were pitied, hated, rejected, and incarcerated. As butches, unable to pass, they rarely had a moment's escape from this reality. It is little wonder that they created or sustained a social system that gave them a little respect and some social prerogatives. "There were certain things that they could do that femmes couldn't do . . . double standards. I think some of the butches took it to extremes. . . . I mean you had to ask another butch if you could dance with her lover—like 'Do you mind if I dance with so and so?' . . . Some social rules [were] established along the way."

Although these rules in part bespoke the competition that existed within bar culture, adherence to them also reflected a camaraderie between butches which some of our narrators remember fondly. "One thing I'll say, though, the butches weren't bad. They would come right up to you [after a breakup], they would say, 'Is it over for sure? Is it all right if I ask her out?' And you'd say, 'Sure, go ahead.' That's the way

[5] Grahn, *Another Mother Tongue*, pp. 30–31.

it was." Another public expression of this role-defined camaraderie, was the butches' night out, which was similar to the boys' night out in straight society. "Oh, yes, we had a ball with that—I loved it. . . . We would go out. We'd go out and drink, go to different bars, cruise up a storm. It was nice, yeah. We'd take maybe a Friday or a Saturday . . . that was when everybody's out." And what did the femmes do on the butches' night out? "Stay at home and have the other femmes visit them." But femmes too had a night out, at least in the circle some of our narrators traveled in. Said one butch:

> Of course we gave them maybe a Monday or a Tuesday. . . . They would go out to a nightclub, you know, to one of the clubs, and our spies would be there anyways; we would get a phone call. . . . [And] it's still another night out for us. We'd go to all the bars and everything and then at the end of the night we'd meet them to take them home. That was their night out! Unless they wanted to see their mother or family—that was even better for us.

Our research, like that of other lesbian historians, indicates that for the most part friendships were butch to butch or femme to femme. Cross-identity friendships were seen as threatening to romantic couplings and thus were very rare.

Relationships among the women who frequented the Lighthouse ran the gamut that might be found in any social setting such as a college campus, a workplace, or a neighborhood. Although many women were drawn there in hope of finding a lover, they also found friends, enemies, social acquaintances, and people who acknowledged each other's existence only begrudgingly because they were, so to speak, in the family. The nature of all of those relationships took on heightened significance because they took place in the bar, the only setting in which most of the women openly acknowledged their sexual preference.

For most of the women in the bar culture, having a good time was a major objective. Mae, who made a great deal of money as a female escort, described her thoughts about the future when she was in her teens and early twenties. "None. Having a good time. Spending it. Taking two, three girls out and having a great time. I wasn't worrying about nothing. You don't think of your future. Some people do. I didn't. No." All of our narrators were enthusiastic when describing the good times they had at the bars and their relief that such places existed. Friends were people to have a good time with, and for butches, good friends were those who stuck by and helped when one was in a jam. Sometimes such aid came not from close friendship but simply from the family feeling of sharing bar life. One narrator recalled the bravery of the butches:

They wouldn't be afraid to come out of the closet. They'd be right there to help you. There's a lot of them like that. In fact, Candy, she used to be dynamite. I was leaving the bar one time and I had these new cowboy boots on and they were kind of stiff. . . . I was walking through Central Square . . . and this cop who is dead now, which doesn't bother me at all. . . . He ripped my jacket, smashed me up against those big beams in Central Square, and literally beat me up. Swore up and down that I was drunk because I was walking funny and then swore up and down that I gave him the finger and that was why he arrested me. I never gave him the finger. He literally beat me in Central Square and everybody in the White Tower saw it and watched. Candy happened to be in the White Tower and she didn't recognize that it was me until they threw me in the paddy wagon. I had blood all over. . . . The next day when I was released from jail, I went down to the club. Candy got a hold of me and even though all the straight people in the White Tower knew I was gay, she got 95 percent of them to come down to the Lynn court and tell them exactly what that cop did to me. . . . Do you know those charges were instantly dropped; the case never got into court! Candy was really good that way. She was right there.

This story of Candy's spunk, courage, and determination illuminates an aspect of political bravery that was relatively rare in the tales recounted to us by the regulars at the bar. In a city like Lynn, to have stepped out as Candy did and to have challenged the police and rallied the patrons of the White Tower to sympathize with the narrator about the indignity she endured is noteworthy.

Outrage at the abuses suffered in the bar at the hands of the police and anyone else who wanted to beat up lesbians created a natural setting for heroines to emerge, and, indeed, such stars were often the butches who could fight. These women made reputations for themselves in the Lighthouse and were looked up to as key figures. Our interviews suggest that acts of bravery in fighting back usually occurred in and around the bar, and in that sense the bar became a public forum for shaping a more self-conscious view of oneself as a lesbian, as well as some nascent political sense.

Amid the oppression they endured, women made lasting friendships and met the essential network of people who would be a part of their lives for years. When asked what she looked for in a friend, Mae replied:

Just to be a friend. I didn't have that many friends either. I probably had many many acquaintances, but my friends . . . there were five of us. . . . I could be gone eight years, ten years, and we're still tight, no matter what, you know what I mean? . . . Maybe on a Christmas or maybe two years down the road I'd pick up a phone, "Hey, Rose, how are you doing? Are you all right? Yeah, I'm all right. All right, take care. Bye-bye." All of us will do that.

The depth of their bonding is significant. Their connections with one another are solid. The friendships have persisted for more than thirty years. Mae recalled, "Like Judy called me four years ago. She needed money. I sent it. She sent it back to me. . . . We all hung together as kids at the Lighthouse, that is why we had this thing. We all roomed together or we starved together." They are like old college chums or perhaps war buddies.

The habit of helping each other out with no questions asked began early in this particular friendship. Mae was in her late teens, traveling between Lynn and Florida, when Judy befriended her.

> I'd come home . . . you know, bunk in with somebody. . . . Then go on my way again. . . . Sometimes I was broke and I would stay with Judy. She put me up. Never asked me no questions. . . . Never asked me nothing. You need a place to stay; here it is. Sometimes I went home sick from drugs and stuff. They never knew it; and I would stay with them for a month until I got myself together and then out and gone.

Acceptance with no questions asked fit in with the codes of silent acknowledgment and acceptance which were a cornerstone of gay and lesbian life at that time. For example, Mae told how at the age of fifteen she went

> five blocks over from where I lived, looking for a job in the factory. . . . Of course I got a job, and as soon as I walked into the walkway where all the women are stitching and doing stuff and the guy showed me where I am going to work and everything, up walks this—it looked like a man to me—come toward me, and I'm looking at it and I figured out it's a girl. And she says to me, "Don't worry, I'll take care of you." And her and I became the best of friends. Anne, she took me to my first gay club, right there on that street—the Lighthouse.

Anne's befriending of Mae seems emblematic of the support and networking that went on. Most of the identification of each other occurred in the bar, but workplaces were another area where butches in particular could find each other.

Although lesbians often found each other jobs and were not afraid to bring other overt butches into their workplaces, many of them hesitated to bring these women home to meet their families. Femmes were reluctant to bring their butches home, and the resulting tension, then as now, was most poignant around the holidays. One of our narrators transformed the rejection she felt into a display of butch solidarity by making holidays at her family's home a special occasion to which she invited many of her friends who were rejected elsewhere. Taking care of each other around holidays meant caring for friends, showing a special kindness and concern. Since most of the women in bars were from the same class background, they tended to understand each other's family situations. In a context in which the private realm of the family did not provide traditional family support, these women forged new families in the public space of the bar.

This sense of appreciation for each other also manifested itself in the respect the women showed each other. Old friends, good fighters, and good pool players, for example, were respected. Mae considers the matter of respect to be a problem for today's younger generation of bar dykes. "Respect, that's it, respect. They don't have that today. That's what a bunch of us were talking about one night when we were sitting here. Phyllis, me, and Red and a bunch—and we said, 'You know what these kids ain't got? They ain't got no respect. None. Not even for each other.' " By example she related the following story about something that happened to her at Fran's Place a few years before:

> It's like I was playing pool there one night and I'm quite the pool player. This girl comes up and says, . . . "I heard you're a good player from way back." I says, "Well, you know, I can play pool." She says, "Well, it would be an honor for me to play you and beat you." AND BEAT YOU. That was the thing. So . . . I said, . . . "Can you play for a hundred dollars a game?" She probably had like ten dollars in her pocket. . . . She ran around and got the hundred dollars and comes back and says, "Yeah." I said, "You know, I'm going to love taking your hundred dollars." . . . And I did. I took her hundred, and she looked at me and said, "You know you are good at pool." And I said, "Oh, give me a break."

Mae's dismay at the apparent lack of respect for her as a good pool player from the old days was heightened not by the challenge to a pool game but by the attitude of the newcomers to the bar. In the old days, she felt, deference would be shown to a recognized pool player. She was dismayed by the erosion of the system of hierarchy from which butches had drawn much of their social status or pride.

Our research indicates, perhaps not surprisingly, that public expression of butch/femme roles was somewhat more uniform than private expression. Within the homes of cohabiting couples there were many variations on the butch/femme theme. In some households, maintenance chores were shared, while in others they were entirely a femme responsibility. In some couples, the femme stayed home and the butch supported her; in some households both partners were employed; and in other cases the femme, who could pass in the straight world, was the more reliable source of income. Similarly, there were different patterns of money management. Said one of our butch narrators:

> I always gave all my money to the person I lived with . . . because I was a drinker. See, then they could handle it, and that money had to go into the

> house. That was the reason. . . . But in other cases, the butches felt that they were the man of the house and they went to work, most of them. They'd bring the money in and they'd come home and their supper would have to be done. You know, stuff like that. They played the part of the man.

Many of the relationships were of short duration. That reality is reflected in the language used such as "I always gave my money to the person I lived with." Many of our narrators reflected back on numerous brief relationships, rather than a significant few. This is a matter about which there is some ambivalence within the community. Couples who stayed together for years sometimes were regarded with respect, sometimes with incredulity. "I don't know how they stayed together twenty-two years. I mean I couldn't stay with a woman twenty-two days, never mind twenty-two years. But I guess everybody is different." Thus spoke a narrator who came out in her early teens and who by her late forties was for the first time in a relationship of more than a year's duration. The duration of a relationship seemed to be inconsequential to her; she respected both long and short ones. As she explained it, "Maybe I wanted to see more; maybe they were satisfied in their own little job and being with each other . . . I don't know. . . . I got bored. Bored is it with me. I'm bored and then I'll be seeking and looking, and something."

For this person, not getting stuck in a rut was important in work as well as in relationships. From her perspective, not being stuck gave her some social status. "They thought it was great. I was the talk of the whole thing. They loved it. 'Oh, Mae, who is she going out with now? Who is she seeing now?' . . . And I'd always bring women up from Florida. I'd bring some classy-looking women up and bring them to the Lighthouse."

One of the ways Mae avoided what she perceived as entrapping relationships was to go out with straight women.

> Probably 'cause you don't have to, let me see how to put it. I probably treat them just like a man would a woman. I come home when I feel like it, I don't have to answer to them. I come and go as I please, and if I felt like staying the night, I stayed the night. If I didn't, I went on my way, you know. I probably had more the role of, almost like a man, you know what I mean? I didn't have to deal with anything.

She said, "Gay women are very, very possessive. They are." That many femmes were bisexual or straight was a recurrent theme throughout our interviews. Most narrators did not feel as positive about it as Mae did. For some, it explained the brevity of relationships.

"It never used to last then because most of the femmes at the time were bisexuals. They would be straight and they would go into this life and it was just something different for them. They'd end up always getting married."

Although some femmes may have been straight women dallying with lesbians, others abandoned gay life, and their butches along with it, for more complex reasons.

> Because I'll tell you why. Most of them at the time were really ashamed. Like they couldn't bring them to their homes or anything. And what they saw in a man they wanted in the woman at the time. . . . The only thing was they couldn't have children. So that's why most of them ended up getting married or they would have stayed with that person. You know like take them home and meet the families and all that. . . . I can remember all of them going here for Christmas or there, and there was a few I went with, I couldn't go. . . . I was bitter about it, of course I was. You're with someone so many years and all of a sudden they up and leave. . . . "I want to get married." You can't trust the next person, you're afraid. Really afraid. You say, "No more, no more, I'm not going to do it."

During the course of our research, we heard more than one story about butches who committed suicide or became alcoholic after being left for a man and the comfort of married life in the straight world. Despite their bravado in the bar or in the home, working-class butches were a painfully vulnerable group. Sometimes this vulnerability drove them to get married. Sometimes it was the power of the state that moved them. "I did a lot of crazy things when I was younger, like I married a fag, just to prove I was not a homosexual. . . . I only married him cause I heard that they could lock homosexuals away for the rest of their lives. I did not want to get locked away for the rest of my life so I married him." For others family pressure drove them to marriage. "And my father said to me, . . . 'Why don't you make your mother happy? Get married, she won't know the difference. Go ahead.' "

These, of course, were marriages of convenience or contrivance. They did not bespeak any ambivalence about sexual identity on the part of the butches, as they sometimes did for femmes. Some butches did, however, experience conflict around the issue of sexual expression within their lesbian relationships.

Although many aspects of butch behavior were taught by one butch to another, lovemaking was apparently considered too private a matter for this process. Perhaps some butches were natural lovers, but most acknowledged that they learned a lot from the femmes. Mae had just turned seventeen when she met an older woman on the beach in Miami. "Some girl walked up to me and all I could see was her navel in front of me. And she says, 'Do you need a place to stay?' I looked up and I thought I was dreaming. . . . So she hopped me into her Jaguar and we went over to her apartment . . . and Susan showed me the ropes."

Mae went from being kept by Susan to serving as an escort for the wealthy straight women of Miami Beach. Though knowing how to dress, dine out, and talk right were prerequisites for being a successful escort, they were not the crux of the matter. "You have to be a good lover. That's for sure. I mean you have to know what you are doing and you have to know how to satisfy these women."

For some butches, satisfying the women is what sex was all about. Their own satisfaction came through that process, rather than through being touched themselves. But it is not clear for how many this was true. We heard repeatedly that the public stories and the private truths on this matter differed more than on any other aspect of gay life at that time. "Years ago the butches did everything. The femmes did not do what the butches did; the butches did it all. Of course, a lot of them now are admitting that they did, but when it came to going down to the club they'd be saying, 'I didn't do that.' " The butch who told us this was in the painful process of change, allowing her lover to make love to her: "I'm really finally coming out 'cause my girlfriend is driving me crazy, but . . . for one I'm not used to it. For another I have trained myself to be an expert. I have to do everything perfectly. She says, 'Don't worry about it.' But for me, if it ain't perfect it ain't right. We've had that discussion for a while now, but I'm getting there. Get me stoned, you know; don't do it sober." Even as Alice talked about lovemaking, she admitted feeling "all screwed up here." The apparent decrease in the number of stone butches, those who refuse to be touched, is a significant difference between bar culture of the 1950s and 1960s and that of the 1980s.

Survival: Legacy for the Future

Some aspects of working-class lesbian bar culture have changed in the past twenty years, but much remains the same. Women still go to bars to meet other women and have a good time. For large numbers of working-class women, the bar is a place to congregate and build solidarity and spirit.

Although in the 1970s and 1980s many gays and lesbians created institutions that became alternatives to the bars, the bars are still the central focus of the lives of many working-class lesbians. Our narrators feel comfortable returning to the bars because they will fit in immediately. For most of them, however, the circumstances of their lives are such that they no longer spend much time in bars. Their sentimental ties to the Lighthouse remain, however, and they would not miss a reunion.

We see the women we interviewed as survivors. They did not go straight and live a more secure heterosexual life, nor did they commit suicide in despair. Both of these routes were taken by other women they mentioned. Their lives are a testimony to survival over conditions of poverty, violence, alcohol, and homophobia. Each of our narrators sees herself as someone who has retained her own sense of life while others who were part of her community succumbed to one pitfall or another posed by the conditions in which they found themselves. The strength of both the friendships and the love relationships that developed in the bar community remains powerful testimony to the humanity and the survival skills of these women.

PART II

CIRCLES OF SOCIAL CONTROL AND RESISTANCE

CHAPTER SIX

Safety and Danger: Women on American Public Transport, 1750–1850

Patricia Cline Cohen

When Nathaniel Hawthorne was a young bachelor, he took a trip on the Erie Canal and later described what he saw as gender dynamics in action from a masculine point of view. He observed a lone woman passenger who intercepted an appraising glance from a man and then "reddened, and retired deeper into the female part of the cabin." Evidently, the woman was discomfited by a male gaze, and conveniently the boat provided a ladies-only space, as did all canal boats, steamboats, and major railway stations in the 1830s. But the young Hawthorne did not interpret her actions as arising from reluctance or fear of contact with a male stranger; instead he suggested that she was overly sensitive and perhaps disturbingly thrilled to be given attention: "Here was the pure, modest, sensitive, and shrinking woman of America; shrinking when no evil is intended; and sensitive like diseased flesh, that thrills if you but point at it; and strangely modest, without confidence in the modesty of other people; and admirably pure, with such a quick apprehension of all impurity."[1]

What this particular blushing woman really thought about being stared at by a man is not known, but there is abundant evidence from other women and men that reveals the contours of a history of gender

Research for this paper was supported by grants from the National Endowment for the Humanities given by the American Antiquarian Society in Worcester, Massachusetts, from the Andrew W. Mellon Foundation given by Radcliffe College for research at the Arthur and Elizabeth Schlesinger Library on the History of Women in America, and by the National Endowment for the Humanities Summer Stipend Program. Special thanks go to Sharon Salinger, Helen Horowitz, Katherine Kish Sklar, Linda Kerber, Sharon Farmer, and Zelda Bronstein for their support and comments on earlier versions.

[1] [Nathaniel Hawthorne], "The Canal Boat," *New England Magazine* 9 (1835): 401.

behavior in public. Commercial travel, a common activity and one essentially new in the early nineteenth century, drew in hundreds of thousands of passengers. Between 1790 and 1850, stagecoach lines, canal boats, steamships, and finally railroads—the components of the famed transportation revolution—connected the cities and villages of the eastern half of the United States and provided a new arena for social interaction between the sexes.

A study of gender deportment on public transport illuminates at least three important and interrelated issues about the gender system in the early national period. First, how did public travel behavior fit with the new middle-class ideology about gender that emerged in the early nineteenth century? This ideology, most faithfully elaborated in prescriptive literature, defined masculine and feminine attributes as a study of extreme contrasts, and investigations of private writings have confirmed that, at least for literate, white, middle-class, eastern seaboard people, the doctrine of separate spheres was accepted as a reasonable description of reality.[2] Men were said to be creatures of the public realm—inhabitants of the halls of government, the countinghouse, the workshop, the field, or the street. Respectable women presided over the private realm as inhabitants of private houses and the custodians of family life. Public transport constitutes a potential breach of the public/private dichotomy, wherein a manifestly public activity, booking passage on a commercial boat, stage, or railroad and traveling in a confined space with strangers, was undertaken by both sexes. Traveling women were visibly in public; was their behavior essentially the same as that of men, or were there special gender-specific rules that constrained the behavior of women in this public space, as if to remind them that they were momentarily out of place?

Second, such a study offers a window on the social construction of gender. The new modes of transport were at the same time new public spaces that encouraged or even required close contact by strangers, unmediated by the usual formal customs of introduction and intercession. No preexisting etiquette of commercial travel instructed men and women on codes of proper behavior under these novel circumstances. Public transport of the early nineteenth century thus presented a possibility for cultural improvisation. Certainly we would expect some carryover from established gender behaviors in daily life into travel behavior, but how could formal customs of social distance

[2] The classic analysis of the prescriptive literature on gender is Barbara Welter, "The Cult of True Womanhood, 1820–1860," *American Quarterly* 18 (1966): 131–75. Substantiation of these values in private writings can be found in Nancy F. Cott, *The Bonds of Womanhood: "Woman's Sphere" in New England, 1780–1835* (New Haven, 1977); Carroll Smith-Rosenberg, "The Female World of Love and Ritual," *Signs* 1 (1975): 1–29; and Katherine Kish Sklar, *Catharine Beecher: A Study in American Domesticity* (New Haven, 1973).

be maintained in a stagecoach crammed with nine passengers sharing quarters over several days, or at a tavern where travelers bedded down for the night in shared rooms? Acceptable gestures, thresholds for physical contact, permissible conversation topics, deference and dominance, in short, general deportment between men and women, had to be negotiated and renegotiated each time the train whistle blew or the stage door slammed shut and a new set of strangers moved through space together. Americans who traveled were engaged constantly in expressing, defining, confirming, and, indeed, creating gender.[3]

Finally, travel behavior offers an index to the amount of independence and automomy afforded to women. Could women travel freely, without escorts and without fear, or was there a pervasive or realistic concern about sexual danger? The French observer Alexis de Tocqueville toured America in 1829 and reported with amazement that even young, single women seemed to enjoy unhampered geographical mobility. He concluded that it was primarily women's behavior (stemming from their strong sense of virtue), not men's, that protected them and prevented them from being led astray.[4] But a very different view of safety and danger was taken by the members of the American Female Moral Reform Society, which spread to over five hundred towns in the North in the 1830s and 1840s. These women, most of them religious evangelicals, were united into activist groups by their alarm over a contagion of male licentiousness, spreading rapidly and endangering women everywhere. They worried especially about the many young, mobile women who moved outside the protection of home and kin in search of mill work, domestic work, or teaching jobs, which were newly open to young females. The moral reformers' monthly newspapers carried constant warnings about the dangers of travel. They were certain that legions of men traveled the coaches and canal boats of America with no other purpose than to seduce and abandon unprotected victims.[5] Who was more nearly right, Tocqueville or the moral reformers?

[3] For sociological approaches to the production of gender in daily life see Erving Goffman, "The Arrangement between the Sexes," *Theory and Society* 4 (1977): 301–31; Judith M. Gerson and Kathy Peiss, "Boundaries, Negotiation, Consciousness: Reconceptualizing Gender Relations," *Social Problems* 32 (1985): 316–31; and Candace West and Don Zimmerman, "Doing Gender," *Gender and Society* 1 (1987): 125–51.

[4] Alexis de Tocqueville, *Democracy in America*, ed. Phillips Bradley, 2 vols. (1835; rpt. New York, 1945), 2:224.

[5] Carroll Smith-Rosenberg, "Beauty, the Beast, and the Militant Woman: A Case Study in Sex Roles and Social Stress in Jacksonian America," *American Quarterly* 23 (1971): 562–84; Mary P. Ryan, *Cradle of the Middle Class: The Family in Oneida County, New York, 1790–1865* (New York, 1981), pp. 116–27; and Barbara Hobson, *Uneasy Virtue: The Politics of Prostitution and the American Reform Tradition* (New York, 1987). The two publications of the reformers are *The Advocate of Moral Reform*, published in New York City starting in 1835, and *The Friend of Virtue*, published in Boston from 1838 to 1851.

The available evidence that bears on these issues is voluminous but untidy. Manuscript collections contain disproportionate numbers of letters and diaries written by travelers of both sexes because a common function of letters was to assure friends and family of one's safe arrival after a trip.

This evidence is biased in three ways. First, travel was expensive although not prohibitively so; costs ranged from about two cents per mile on the stage, three to four cents on canal boats, up to four or five cents on trains, which means that a rail ticket from Boston to Worcester was just under two dollars—nearly a whole week's wages for a Lowell mill girl. Consequently, middle- and upper-class women were most likely to be among the traveling public, although working-class women could be found there. Second, the documentary evidence is weighted toward the literate classes, which makes it all the harder to learn about the travel behavior of unschooled females. Very often, however, letter writers described all their fellow travelers, thereby affording a glimpse of women who were unlikely to have left a written record of their perceptions. A more serious bias in women's letters is that their purpose often was to reassure worried kin. Letters describing moments of actual sexual danger were both unlikely to be written and very unlikely to be saved and donated to libraries. No official agencies then collected statistics on sexual crime so newspaper accounts provide the best direct evidence of instances of sexual danger. The private letters of reassurance are very useful, however, for they often include indirect evidence of a woman's sense of sexual peril, as revealed by the measures taken in anticipation of danger.

The goal of this essay is to learn what gender behavior on public transport can tell us about women in the public sphere, about sexual tensions and fears, and about female autonomy or dependence. At heart, this study is an effort to tap into the collective mentality about gender shared by white Americans in a transitional and defining period in American history.

In the eighteenth century, travel in the colonies was difficult and time-consuming. Poor roads, irregular conveyances, unpredictable lodging, and long stretches of uninhabited land between major settlements created serious obstacles to travel. A traveler needed the financial resources to own or rent a horse or carriage, the ability to handle a horse, and a sense of direction or a guide. The first regular stagecoach lines were established in the colonies in the 1730s, connecting New York and Philadelphia with scheduled trips only once a week, taking five days one way. Passenger traffic was thus limited, and it remained so until the 1790s.

Probably the earliest written account by a woman traveling on her own dates from 1704, when Sarah Knight, a thirty-eight-year-old widow from Boston, went to New York City and back on a horse. The trip took about two weeks each way, and nearly every day she hired a guide, some young man of the locality. Innkeepers along her route expressed amazement that she was traveling alone. Knight did encounter dangers in the form of uncertain river crossings, dark swamps, and stumbling horses. But her most difficult moment came on the return trip, at a Norwalk, Connecticut, tavern, which had "poor entertainment, and the Impertinant Bable of one of the worst of men, among many otheres of which our Host made one, who, had he bin one degree Impudenter, would have outdone his Grandfather. And this I think is the most perplexed night I have yet had."[6]

Perplexed at first seems an odd word choice; Knight did not report fear or outrage at the men's behavior, but rather confusion. Something in the normal course of gender interaction was askew in this scene for her so that impertinent and impudent male behavior—adjectives suggesting cockiness and boldness—threw her off balance; she did not read the men's behavior as a customary expression of male dominance. Perhaps her social status conflicted with such a reading, for she was the daughter of a Charleston merchant and the widow of an American agent once stationed in London, whereas the men were small-town tavern habitués. This travel story suggests that a woman alone on the road at this early point was unusual and that male impudence toward an unprotected woman in this case did not create automatic fear but instead simply confusion.

By far the largest class of documented women travelers in the eighteenth century consisted of Quaker women, who traveled in the ministry. Older married women more often than single women were itinerant ministers, and they almost always traveled in pairs on horseback. Usually the women employed local male guides, as had Sarah Knight, to help them find their way and to assist in the event of road hazards, but there was nothing remarkable about two women traveling without a male escort. Their home meetings directed them to keep diaries of their travels so these trips are unusually well documented, but their accounts contain surprisingly little gender commentary.[7] Mainly the Quaker women emphasized confidence in Divine Providence to see them through all difficulties.

One unusual Quaker minister of the revolutionary period did use her journal to advise younger women of the sexual perils of this special

[6] [Sarah Kemble Knight], *Journal of Madam Knight,* ed. George Parker Winship (New York, 1935), pp. 5–6, 61–62.

[7] Swarthmore and Haverford College libraries, in Pennsylvania, have large and rich collections of Quaker travel and spiritual diaries from the period 1740 to 1850.

calling. Catherine Phillips of Philadelphia wrote of "some cautions necessary to be observed by young women in a single state, who travel in the service of the ministry, towards those of the other sex, who are also unmarried." Her concern was with unfamiliar single men, who might confuse the intimacies of spiritual consultation with the intimacies of initial courtship display. The peril involved mixed signals, not attack by predatory males. She warned young women to guard against "slid[ing] into a familiarity and freedom of conversation and behaviour" and to watch closely the conduct of young men so they could "wisely check any forward thought which looks beyond friendship."[8]

In the early nineteenth century, American travel became much more frequent and regular, as hundreds of stagecoach lines competed to shorten the travel time on main routes and roads extended to connect even remote spots. Commercial travel obviated the need for map skills or an adventurous spirit; the route was preordained, defined, and controlled. Letters and accounts of trips by women also became much more frequent as a result of both higher numbers of trips and a higher level of female literacy. The vast majority of trip accounts up to 1820 do not betray any concern for sexual danger. A smaller set of letters take for granted that a male escort is necessary, but for most it appears that lack of a protector was no obstacle to travel. The most common purpose for female travel before 1820 was to visit relatives, and the letters stemming from such trips only rarely remark directly on issues of safety and danger.

One unusually explicit early instance of vulnerability and fear of danger comes from the diary of Margaret Dwight, who went from New Haven to Ohio in 1810. The twenty-year-old Dwight traveled in a private wagon with another family and stayed in public inns with strangers each night, among them rough wagoneers and teamsters. At one inn, she had her first close encounter with a man who presumed to touch her familiarly: "I was very much frighten'd by a drunken waggoner, who came up to me as I stood by the door waiting for a candle, he put his arm around my neck & said something which I was too frighten'd to hear—It is the first time the least insult has been offer'd to any of us."[9]

But it was not the last such experience. A few nights later Dwight had bedded down in a crowded room with Mrs. Jackson, a widow recently met on the road; also in the same room were Mrs. Jackson's son and daughter-in-law, in another bed, and the innkeeper and his wife, on

[8] Catherine Phillips, *Memoirs of the Life of Catherine Phillips* (Philadelphia, 1798), pp. 111–12.

[9] Margaret Van Horn Dwight, *A Journey to Ohio in 1810*, ed. Max Ferrand (New Haven, 1913), p. 36.

the floor. The wife and daughter of the family Dwight traveled with were in another room, and the husband was asleep outside in their wagon.

> I took off my frock & boots, & had scarcely lain down, when one of the wretches [a wagoneer] came into the room & lay down by me on the outside of the bed—I was frighten'd almost to death & clung to Mrs. Jackson . . . & I lay for a quarter of an hour crying, & scolding & trembling, begging of him to leave me—At last, when persuaded I was in earnest, he begg'd of me not to take it amiss, as he intended no harm & only wish'd to become acquainted with me—A good for nothing brute, I wonder what he suppos'd I was—I don't know of any thought word or action of mine that could give him reason to suppose I would authorise such abominable insolence.[10]

What is amazing about this story is the timidity of the twenty-year-old in rebuffing a man who took extraordinary liberties. For fifteen minutes she trembled and begged the man to leave her bed and wondered what she had done to encourage him, but she did not rouse the many other occupants of the room. The man left only when he realized that she really meant *no;* his intention was evidently consensual sex (termed seduction in 1810), not rape. That he thought he could accomplish it so easily suggests that women in backcountry Pennsylvania in 1810 did not yet have the armor of moral virtue to protect them as Tocqueville assumed they had by 1830.

In the next few minutes of Margaret Dwight's story, the plot thickened. She put her outer dress on, to reduce her sense of vulnerability, and returned to bed, when the mother and daughter across the hall flew into the room complaining of a similar attack on them. Now the guests tripled up in the two beds, the daughter joining Dwight and Mrs. Jackson and the mother clambering in with the younger Jackson couple, and yet again a determined wagoneer crawled into the room. This time, the women were emboldened by their shared status as victims and their general outrage, and they sprang from the beds and chased the man out. Interestingly, no one woke the father sleeping outside in the wagon: the wagoneer begged them not to, and the women decided that the father would be so unpleasant all the next day if he lost any sleep that they let the incident pass.

By the mid-1820s, extensive stage routes were linked with steamboats and canal boats, and passenger traffic continued to mushroom. Women's letters about travel increasingly begin to reflect distancing strategies based on gender. For example, a Massachusetts girl in 1828 wrote to her mother about her discomfort with strange men:

[10] Ibid., p. 40.

> My Dear Mother, Through the watchful care of a kind Providence I arrived here in safety. When I had said farewell to Edward, and found myself shut up in the stage without friend or protector my heart almost failed me. There were two men in the stage and I knew not what sort of company they might prove. As the carriage conveyed us along I was unhappy some; but soon I felt that though away from friends and acquaintances, there was One with me who would be my guide and who would preserve me from harm . . . my fears were calmed. I even felt happy. In his presence there is fullness of joy.

By evening there were six men on the stage, and the young traveler commented that she did not have "the pleasure of a Lady's company" except for a few miles in the midday.

> The gentlemen were civil, but I was in no enviable situation. I sat in a corner, seldom enclosing [unclosing] my lips excepting when spoken to and that was an infrequent occurrence. When silence was interrupted by conversation it was upon subjects that ladies are not often consulted about, such as the presidential election, tariff, canals, slave trade, smuggling, &c &c. Some part of the time I felt somewhat more alone, than if alone.[11]

This young woman could find comfort in summoning God to escort her, much as the Quaker women ministers did. She also insulated herself by defining the conversation topics as masculine and therefore off-limits to women. The most unusual feature of this letter is that the author wrote so fully to her mother about her feelings and discomforts. She did not feel the need to explain why she felt vulnerable—the mere fact of being the only woman was sufficient. She was telling her mother that she knew how to conduct herself with modesty and reserve.

If having an escort provided security, a woman without an escort might invent one if traveling companions made her uneasy. Lucy Pierce of Brookline, Massachusetts, an experienced traveler, got on a stage in Worcester one morning in 1819 to find it filled entirely by large and unruly men. She sensed a need to invoke her class privilege as a form of escortage. "I looked around on *all,* to discover my *protector,* and anxiously inquired if either of them had a letter for me, 'from Mr. Lewis Tappan, merchant, Boston.' The answer was no. I then observed to the gentleman on my right hand, that I was very much dis-

[11] S. to Mother, November 7, 1828, Bradley-Hyde Papers, The Arthur and Elizabeth Schlesinger Library on the History of Women in America, Radcliffe College, Cambridge, Mass.

appointed, for my *brother* had promised me a protector, in the gentleman I inquired for."[12] Pierce manufactured the ruse about the letter and thereby cleverly announced her privileged status as the sister of a well-known Boston merchant.

A similar ruse was observed by the Englishwoman Harriet Martineau in her travels in Kentucky in the mid-1830s. She encountered a young woman with extraordinary freedom of manners; the woman was dressed oddly, but she was so friendly and open that Martineau "concluded that she belonged to one of two gentlemen in the stage, and we rather wondered that any gentleman should like to travel with a companion so untidily dressed as she was." But when it came time to change stages next day, the woman "cooly inquired if any gentleman would ask a free passage for her till she could send the money out of Indiana, where she was going. It was now evident that she was alone, every passenger having supposed that she was of the party of someone else." One of the men volunteered to pay her way, and Martineau carefully noted that he was an elderly gentleman, who presumably had only honorable motives. Concluded Martineau, who was in her early thirties and touring America with a female companion, "Though the freedom of travelling is not such as to admit of young ladies making their way about quite alone, in a way so unceremonious as this, the liberty of intercourse on the road is very great, and highly amusing to a stranger."[13]

These last three stories suggest that young women could and did travel alone, just as Tocqueville reported, but they were aware of and took precautions to subdue sexual tensions, as the moral reformers said they must. (Martineau's girl even manipulated the sexual dynamics for her own benefit.) Women were not "out of place" in public, but they were not traveling on the same terms as were men.

An amusing newspaper piece of 1844 confirmed this view with a mock proposal for an escort service for hire: a series of "civil agents" would see women from station to station along the stage or rail route and would procure seats, book hotel rooms, attend to baggage, and fetch lemonade. The article had a whimsical tone, as if all gentlemen ever did for women was to carry bandboxes, but its final argument got to the heart of the gender exchange: "Another great point would be an entire absence of any feeling of obligation on the part of the ladies; they would receive every possible care and attention, and would pay accordingly. It would be a perfect business transaction."[14] This

[12] Lucy Tappan Pierce to John Pierce, July 19, 1819, Poor Family Papers, ibid.

[13] Harriet Martineau, *Retrospect of Western Travel,* 2 vols. (New York, 1838), 2:198–200.

[14] Letter to the editor from H.T.M., *New Mirror* 3 (May 11, 1844): 87.

courtesy-for-hire scheme reveals a fundamental fact about the character of customary courtesy: women became obligated to men for their protective function.[15]

It was just this sense of obligation that worried the Female Moral Reformers, who were sure that licentiousness was on the rise in America. In the 1840 issue of *The Advocate of Moral Reform*, the women warned that "men journey to and fro through the country, who have no other object in view than the pursuit of unprotected females with whom they may chance to travel. It is at your peril that you become familiar with such men. . . . As you cannot know them from any given marks, the only course left you is to trust no man with whom you are not acquainted. And those you do know as neighbors and associates, should not be trusted beyond the limits of rigid delicacy and personal security."[16]

The reformers published numerous cautionary tales. In one, an inexperienced young traveler boarded a train in Worcester, headed for Harrisburg, Pennsylvania. The person who sent her off entrusted her to the conductor, but soon a "pretended gentleman" sat down and asked her about her plans. When he offered to show her around New York City, she became alarmed and called the conductor. The man lied to the conductor, saying "the lady was an acquaintance of his, and was placed under his care. The conductor, then going into a seat behind the lady, inquired, in a whisper, if she wished this stranger's protection. She told him decidedly, NO—that she never saw the man before, and hoped he, himself, would not fail to protect her." The conductor seems to have been a little slow to do his duty here, since the woman had been put in his care and he was evidently familiar enough with the man to snarl at him, "This is not the first lady you have insulted."[17]

Railroad conductors themselves might presume on their protective custody of women. In a well-publicized criminal case of 1847, a conductor in Albany, New York, was accused of misinforming an Ohio girl about her correct train and then directing her to a hotel where she could have a Sabbath layover; the hotel turned out to be less than reputable, and the conductor allegedly assaulted her in her room, followed by two other men. The message for young women was clear: know your route, know how to recognize a reputable hotel, carry adequate

[15] Kathy Peiss, *Cheap Amusements: Working Women and Leisure in Turn-of-the-Century New York* (Philadelphia, 1986), explores the sexual trade-offs and obligations incurred in an early dating system in an urban environment. The behaviors of antebellum women travelers did not, of course, constitute a dating system, but the situation is similar in that men and women were continuously engaged in negotiating the boundary between complimentary service and service that puts women under obligation.

[16] *Advocate of Moral Reform* 4 (February 15, 1840): 23.

[17] *Friend of Virtue* 14 (July 1, 1851): 197–98.

money, and always be on the lookout for libertines.[18] Another cautionary tale from 1836 described a stage trip on which a young woman with inadequate funds had to appeal to the stage proprietor for money; he arranged for a hotel for her, escorted her there, and then raped her in the room. The moral reformers circulated this story and advised all women to make direct inquiries about the owner of any hotel they contemplated using: "Is it respectable? Is the landlord a libertine?"[19]

Other signs of a rising preoccupation with sexual danger for women in public in the 1830s can be seen in the provision of waiting rooms for "ladies only" in railroad stations and in the establishment of special temperance hotels in the Northeast open to nondrinking travelers of both sexes but with ads pitched particularly to women. The American Temperance House in Worcester rented rooms to about two hundred men and eighty-five women in June and July 1834; forty-eight of the women were without apparent male escorts.[20] Sexual danger also shaped the emergence of a formal etiquette of travel, set forth in new chapters in etiquette books, some seventy of which were published between 1830 and 1860.[21] Typically the advice-givers instructed women to use male protectors or to follow strict rules of behavior (such as modest dress, veils, and reserved conversation) to avoid overfamiliarity with strangers.

To some extent, changes in the technology of transportation help explain the rising apprehension about personal security for women in public. Stagecoaches, the earliest and most local form of transport, provided fixed and close seating; travelers experienced physical and sometimes distressing closeness, but that very crowdedness made it

[18] "Attempted Rape by a Railroad Conductor," *National Police Gazette* 3 (July 31, August 7, 21, 1847): 373, 380, 397.

[19] "Public Houses—Stage Proprietors: A Warning to Females Traveling Alone," *Journal of Public Morals* 1 (March 1, 1837): 3. This New York publication was issued by the Seventh Commandment Society, an organization of male ministers affiliated with the Female Moral Reformers.

[20] Register of the American Temperance House in Worcester, May 1834 to November 1836, American Antiquarian Society, Worcester, Mass. This hotel was not 100 percent dry, however; the one nipper was a Miss Fenten of Virginia, traveling with the Carter family, who charged a bottle of port to her room bill on July 5, 1834.

The female help of the Temperance Hotel in Hartford, Connecticut, saved a young woman abducted under false pretenses from Boston by a con man who meant to deliver her to her ruin in New York City. Probably to allay her suspicions, he lodged her at the Temperance Hotel in transit; she told her plight to a sympathetic maid whose employer then arranged for the police to follow the absconding pair (*Advocate of Moral Reform* 2 [February 1, 1837]: 17–18).

[21] Karen Halttunen, *Confidence Men and Painted Women: A Study of Middle-Class Culture in America, 1830–1870* (New Haven, 1982), p. 92. A good third of advice books devoted a separate section or even an entire chapter to travel behavior. For two early examples, see *The Laws of Etiquette, or, Short Rule and Reflections for Conduct in Society*, by a Gentleman (Philadelphia, 1836), pp. 191–95; and Mrs. John Ferrar, *The Young Lady's Friend* (Boston, 1838), pp. 104–15.

more difficult for a man to make an inappropriate advance toward a woman because everyone else would see or hear it. For example, in a legal dispute about an incident in upstate New York in 1838, witnesses in a stagecoach observed that a minister stroked the hand of an unfamiliar woman passenger, who disembarked prematurely at the next stop; the dispute was about his intentions, not his action.[22]

In contrast, steamboats, canal boats, and railroads allowed for more space and mobility among passengers; a man on the make could target a vulnerable female and press his attentions. In boat danger stories, female passengers found it easier to move away than in train stories, for on a train it apparently took more gumption for a seated woman to stand up and leave.[23] Railroad noise also reduced the potential for intercession of bystanders. It is probably not too much to claim that railroads required markedly new negotiations of gender behaviors in public. And indeed, the swift beginnings of railroad travel in the 1830s coincided with the rise of the American Female Moral Reform Societies and their insistence on the dangers of sexual predators. The earliest passenger railroads were built in 1829, and by 1835 thousands of passengers were moving by rail.[24] The sheer volume of people meant that many more strangers shared space, and that changed the dynamics of travel interaction as well. Nine people (at a maximum) in a stagecoach could easily connect and actually share a journey; a train traveler in the 1830s was much more in the new world of anonymous mass transport.

Not only the technology of travel but the demographics of passenger traffic were changing in the 1830s. Work opportunities pulled young women out of marginal rural economies and propelled them to factory towns and urban centers, where they could find employment as mill hands, shopgirls, and domestic servants. Increasingly the warning stories about the pitfalls of travel had a class dimension, wherein well-meaning respectable women undertook to protect naive youngsters in

[22] *The Proceedings of the Court Convened under the Third Canon of 1844, on Tuesday, December 10, 1844, for the Trial of the Right Reverend Benjamin T. Onderdonk, D.D., Bishop of New York, on a Presentment Made by the Bishops of Virginia, Tennessee, and Georgia* (New York, 1845), pp. 30–39.

[23] Sarah Mendell, a plucky twenty-five-year-old from northern New York who spent a year roaming the East Coast, reported that she encountered a "wolf" on a train to Washington, D.C., in 1852. Mendell generally flaunted travel etiquette rules and could hold her own against intrusive males, but in this case she trembled in anxiety when the man began to tell her what beautiful eyes and hands she had. The unhappy story of Little Red Riding Hood immediately came to her mind (The Misses Mendell and Hosmer, *Notes of Travel and Life* [New York, 1854], pp. 113–14).

[24] In 1835, passengers numbered over four hundred daily between Boston and Lowell, nearly sixteen thousand in six months between Charleston and Hamburg, South Carolina, and over ninety-seven thousand on the sixty miles of track belonging to the Baltimore and Ohio (Seymour Dunbar, *A History of Travel in America* [New York, 1937], 1009).

coarse-cloth dresses from the devious men who were chatting them up.[25] In the eyes of the respectable woman, youthful age and rural clothes marked these girls as inexperienced, out of their element, and hence especially vulnerable.

The point of view of the rural girls, however, might have been entirely different. If the apprehension of danger of travel frightened some, it is clear that the liberation and escape afforded by travel was attractive to others. Travel carries the possibility of being a liminal or in-between sort of experience; the traveler is not in the secure, predictable environment of home and is thus not necessarily bound to adhere to secure and predictable behaviors. Adventure is possible when one is freed from the moral restraints of one's home community. In an extreme example of a female con artist, a rural girl arrived in Buffalo in 1848 and convinced the owner of an inn that she was a rich heiress who had been imprisoned in a convent; the man bought her story and went halfway across New York with her to help her recover her fortune from the evil relatives, meanwhile running up lodging and travel bills at his own expense. The story eventually unraveled, and the man returned home sadder and poorer, while the girl moved on, presumably to play her game again.[26] A Canadian minister traveling by stage near Lockport, New York, in 1832, met two young women "rather singular in their dress and manners . . . [and] more free in conversation, and with less of reserve, than any American women I had seen before." A whispered inquiry to an innkeeper at a rest stop confirmed his slow-to-form suspicions: these women "were not of good reputation," and further, he was told, there were many similar young women floating about the region on stages and canal boats.[27]

Whether such women really were of questionable character cannot be known; the essential point is that men who saw women alone exhibiting freedom of manners, sociability, and splendid dress marked them as disreputable women and treated them accordingly. A woman who wanted to appear reputable, therefore, had to constrain her actions, draw her cloak close, maintain reserve, and accept male escortage wherever possible.

Women travelers in the 1830s thus negotiated with men in developing a set of behaviors that allegedly protected them from danger in public. A realistic apprehension of fear as a result of changes in the modes and demographics of travel as well as publicity about crimes impelled women to adopt distancing strategies such as personal coolness, use of female-only space, and reliance on courteous men to buy

[25] *Advocate of Moral Reform* 2 (November 15, 1836): 165–66.
[26] *Rochester Daily American*, February 3, 1848.
[27] Isaac Fidler, *Observations of Professions, Literatures, Manners, and Emigration, in the United States and Canada* (New York, 1833), pp. 122–23.

tickets, secure lodging, and lift baggage. The construction of gendered travel behaviors during the transportation revolution was thus fully congruent with the social construction of womanhood that historians have come to call the cult of domesticity. Women could certainly travel in public, and even travel alone, but for many their freedom was circumscribed by a system that dictated different rules of deportment and carried heavy potential penalties for nonconforming women.

Two serious and long-lived consequences flowed from the particular arrangement of the sexes in public. First, its bedrock assumption was just as Tocqueville had conjectured: female behavior became the determinant of male behavior. A truly virtuous woman who behaved appropriately was allegedly assured of safe passage; safety had become the responsibility of women. And second, part of the price of respectability was a denial of female competence in negotiating public space. A few women were shrewd enough to laugh at the bargain that had been struck: a nineteen-year-old was amused by a boat captain at Fall River, Massachusetts, who rounded up all the "unprotected" women on board and hustled them to a waiting train:

> You should have seen him rally us all to one spot, and charge and recharge us to stay there till he came to "take" us, as though we could not step from the boat to the cars without having the way marked out, and being led step by step. But we all demurely kept our places, and waited till our leader came; and to give you a perfect picture of us, hurrying along from the boat to the cars, you must fancy a hen with an immense brood of chickens, when there is danger near. . . . As, however, the other ladies didn't seem to consider it [annoying], I think I must be strong-minded and masculine, and lack the helplessness becoming my sex.[28]

This young woman was joking about being masculine, but the studied helplessness of "respectable" women in public was surely no joke.

[28] Mendell and Hosmer, *Notes of Travel and Life,* pp. 285–86.

CHAPTER SEVEN

Disordered Bodies/Disorderly Acts: Medical Discourse and the Female Criminal in Nineteenth-Century Paris

Ann-Louise Shapiro

In 1826, Ch.-C. H. Marc, a prominent doctor of mental medicine (an alienist), argued for the first time in a criminal case that the defendant, Henriette Cornier, could not be held responsible for the murder of her nineteen-month-old neighbor because at the time of the attack Cornier had her period. Marc contended that she had been overcome by an irresistible homicidal impulse, provoked by menstruation, that induced a "profound lesion of the will," destroying her moral freedom.[1] Rejecting the logic of this position, the judge found Cornier mentally competent, hence responsible; she was condemned to forced labor for life. Marc's claim was novel and, at the time, unconvincing.

By midcentury, however, it was commonplace for alienists, serving as expert witnesses in the courtroom, to argue that female reproductive biology caused a broad range of mental disturbances that attenuated women's responsibility for their behavior. Marc's somewhat quirky defense of Cornier moved quickly from the periphery to the center of a medical discourse that increasingly drew tight conceptual links between female criminality and reproductive functions. Alienists identified themselves as privileged, that is "scientific," interpreters of female behavior. But their discourse reverberated beyond the private realm of women and their bodies (although women's experience of their bodies would be affected) and beyond the development of

This essay is a slightly revised version of an article by the same title first published in *Genders* 4 (Spring 1989): 68–86. Reprinted by permission of the University of Texas Press.

[1] Ch.-C. H. Marc, *Consultation médico-légale pour Henriette Cornier, femme Berton, Précédée de l'acte d'accusation* (Paris, [1826]).

the profession of mental medicine (although women's alleged reproductive anomalies helped to consolidate the categories of medical jurisprudence). In producing a knowledge in the Foucauldian sense, alienists placed women, defined by biology, at the crossroads of several intersecting cultural developments. This metaphoric woman sat at the conjuncture of nineteenth-century efforts to redraw the boundaries between men and women, between reason and madness, between the criminal and the sick, between law and medicine, and between medicine and politics. Each of these processes was both independent and linked to the others; none was focused exclusively on the reproductive female. Yet medical discourse, even with its internal inconsistencies and contested conclusions, created a powerful construct that moved readily outward from the bodies of individual women to shape more broadly symbolic forms and social practices. The most personal and intimate female experiences would provide a mechanism for rearranging the contours of public life.

In a penal system newly responsive to pleas for judicial leniency based on extenuating circumstances (including the mental competency of the accused),[2] alienists in the 1830s began to claim that only specialized clinicians could separate illness from moral weakness. By challenging assumptions about the transparency of madness, calling into question customary understandings of mental health as well as the ability of a lay person to recognize the subtle manifestations of disease, alienists sought to secure, publicly and institutionally, the stature of their new specialty and their presence in the criminal justice system. In this context, the concerns of legal reformers seeking to reduce the severity of punishments coincided with the professional ambitions of alienists; humanitarianism would march hand in hand with science.[3]

Although acceptance of the role of the alienist in the courtroom was by no means automatic, an expansion of the judges' discretionary power promoted a heightened receptivity to the definition of states of being which existed in the space between reason and unreason—intermediary mental states that might provide some insulation against the full force of the law though not entirely absolving the accused of personal responsibility. The diagnosis of monomania emerged to explain the so-called intermediary mental states. First elaborated by J. E. D. Esquirol, and formally admitted into the French language by the Académie française in 1835, monomania referred to behavior characterized by a "profound perversity" that could not be explained as complete

[2] See Jan Goldstein, *Console and Classify: The French Psychiatric Profession in the Nineteenth Century* (Cambridge, Eng., 1987), pp. 177–80.

[3] Ibid, pp. 180–89.

mental alienation.[4] Alienists described "a delirium more silent and more restricted" than the burning, generalized delirium of the maniac—a partial mental impairment among people who, absent the interpretive skills of the specialist, might indeed pass for sane. Even though the theory of monomania had little clinical relevance, it became a central theme of medical jurisprudence and forensic psychiatry and remained a common diagnosis until the 1870s.

When applied to female behavior, the monomania diagnosis was strikingly apt as a means to connect mental illness, which could be intermittent and limited, to organic function, thus reinforcing a dominant somaticist current within nineteenth-century alienism. The reproductive life cycle of women—punctuated by puberty, childbearing, and menopause—offered a convincing material ground from which to account for mental derangement. Woman could, at any point, cross the boundary between reason and unreason in the throes of "menstrual psychosis," "puerperal insanity," or "menopausal mania." More specifically, the periodicity of menstruation and the episodic nature of the "critical ages" of woman provided a model for applying judicial leniency in cases that did not conform neatly to traditional all-or-nothing definitions of insanity.

In both medical theory and clinical practice, alienists produced evidence that the female reproductive cycle was a kind of pathology that placed women chronically at risk. A woman's life divided, according to medical texts, into three phases—before, during, and after reproductive functioning—placing her in a permanent state of physical, mental, and spiritual disequilibrium in which she fluctuated between reason and unreason. Paraphrasing Mme de Stael's epigrammatic remark that love, merely an episode in the life of a man, is the entire life of a woman, Dr. Aimé Schwob explained that woman's reproductive cycle was her life *en tout.*[5] In a major treatise on menstrual neuroses, the alienist Dr. Pierre Berthier laid out the terrain:

> In effect, from birth to death, a woman who experiences the full range of her obligations finds herself, each day, in submission to a multitude of impressions and mishaps. From one side, the nervous temperament that is her fate predisposes her to reactions from the brain to the uterus; from the other side, she is compelled to obey the operations of the uterus on the brain. . . . During the period of her fecundity, a woman must be regulated,

[4] Aimé Schwob, *Contribution à l'étude des psychoses menstruelles considérées surtout au point de vue médico-légal* (Lyons, 1893); Raymond de Saussure, "The Influence of the Concept of Monomania on French Medico-Legal Psychiatry (from 1825–1840)," *Journal of the History of Medicine* 1 (July 1946): 374.

[5] Schwob, *Contribution à l'étude,* p. 31.

because her organism is the theater of a general and local inflammation that disturbs the harmony of her economy.[6]

Medical language unequivocally conveyed alarm, speaking equally of puberty, menopause, pregnancy, and ordinary menstruation as "attacks," "eruptions," "crises," "outbreaks," and "critical moments." Citing ancient texts which claimed that if a menstruating woman walked through a garden, her presence would prevent flowers from growing and kill all the insects, contemporary doctors stated that, although menstrual blood had proved to be chemically innocuous, classical beliefs gained credibility because the ancients had rightly perceived that menstruation was essentially fearsome and could, in fact, "annihilate reason."[7] A. A. Tardieu summarized the medical consensus: "It is certain that the menstrual cycle, when it involves the suppression of the period, when the flow is moderate, even when it presents nothing out of the ordinary, plays a large role in the production of neuroses and madness."[8]

Following Tardieu's lead, alienists identified all experiences of menstruation as inherently pathological—as a departure from, or disturbance of, a never identified normal condition; the unspecified state of health against which aberrant functioning was measured became a vanishing point that receded into the infinite distance. In this context, the underlying assumption seems to be that, in normal states, biology is silent, missing; pathology becomes, then, the condition in which biological functions are visible.[9] The menstrual anomaly was, quite simply, menstruation itself. Both the early and late arrival of puberty were construed as warning signs of immanent mental illness; both a light and a heavy menstrual flow were dangerous. The beginning of puberty was likely to disequilibrate the young woman, but the suppression of periods was even more likely to throw her into a state of unreason, and menopause could either produce madness or cure it. Rather than disabling the authority of medical discourse, these contradictions, by rendering the theory infinitely malleable, constituted, in large part, its power.

In its most acute expression, the mental imbalance produced by menstruation became monomania. Each of the variable symptoms could, according to medical theory, readily deteriorate into its charac-

[6] Pierre Berthier, *Des névroses menstruelles ou la menstruation dans ses rapports avec les maladies nerveuses et mentales* (Paris, 1874), pp. 9, 22. All translations in this essay are my own.

[7] Schwob, *Contribution à l'étude*, p. 17.

[8] Tardieu quoted in Berthier, *Des névroses menstruelles*, frontispiece.

[9] For an interesting contemporary discussion of these issues, see Hilary Allen, "At the Mercy of Her Hormones: Premenstrual Tension and the Law," *m/f* (1984): 19–44.

teristic form of madness: melancholia became suicidal monomania; excitability became erotic monomania or homicidal monomania; irritability became religious monomania; and so on. It was but a short jump from the ordered symptoms—the illness—to the assumption that biology was the cause of behavior. The argument had come full circle: female reproductive biology was construed as recurrently morbid; biological symptoms were codified as disease entities that were manifest, especially, in temporary, partial loss of reason; and unreasonable or problematic behavior confirmed the presence of disease. By pathologizing behavior that did not conform to a hypothetical normal state, medical discourse ignored all the possible mediations that intervene between biology and action. The label of mental disease effectively obscured the personal meaning of behavior and drained it of social content. Murder, theft, despair, and eroticism all became equally, unproblematically, the product of biology and manifestations of disease.

More and more, medical journals and treatises reported cases of homicides (or merely murderous intentions) and thefts that coincided with menstruation or with a prior disturbance in menstrual functioning. In these accounts, menstruation emerged as the *cause* of the criminal acts, identifying behavior as mad rather than criminal and providing the basis for a legal defense of attenuated responsibility. The relation of behavior to body functions was assumed to be direct, unmediated, and determinative. The case of Mme R. is exemplary:

> Mme R. had been married for one year, but the marriage was not a happy one. Her husband developed chronic bronchitis and worked for only four months. Mme R. had to abandon her trade of waistcoat maker in order to complete her housework and care for her ailing spouse. She was pursued unrelentingly by demanding creditors. She no longer ate or slept properly, became anemic, and her periods ceased. She developed sensations of congestion in her head, irritability, bizarre forgetfulness, and "poorly restrained compulsions." During this time, Mme R. stole 1,500 francs. Medical experts argued that the cessation of her periods produced a condition of physical and moral debility that attenuated her criminal responsibility. The court decided not to prosecute Mme R. (1868)[10]

At her first interrogation, Mme R. offered a complete confession. But interestingly, the story shifted a bit over time. Although there is no conclusive evidence that Mme R. was influenced by medical experts, it is at least suggestive that the medical report notes that, though "today she still maintains this story [her original confession], she adds

[10] Paul Dubuisson and A. Vigouroux, *Responsabilité pénale et folie: Etude médico-légale* (Paris, 1911), pp. 464–66.

that if she had not been in a weakened physical and moral condition, she would have been able to resist the suggestions of poverty." The report concludes with the observation that "Mme R. found herself in a state of physical and moral disturbance, produced by the cessation of her periods, which considerably attenuated her criminal responsibility and merits the court's indulgence."[11] What we see here, then, is the interpretive filter that medical expertise provided. Of all the possible ways of explaining or understanding this theft, the one that resonated most deeply, that seemed to link all the circumstances most logically, that proved most convincing for all parties, was the medical explanation.

In the 1880s, the advent of department stores and the new leisure activity of "just looking" generated both increased shoplifting and a renewed medical interest in *monomanie du vol* (kleptomania).[12] Medical case histories described moments of physical weakness, confusion, vertiginous sensations, hot flashes, and headaches that preceded the impulsive act, all pointing to its source in some form of "genital or ovarian debility." The alienist Tardieu reported, for example, the case of a woman who "had matured late, without regular periods which sometimes were missed for three or four months; she had been subject to headaches, to sensations of suffocation, to cramps that doubled in intensity with her periods; it was after a miscarriage that she performed her first larceny. Is it not evident," Tardieu asks, "that the instinctive impulsion, as well as the convulsive state, emerged under the sway of menstruation?"[13] From Tardieu's perspective, the logic of this conclusion was beyond question.

The accounts of shoplifting, as well as discussions of other forms of mental disturbance, contain a characteristic subtext that arises not only from a concern with the female body in its biological functioning, but from a (veiled) focus on the sexual body. Although it was the operation of her reproductive system that allegedly catapulted the woman into a state of mental disequilibrium, this clinical picture was inseparable from, and perhaps embedded in, what Michèle Ouerd has called the persistent fantasies and formulaic nightmares that have informed discourses on the deviant woman.[14] In the construction of female deviants (the witch and the hysteric, for example), sexuality

[11] Ibid., p. 466.

[12] See Patricia O'Brien, "The Kleptomania Diagnosis: Bourgeois Women and Theft in Late Nineteenth-Century France," *Journal of Social History* 17 (Fall 1983): 65–77; Elaine Abelson, *When Ladies Go A-Thieving: Middle-Class Shoplifters in Victorian Department Stores* (Oxford, 1989).

[13] Tardieu, in Berthier, *Des névroses menstruelles*, pp. 156–57.

[14] Michèle Ouerd, "Dans la forge à cauchemars mythologiques, sorcières, praticiennes et hystériques," *Les Cahiers de Fontenay* 11–12 (September 1978): 139–213.

proliferates; woman is infinitely and problematically sexualized. This subtext in its nineteenth-century mode of seeing and telling is evident in a prominent alienist's discussion of department store theft:

> The new stores contain and expose, competing for attention, the richest materials, the most sumptuous *objets de toilette* and the most seductive excesses. Women of every rank, attracted to this elegant milieu by the instinct that is natural to their sex, fascinated by so much imprudent provocation, dazzled by the profusion of laces and trinkets, find themselves surprised by a sudden incitement which is not premeditated and is nearly brutal: they place an inexpert, but furtive, hand on the exposed goods, and, there it is; they cancel, in a thoughtless touch, the most respectable past, becoming thieves, making themselves into delinquents.[15]

This text operates on several levels. The department store is at once the scene of a sexual encounter and the occasion for a psychosexual discourse. The author links instincts with excesses, exposure, and imprudence; unpremeditated excitement with delinquency and punishment; touching with crime. What is it here that is stolen? Who is, in fact, the author of the furtive, fatal touch? What is the danger that links instinct and exposure? And whose fears and fantasies are most clearly in evidence here?

The discussion of disturbances in female reproductive biology has led, then, to the disturbing mystery of female sexuality—a connection most explicit in the medical literature that linked menstruation with the "disease" of erotomania. Typically, alienists described erotomania as a temporary mental illness that recurred periodically, most often with the onset of both puberty and menopause (that is, in women whose sexual life was not likely to be bounded by pregnancy and childbirth), and especially in women organically predisposed by a "genital temperament." It was characterized by a "morbid excitement of the genital organs" that rendered the victim/patient unable to dominate her desires or control her inclinations. Alienists argued that the alleged disappearance of symptoms on "noncritical" days confirmed their theory of a periodic pathology, that is, a contained insanity or monomania.[16] In his social history of psychiatry, Klaus Doerner has argued that monomania was, above all, a framework for containing the excessive, a pathologizing of imbalance, one-sidedness, irregularity that invited medical intervention to restore the equilibrium.[17] Medical descriptions of erotomania support Doerner's thesis. But I would

[15] Henri Legrand du Saulle, *Les hystériques: Etat physique et mental, actes insolites, delictueux et criminels* (Paris, 1883), p. 437.

[16] Dubuisson and Vigouroux, *Responsabilité pénale,* p. 459.

[17] Klaus Doerner, *Madmen and the Bourgeoisie: A Social History of Insanity and Psychiatry,* trans. Joachim Neugroschel and Jean Steinberg (Oxford, 1981), pp. 131, 150.

argue that this focus on setting sexual limits is, perhaps, too simple; the language of the texts is somewhat more equivocal, suggesting a preoccupation with the release of female sexuality—with the opportunities for, and conditions of, a seduction—as well as with the desire to contain it. Erotomania does not simply erupt, as do menstrual periods; within the rhetorical structure of the case history, the woman is seduced, struggles, and inevitably succumbs. Let us listen to the words of one alienist: "[The ill woman] . . . resists at first the thoughts, the desires that besiege her; little by little she allows herself to be dominated by her inclinations . . . she pleases herself with the most lascivious ideas, the most voluptuous conversations, the most obscene reading, until finally . . . the most timid young girl [is transformed] into a lewd woman and the most delicate modesty into a furious audacity.[18] The metaphor of seduction, with its denouement in the act of succumbing, is similarly sustained in the alienist Henri Legrand du Saulle's advice to medical experts testifying in cases of kleptomania. He maintained that, in evaluating criminal behavior, it was necessary to consider both a powerful incitement to act and an insufficient resistance to temptation. In the end, he urged doctors to evaluate the defendant on the basis of the passive side—the pathological loss of will to resist—rather than the strength of the compulsion.[19] In this scenario, the seduction was not complete unless it vanquished resistance. These descriptions of pathologies—sexual and criminal—provide, then, the opportunity for a recurring discussion of the threshold, the point at which will is overcome, pointing to the moment at which female sexuality is released. We seem to have arrived here at the intersections of fantasy, myth, fear, and medical science.

In medicalizing both women's reproductive functioning and alleged anomalies of female sexuality, medical discourses generated a pathologized conception of femaleness that preempted alternate understandings of women in relation to their bodies, their sexuality, and their social environments. In effect, by arguing that women could not be held fully responsible for their acts, by insisting that at various points in their reproductive cycles they slipped into behaviors they were unable to control, medical testimonies promoted the disabling of the feminine. Alienists were not alone in this project and did not, by themselves, codify the meanings attributed to biological difference. The historian Jules Michelet, for example, had published at midcentury *L'Amour*, in which he discussed such topics as the female body, sexual hygiene, menstruation, and female pleasure, causing a contemporary scandal. Michelet claimed that the silence surrounding these subjects preserved ancient, obsolete taboos that associated women

[18] Loyer Villermay, quoted in Schwob, *Contribution à l'étude*, pp. 70–71.
[19] Legrand du Saulle, *Les hystériques*, pp. 450–51.

with impurity and depravity. Instead, he invoked the discoveries of ovariology and embryology to link women to the advance of civilization, connecting menstrual blood to the beneficent functions of reproduction and motherhood. Spiritualizing and purifying *la crise périodique,* Michelet created what Thérèse Moreau has called the sacred cult of the bleeding womb. This sanctification of reproduction was, of course, little different in its effects from the pathologizing of the alienists; both generated a construction of woman as partial, dominated by biology, and needing protection. According to Michelet,

> [Woman] is generally unwell one week of four. The week that precedes the crisis is already troubled. And in the eight or ten days that follow this painful week there is a prolonged langour, a weakness, that could not be defined. But we now understand it. It is the healing of an internal wound which, at bottom, is the source of the whole drama. So that in reality, fifteen or twenty days out of twenty-eight (one might say nearly always) the woman is not merely sick, but wounded.[20]

In seeking a means of ordering social and political life, Michelet had rediscovered the multiple symbolic possibilities of the methaphoric woman and endowed his schema with the imprimatur of science. Michelet explained his project, his conscious rewriting of the imagery of female biology, as a design for implanting and reproducing republican values. Michelet's construction was indeed a political move—one that made woman a being apart, whose essential life experiences and possibilities were articulated from within her body. His work, like that of the alienists, both reflected and constituted more general nineteenth-century commitments to the centrality—in fact, the foundational status—of biological difference. Rousseau's dictum—that "the male is only a male now and again, the female is always a female"—had broad currency by the middle decades of the nineteenth century. Woman was, then, both an empty sign, the universal repository of otherness, and an overflowing category, suffused by her sex.[21]

In their role as expert witnesses in the criminal justice system, alienists provided the specific terms in which the "disabilities" of the reproductive female would be interpreted. Rarely did they argue that women ought to be absolved of all responsibility for their criminal behavior. Such a claim was not congruent with their preoccupations with the periodicity of the female life cycle, which suggested, more

[20] Thérèse Moreau, "Sang sur: Michelet et le sang féminin," *Romantisme,* no. 31 (1981): 151–65; quotation on p. 159.

[21] For a broader discussion of this theme, see Joan Landes, *Women and the Public Sphere in the Age of the French Revolution* (Ithaca, 1988); and Denise Riley, *"Am I That Name?": Feminism and the Category of Women in History* (Minneapolis, 1988).

vaguely, intermittent incapacity, nor was it likely to be acceptable in a system that had begun to worry about the "misguided philanthropy" of medical diagnoses that left society disarmed and criminals unpunished.[22] Rather, alienists searched the histories of accused women for biological evidence foreshadowing the "extenuating circumstances" that justified a conclusion of attenuated responsibility and a plea for judicial leniency. Medical reports of female defendants typically began with a discussion of the onset of menstruation followed by details of menstrual functioning (regularity, emotional responses, and so on) and, if appropriate, similar investigations of the physical "symptoms" generated by pregnancy, childbirth, or menopause. Although they most often found that the accused woman's mental faculties had not been entirely impaired, they argued that menstrual anomalies produced "exaltations" that left her prey to "instinctual impulses." Medical discourse in these instances closed the space between biology and behavior, constructing a female subject confined in a system of physical responses.

By the final two decades of the century, the monomania diagnosis had largely fallen out of favor;[23] monomaniacs disappeared from both the asylum and the courtroom. Many alienists had argued that monomania presumed too complete a separation among intellect, will, and emotions and failed to provide acceptable criteria for distinguishing between morbid passions and merely exaggerated ones. Following larger currents in medical and social theory, alienists in the closing years of the century were more likely to connect mental disturbance to a hereditary defect. Within this shifting conceptual framework, the most common female nervous disorders were degeneracy and, especially, hysteria—disease categories that were so inclusive, so compelling, so evocative and economical that they displaced most other diagnoses. Female reproductive biology remained a signpost in locating mental disorder; but in this new medical climate, menstruation, puberty, and menopause were typically described less as cause than as triggers that released latent pathology. According to Dr. Séverin Icard, for example, "menstruation is only the occasional cause; it is the drop which overflows the vase, the spark which ignites . . . but the seed has already been sown in fertile ground."[24] The discussion of menstrual anomalies and criminal responsibility did not disappear; rather, its position in the discourse shifted. Because the monomania diagnosis had

[22] Goldstein, *Console and Classify*, pp. 181, 183.

[23] Ibid., p. 191.

[24] See esp. J.-P. Coutagne, *La folie au point de vue judiciaire et administrative: Leçons faites à la Faculté de droit de Lyon* (Lyons, 1889); Alexandre Paris, *La folie des femmes enceintes, des nouvelles accouchées et des nourrices* (Paris, 1897); Séverin Icard, *La femme pendant la période menstruelle: Etude de psychologie morbide et de médecine légale* (Paris, 1890), p. 274.

operated most effectively on the level of discourse, it could be discarded readily and without practical consequence.

But even as disease etiology shifted and old concepts became obsolete, the metaphorical and perceptual overlay of earlier doctrines did not necessarily disappear. The centrality of female reproductive biology in confirming the monomania diagnosis and in authorizing medical expertise in the definition of criminal responsibility had produced a "scientific"/symbolic representation of the female life cycle as essentially pathological. Thus Dr. Georges Morache, professor of legal medicine at the University of Bordeaux, could argue in the 1890s that women could not be held to the same standards of responsibility as men. He pointed to "troubles in various stages of genital life"—especially connected to accumulations and transformations of menstrual blood—that produced a veritable condition of "autointoxication." Because of this "poisoning," rendering her not insane, not sick, but "troubled in her psychicity," she could not be held fully responsible. In Morache's words, "she feels differently (*autrement*), she thinks differently, she acts differently. In everything, she is *Other*, and the same principles of justice cannot be applied to her." Imploring the criminal justice system to take account of the physical and moral tempests to which a woman was subject, he concluded, "If these principles constitute feminism, then feminism it is."[25]

Ironically, perhaps, Morache's linking of his theories of female "otherness" to feminism is not entirely inappropriate (although for reasons other than he intended). In actual practice, medical expertise did not gain for women a judicial leniency that they did not already possess. Medical testimony was not automatically authoritative, and jury verdicts often had no obvious connection to formal legal principles or to medical tests of responsibility. By the final decades of the century, the courtroom had become a melodramatic theater that sought not only to punish but to clarify social and moral codes; many female defendants, positioned in these criminal scenarios as victims needing the protection of the (paternal) court, profited from the logic of this environment and were acquitted without the intervention of the medical expert.[26] But the pathologizing of the female life cycle became ever more important in the final decades of the century when the question of women's rights again came to the fore. As the issues of divorce, adultery, paternity, female education, and political and economic rights for

[25] Georges Morache, *La responsabilité criminelle de la femme, différente de celle de l'homme* (Paris, n.d.), p. 587.

[26] See Judith R. Walkowitz, "Melodrama and Victorian Political Culture," paper presented at the Pembroke Center Conference on Melodrama, Popular Culture, and Gender, January 1987; Ann-Louise Shapiro, "Love Stories: Female Crimes of Passion in Fin-de-Siècle Paris," paper presented to the Feminist History Group, University of Melbourne, Summer 1989.

women became subjects of public debate in the final third of the century, medical discourse, in its claims to scientific verity, could provide the justification for restoring and reinforcing ideas about gender difference that seemed to have become dangerously slippery.

Social critics had begun to argue that women's increased physical freedom and ungendered role expectations were producing a pathological social universe. In an especially apt summary of contemporary anxieties about the "new woman," Dr. Julien Chevalier noted that the dualities that had ordered social life were increasingly unreliable, that "in a multitude of matters, feelings, ways of thinking, activities, there is a resemblance" between men and women:

> Little by little woman tends to approximate man, to appropriate his ways of being, his kind of independent and free existence. Instead of woman's life being constituted, as it was not long ago, by calm, by private life, by intimacy, the life of the woman of today is lived beyond her home, within preoccupations where the family does not count. . . . Determined, she affects in everything the independence, the turbulent audacity, the self-confidence of a boy. She shocks and disconcerts without being shocked or disconcerted herself.[27]

This woman who was, for Chevalier, "without limits" could not, then, be counted on for definitions of alterity, for fixing difference. A world set free from its moorings in this way became, in consequence, unimaginable and, even more, sick. Medical men with their definitions of the normal and the abnormal could help to restore the world "as it was not long ago." Through the interpretation of female reproductive biology, medical discourse sought and "found" the limits of woman's self-control, her problematic sexuality, her intermittent incapacity, and, above all, her unsuitability for a full public life. In exploring the private realm of female biology, medical men participated in the gendering of the patterns of public life; in their public functions in the judicial process, medical men not only consolidated their role as privileged interpreters of deviancy but, even more, articulated meanings that would affect women's intimate experiences of their own biology and sexuality. These processes were interactive and mutually reinforcing. Both public and private life would continue to respond to this medical, gendered vision of the right order of things.

[27] Julien Chevalier, "De l'inversion sexuelle aux points de vue clinique, anthropoligique et médico-légal," *Archives d'anthropologie criminelle* 6 (1891): 500–501.

CHAPTER EIGHT

The Unruly Woman of the Paris Commune

Gay L. Gullickson

Analyzing historical and literary accounts of the French revolutions of 1789, 1848, and 1871, Neil Hertz pointed out in 1983 that it is not unusual for a political threat to be represented as a sexual threat. Indeed, he observed, revolutionary violence has often been emblematized not simply in female form but "as a hideous and fierce but not exactly sexless woman."[1] In 1986, Joan Scott called our attention to the similar tendency of both right-wing and left-wing authoritarian regimes to perceive political threats in gendered terms; to represent "enemies, outsiders, subversives, [and] weakness" as feminine; and, when they acquire political power, to use it to limit women's freedom of speech, assembly, or conduct, even though the new regime has had "nothing immediate or material to gain from the control of women."[2]

Nowhere is a political threat more clearly represented as a sexual threat than in writings about the Paris Commune of 1871. Particularly significant are the descriptions of the *pétroleuses,* the women who were accused of burning Paris during the final week of the Commune, when Versailles troops and the Parisian National Guard fought in the streets of Paris. Despite good evidence that most of the fires were set by men, fear of the *pétroleuse* was so widespread and so long-lasting that to its opponents she came to represent the crimes of the Commune, and its supporters found themselves denying her existence and unable to focus public attention on the willingness of the Versailles

Another version of this essay appeared in *Feminist Studies* 17 (Summer 1991): 241–65, and is reprinted by permission of the publisher, Feminist Studies, Inc., c/o Women's Studies Program, University of Maryland, College Park, MD 20742.

[1] Neil Hertz, "Medusa's Head: Male Hysteria under Political Pressure," *Representations* 4 (Fall 1983): 27.

[2] Joan W. Scott, "Gender: A Useful Category of Historical Analysis," *American Historical Review* 91 (December 1986): 1072.

government to kill thousands of its own citizens, many after they had surrendered or been taken prisoner.

The *pétroleuse* was almost entirely a figment of the government's and the conservative press's imagination. Why, in the first place, did the government think that women were setting fires, and, in the second place, why did people so readily believe the rumors? Or, to paraphrase Neil Hertz, how did the political threat posed by the Commune come to be represented by a hideous and fierce but sexually compelling female figure?

The Paris Commune

In July 1870, Otto von Bismarck finally goaded Louis Napoleon into declaring war, and France was catapulted into a year of warfare, civil strife, political experimentation, and tragedy. Louis Napoleon (and with him the Second Empire) was defeated less than two months after the war with Prussia began. In the political vacuum that followed, Republicans in Paris announced the establishment of the Third French Republic and mounted an attempt to defend the city against the advancing Prussian troops. Paris was quickly surrounded by the Prussian army, and the Parisians hunkered down to endure four months of hunger, disease, cold, and finally bombardment while the Prussians waited for them to surrender. Paris never surrendered, but the provisional French government did in January 1871.

Adolphe Thiers, the ultraconservative politician at the head of the provisional government, accepted the Prussians' peace terms (which included the secession of Alsace and Lorraine to the new German state and a triumphal march of Prussian troops down the Champs Elysées in Paris) and then proceeded to sponsor and endorse a series of decrees from the National Assembly that further alienated and humiliated Paris. Radical newspapers were suppressed; the moratorium on rents and debts that had been established during the Prussian siege was lifted, confronting Parisian workers, craftsmen, shop owners, and even wealthy apartment dwellers with imminent eviction; and the National Assembly (which had been meeting in Bordeaux during the siege) voted to establish itself in Versailles, in essence "decapitalizing" Paris.[3]

Finally, in a poorly planned and subsequently much debated decision, Thiers sent French army troops in the early hours of March 18, 1871, to remove the cannons which the city had used to defend itself

[3] The phrase is Frank Jellinek's in *The Paris Commune of 1871* (1937; rpt. New York, 1965), p. 98.

against the Prussians. The predawn raid on the cannons was detected when the government failed to send horses to pull the heavy guns. While the soldiers waited for the horses, they fraternized with the people, military order was lost, and eventually two French generals were killed. These events led to the establishment of a separate government in Paris (the Commune) and a second siege, this time by provincial French troops.

Despite the siege, Paris ruled itself for two months, electing representatives to a governing body (also known as the Commune) and passing laws that have earned it a place among the most radical of French governments. A general moratorium was placed on rents; the interest due on debts was abolished; fines in factories were eliminated; the pay for legislators was set at the daily wage for ordinary workers; and the tools, furniture, and clothing that people had pawned during the Prussian siege were returned to their owners free of charge.[4]

Finally, on the night of May 21–22, Versailles troops entered the city through a temporarily unguarded gate, and five days of bloody fighting began. Left largely to their own devices, the National Guard troops, women, and children defended their neighborhoods behind hastily constructed barricades. The provincial army troops, well indoctrinated at Versailles to hate the insurgents of Paris and following orders to take no prisoners, slaughtered twenty thousand Parisians.[5] The Communards, in turn, killed very few Versailles soldiers but executed some of the hostages they had been holding.

From beginning to end, women were actively involved in the Commune. They were major participants in the March 18 battle over the cannons and the execution of the generals that precipitated the split between Paris and the National Assembly. Louise Michel, who would become the most famous of the Communard women, alerted the citizens of Montmartre—the district of Paris where most of the cannons were stored—that the army was trying secretly to remove the cannons.[6] Women debated issues in political meetings, served on committees, established schools for children and workshops for women, risked their lives as nurses and aides to the National Guards in their endless skirmishes with the Versailles troops, and defended the barricades during the final battle. Several barricades were defended entirely

[4] Numerous histories of the Franco-Prussian War and the Paris Commune exist in English. Among the best are Prosper-Olivier Lissagaray, *History of the Commune of 1871*, trans. Eleanor Marx Aveling (New York, 1898); Jellinek, *Paris Commune*; Michael Howard, *The Franco-Prussian War* (New York, 1961); and Stewart Edwards, *The Paris Commune, 1871* (Chicago, 1971).

[5] Robert Tombs, *The War against Paris, 1871* (Cambridge, Eng., 1981), pp. 119, 171–93. The first executions of prisoners by the Versailles soldiers took place on May 22 (ibid., p. 171).

[6] Edith Thomas, *Louise Michel* (Paris, 1971), p. 84.

by women.[7] These activities have been little heralded by historians, however, and the Communard women are remembered primarily for having set the fires that consumed much of Paris during the final battle. Hundreds of women were arrested for this and other "crimes." Some were shot on the spot, others while being marched to Versailles; some were tried, and those who were found guilty were exiled to French penal colonies in New Caledonia.[8] For months after the fighting, Parisians continued to fear that women were sneaking around the city lobbing bottles of petroleum into open cellar windows.

Rumors and exaggerated fears are understandable in a city that had lived on the edge of disaster for nine months and was under attack and literally burning. So is a lingering bourgeois paranoia and vengefulness about the destruction of property. Why women were accused of setting the fires, why the fear did not subside once the fighting was over and the fires were out, and why the *pétroleuse* rather than some other figure came to stand for the "horrors" of the Commune is not so readily understandable.[9]

The Fires

Versailles troops entered Paris late Sunday night, May 21. On Tuesday, May 23, Communard troops set the first fire to protect their battle position. By that evening other fires had been set, some for strategic reasons, some in revenge against the monarchy and upper-class "justice." Still others were ignited by the incendiary shells used by the Versailles troops.[10] By Wednesday, rows of houses, the Tuileries Palace, the Ministry of Finances, and the Hotel de Ville were on fire. Charred paper from the library of the Louvre floated on the wind, and people feared that the museum itself was on fire. The city glowed red by night; smoke, sparks, and charred paper filled the air; and observers who watched from the hills outside Paris were convinced that the entire city was burning to the ground. The disaster was not as great as it appeared to those who watched from a distance, but a considerable number of houses and other structures were destroyed or damaged.[11]

[7] Lissagaray, *History of the Commune*, pp. 329, 344.

[8] For a general history of women's activities during the Commune see Edith Thomas, *Les pétroleuses* (Paris, 1963).

[9] The killing of the hostages, who included the archbishop of Paris, priests, and policemen, was also used by opponents of the Commune to brand it as evil, but no lasting symbol emerged from this episode. See Tombs, *War against Paris*, p. 170.

[10] For accounts of the causes of the fires, see Jellinek, *Paris Commune*, pp. 331–32; Tombs, *War against Paris*, p. 152; Alistair Horne, *The Fall of Paris* (New York, 1966), pp. 390–91.

[11] See, for instance, the London *Times*, May 25, 1871, p. 5.

Why women were held responsible for setting the fires is an intriguing question because there is clear evidence that the majority of the fires were set by men.[12] Nor were women the first to be accused. On Wednesday, May 24, Adolphe Thiers excoriated the setting of the fires in a speech to the National Assembly at Versailles, calling it a desperate military tactic carried out by men: "The odious act—one unparrelleled in history—of which some villains have just been guilty, is the crowning act of their despair. . . . No one could have prevented the crime of these wicked wretches. They have made use of petroleum for their incendiary purposes, and have sent petroleum bombs against our soldiers." By Thursday, May 25, however, the opponents of the Commune suggested that vengeance rather than strategy was the motivation for the fires. The London *Times* reported that the fires were "wrought without a shadow of provocation; . . . it is an act of deliberate and demoniacal malice. . . . A mere act of revenge." Rumors escalated, and suspicion began to fall on noncombatants, including male firefighters (*pompiers*) and women and children. The *Times* on May 26 and *La Gaulois* (a pro-Versailles newspaper) on May 29 reported that *pompiers* had been shot when they were found to be pumping petroleum rather than water into the flames and announced that windows were being barricaded to prevent the firebombing of houses by women and children. Walking through the city, the *Times* correspondent had discovered that "the fears of petroleum and explosions are universal. The inhabitants had either stopped up, or were engaged in stopping up, every chink through which petroleum might be thrown into their houses. . . . The precaution was taken because women and children, partisans of the Commune, have in numerous instances been detected throwing petroleum into houses."[13]

[12] Even the most conservative of historians no longer credit the rumor of the *pétroleuses.* See, for instance, Edward S. Mason, *The Paris Commune: An Episode in the History of the Socialist Movement* (New York, 1930), pp. 281–82; Horne, *Fall of Paris,* pp. 391–93. For similar views from a more liberal historian, see Edwards, *Paris Commune,* pp. 322–27.

[13] Reported in the *London Times,* May 25, 1871, pp. 5, 9, May 26, 1871, p. 5. Because of the fear of such activities by the *pétroleuses,* the cellar windows of Paris would remain closed throughout the long, hot summer that followed the Commune. The absurdity of this was well remarked by Colonel Wickham Hoffman, the secretary of the U.S. legation, who pointed out that "the windows were barred, and the cellars in Paris are universally built in stone and concrete. How they [the *pétroleuses*] effected their purpose under these circumstances is not readily seen. If this was their *modus operandi,* they were the most inexpert incendiaries ever known" (Wickham Hoffman, *Camp, Court, and Siege* [New York, 1877], p. 283). The Reverend William Gibson also recorded the "information" about the *pompiers* as well as about the women incendiaries in his journal on May 25, 1871. (Reverend William Gibson, *Paris during the Commune* [New York, 1974], p. 285). Gibson's letters were originally published in the *Watchman* and subsequently republished.

Rumors about the number of women working as incendiaries grew rapidly, and reports soon claimed that "many" of the arrested women were *pétroleuses.*[14] On May 28 and 29, *Le Gaulois* reported that men, women, and children had been hired and paid ten francs per building to start fires. Elihu Washburne, the American minister to France, repeated this story in his memoirs, apparently still believing it and embellishing it with the "information" that immense numbers of men, women, and children (Washburne claimed eight thousand) had been employed to distribute incendiary devices.[15]

The credibility of the reports was enhanced by their specificity. *Le Gaulois* was especially inclined toward detail. On May 28, it reported that the incendiaries were "armed with tin boxes, about the size of a large sardine can and containing a mixture of *pétrole* [kerosene], tallow and sulfur," which they lit with a match. The next day the paper reported that during the month of April the Commune had infiltrated into the ranks of the *pompiers* "its most fanatical partisans whose mission was to stir up the fires when they were beginning to die out."

Although men were employed in setting fires, women were widely regarded as being more active in the "work" and as the greater villains. M. Chastel, a librarian, reported in a letter on Wednesday, May 24, that it was "especially the women who are setting fires to the houses. Many have been taken in the act and shot at once." Ambassador Washburne reported in his memoir: "Of all this army of burners, the women were the worst. They were a separate force, and called *pétroleuses.* . . . Whenever it was possible, the *pétroleuse,* who was to receive ten francs for every ten houses burnt, would find some little boy or girl whom she would take by the hand and to whom she would give a bottle of the incendiary liquid, with instructions to scatter it in certain places."[16]

Children were commonly thought to be women's accomplices, and suspicious-looking children, like the women, were arrested and executed. Residents and journalists reported seeing the bodies of dead children as well as child prisoners. Washburne reported the death of eight children and Wickham Hoffman mentioned six, the eldest "ap-

[14] See, for instance, the reports in *Paris under Siege: A Journal of the Events of 1870–1871 Kept by Contemporaries and Translated and Presented by Joanna Richardson* (London, 1982), pp. 180–98.

[15] E. B. Washburne, *Recollections of a Minister to France, 1869–1877* (New York, 1887), p. 155. One of the most amazing aspects of Washburne's account of the *pétroleuses* is that it appears in a memoir rather than in an unedited or unpublished diary. By the time Washburne's memoirs were published in 1887, many, like Colonel Wickham Hoffman, no longer believed the rumors about the *pétroleuses.* For Hoffman's views see his *Camp, Court, and Siege,* pp. 282–83.

[16] Chastel, "Letter," May 24, 1871, quoted in Gibson, *Paris during the Commune,* p. 283; Washburne, *Recollections,* pp. 222–23. Washburne's account of the amount of money paid to the *pétroleuses* differed from that in *Le Gaulois.*

parently not over fourteen," who were "caught" carrying petroleum in the Avenue d'Autin. Edmond de Goncourt recorded in his diary on May 26 that he had seen "a band of frightful street urchins and incendiary hooligans" who were being held in the train station at Passy. And on May 28 Chastel reported that he had seen a large number of prisoners, among whom were "women and children, who sometimes were obliged to run to keep up with the rest, or they would have been trampled on by the horses."[17]

Women were also accused of poisoning the Versailles troops. The number of women assumed to be involved in this "crime" and the number of their victims escalated rapidly. On May 27, the *Times* reported that ten soldiers had been poisoned by a *cantinière;* on May 28, Edwin Child, a young Englishman in Paris, wrote to his father that forty men had been poisoned.[18] These accusations did not have the staying power of the accusations of incendiarism in a city that had seen huge fires, however, and the press and public devoted far more attention to the *pétroleuses.* Indeed, on June 2, *Le Figaro* carried an article about the last group of prisoners to be marched from Paris to Versailles. The article reported that the crowds that gathered along the route had the greatest interest in the women. "People devoured them with their eyes, they tried to discern the leaders who had inspired this terrible battle in the sinister heads of these witches, they stared at the hands that had poured the incendiary petroleum on the monuments of Paris."

The *Pétroleuses*

The male "eyewitness" descriptions of the women prisoners, many but not all of whom were accused of being incendiaries, reveal both fear of and considerable fascination with the women who had fought for the Commune. Virtually every account likened these women to the furies of Greek mythology, wild animals, or mad women.

Edwin Child, in a letter dated Sunday, May 28, 1871, reported to his father that "the women behaved like tigresses, throwing petroleum everywhere & distinguishing themselves by the fury with which they

[17] Washburne, *Recollections,* p. 155; Hoffman, *Camp, Court and Seige,* p. 281; Edmond and Jules de Goncourt, *Journal: Mémoires de la vie litteraire, 1864–1878,* x vols. (Paris, 1956), 2:815; Chastel quoted in Gibson, *Paris during the Commune,* p. 290. The Versailles government held 650 children aged sixteen or under as prisoners. How many were killed in the streets of Paris or on the forced marches from Paris to Versailles is unknown. See *Rapport d'ensemble de M. le général Appert sur les opérations de la justice militaire relative à l'insurrection de 1871* (Versailles, 1875), p. 180.

[18] The London *Times,* May 27, 1871, p. 5; Edwin Child, letter, May 28, 1871, published in *Paris under Siege,* p. 197.

fought, a convoi of nearly four thousand passed the Boulevards this afternoon, such figures you never saw, blackened with powder, all in tatters and filthy dirty, a few with chests exposed to show their sex, the women with their hair dishevelled & of a most ferocious appearance."[19] The conservative *Paris-Journal* reported on May 31 that "in the midst of the atrocious scenes which shock Paris, the women are particularly distinguished by their cruelty and rage; most of them are widows of Communards. Madness seems to possess them; one sees them, their hair down like furies, throwing boiling oil, furniture, paving stones, on the soldiers, and when they are taken, they throw themselves desperately on the bayonets and die still trying to fight."[20]

The Reverend William Gibson was not in Paris during the week of fighting and did not see the prisoners. Nevertheless, he recorded in his diary on May 27 that "we learn that women, more like furies than human beings, have taken a fiendish part in the work of destruction." Denis Arthur Bingham, an English correspondent for the *Pall Mall*, who was highly critical of the Commune, recorded in a diary which he later published that the female prisoners whom he saw were "*hideous viragoes . . . furies* intoxicated with the fumes of wine and blood."[21] The Reverend Mr. Ussher of Westbury, who was more sympathetic to the Parisians who had endured both the Prussian siege and the French bombardment, nevertheless reported that he was "particularly struck by the awful expressions which he noticed on the [women's] faces. . . . It was, indeed, for the most part something unnatural, a compound of savagery, revengefulness, despair and ecstatic fervour. . . . Many of them were now sheer furies."[22]

Fascinated rather than repelled by the women who passed through the streets of Paris as prisoners, the men who observed them frequently contrasted their behavior with that of their male comrades. Edmond de Goncourt reported that none of the arrested women whom he saw had the same "apathetic resignation" as the men. "There is," he wrote, "anger and irony on their faces. Many of them have the eyes of mad women." *Le Figaro* reported on June 1 that the women and children in the convoys of prisoners "marched with a hardier step than the men. . . . The men are more solemn and seem to be asking themselves if it would not have been better to think before serving against their brothers in the army." The *Times* correspondent, reflecting back on the fighting, reported that, "more courageous than the men, the

[19] Child, letter, in *Paris under Siege*, p. 197.

[20] *Paris-Journal*, May 31, 1871, quoted in Mason, *Paris Commune*, p. 291. Only the conservative newspapers were still publishing at this point.

[21] Gibson, *Paris during the Commune*, p. 270; D. A. Bingham, *Recollections of Paris*, 2 vols. (London, 1896), 2:124.

[22] Reported by Ernest A. Vizetelly, *My Adventures in the Commune* (London, 1914), p. 316.

women show fight to the last moment, and meet their death, according to the accounts of those who have witnessed their executions; with an undaunted courage."[23]

Ussher and Goncourt quickly began to find it painful to watch the columns of prisoners marching through the city, often to be shot without trial. But even in his distress at the government's treatment of the prisoners, Goncourt remained fascinated by the defiant (sexual) demeanor of the women: "The rain increases in force. Some of the women pull up their skirts to cover their heads. A line of horsemen in white coats has reinforced the line of foot soldiers. The colonel . . . shouts: 'Attention!' and the African riflemen load their guns. At this moment the women think they are going to be shot and one of them collapses with an attack of nerves. But the terror only lasts a moment; at once they renew their irony, and some their coquetry with the soldiers."[24]

The convoys of prisoners were treated in an appallingly inhumane and humiliating manner. Forced to march bareheaded and without food and water through the hot summer sun, some who could not keep up with the pace of the march, others for no discernible reason, were executed along the roadside, and all were subjected to the taunts and abuse of Parisians and Versaillais who had opposed the Commune. Chastel reported, for instance, that "the crowd hooted" the prisoners as they passed along. Bingham, the *Pall Mall* correspondent, recounted that "for many a long day after the insurrection was quelled long caravans of prisoners were to be seen wending their way to Versailles, innocent and guilty alike, to the great delight of substantial citizens . . . [who] revenged [them]selves indiscriminately." The *Times* reported that "escorts with prisoners are continually passing through the streets followed by a jeering mob." Even *Le Gaulois* reported that "the crowd, exasperated by the preceding days, accosted them [the prisoners] with invectives and cries of 'Kill them!' " and "even some stones were thrown at the prisoners."[25]

There was a sexual dimension, however, to the punishment meted out to the women that was absent in the treatment of the men. Several correspondents reported that the women were stripped, either partially or completely, before they were executed. On Friday, May 26, the *Times*'s correspondent reported that thirteen women, "caught in the act of spreading petroleum," had been executed "after being publicly disgraced in the Place Vendôme." Although the form this public disgrace took is unknown, it is likely that it involved at least the ripping

[23] Goncourt, *Journal*, p. 814; the *Times*, May 29, 1871, p. 10.

[24] Goncourt, *Journal*, p. 815.

[25] Chastel, "Letter," quoted in Gibson, *Paris during the Commune*, p. 290; Bingham, *Recollections*, p. 121; the *Times*, May 27, 1871, p. 5; *Le Gaulois*, April 5, 1871, p. 1.

of the women's bodices to reveal their breasts. Child, for instance, reported that some of the prisoners who were marched through the streets had their "chests exposed to show their sex." Goncourt reported that some of the women he saw were concealed behind veils until a "noncommissioned officer touched one of the veils with a cruel and brutal flick of his whip" and demanded, " 'Come on, off with your veils. Let's see your hussy faces [*vos visages de conquines*]!' " Louis Bergeret, an early leader of the Commune, reported that all the arrested women who were taken to the Place Vendôme were "undressed, raped and killed."[26] For male prisoners, punishment included turning their uniform jackets (if they wore one) inside out, a form of humiliation that lacked the sexual dimension that was involved in the treatment of the women.

The at least partial stripping of a woman accomplished several objectives. First, it determined her sex. Since some of the women were dressed in National Guard uniforms, revealing their breasts confirmed that they were women. More than a simple identification was involved, however. For men, simply being captured and thus rendered powerless was humiliating, as their reportedly passive behavior demonstrated to the observers. But women were supposed to be powerless so their humiliation had to take another form. Indeed, the reported defiance and coquetry of some of the female prisoners indicated to the observers that merely imprisoning them was not sufficient punishment. Stripping a woman would reveal to the world (or at least to the spectators and firing squads) that she was only a weak woman after all, not a fury with the power to burn houses or kill men.

Stripping a woman did not always remove her power, however, even when that was the intent. Men were, after all, fascinated with beautiful naked women, and any *pétroleuse* who resembled one of the prisoners described by Goncourt might have retained a great deal of power even when stripped naked: "Among these women there is one who is especially beautiful, beautiful with the implacable fury of a young Fate. She is a brunette with wild curly hair, with eyes of steel, with cheeks reddened by dried tears. She is *planted* in an attitude of defiance."[27] In the eyes of the British and French observers, the *pétroleuse* was a frightening but compelling figure—a fury with unbound, flying hair; a defiant madwoman; captured but wild; sometimes ugly and sometimes beautiful; often seductive; and always more powerful and more fascinating than her cowed male counterpart, who,

[26] The *Times*, May 27, 1871, p. 5; Child, letter, in *Paris under Siege*, p. 197; Goncourt, *Journal*, p. 815. Jules Bergeret, *Le 18 Mars, Journal Hebdomadaire*, (London, 1871), p. 24. Bergeret's *Journal* was published in three installments on August 21, August 28, and September 6, 1871. The French phrase translated here is "deshabillées, violées et massacrées."

[27] Goncourt, *Journal*, p. 814.

once arrested, became serious and unnaturally passive, while she remained unnaturally aggressive.

The *Bourgeoises*

Several observers were as fascinated by and as critical of the unladylike behavior of the *bourgeoises* who taunted and tortured the prisoners as they were of the behavior of the *communardes.* The *Times* reported on May 27 that the jeering mob following the prisoners contained "more women than men among its ranks—women who hoot and clap their hands and insult their victims to their hearts' content. Verily, it was with truth that Voltaire declared that a Parisian woman was half tiger and half monkey!" The misogynist nature of this critique indicates that The *Times*'s correspondent was at least as alarmed by the behavior of the *bourgeoises* as by that of the *pétroleuses.*

Gaston Cerfbeer, who was only twelve years old in 1871, long remembered the columns of prisoners and their treatment by the spectators. As the prisoners made their weary way through the city, he recalled in 1903, "one heard no cry of pity; [but] horrible epithets, insults, *injuries,* rained down upon them along with pieces of charred wood and stones. . . . Above all, the women were without pity, screaming 'Kill-them! To death!' "[28]

Even Maxime DuCamp, one of Versailles's strongest proponents, was distressed by the spectators' lack of charity, in general, and the women's behavior, in particular: "When a band of prisoners appeared, people rushed toward them and tried to break through the cordon of soldiers who escorted them and protected them; the women were, as always, the most agitated; they broke through the military ranks and beat the prisoners with umbrellas; crying: Kill the assassins! Burn the incendiaries!"[29]

Archibald Forbes, correspondent for the London *Daily News,* witnessed the lynching of a Communard by a mob and some Versailles soldiers on May 24 and reported in his memoir: "Very eager in their patriotic duty were the dear creatures of women. They knew the rat-holes into which the poor devils had squeezed themselves, and they guided the Versaillist soldiers to the spot with a fiendish glee. . . . They [the crowd] yell, . . . 'Shoot him! Shoot him!'—the demon-women most clamorous of course."[30] The *bourgeoises* might not have

[28] Gaston Cerfbeer, "Une nuit de la semaine sanglante," *La Revue Hebdomadaire* 6 (May 23, 1903): 423.

[29] Maxime DuCamp, *Les convulsions de Paris,* 4 vols., 5th ed. (Paris, 1881), 2:299.

[30] Archibald Forbes, "What I Saw of the Paris Commune," *Century Magazine* 44 (1892): 54.

been as compelling or as frightening as the *pétroleuses,* but their behavior broke the gender rules of Western culture just as that of the female Communards had, and it, too, was a threat to social order and not to be tolerated or condoned.

The *Pétroleuse* and the Artist

Artists and caricaturists produced visual representations of the *pétroleuses,* sometimes to accompany the verbal descriptions of the reporters, sometimes to stand alone. These visual images, perhaps more than the written descriptions, gave power to the myth of the *pétroleuse.* In the artists' hands, however, the variety of attributes that appeared in the accounts of reporters and other eyewitnesses—the implacable fury, her hair disheveled and unrestrained, her eyes wild with insanity; the stunning beauty; the madwoman, her face distorted by rage; the coquettish and seductive young woman—was lost. Replacing them were two major images—the hag and the victim.

In unsympathetic representations, artists emphasized the hideous, stripping the women of their compelling fury and sexuality. They became banshees racing around Paris with their cans of petrol (see Figure 8.1); hags pouring petrol through windows, sometime assisted by their corrupted children (see Figure 8.2); or, in one of the most vicious of the anti-Communard cartoons of the period, a pig (see Figure 8.3), a reversal of the myth of Circe, who seduced the companions of Ulysses with her beautiful voice and hair and turned them into swine.

The horror and rage which conservatives felt toward the *pétroleuses* is obvious in the caricatures, as is their sense that they were unnatural women. Natural women do not have pigs' snouts, crouch around cellar windows like Macbeth's witches around a caldron, or race through the streets with burning faggots and cans of petrol. By emphasizing the hideous in their drawings of the *pétroleuse,* the anti-Communard cartoonists went one step further than the verbal descriptions in displaying their hatred of women. But they missed one of the attributes that made the *pétroleuse* so horrifying and hence so hated—her sexuality.

For the conservative artist, the *pétroleuse* was the embodiment of evil, not a sexually attractive woman or one who could be humbled or humiliated. To depict her as sexually compelling or as sexually humiliated might evoke unwanted sympathy for her in the viewer, thereby interfering with the message the artists wished to convey. Moreover, baring the breasts of the *pétroleuses,* as the written accounts indicate

Figure 8.1. Eugene Girard, *The Emancipated Woman Shedding Light on the World.* Courtesy Vinck Collection, Bibliotheque Nationale

Figure 8.2. M. Lix, *The Incendiaries—The* Pétroleuses *and Their Accomplices*. *Le Monde Illustré*, June 3, 1871. Courtesy Vinck Collection, Bibliotheque Nationale

Figure 8.3. Anonymous, "Ah! If her man could see her." Courtesy Vinck Collection, Bibliotheque Nationale

occurred, might have confused the message by reminding viewers of the powerful and virtuous naked, semiclothed, and bare-breasted goddesses of contemporary and classical art and caricature.[31]

In sympathetic representations, artists stripped the *pétroleuses* of their sexuality and fearfulness and hence of their power. Their *pétroleuses* were young, attractive women (see Figure 8.4), captured and afraid, who shrank back in fear against the wall where they were about to be executed. Powerless and helpless, these *pétroleuses* were not the furies of the bourgeois imagination but innocent victims of the Versailles soldiers. Just as they could not appear to be strong or frightening, they could not be sexually seductive. They were victims in need of help. Imminent death or imprisonment was the key element in these representations. If the *pétroleuse* was to appear seductive or coquettish or strong, she might appear to be in some way responsible for her fate.

Although the artists eliminated sexuality from their drawings, they made sure that the *pétroleuse* was immediately recognized as female. For sympathetic artists, her femininity (as distinct from her sexuality) was integral to her victimhood. For unsympathetic artists, femaleness rather than femininity was the issue. If the figure could be misconstrued as male, the power of the message would be lost. Some caricaturists did draw an occasional *pétroleur,* but this figure soon disappeared from the histories and memoirs of the Commune. The horror of the fires could be adquately represented only in the figure of the unnatural woman—the female incendiary. As a result, the drawings always depicted the *pétroleuse* in a dress, even though the written accounts indicate that the *communardes* often wore male clothing. Indeed, one reason given for the tearing of the women's bodices was to reveal that they were women in men's clothing.

Revolution and the Unruly Woman

Why was the political threat of the Commune represented as a fury, a hideous, powerful, avenging, mad, sexually compelling woman? The answer lies, I think, partially in the defeat of the Commune, which meant that it could not be satisfactorily represented by a goddess as other revolutions might be. Nor could it be represented by a barricade

[31] For an analysis on the role of female nudity in art, see Marina Warner, *Monuments and Maidens: The Allegory of the Female Form* (New York, 1985), and Ann Hollander, *Seeing through Clothes* (New York, 1978). During this period of war and civil war, it was common for artists to depict both France and Paris as semiclad goddesses being raped or stabbed in the back by evil men. See, for instance, James Leith, "The War of Images Surrounding the Commune," in *Images of the Commune/Images de la Commune,* ed. Leith (Montreal, 1978), p. 111.

THE GRAPHIC

AN ILLUSTRATED WEEKLY NEWSPAPER

VOL III—No. 80
Regd. at General Post Office as a Newspaper

SATURDAY, JUNE 10 1871

PRICE SIXPENCE
Or by Post Sixpence Halfpenny

THE END OF THE COMMUNE—EXECUTION OF A PÉTROLEUSE

Figure 8.4. R. M., *The End of the Commune—Execution of a* Pétroleuse. The Graphic, June 10, 1871. Courtesy Vinck Collection, Bibliotheque Nationale

fighter, either male or female, because that figure evoked sympathy, not criticism, from many French women and men, and was too closely allied with the avenging, virtuous *Liberté* of Delacroix and other artists.

The defeat of the Commune is only part of the explanation for the representation of it as the *pétroleuse,* however. Another part is revealed by the punishment meted out to one of the female "poisoners." William Gibson reported that a woman who had poisoned forty soldiers was "taken to her home to be shot at the door of her house as an example."[32] An example of what? one might ask. In 1871, Gibson assumed the answer was so obvious that it did not need to be stated. The execution of the woman on her doorstep was an example of the punishment the unruly woman who tried to usurp male power could expect. Had she stayed in her home, the woman would have been safe. Having left it and having challenged male dominance, she was no longer truly a "woman," no longer deserving of a "man's" protection, and she would be killed as an example to other women of what they could expect if they stepped out of the proper female role.

The *pétroleuse*'s crime was even more threatening than that of the poisoner. The poisoner threatened the lives of a few men, whereas the *pétroleuse* threatened to overturn the social order. She not only challenged male authority by leaving her home and acting in the public sphere; she attacked male property, the source of the bourgeois male's sense of importance; she burned down the home in which she was supposed to care for her children; and she corrupted her children by encouraging them to aid her in this deed. What more unnatural and symbolically significant action could she have taken? She was the evil mother, capable of killing her children, controlling men, and destroying their power base. These were the ends socialism and feminism would lead to.

It is no accident that the caption for Figure 8.1 identifies the *pétroleuse* as "the emancipated women." Feminists (the emancipated women of the nineteenth century) had left the domestic sphere for the political arena. They were challenging bourgeois men's sense of order, power, and well-being. The conflation of the image of the feminist with that of the *pétroleuse* is thus hardly surprising. In a sense, the *pétroleuse* was simply a representation of what men feared about feminism.

To make it all worse, the *pétroleuse*'s fury, her wild eyes and unruly hair, and her uncowed behavior when arrested made her sexually alluring. She had to be tamed, turned into the hideous, nonalluring *pétroleuse* of the cartoonists, and summarily killed when apprehended,

[32] Gibson, *Paris during the Commune,* p. 293. Here Gibson quotes a letter from a member of his congregation.

or turned into the helpless female victim of the pro-Commune artists. Otherwise, her sexual power might turn the world upside down, and she might come to dominate men.

By giving physical form to the *pétroleuse,* the artists helped to make her memorable. But by eliminating her sexuality, they obscured the attribute that made this mythical figure so powerful and so likely a representation of the revolutionary Commune. She was fearful, in part, because she was sexually compelling. Not because she acted like a man but because she was a woman, she might be able to lure men to their destruction and to the destruction of their civilization. The sexual nature of the *pétroleuse*'s appeal to the men who watched her march through the city and feared her presence in dark alleys was integral to her power.

Revolution was like the unruly woman: it threatened to turn on its head the social order that was assumed by its beneficiaries (bourgeois men and, to a certain extent, bourgeois women who taunted the female prisoners, although men also saw their behavior as threatening social order) to be natural. In the political arena, revolution was the ultimate threat, just as in the personal arena women's sexuality was the ultimate threat. These were the two forces which, if they got out of control, would give power to the powerless. It is not surprising that the image so often used to represent the political threat of revolution was that of the unruly woman. One fear represents the other.

Unfortunately for women, men have often demonstrated their mastery of the revolution by mastering the representation, that is, by repressing women. In the case of the Paris Commune, such repression was particularly easy because women had participated in the revolt and had defended the city at the barricades. Whether or not they had burned the city, they were fully implicated by their other unladylike or "feminist" activities, and they would be severely punished for their "unnatural" acts. Given the roles women did play during the Commune and men's fear of powerful women, it is difficult to imagine the *pétroleuse* not emerging in the bourgeois imagination and, once she had emerged, any other representation of the Paris Commune having any power.

CHAPTER NINE

True Women, Real Men: Gender, Ideology, and Social Roles in the Garvey Movement

Barbara Bair

The concept of difference is an essential theoretical framework for understanding the complex intersection of race and gender in the Garvey movement. The movement began with the formation in Jamaica of the Universal Negro Improvement Association (UNIA) as a benevolent organization in 1914. It took root among West Indian immigrants and African Americans in Harlem in 1918–19, after its founder, Marcus Garvey, migrated to the United States and reformulated the UNIA within the sociopolitical context of the New Negro era. In the early 1920s the UNIA became a major black grass-roots movement, with local divisions throughout the United States, in the Caribbean, Central America, and abroad. The UNIA was a separatist organization; its membership was open only to blacks—both men and women. It was dedicated to principles that had become well-formulated within the African-American community by the turn of the century: the development of black economic independence through enterprise and production; industrial education; social and moral uplift; and self-reliance. The principles of socioeconomic self-help had been most famously articulated in the earlier career of Booker T. Washington and in institutions such as the National Negro Business League and southern black colleges. The philosophy of social uplift and racial solidarity had also been exemplified in a number of black women's community organizations, as well as in the black women's club movement. In addition to these precursors, the UNIA, as a Pan-African organization, had intellectual debts to colonization movements of the nineteenth century as well as to modern New Negro consciousness. The UNIA represented race pride and identification with Africa; through its conventions and its publication, *The Negro World,* it fostered the idea of nationalist independence from colonial rule; and its officers made (ultimately unsuccessful) efforts to develop a colonization program in cooperation with Liberia to provide an opportunity for repatriation to an African homeland to the descendants of members of the African diaspora.

From its inception, the structure of the organization and the philosophy that guided its purpose were laden with culturally constructed concepts of gender that in turn helped define highly gender-specific social roles. Women were technically granted an equal share of power based on the division of authority by gender. In practice, however, the organizational pattern of men's and women's leadership roles was not separate and equal but separate and hierarchical. The predominant model of gender relations was similar to that of the companionate marriage, with wife/woman and husband/man cooperating while asserting authority over separate spheres of influence. In this scheme, the wife/woman's sphere (and her roles as mother, teacher, nurse, or office worker) was deemed important but secondary to and supportive of that of the husband/man (and his roles as policy maker, executive, or diplomat). Many women accepted these gender definitions and their attending roles, but others rebelled against them, creating modified positions of authority for themselves and reconstructing the prevailing views of womanhood and manhood in the process.

The UNIA was strongly formulated around the sociopolitical concept of difference—both gender and racial. Maximalist in its rhetoric, it celebrated separate spheres of influence and expertise for women and men; it exalted the association of manhood with public roles and the constructions of independence, authority, and power, while celebrating the association of womanhood with private roles and the qualities of cooperation, nurturing, and uplift. Similarly, its program of racial independence presented a polar framework. It supported separatism and race pride and opposed other black organizations' efforts at integration and assimilation. Just as feminists are now debating the nature of gender difference—whether it is biologically innate or economically and culturally constructed, whether it is positive in its manifestations or repressive—so too were black activists split over the racial meanings embedded in the philosophy of the UNIA. For many activists of the period, voluntary separatism was too closely related to forced segregation and to patterns of black accommodation and repression (or, when it took the form of nationalism, with reactionary authoritarianism). For others, including members of the UNIA, separatism offered a liberating vision, a concrete alternative to the realities of discrimination and exclusion suffered in a world dominated by whites and a utopian model for future independence and strength that would belie negative white constructions of black ability and value. This radical power to reverse dominant white definitions also informed the dichotomous vision of gender. The self-definition of separate spheres for black women and men can be seen as a direct reaction against racist attribution of stereotypical "feminine" qualities (passivity, subordination, exclusion from skilled and professional employment) to black males and of stereotypical "masculine" qualities (strength, authority, and physicality) to black females. It was also a reversal of the double standard applied by whites in which white women belonged in the home, black women in the work force. The concept of protection implied in dichotomous relations was also a reversal of a long history of black women's sexual subjugation to whites and their vulnerability to exploitation in the workplace. Thus the very Victorian ideology of true women and real men against which many privileged white feminists revolted held attractions for black women and men, who saw the minimalist gender constructions applied to them as part of a repressive history of racism, denigration, and lack of choice.

True Women, Real Men

As an article in *The Negro World,* June 9, 1923, put it:

> Let us go back to the days of true manhood when women truly reverenced us and without any condescension on our part, for all true women will admire and respect a real man: therefore let us again place our women upon the pedestal from whence they have been forced into the vortex of the seething world of business. . . . We would have many more mothers, many more virtuous wives, many more amiable and lovable daughters if man would play his part as he should.

Black soldiers' experience in World War I has long been considered a determining factor in the emergence of the UNIA in the postwar period. In the mid-1920s Garveyite Edgar Grey described the UNIA as "the new manhood movement,"[1] voicing the fact that for many people the organization represented militant values that have been conventionally defined as "masculine"—pride, power, self-determination, and dominance. Marcus Garvey hinted at his own conception of real black manhood when he told his audiences in 1923 that "this is the age of men, not of pygmies, not of serfs and peons and dogs, but men, and we who make up the membership of the Universal Negro Improvement Association reflect the new manhood of the Negro."[2]

[1] *New York News,* February 21, 1925.
[2] *Negro World,* June 23, 1923.

The conceptualization of new black political power as a masculine construction was reflected in the structure of the UNIA. Initially it was governed by a slate of male national officers headquartered in New York; in 1922, one national leadership position was reserved for a woman. Women had similar minority representation on UNIA corporate boards, as delegates at its conventions, and in the editorial ranks of its newspaper. The operation of the UNIA headquarters office divided along white- and pink-collar lines, with men in executive and field positions and women forming the foundation of the clerical staff, which also included many men. On the local level, each division had a male and a female president. Although the lady president had charge of the local ladies' auxiliaries, she was under the general supervision of the male president, who was in turn answerable to Garvey and the national office.

The gender ideology that informed the status and function of representative men and women in the movement in nonleadership roles is illustrated in the design of the local male and female auxiliaries. The Black Cross Nurses and the Universal African Legions offer two contrasting constructions of gender; indeed, they encapsulate two dichotomous sets of genderized values which can be listed under the headings of "motherhood" and "militarism." The Black Cross Nurse auxiliaries, who were based on the model of wartime Red Cross canteen workers, offered support services to black soldiers, who were in turn the models for the African Legions. Local groups were headed by a matron, often the lady president of the division, and by a head nurse who preferably had three years of practical experience. Although many of the nurses had no formal training, others were graduates of nursing programs, and in some areas classes and examinations for certification were instituted for Black Cross members in affiliation with local hospitals. The nurses performed social welfare and organizational functions—visiting the sick, providing clothing, running food banks and supper kitchens, and appearing as contingents in UNIA parades. In many instances they provided essential public health services in black neighborhoods not reached by government programs. Wearing recognizable uniforms, they were highly visible and highly respected members of their communities. They were important as role models and recruiters of young women into the movement, and their outreach was primarily to other women, particularly mothers, who were in charge of the health and well-being of their families. The nurses—heirs to decades of black women's charitable work—personified the benevolent, nurturing, and uplifting aspirations of the UNIA and the communitarian principle of black survival and mutual care.[3]

[3] See *Negro World*, February 19, August 21, 1921, March 17, 31, April 7, 21, 28, May

The African Legions personified the prestige and purpose associated with independent black manhood. They represented the ideas of power and dominance and the military might necessary to achieve and maintain Negro nationhood. Modeled on U.S. infantry protocol and regimentation, the paramilitary wing of the movement was made up primarily of black veterans of World War I. They provided a dress military function within the UNIA, marching in UNIA parades, supplying bodyguard and crowd-control services in mass meetings, and adding to the pomp and ceremony associated with the public appearance of UNIA officials—serving in each case as bodily symbols of the movement as a nation within a nation. Many also were involved in street speaking and, in some cases, street violence.

Garvey referred to the militant nationalism of the African Legions in 1937 when he told journalist Joel Rogers: "We were the first Fascists . . . when we had 100,000 disciplined men, and were training children, Mussolini was still an unknown. Mussolini copied our Fascism."[4] A few years earlier he had praised Hitler as "dominant . . . of the true-man type."[5] The quality of dominance that Garvey admired in the rising fascist leaders was linked to his similar love of the idea of the self-made man. Rejecting the class analysis and identification with labor propagated by other black leaders of the period, Garvey frequently offered his audiences the examples of white captains of industry as models to emulate. "Wealth is strength, wealth is power, wealth is influence," he told the readers of his London-based journal, the *Black Man,* "wealth is justice, is liberty, is real human rights."[6] Garvey's paradigm of black manhood, with its complements of power, pride, and economic success, was the standard white paradigm of power turned inside out. Black men had been slaves but would become their own masters; rather than workers, they would become owners, achieving a level of financial success that would defy the definition of themselves as an underclass. "The black man is tired of eating food and never selling it," Garvey said in 1923, "the black man is tired of laboring in the bowels of ships and not keeping watch on the bridge."[7]

The self-made construction of manhood translated in the movement into the fostering of a petty bourgeois ideal, including the ideals of the

---

19, 26, 1923, August 14, 1924; see also Eleanor Krohn Herrmann, "Black Cross Nursing in Belize: A Labour of Love," *Belizean Studies* 8 (March 1980): 1–9.

[4] Joel Rogers, "Marcus Garvey," in "Negroes of New York," WPA Writers' Program of New York City, 1939, manuscript/microfilm collection, Schomburg Center for Research in Black Culture, New York.

[5] *Black Man* 1 (March–April 1934): 2.

[6] Marcus Garvey, "Let the Negro Accumulate Wealth: It Will Bring Him Power," *Black Man* 1 (late July 1935): 4–5.

[7] *Negro World,* June 30, 1923.

nuclear family and of a sexual division of labor in which women's roles were largely privatized. Ladies' division meetings and Women's Day exhibits at UNIA conventions often presented a bourgeois view of UNIA women as leisured ladies, featuring teas and fashion shows with a full array of afternoon frocks, golf costumes, and evening gowns.[8] This presentation of womanhood was prescriptive rather than representative, however. In reality, many, if not most, women members of the UNIA were involved in the wage work force; in the South, many of them were engaged in agriculture. Many of the clerical workers who worked in UNIA offices in urban areas were unmarried women who held second jobs, often as domestic workers or beauticians, and lived in extended family situations. Many of the female UNIA officers, whether married or single, were involved in small businesses or had careers as teachers, editors, social workers, musicians, or elocutionists. Nevertheless, the ideal presented to UNIA members was that of marriage, motherhood, and the single-income family—the woman not as worker or professional but as helpmate and partner to the man, a moral influence, a charitable volunteer, and an educator of children. The two options of paid labor and family life were not, of course, mutually exclusive; but the reality of black women's participation in the labor force was often described negatively as a problem stemming from the inadequacies of black men. UNIA women used the phrase "real manhood," too; they even emblazoned it on their banners in UNIA parades—but in their usage it meant a code of chivalry, men who were gentlemen and providers, responsible fathers and husbands, who respected black women, supported black children, and did not reject them for white girlfriends and wives.[9]

At the same time that the dominant construction of womanhood in the movement endorsed the middle-class dynamic of the male wage earner and the non-wage-earning wife and mother, it also valorized the special qualities women were said to possess. Garveyite Eunice Lewis wrote to the *Negro World* to describe the "New Negro Woman," who "is conscious of the value of pure womanhood that has the power to win and conquer the beastly side of man."[10] Garvey underscored the idealized vision of black womanhood in his poetry, depicting the ancient African woman as a regal figure of beauty in "The Black Woman" and the black mother as the source of unconditional love and support for the black man in "The Black Mother."[11] The combination of this

[8] Ibid., September 2, 1922.

[9] Theodore Vincent writes that the marchers at the head of the ladies' auxiliary in the 1920 convention parade carried a banner reading "God Give Us Real Men!" (*Black Power and the Garvey Movement* [San Francisco, 1972], p. 114).

[10] *Negro World*, April 19, 1924.

[11] *The Poetical Works of Marcus Garvey*, comp. Tony Martin (Dover, Mass., 1983), pp. 44–45, 59.

construction of woman as virginal goddess and as mother came in the UNIA's formal canonization of the Virgin Mary as a black woman in 1924.[12]

The dominant constructions of manhood and womanhood in the movement thus served to reverse negative racial stereotypes—overturning the status of the black man as a powerless member of an underclass and the status of the black woman as a white-oriented servant; replacing white standards of beauty with black standards; and exchanging conceptualizations of a white deity for a black one. Women's own reaction to this purity/helpmate model of womanhood was ambivalent. Women saw themselves primarily united with men in the cause of racial solidarity and uplift, yet many questioned the dichotomous construction of their roles that consigned them to act within the realm of reproduction, morality, and support while men were involved in leadership, business, and policy making. These women lobbied forcefully for greater agency, rejecting the maximalist position reflected in much of the UNIA rhetoric and arguing that they possessed intellectual and leadership abilities that made them as capable as men to assume policy positions in the organization.

That many women within the movement felt stifled in their roles and wanted greater autonomy is illustrated in a protest staged by women delegates at the 1922 UNIA convention. When Garvey was out of the room, Victoria Turner, a delegate from St. Louis, approached the podium with a set of five resolutions that had been ratified by a majority of the women delegates, requesting that women be granted greater recognition and authority as delegates, as committee members, as local officers, and as field representatives, and ending with a general resolution on the need for a woman to be involved in setting international policy "so that the Negro women all over the world can function without restriction from the men." After Turner presented the resolutions, women rose one by one to express their dissatisfaction over the limitations placed upon them in the movement. Clara Morgan, a Black Cross Nurse, declared that "she was not in favor of the women standing behind and pushing the men; they wanted to be placed in some of the executive positions because they felt they were entitled to them." Mrs. M. M. Scott of Detroit stated that "she found that whenever women began to function in the organization the men presumed to dictate to them." Aladia Robertson, a field representative and leader, with her husband, of the New Orleans division, ironically championed a "special protection" view, arguing that women should not be in the field as organizers "if they wanted to hold the proper respect of the men." Lillian Willis, a fellow field organizer, challenged

[12] *Negro World*, September 6, 1924, June 6, September 5, 1925, March 16, 1926.

Robertson, stating that "she believed the women were as competent as the men to be field representatives." Mrs. Hogue of Chicago responded to the implicit threat to male hegemony contained in the resolutions, saying that women had no intention "to get in the way of the men or to take the men's places, but they wanted to be at their side." Delegates from Florida, Maryland, Indiana, and Ohio spoke before Garvey made his entrance and reassumed control of the session, informing the women that there was no need for their resolutions because their interests were already protected under the UNIA constitution.[13] During the same convention, when delegate Henry Plummer rose to nominate a woman as a member of the UNIA delegation to the League of Nations, Garvey vetoed his action, remarking "that it would be entirely improper to send a lady as a delegate, since it would be contrary to diplomatic custom, ladies never being chosen as members of diplomatic missions."[14]

Garvey himself tacitly recognized the realities experienced by black women in the wage labor force when he praised the UNIA as an employer that had lifted women from domestic work in white homes to dignified clerical positions in a black-owned organization. He also recognized that it was women who were the stalwarts of the movement and the backbone of local divisions.[15] In a movement marked by factionalization, impeachments, purgings, and continual turnover in male personnel, women like Amy Jacques Garvey, Henrietta Vinton Davis, Maymie Lena Turpeau De Mena, and Ethel Collins stand out as constants whose involvement in the movement spanned many years and various regimes.

Henrietta Vinton Davis, born in Maryland, was a leader in the UNIA for some twenty years. She worked as a schoolteacher and as an assistant to Frederick Douglass in Washington before establishing a successful career as an elocutionist. She volunteered as an organizer for the Populist movement in the 1890s and in the early 1900s toured the Caribbean raising money for a Jamaican school for girls. She joined the UNIA in New York in 1919 and was one of the original directors and officers of the Black Star Line. As international organizer of the UNIA, she presided regularly at major mass meetings, including those at Carnegie Hall and Madison Square Garden. She became the only woman in the main slate of officers when Garvey created the position of fourth assistant president general for her in 1922. In 1924 she became the only woman member of the UNIA delegation to Liberia.[16]

[13] Ibid., September 9, 1922.
[14] Ibid., August 12, 1922.
[15] Ibid., June 23, 1923; *Pittsburgh Courier,* May 31, 1930.
[16] *Negro World,* June 14, 21, 1919, September 11, 1920, February 12, 1921, September 9, December 23, 1922, June 2, 1923, March 29, July 5, 1924; correspondence, John E.

Davis's companion on a 1925 organizing tour of the Caribbean was Maymie De Mena. De Mena was born in Nicaragua. She joined the tour as a Spanish translator and organizer. Significantly, her rise to prominence in the movement coincided with Garvey's imprisonment. With Garvey removed from visibility, his second wife, Amy Jacques Garvey, and De Mena assumed compensatory leadership in his name. Jacques was Garvey's unofficial lieutenant, exercising great authority but never holding an official office in the organization, whereas De Mena was his official representative, traveling widely during his imprisonment, first as assistant international organizer (1926), then succeeding Davis as fourth assistant president general (1927). At the first international UNIA convention held after Garvey's release and deportation from the United States, De Mena became a female symbol of the crusading spirit of the organization when she led a massive UNIA parade through the streets of Kingston, on horseback, brandishing a sword like a black Joan of Arc. She was central in Garvey's 1929 reorganization of the movement, becoming international organizer and officer in charge of the American Field in 1929 and 1930. She briefly assumed the directorship of the *Negro World* in the early 1930s, then moved to Jamaica, where she remained involved in the UNIA in the 1940s while working as a social worker and as owner/editor of her own newspaper, the *Ethiopian World.*[17]

Amy Jacques Garvey had been an important figure in the movement since she became the business manager of the UNIA headquarters in 1920, but her recognition and influence within the organization burgeoned when her husband was convicted on mail fraud charges in 1923 and imprisoned in 1925–27. Although many men voiced their resentment at taking orders from a woman, even if many of those orders were being relayed from the president general in his prison cell, Jacques wielded power successfully, carrying out her husband's wishes in the ongoing operation of the movement and gaining admiration from members for her ready ability to assume control. Jacques became the premier propagandist of Garveyism, traveling to division meetings throughout the country, lobbying for Garvey's release in Washington, publishing the two-volume *Philosophy and Opinions* in 1923 and 1925, and becoming associate editor of the *Negro World* in 1924. As

Bruce Papers, Schomburg Center for Research in Black Culture, New York; Barbara Bair, "Henrietta Vinton Davis," in *Marcus Garvey: Life and Lessons*, ed. Robert A. Hill and Barbara Bair (Berkeley, 1987), pp. 375–76.

[17] *Negro World*, July 11, September 5, 1925, March 27, December 11, 1926, March 19, 1927, April 15, October 17, 1933; *Daily Gleaner* (Kingston), August 2, September 3, 1929, August 3, 1937; Barbara Bair, "M. L. T. De Mena," in *Marcus Garvey*, ed. Hill and Bair, pp. 376–77.

editor, she introduced a new page called "Our Women and What They Think," for the first time providing a public forum for women members of the movement. Although Jacques exercised independent leadership, she was almost always viewed as an extension of Garvey's identity—the ultimate example of the companionate wife model exalted by the movement. A *Negro World* reporter who interviewed her in 1923 described her as a woman "helping a man to make the present and future of Negroes secure and happy; doing her full share as a good wife and helping him to accomplish his task as a Negro leader. Here indeed, was the better half of Marcus Garvey!" When, a few months later, the *Negro World* characterized Jacques as "an innocent and helpless woman [thrown] into an arena where she cannot properly defend herself," Jacques retorted that she felt she had a "fair knowledge of men and the methods they employ in the organization and out of it" and suggested that "the word 'helpless' " had been "misapplied."[18]

Thus the success of Davis, De Mena, and Jacques as UNIA leaders was seemingly owing not only to their own merit as strong intellects and forceful organizers but to their perceived status as Garvey's representatives—a status that prevented them from being seen as "real" leaders in their own right and therefore as threats to his autocratic authority. The case of Laura Kofey offers an extreme example of the animosity that could meet those (women and men) who challenged that authority, rather than serving as extensions of it. Kofey emerged as a prominent figure at about the same time as De Mena. An extremely charismatic woman, she drew enormous crowds when she began organizing for the UNIA in Florida in 1927. Newspaper accounts claimed that hundreds of new members joined the UNIA in each location on her tour and thousands attended her camp meetings. Kofey considered herself a prophet of Garveyism, and she visited the UNIA leader in prison in August 1927. Her phenomenal success in moving audiences soon won her a personal following, however, and her status as organizer par excellence shifted to that of rival to Garvey. Bitter factionalization resulted, and Kofey established her own parallel organization, the African Universal Church and Commercial League, in 1928. Her meetings were regularly heckled by African Legion members who were loyal to Garvey and represented her rise to power. The rivalry between Garvey and Kofey loyalists culminated in March 1928, when Kofey was assassinated by a gunman from the audience while she read from the Bible in a meeting in Miami. An African Legionnaire loyal to Garvey was arrested for the crime.[19]

[18] *Negro World*, March 17, July 14, 21, 1923.

[19] Ibid., May 7, May 21, June 4, 11, July 2, 9, 23, October 22, 1927, January 21, April 21, July 27, 1928; Richard Newman, "Warrior Mother of Africa's Warriors of the Most High God: Laura Adorkor Kofey and the African Universal Church," in *Black Power and*

As the movement progressed, hundreds of women learned organizational skills and cooperative/empowering patterns of leadership through involvement in their local divisions or the women's auxiliaries. Many of them ultimately employed these skills for causes outside the Garvey movement—in religious and benevolent groups, in party politics, or in women-oriented careers. Examples include Adelaide Casely-Hayford, lady president of the Freetown, Sierra Leone, UNIA division, who was active in the International Council of Women of the Darker Races and founded a technical school for African girls.[20] Mittie Maud Lena Gordon, lady president of the Chicago division, founded the Peace Movement of Ethiopia, a grass-roots movement that became a powerful lobbying force for legislation to aid black repatriation to Africa.[21] Black Cross Nurse Frances Albrier became a union organizer with the Brotherhood of Sleeping Car Porters and worked to desegregate the teaching staffs of Oakland city schools.[22] Journalist Charlotta Bass, lady president of the Los Angeles division and managing editor of the influential *California Eagle,* left the UNIA in protest over Garvey's autocratic handling of organizational policy. She became a local leader in fights against residential segregation, racial violence, and discrimination against blacks in employment, union membership, and public transportation. She also worked as an organizer in Republican and Progressive party politics and was the latter party's vice-presidential candidate in 1952.[23] Amy Ashwood Garvey, Garvey's first wife and an avowed and dedicated feminist, was seventeen years old when she co-founded the UNIA with Garvey in Jamaica in 1914. She established the ladies' wing of the movement and was the organization's first secretary. When she joined Garvey in New York in 1918, she became what a Bureau of Investigation agent described as Garvey's "chief assistant, a kind of managing boss," and was instrumental in

---

Black Religion, ed. Richard Newman (West Cornwall, Conn., 1987), pp. 131–45.

[20] See Adelaide Casely Hayford, "A Girls' School in West Africa," *Southern Workman* 55 (October 1926): 449–56; Rina Okonkwo, "Adelaide Casely Hayford: Cultural Nationalist and Feminist," *Phylon: A Review of Race and Culture* 42 (March 1981): 44; Adelaide M. Cromwell, *An African Victorian Feminist: The Life and Times of Adelaide Smith Casely Hayford* (London, 1986).

[21] See Ethel Hedlin, "Earnest Cox and Colonization: A White Racist's Response to Black Repatriation, 1923–1966" (Ph.D. diss., Duke University, 1974).

[22] "Frances Mary Albrier," interview by Malca Chall, Black Women Oral History Project, Schlesinger Library on the History of Women in America, Radcliffe College, and Women in Politics Oral History Project, University of California, Berkeley, 1977–78.

[23] Charlotta Bass, *Forty Years: Memoirs from the Pages of a Newspaper* (Los Angeles, 1960); Gerald R. Gill, " 'Win or Lose We Win': The 1952 Vice-Presidential Campaign of Charlotta A. Bass," in *The Afro-American Woman Struggles and Images,* ed. Sharon Harley and Rosayln Terborg-Penn (Port Washington, N.Y., 1978), pp. 109–18; Emory J. Tolbert, *The UNIA and Black Los Angeles* (Los Angeles, 1980); Charlotta Bass Papers, Southern California Library of Social Science and Research, Los Angeles.

drawing women into the affairs of the organization.[24] She married Garvey in 1920, but the marriage lasted only a few months before dissolving into separation and finally divorce in 1922. Ashwood offered a feminist analysis for its failure, citing the clash between Garvey's dominating ways and her own forceful and extroverted personality and stating her unwillingness to meet Garvey's expectations of a wife who would sacrifice her own goals to devote herself to the career of her husband. Ashwood went on to have a long international career as a playwright and producer, journalist, public speaker, and political activist in Pan-African, women's, and labor causes.[25]

Ethel Collins is a less flamboyant and more representative example of a woman who acquired skills through her work with the UNIA. Like De Mena and Davis, Collins was a Garvey loyalist who was active in the movement for over twenty years. Unlike them, she worked mainly behind the scenes, providing the day-to-day labor that kept the association operating. Born in Jamaica, Collins immigrated to New York in 1919 and joined the UNIA the following year, becoming a member of the New York division and a stockholder in the Black Star Line. By the mid-1920s she was a regular speaker and soloist at UNIA meetings, and by the late 1920s, lady president of the local Garvey Club. Collins was unmarried and lived with siblings. She worked as a secretary at UNIA headquarters; she also worked as a beautician and a typist. By 1929 she was acting secretary general of the UNIA and an American delegate to the 1929 convention in Jamaica. She was also a delegate to the Canadian conventions in the 1930s and a top graduate of Garvey's African School of Philosophy, a course designed to train members for leadership positions. After Garvey's death in 1940, Collins maintained close correspondence with Amy Jacques Garvey in Jamaica and also communicated regularly with Daisy Whyte, Garvey's personal secretary, who had nursed him in London during his final illness and was left in charge of his affairs. Collins and Whyte were among the three women elected to the five-person slate of new UNIA officers at an emergency convention held two months after Garvey's death, and Collins participated in the relocation of the headquarters of the movement to Cleveland.[26] Collins thus is representative of the

[24] Robert A. Hill, Emory J. Tolbert, and Deborah Forczek, eds., *The Marcus Garvey and UNIA Papers*, vols. 1 and 2 (Berkeley, 1983), 2:15, see also 1:74 n. 2.

[25] *New York Amsterdam News*, November 3, 10, 1916, September 21, 1940, March 4, 1944; Amy Ashwood Garvey, "The Liberian Woman Emerges," *People's Voice*, June 8, 1946; Barbara Bair, "Amy Ashwood," in *Marcus Garvey*, ed. Hill and Bair, pp. 358–59; Lionel M. Yard, *Biography of Amy Ashwood Garvey: Co-founder of the Universal Negro Improvement Association* (New York, 1989).

[26] See *Negro World*, August 28, 1926, March 12, 1927, September 15, 1928, June 15, August 24, September 7, 1929, and all January, February, March, and April 1931 issues;

working-class woman who developed organizational skills and rose within the movement, networking with other women and with men and participating in, or personally shaping, some of the key events in the organization's history.

For each of these brief profiles of UNIA women, there are hundreds of others that would aptly illustrate the spectrum of roles, self-images, class affiliation, marital status, routes to power, and philosophies of leadership represented by women in the Garvey movement—a spectrum of thought and achievement that to some extent belies the dominant construction of womanhood presented by Garvey and by many of the women themselves. The centrality and longevity of their participation, particularly on the local level, is a testament that Garveyism was not only a "new manhood movement" but a new womanhood movement as well.

Black Man 4 (June 1939): 8; UNIA Central Division Papers, Schomburg Center for Research in Black Culture, New York; Amy Jacques Garvey Papers, Fisk University.

CHAPTER TEN

Learning to Live "Just Like White Folks": Gender, Ethnicity, and the State in the Inland Northwest

Dolores Janiewski

"We live just like white folks," a Native American husband was quoted as saying in a 1933 report issued by the Bureau of Indian Affairs, "since my wife joined the extension club."[1] True or not, his words expressed the aims of centuries of effort by government officials, missionaries, scholars, and reformers, including many women. As Carl Schurz, former secretary of the interior, enunciated the goals of Indian policy in 1881, "Nothing will be more apt to raise the Indians in the scale of civilization than to stimulate their attachment to permanent homes, and it is the woman that must make the atmosphere and form the attraction of the home. She must be recognized, with affection and respect, as the center of domestic life."[2] Associate Justice William Strong, speaking to a group of Indian reformers, declared that Indians "should not maintain their own language and habits" but should "ultimately be Americanized."[3] Refashioning the gender, ethnic, and economic identities of Native Americans was a goal jointly espoused by public authorities and voluntary associations.

As elsewhere, the colonizing process by which the United States established control over indigenous peoples involved the "domestication" of women, which included vesting "sole ownership of family

[1] Quoted in Bureau of Indian Affairs, Division of Extension, "Annual Report for 1932," Bureau of Indian Affairs, Record group 75, National Archives, Washington, D.C. (hereafter cited as RG 75/DC).

[2] Carl Schurz, "Present Aspects of the Indian Problem," *North American Review* 133 (July 1881): 12–14.

[3] William Strong, *Proceedings of the Third Annual Meeting of the Lake Mohonk Conference* (1885), quoted in Francis Paul Prucha, *Americanizing the American Indians: Writings by the "Friends of the Indian"* (Lincoln, 1978), p. 39.

assets" in the "head of the household."[4] In the terms of nineteenth-century middle-class ideology, women were to be sheltered within the private space of the home while their husbands were to "be allowed a man's rights and privileges and be held to the performance of a man's obligations" and enjoy "the autonomy of the individual." But these efforts to demarcate the domestic world of women from the public world of men inadvertently but unavoidably caused their advocates to violate the very boundaries they sought to establish between the sexual and political economies. As Thomas J. Morgan, commissioner of Indian affairs, insisted in his 1889 report to Congress, "The Indians must conform to 'the white man's ways,' peaceably if they will, forcibly if they must."[5] Even while insisting that their proposed reforms obeyed "the laws which grow naturally out of the family," the reformers and officials admitted that they would have to "force law" upon the Native Americans they were seeking to transform.[6]

Although the reform process was complex, involving many Native American cultures, this examination will concentrate on some of the indigenous peoples of the inland Pacific Northwest.[7] Descendants of the participants in the plateau cultural complex based on fishing, gathering, and hunting now live on the Colville Confederated Tribes reservation in eastern Washington, the Coeur d'Alene reservation, and the Nez Perce reservation in northern Idaho. Among these peoples women played a major role in the production and trade of subsistence items, principally through gathering roots, berries, and other edible plants. Women also shared in the collective work of fishing that supplied most of the protein in their diets, caught small animals for food, and joined the buffalo hunts that ventured across the Rocky Mountains into the Great Plains. By virtue of their contributions, women controlled the distribution of the food, the dwellings their labor had built, and all the products of their labor.

Living under a system of bilateral kinship, not bound to a specific husband by economic dependency or a code of sexual passivity, women, in the words of one horrified missionary, could "think it nothing more than fun to steal a man."[8] Indeed, a fluid notion of gender identity enabled some men and women to assume the activities

[4] Barbara Rogers, *The Domestication of Women: Discrimination in Developing Societies* (New York, 1979), p. 38; and *Women's Work: Development and the Division of Labor by Gender*, ed. Eleanor Leacock and Helen I. Safa (South Hadley, Mass., 1986).

[5] Thomas J. Morgan, Commissioner of Indian Affairs, Report of October 1, 1889, in *House Executive Document*, vol. 2, 51st Cong., 1st sess., serial 2725, quoted in Prucha, *Americanizing the American Indians*, p. 75.

[6] Merrill E. Gates, quoted ibid., pp. 51–52.

[7] The research on which this essay is based was supported by the John Calhoun Smith Fund and the Faculty Seed Grant program of the University of Idaho.

[8] Judith Giniger, "Aboriginal Female Status and Autonomy on the Columbia Plateau" (M.A. thesis, Washington State University, 1977); and Michael C. Coleman, *Presbyterian Missionary Attitudes towards American Indians, 1837–1893* (Jackson, Miss.,

"customarily pursued" by the other sex.[9] In a society in which political institutions were little developed, wars were infrequent and small scale, and spiritual power could pass through female and male hands, gender relations differed markedly from those then existing in the Euroamerican societies that began to expand into the inland Pacific Northwest.[10]

Beginning in the 1830s, these peoples first began to encounter conscious agents of cultural transformation in the form of Presbyterian missionaries sent by the American Board of Foreign Missions.[11] Henry and Eliza Spalding traveled with the more famous Marcus and Narcissa Whitman to establish missionary stations among the Nez Perces and the Cayuses in 1836. The oral tradition of the Nez Perces held that "the real purpose of missionaries was to pacify those Nez Perce and others who opposed the movement of settlers into the northwest. . . . But we were not inclined to change our old way of life. . . . We felt that a man's status depended upon his ability as a hunter and fisherman and it was woman's work to gather berries and such."[12] Henry Spalding recalled that for the missionaries domestic training for women and farming for men was a major part of the campaign for elevating the condition of the natives. "Myself and my angel wife left the following as the fruits of these eleven short years: a school of 234 most enthusiastic learners . . . a large class of girls taught to spin and weave . . . patriarchal religion night and morning . . . filthy habits supplanted by cleanliness and decency. . . . We left the whole people happily at work on their little farms."[13] Through such efforts, the Spaldings and others sought to transform the sexual and economic traditions of their converts.[14]

1985), p. 85. See also Robert H. Ruby and John A. Brown, *The Spokane Indians: Children of the Sun* (Norman, Okla., 1970); Angelo Anastasio, "The Southern Plateau: An Ecological Analysis of Intergroup Relations," Laboratory of Anthropology, University of Idaho, Moscow, Idaho, 1975; David Haydn Chance, "Influences of the Hudson's Bay Company on the Native Cultures of the Colville District" (M.A. thesis, University of Idaho, 1973); and E. Jane Gay, *With the Nez Perces: Alice Fletcher in the Field, 1889–92*, ed. Federick E. Hoxie and Joan T. Mark (Lincoln, Nebr., 1981).

[9] Claude E. Schaeffer, "The Kutenai Female Berdache: Courier, Guide, Prophetess, and Warrior," *Ethnohistory*, 12, no. 3 (1965): 193–236.

[10] Verne F. Ray, "Cultural Relations in the Plateau of Northwestern America," *Southwest Museum Publications* 3 (1939): 1–154; Lucullus McWhorter Papers, Washington State University, Pullman, Wash.

[11] Clifford Merrill Drury, *First White Women over the Rockies*. 2 vols. (Glendale, Calif.; 1963), 1:213.

[12] Allen P. Slickpoo and Deward E. Walker, *Noon-Nee-Me-Poo* (*We, the Nez Perces*) (Lewiston, 1973), pp. 71–72.

[13] Henry S. Spalding, in *States Rights Democrat*, November 29, 1867.

[14] For a broader view of the missionary agenda, see Coleman, *Presbyterian Missionary Attitudes*; Eleanor Leacock, "Montagnais Women and the Jesuit Program for Colonization," and Diane Rothenberg, "The Mothers of the Nation: Seneca Resistance to

The Catholic missionaries who followed Protestants into the region in the 1840s concurred with the necessity of making Native American men into farmers and women into housewives. Perhaps following a peasant model of the family economy, they allowed more scope for women's involvement in productive work in the fields as well as the household. But both groups of missionaries agreed on the need to place power in male hands at the household and the band levels. Catholic priests preached to the Colvilles and the Coeur d'Alenes about the "'Christian' sense of female submission" to a population that contained too many "viragos," unwomanly women who aspired to be "absolute" masters of themselves and their actions. They praised as ideal the woman who "never neglected the care and ordering of her own house."[15] Sixty years later, their successors were still trying to teach female converts to "dress better, to put aside the blanket, and to make bread" so they would become "refined, talented, learned American ladies."[16]

Under President Ulysses S. Grant's "peace" policy, the Nez Perce reservation was briefly allocated to Catholic control, as were the Colvilles and Coeur d'Alenes. In the 1870s Sue and Kate McBeth, together with other Presbyterian missionaries, arrived to reclaim the Protestant missionary effort, continuing the lessons in proper gender relations. The McBeths insisted that the father and husband must assume "his proper place at the head of his family." They warned against the dangers of several families cohabiting in the same long house, emphasized the primacy of the conjugal unit over relations with other kin, attacked polygamy, easy divorce, "permissive" child rearing, and the "false ideas of dignity and labor" that kept men out of the fields and women out of their households. In the eyes of the missionaries, these women, descended from "generations of burden bearers," needed to learn "wifely duties and civilized ways," which would "shape and beautify their future."[17]

Quaker Intervention," in *Women and Colonization: Anthropological Perspectives,* ed. Mona Etienne and Eleanor Leacock (South Hadley, Mass., 1986), pp. 25–42, 63–87; Joan M. Jensen, "Native American Women and Agriculture: A Seneca Case Study," *Sex Roles* 3 (1977):423–41; Theda Perdue, "Southern Indians and the Cult of True Womanhood," in *The Web of Southern Social Relations: Women, Family, and Education,* ed. Walter J. Fraser, Jr., R. Frank Saunders, Jr., and Jon L. Wakelyn (Athens, Ga., 1985); and *The Hidden Half: Studies of Plains Indian Woman,* ed. Patricia Albers and Beatrice Medicine (Washington, D.C., 1983).

[15] Father Pierre DeSmet, "Louis Sighouin," *Coeur d'Alene Teepee,* April 1938.

[16] S. M. DeRougé to J. M. Johnson, Superintendent of the Colville Agency, February 25, 1915, Colville Agency, Central Agency Files, RG75/DC.

[17] Coleman, *Presbyterian Missionary Attitudes,* pp. 125, 94, 88; Allen C. Morrill and Eleanor Dunlap Morrill, *Out of the Blanket: The Story of Sue and Kate McBeth, Missionaries to the Nez Perces* (Moscow, Idaho, 1977), pp. 214, 278; *Women's Work for Women* 1 (July 1886): 146.

In the 1850s, the United States government arrived on the scene. Seeking to clear a path for white settlers and a future railway, Isaac Stevens, governor of Washington Territory, conducted a treaty council in 1855 among the Nez Perces, Cayuses, Palouses, Spokanes, and other groups. Stevens's treaty enunciated a political, economic, and sexual agenda. The "Great Father," the 1855 treaty declared, desired that "the men will be farmers and mechanics . . . like white men, you women and your daughters will then teach their children to spin and to weave, to sew and all the work of the house and lodges." To ensure that result, "We shall spend a certain amount . . . in breaking up [the land] and fencing your farms . . . in building houses . . . in cooking utensils for your houses."[18] The subsequent 1863 Nez Perce treaty took away Nez Perce territory but gave each male head twenty acres of land.[19] It was equally significant that both negotiations took place between male leaders, who disregarded women's claims to resources.

Government agents, now active on the newly established reservations, farmers appointed by the Bureau of Indian Affairs, missionaries, and teachers preached to the reservation inhabitants. Agents reported to the bureau headquarters in Washington, D.C., that fields were under cultivation in the 1870s and 1880s, especially praising the Coeur d'Alenes and the Nez Perces around Kamiah. Like the McBeth sisters, Catholic nuns placed girls "in the charge of the matron, seamstress, cook, and launderess" at the Coeur d'Alene school. Female missionaries, Catholic and Protestant alike, paid particular attention to training "helpless little Indian girls in rising up to the habits of our Christian women" and teaching them to wear "white women's dresses, cared for and worked for by their husbands."[20] The commissioner of Indian Affairs reinforced such efforts by insisting upon a sex-specific curriculum. An 1878 educational circular specified that boys were to be given instruction "in cultivating the farm and garden . . . to contribute to their own support" while girls were to be "taught all household industries such as breadmaking, plain cooking, cutting, making and mending garments for both sexes; the work of the dairy, and the proper care of their own homes."[21] Indian agents, agency

[18] The 1855 treaty quoted in Slickpoo and Walker, *Noon-Nee-Me-Poo,* pp. 92, 94. See also Alvin M. Josephy, Jr., "The Walla Walla Council of 1855," in *The Western American Indian,* ed. Richard N. Ellis (Lincoln, Nebr., 1972), pp. 2–22.

[19] C. H. Hale, Superintendent of Indian Affairs, Washington Territory, to Commissioner of Indian Affairs, June 30, 1863, and Oscar H. Lipps to Commissioner, November 18, 1925, both in Fort Lapwai Agency, RG 75/DC.

[20] Sister Amadeé, Superintendent, Providence of Mary Imaculetta, Coeur d'Alene Reservation, Idaho Territory, to S. D. Waters, U.S. Indian Agent, Colville Agency, July 23, 1884, Letters Received, Bureau of Indian Affairs, RG 75, National Archives, Seattle Branch (hereafter cited as RG75/Seattle); Coleman, *Missionary Attitudes,* p. 85.

[21] E. A. Hayt, Commissioner, Office of Indian Affairs, January 9, 1878, Educational

farmers, and field matrons received the orders to be implemented on the reservation and in the off-reservation boarding schools at Carlisle, Hampton, and Chemewa.

In the 1880s legislation was proposed to "help the Indians to become independent farmers and stockmen by making them individual land holders," loosen "the fatal tribal bonds," and open the way "for their entrance into citizenship."[22] A coalition composed of western congressmen and eastern Republicans, settlers, missionaries, former abolitionists, and others interested in the "Indian question" secured the passage in 1887 of the Land in Severalty Law, which was named the Dawes Act after the chairman of the Senate Indian Affairs Committee. After land was allotted to individual Native Americans, the rest of the reservation acreage would be opened to white settlement. According to Philip C. Garrett of the Indian Rights Association, the Dawes Act constituted an Indian Emancipation Proclamation that "will buy them life, manhood, civilization and Christianity, at the sacrifice of a few chieftain's feathers, a few worthless bits of parchment, the cohesion of the tribal relations, and the traditions of their race."[23] Each head of household would receive 160 acres, the ownership of which would teach Native American men to become independent, possessive individuals whose wives, denied property in their own names, would become dependent, domesticated beings.

Women missionaries, educators, reformers such as Amelia Quinton, and the feminist anthropologist Alice Fletcher played an important part in the deliberations and the lobbying that led to the enactment of the Dawes Act and the shift in gender relations it entailed. Under the auspices of Quinton's Women's National Indian Association, in which Fletcher was active, women encouraged the passage of the Dawes Act. Believing, as Sara T. Kinney, the head of the Connecticut branch, put it, in "one roof sheltering father and mother and their children secure in the sharing and inheritance of property," the association sent Native American couples to be educated jointly at Hampton, built model houses on reservations, and missionaries equipped with domestic knowledge to reservations. Quinton described the association's work as fulfilling women's divinely appointed role as "mother," "growth-nourisher," and "love parent".[24] Like many other women reformers of

---

Circular No. 3, Colville Agency, Letters Received—Commissioner, 1865–78, Box 4, RG75/Seattle.

[22] Indian Rights Association, *Fourth Annual Report* (Philadelphia, 1887), p. 9, Indian Rights Association Papers, Historical Society of Pennsylvania, Philadelphia.

[23] Francis Paul Prucha, *Indian Policy in the United States: Historical Essays* (Lincoln, Nebr., 1981), p. 240.

[24] See Helen M. Wanken, " 'Woman's Sphere' and Indian Reform: The Women's National Indian Association, 1879–1901" (Ph.D. diss., Marquette University, 1981).

the late nineteenth century, these women justified their activism in the public realm on the basis of the special qualities they had acquired through their location in the private world of home, family, and motherhood. Indeed, they rejected any more active role in bringing women into the public realm by refusing to endorse suffrage or temperance. They welcomed the opportunity to insert Native American women into the same divinely ordained division between public and private that they honored as an ideal but violated in practice.

Although most of the members of the Women's National Indian Association refused to recognize any conflict between their ideals of female domesticity and their activities, Alice Fletcher could not. Her organizational activities and her efforts to open anthropology as a career for women placed her among those committed to women's emancipation from the exclusively domestic realm. As an organizer of the Association for the Advancement of Women in the 1870s, Fletcher, like Quinton, participated in the 1888 founding conference of the International Council of Women. Predictably, Fletcher's remarks expressed doubts about the benefits Native American women would receive from enclosure in an exclusively private, dependent domestic space. Introduced to the conference by Susan B. Anthony, Fletcher noted that the Native American woman was "free to choose her husband if she so desires" and "independent in the use of her possessions." She described her own dilemma at having to "explain to Indian women their legal conditions under the law" in her duties as allotting agent on the Omaha and Winnebago reservations. Her task had led to her to "realize how much woman has given of her own freedom to make strong the foundations of the family and to preserve the accumulations and descent of property in order that the pressure of want should be removed." After reassuring her listeners that women's sacrifices were necessary for "the development of civilization," she told them, "I crave for my Indian sisters your help, your patience, and unfailing labors, to hasten the day when the laws of all the land shall know neither male nor female, but grant to all equal rights and equal justice."[25] Evidently her belief in the evolutionary necessity of her task did not allow her to submerge completely her feminist doubts concerning the costs of the civilization she was helping to impose on her "Indian sisters."

Only a year after her debate with Quinton, Fletcher journeyed to the Nez Perce reservation to undertake her third assignment from the Bureau of Indian Affairs to allot a reservation. From 1889 to 1892 she determinedly persisted in the work of allotting agent issuing individual titles to the land under the terms of the Dawes Act. She disregarded

[25] *Women's Tribune,* March 31, 1888.

the opposition from the Nez Perces, who could "hear in the near future the tramp-tramp-tramp of the incoming whites on the homeland." On the reservation she joined forces with missionary Kate McBeth, whose pupils were more receptive to Fletcher's goals than the "heathen" Nez Perces. Like McBeth, Fletcher believed that "citizenship and Christianity should go hand in hand" with individual land title.[26] In an 1895 letter to the Women's National Indian Association, Fletcher praised the association's work and gave a justification for her own activities: "We cannot stop the rush that is engulfing the Indians, but . . . we shall help and save hundreds of struggling individuals in the future."[27] Despite the cost to women, Fletcher remained convinced that she was ameliorating the worst effects of an inevitable process. Even women sensitive to the "woman question" believed that Native Americans must become "like white folks."

Fletcher's feminism, however, may have motivated her to support the campaign to amend the Dawes Act to give "80 acres to every man, woman, & child, irrespective of age or relation."[28] Like her male allies, she saw women's ownership of land as protection "so that she cannot be put away by her husband landless," but she did not question the somewhat antifeminist assumptions also present in the proposed change in policy desired by the Indian Rights Association. Even as land was being allocated to "each Indian," provision was being made for "the leasing of Indians lands when, for any reason, the allottee is unable to cultivate *his or her* allotment."[29] At the same time, she encouraged the establishment of an all-male governing committee among the Nez Perces when they ceded 542,000 unallotted acres to the U.S. government in 1893. Nez Perce women received some land because of the change in the Dawes Act, but they lost far more in the cession and subsequent "opening" of the reservation, which took place without their consent.[30]

Lacking Fletcher's appreciation for women's position in aboriginal society, reformers and federal officials deliberately formulated Indian policy with little regard to its consequences for Native American women who might actually wish to become farmers. Even though they received land under the revised Dawes Act, women were to be provided instruction only in household duties. Agricultural extension

[26] Kate McBeth, *The Nez Perces since Lewis and Clark* (New York, 1908), p. 185.

[27] Alice Fletcher to Women's National Indian Association, November 20, 1895, in "The Indian's Friend" Alice Fletcher–Francis LaFlesche Papers, National Anthropological Archives, Smithsonian Institution, Washington, D.C.

[28] Alice Fletcher, Fort Lapwai, Idaho, Gen. T. J. Morgan, Commissioner of Indian Affairs, May 26, 1890, Fletcher-LeFlesche Papers.

[29] Indian Rights Association, *Eighth Annual Report* (Philadelphia, 1891), pp. 9–10; emphasis added.

[30] Slickpoo and Walker, *Noon-Nee-Me-Poo*, p. 224.

agents directed their efforts to men while field matrons and home economics specialists, where available, served a female clientele. They insisted that Native Americans undertake the risks of small farm agriculture at a time when white farmers were struggling to survive. Having denied women the education and skills necessary for farming, they proceeded to define women as unable to farm. In drawing up regulations "relating to the Indians and Their Lands," Oscar Lipps, the chief official of the Northern Idaho Agency, included among those too disabled to cultivate their own land "unmarried women," "widows who have no sons of suitable age," and "all married women whose husbands and sons are not in a condition to cultivate." Only adult males were defined as "able-bodied."[31] As a consequence, land owned by women readily passed into white hands. Administrators condemned the backwardness of Native Americans as the major reason for their failure to become self-supporting agriculturalists and housewives, yet their own policies reflected a rigid adherence to gender ideology that limited the possibility of success.

By the 1910s evidence began to accumulate about the failures of the policies pursued since the 1880s. Native Americans in the inland Pacific Northwest had neither become enthusiastic farmers nor abandoned their traditional subsistence practices. Rather than achieving self-sufficiency, the Coeur d'Alenes had become dependent on "easy" money acquired through the land leasing system.[32] The Colvilles petitioned the commissioner of Indian affairs against opening the southern half of their reservation until "the older people have passed way" because "the older people can not be made over. They remain as the Great Spirit made us and can not change."[33] Two years later, Corbett Lawyer reported that only 967 allotments remained in Nez Perce hands out of the 2,009 issued by Alice Fletcher thirty years earlier. "Practically the entire tribe depends largely on rentals. . . . The Nez Perce reservation is for all practical purposes a white man's country." Home and Farm associations were instituted among the Nez Perces and the Coeur d'Alenes to put men into the fields and "get the women interested in home improvement," but the organizations languished.[34] The annual report of the chief official for the Northern Idaho Agency in 1928 reported that the Nez Perces "are in the main a

[31] Oscar H. Lipps, "Laws and Regulations Relating to the Indians and Their Lands" (Lewiston, Idaho, 1913), pp. 44.

[32] M. D. Colgrove to Arthur C. Parker, Secretary-Treasurer of the Society of American Indians, May 19, 1915, Coeur d'Alene Agency, Central Agency Files, RG75/DC.

[33] Jim Harris et al. to Honorable Commissioner of Indian Affairs, January 19, 1915, Colville Agency, ibid.

[34] *Indian Leader* 1924; Nez Perce Home and Farm Association, "Declaration of Purpose and Program," Slickpoo and Walker, *Noon-Nee-me-poo*, pp. 243–51; Couer D'Alene Home and Farm Association, Central Agency Files, Coeur d'Alene Agency, RG75/DC.

race of landlords whose personal agricultural activities are limited to the raising of a garden" and who knew "by bitter experience that large farming is a hazardous financial occupation." He also reported that the women "seem to delight to steal each others' husbands" and the "nomadic spirit inbred for generations" was "one of the chief obstacles to the building up of a stable standard home life among our people."[35] By the late 1920s agricultural statistics revealed that the Nez Perces, Coeur d'Alenes, and Colvilles were farming fewer acres than they had cultivated before the allotment.

Because of this evidence, a report by Lewis Meriam to the Secretary of the Interior recommended that the Bureau of Indian Affairs shift from promoting commercial to "subsistence farming for the support of Indian families." But according to the report, the ideal remained a "permanent home for every Indian family, supported, in the main, by the earnings of the husband" to restore "the balance in the division of labor between men and women." Women should not become "the sole or chief dependence of the family." The report also criticized women's "quests for vegetable foods" and the tendency to continue to follow the "care-free camp life existence." But it did acknowledge the failure to educate women in "directly productive work," which "plays an exceedingly important part in successful subsistence farming."[36] Thus the report advised that the previous policy be continued while recognizing the necessity for women to assume some productive tasks on the family farm.

When John Collier, an advocate of "cultural pluralism" instead of cultural assimilation, became commissioner of Indian affairs in 1933, his guarantee of "religious and social freedom" made no specific reference to women.[37] Denouncing the Dawes Act, he wrote, "The so-called individualization policy was pressed beyond the negative outlawing of tribal institutions to the attempted summary transformation of the individual Indian. He was to be made, as an individual and at once, into a white man." Collier criticized the only provision of the revised act that had responded to feminist concerns—the granting of land to individuals rather than to the male heads of households—as "a blow not only at tribal unity but at the family unity. Parcels of land went to individual Indians only." Native American women were not included among his major advisers. Although the constitutions that were drawn up under Collier's Indian Reorganization Act included woman suffrage, their policies concerning land and resources often

[35] O. C. Upchurch, "Review of the Report of the Committee from the Institute for Governmental Research," Northern Idaho Agency, RG 75/Seattle.

[36] Lewis Meriam et al., *The Problem of Indian Administration* (Baltimore, 1928), pp. 490–91, 523, 530, 499.

[37] Kenneth R. Philp, *John Collier's Crusade for Indian Reform, 1920–1954* (Tucson, 1981), pp. 46–47.

placed ownership in the hands of male household heads. Collier's director of Indian education reorganized the curriculum to teach girls some farming skills, but the Bureau of Indian Affairs continued to emphasize women's primary role as domestic. Like other New Deal agencies, it placed the need to restore men's jobs and men's place in the economy before any feminist concerns about women's economic independence.[38]

Skeptical of government promises because of past experience, Native Americans in the Inland Northwest expressed little enthusiasm for Collier's "Indian New Deal." All the major groups voted against a return to self-government under the terms of the Indian Reorganization Act of 1934. The Nez Perce Tribal Business Committee spoke for those who had followed the path of Christianity and citizenship, telling Collier, "We object most strenuously to the taking away of our independence to control our own affairs and transact our own business. . . . We object because we do not think your plan is workable. Now it is only an untried experiment. Should it fail, the situation will be worse . . . for we would neither have land nor money."[39] The Coeur d'Alenes sent a Christmas card to Collier complaining about "outsiders who are trying to run our business and tell us how to run our place."[40] The Native Americans' doubts about the benefits to be expected from Collier's reforms were reinforced by the inadequate resources that Collier was able to draw upon to support his approach. New Deal and congressional priorities placed the needs of Native Americans behind other goals. Within the Department of the Interior more powerful agencies successfully pressed for the erection of dams along the Columbia River that would flood Native American lands and interrupt the salmon runs.[41] The Indian New Deal could not restore the economic resources essential to the cultural autonomy it promised and the sexual autonomy it did not.

As the Indian New Deal gave way to efforts to terminate the tribal and reservation system, the actions of men and women among the Coeur d'Alenes, the Colvilles, and the Nez Perces determined the extent to which the sexes conformed to the official policy of female exclusion from productive and public activities. Already by the 1910s there was

[38] See Alison Bernstein, "A Mixed Record: The Political Enfranchisement of American Indian Women during the New Deal," *Journal of the West*, 13–20.

[39] Nez Perce Tribal Business Committee to John Collier, February 8, 1934, enclosed with letter from Mary Crawford, McBeth Mission, to Senator William Borah, March 16, 1934, who also reported opposition from the Nespelem, Coeur d'Alenes, and Spokanes, in William J. Borah Papers, Library of Congress.

[40] Ernest Williams et al. to John Collier, December 1937, Coeur d'Alene Agency, Central Agency Files, RG75/DC.

[41] Archie Phinney, "The Nez Perces of Idaho," February 26, 1932, submitted to Honorable Charles J. Rhoads, Commissioner of Indian Affairs, Central Agency Files, Fort Lapwai Agency, RG 75/DC.

evidence that women had not left the arena of public decision making entirely to men. Petitions from the Coeur d'Alenes, the Nez Perces, and the Colvilles to the Bureau of Indian Affairs carried female and male names. According to the *Lewiston Tribune,* four Nez Perce women, including "one of the famous Joseph band," "made eloquent appeals for temperance from a mother's standpoint" in what was "probably the first meeting of its kind in which women have spoken."[42] By the late 1920s Nez Perce women from the Joseph band were submitting testimony "in support of the claims of Chief Joseph's Band of the Nez Perce Indians" for the land from which they had been expelled in the 1870s.[43] At the 1934 northwestern conference to discuss the Indian Reorganization Act, Christine Galler told the assembled delegates, "I am a woman and you might think it funny that the Colvilles elect a woman . . . but the capacity of an Indian woman's head has the same amount as a man or a white man."[44] Almost half the signators to the Coeur d'Alene petition to President Franklin D. Roosevelt in 1936 asking him "to protect our natural rights as the aborigines of this continent to hunt and fish in and outside of the reservation" were women.[45] Clearly, women would not leave the task of defending their community's interests solely to men.

In addition to contributing to the ongoing struggle to restore the territory essential to their traditional subsistence practices, women continued to "go on digging parties, sometimes bringing along the entire household," to engage in trade in the products of women's work, and to participate in religious ceremonies that celebrated their skills.[46] Mary Moses, widow of Chief Moses of the Columbias on the Colville reservation, carefully instructed her granddaughter Lucy. She taught her to "take land before you ever take money" and not to "fall in line with the white peoples' demands that we should blend in with civilized people."[47] Even into the 1980s women passed "the power down from generation to generation" that came from sustaining a traditional relationship to the land.[48]

[42] *Lewiston Tribune,* July 12, 1912.

[43] General Council minutes, August 26, 1927, Fort Lapwai Agency, General Classified Files, RG75/Seattle.

[44] "Proceedings of the Conference at Chemewa, Oregon, 8–9 April 1934, to Discuss with the Indians the Howard-Wheeler Bill," in Borah Papers.

[45] Louie Sam et al. to the President, November 19, 1936, Fort Lapwai Agency, Central Classified Files, RG75/DC.

[46] Lucy Jane Harbinger, "The Importance of Food Plants in the Maintenance of Nez Perce Cultural Identity" (M.A. thesis, Washington State University, 1969), pp. 25, 44; Lucullus Virgil McWhorter to Mrs. Hedge, 1935, McWhorter Papers, Washington State University, Pullman, Wash.

[47] *Lucy Covington: Native American Indian,* 1978, Encyclopedia Britannica Educational Film, American Character Series.

[48] Leah Talalippinmy Slaney, "The Effects of Supernatural Forces on Nez Perce Life," unpublished paper in possession of the author.

By the 1930s women began to occupy formal political office in the tribal governments and in the larger organizations Native Americans formed to defend their interests. Christine Galler was the first. Lena Luie served as secretary for the Coeur d'Alene Tribal Council. Women also worked in movements in opposition to tribal governments. The Nez Perce "warriors" faction, formed in 1950 to organize war dances and challenge the constitution imposed by the Bureau of Indian Affairs, included women as well as men. At the national level, the Nez Perces, Columbias, and Coeur d'Alenes played an active part in the campaign sponsored by the National Congress of American Indians against termination of reservations, and increasing numbers of women were elected to the Colville Tribal Business Council and the Nez Perce Tribal Executive Committee.[49] Lucy Covington, granddaughter of Mary Moses, campaigned against termination, insisting that her people should never give their "eagle feather away" by allowing their tribal organization and territory to be abolished.[50] In 1980s, female political activism increased. Jeannie Givens of the Coeur d'Alenes was elected to the Idaho state legislature and ran as the unsuccessful Democratic nominee for the U.S. Congress in the 1988 election. The women of the Nez Perces, Coeur d'Alenes, and Colville confederated tribes actively defended their cultural traditions and economic resources through the skillful use of political power in the "white man's" arena as well as their own.

In this frontier, as in many other times and places, the meeting of Native American and Euroamerican cultures inescapably involved issues of gender as well as economics, politics, and ethnicity. Commissioner Thomas J. Morgan had decreed: "The tribal relations should be broken up, socialism destroyed, and the family and the autonomy of the individual substituted."[51] As the colonizers recognized, gender identities together with control over resources were essential to the maintenance or transformation of ethnic communities. Imposing a split between men and women that corresponded to a separation between the public arena of the autonomous, competitive, possessive individual and the private, selfless world of familial domesticity was as essential to the colonizing process as it was to the organization of the expanding nation-state and its market-oriented economy. By eliminating alternatives to the sexual and political economy that dominated their own society, the colonizers simultaneously facilitated its

[49] National Congress of American Indian Papers, National Anthropological Archives, Smithsonian Museum of Natural History, Washington, D.C.; Peter Maurice Well, "Political Modernization on the Nez Perce Indian Reservation, 1940–1963" (M.A. thesis, University of Oregon, 1965).

[50] *Lucy Covington, Native American Indian.*

[51] Thomas J. Morgan, "Report of 1 October 1889," quoted in Prucha, *Americanizing the American Indians*, p. 75.

expansion and attempted to deprive its feminist and socialist critics of subversive examples that might suggest that those arrangements could and should be changed.[52]

Resisting a civilization that sought "to tame and domesticate wild Indians," the Nez Perces, Cayuses, Coeur d'Alenes, Colvilles, Columbias, and other Native Americans of the inland Pacific Northwest continued to exist as distinct peoples. Their women refused to be domesticated.[53] Their success in sustaining a distinct ethnic and gender pattern was, of course, only partial. But their example provides yet another demonstration of the ability of women to determine for themselves the meaning of womanhood. These women, like the female reformers, never acted as powerless, domestic beings isolated within the private world of the home and family.

[52] Among these "subversive" critics might be included Lydia Maria Child, Elizabeth Cady Stanton, Matilda Joslyn Gage, Alice Fletcher, and Friederich Engels, who drew inspiration from their study of Native American women to support their feminist and, in Engels's case, socialist programs. See, for example, Fletcher's article in *Women's Tribune,* August 3, 1901, in which she criticizes the "domination" the Indian woman faced "if she be married" and the effects of the "crude teaching that evil and sin came to the race solely through woman," supported by "the white man's authority backed by the unseen hand of the law."

[53] The phrase comes from the "Report of the Commissioner of Indian Affairs, 24 October 1881," U.S. House of Representatives, *Executive Documents,* 47th Cong., 1st sess., 1881–82, p. 1.

PART III

CONTRADICTIONS OF SOCIAL WELFARE

CHAPTER ELEVEN

Women in the Public Sphere in Early Modern England: The Case of the Urban Working Poor

Diane Willen

I

In August 1553, the treasurer of Christ's Hospital in London recorded an expenditure of 12*d.* for outdoor relief, "Paid in rewarde to a poore woman for takinge paynes with a verie syck person."[1] Local officials had every reason to be satisfied with such an arrangement because it provided public relief at minimum cost. Unfortunately, the sources tell no more about the individuals involved than that one, "verie syck," was a recipient of medical poor relief and the other, "a poore woman," earned her own relief through her services as a nurse. The episode would be unremarkable were it not symptomatic of English social policy in an important aspect of its treatment of pauper women during the years 1550–1700.

Such social policy required and reflected a close relationship between local patriarchal political authorities and the women of the working poor who lived under their jurisdiction. It questions or at least severely qualifies the idea that separate private/public spheres existed in the early modern period. Joan Kelly, in a series of influential articles, has established a very different conceptual model. Kelly argues that "a new division between personal and public life made itself

This essay originally appeared in the *Sixteenth Century Journal* 19 (Winter 1988): 559–79. I wish to thank the publisher for permission to publish this revised version. I am grateful to Barbara Harris, Marjorie McIntosh, Sherrin Marshall, Ronald Berger, Esther Cope, and Merry Wiesner for their comments on early versions of the essay.

[1] Guildhall Library (hereafter cited as GL), MS 12819/1, fol. 33v.

felt as the state came to organize Renaissance society."[2] Recognizing that the meaning of domestic varies in different cultures and not discriminating between the personal, the domestic, or the familial, Kelly asserts that "where familial activities coincided with public or social ones, the status of women is comparable or even superior to that of men." Conversely, the greater the differentiation between private, domestic roles and public roles, the more restricted are the status and activities of women. She attributes change in status, that is, increased separation between the two spheres, in some instances to economic shifts (the end of subsistence production) and in other instances to a political shift (the consolidation and centralization of public authority). Although she does not clearly distinguish between economic and political change, she nevertheless identifies the early modern period as a time of crucial transition.[3]

Increasingly, however, historians of early modern England are challenging the relevance of this model to Tudor and Stuart society. Women's involvement at court, in religious change, in the household economy, in service occupations, in poor relief, even in the family cannot be understood in terms of a separate domestic sphere of activity. In intellectual, political, religious, and economic terms, the early modern English family was integral to society and state.[4] This essay examines social policy and women, especially women among the working poor: women who were menial laborers, recipients of poor relief, caretakers, nurses, and teachers, employees in both the private and public spheres. It argues that a paternalistic social policy confounded the private with the public sphere at the very time that the state assumed new functions and women remained excluded from public office.

II

Throughout the sixteenth and seventeenth centuries, the English state did not hesitate to interfere or intrude itself into affairs which modern society would categorize as private matters. In the early modern context, however, the individual was so integral a part of a larger organic community that his or her private life was deemed to have public consequence. Religion provides one clear example. As long as

[2] Joan Kelly, *Women, History, and Theory* (Chicago, 1984), p. 47.

[3] Ibid., pp. 10–12.

[4] See Susan D. Amussen, *An Ordered Society: Gender and Class in Early Modern England* (Oxford, 1988). For other scholarship, see the original version of this essay, *Sixteenth Century Journal* 19 (Winter 1988): 560 n. 4. This essay focuses on the working poor, but when court, religion, and the household economy are considered, the public/private dichotomy loses validity for other social classes as well.

the state placed a high priority on religious conformity and the men who controlled the machinery of church and state saw in religious pluralism a threat to social and political stability, religious worship could not become a private matter relegated to a separate sphere. The religious practices of both recusants (Catholic dissenters) and sectarians (Protestant nonconformists) were perceived as legitimate matters of public concern for the body politic.[5]

As in religious matters, so too in economic affairs, the state pursued intrusive, paternalistic policies. On the local level, urban authorities, anxious to minimize the numbers on relief rolls, frequently intervened to mitigate the poverty of women while at the same time reinforcing women's economic dependency. Although they protected the employment rights of widows, city fathers prohibited single women from living on their own, assuming they would come to no good. Single women posed an economic threat because their illegitimate children would likely need the support of the community. Moreover, as "masterless" women without a household, they represented a threat to the patriarchal social order.[6] Time and again, the mayoralty court of Norwich ordered a female "lyvinge idely at her own hand" either to be retained in service, usually within a fortnight, or be committed to Bridewell, where work would be provided for her.[7] In arbitrating disputes between masters and servants, the court showed paternalistic tendencies that might benefit an individual female but were intended to serve the economic interests of the greater community by keeping her off public relief.[8] The Norwich court also intervened to ensure that husbands, whether in legitimate service or in Bridewell, contributed to the support of their families. In the majority of such cases, the employer paid a portion of a man's wage directly to his wife; in one case, city fathers went so far as to require an employer "to pay wekely into this court" to guarantee a specific sum for the employee's wife and children.[9]

Notwithstanding such precautions, women more easily than men earned the dubious distinction of "deserving poor" and often predominated on the rolls of relief recipients. When the towns of Warwick, Salisbury, Ipswich, and Norwich drew up surveys or censuses of the

[5] Diane Willen, "Women and Religion in Early Modern England," in *Women in Reformation and Counter-Reformation Europe: Private and Public Worlds*, ed. Sherrin Marshall (Bloomington, 1989), p. 154 and passim.

[6] Merry E. Wiesner, *Working Women in Renaissance Germany* (New Brunswick, 1986), pp. 191–92, 187, 237 n. 1.

[7] Norfolk and Norwich Record Office (hereafter cited as NNRO), D. 16a, no. 14, fol. 4v; no. 15, fols. 19v, 208r, 396v; D. 16b, no. 25, fol. 2.

[8] For example, the mayoralty court ordered a master to retain a pregnant servant because he had not fulfilled his obligation to provide her with proper housing (NNRO, D. 16a, no. 15, fol. 166r. Cf. fol. 37r).

[9] NNRO, D. 16a, no. 15, fol. 73r.

poor to facilitate the implementation of poor relief, women formed the majority of their indigent populations. In the Warwick census of 1587 women outnumbered men two to one, although in the general population women would have been only barely in the majority.[10] In the Salisbury census of 1625, which listed "the irreducible minimum of the poor," two-thirds of the adults were women.[11] The Norwich census of 1570, the most comprehensive of those that survive, included 860 women to 525 men; of 926 children in the census, 171 belonged to female heads of household.[12]

Censuses sometimes included the underemployed and the marginally poor, whereas records of hospitals focus on the neediest and the most dependent of the poor. Here, in cases of indoor relief, women's predominance is even more striking.[13] Moreover, in some instances, special forms of relief were given to women, usually widows. Evidence suggests that York may have provided subsidized housing for poor widows during the sixteenth century, and in the seventeenth century, when eight hospitals or almshouses were newly endowed or rebuilt in the city, at least four were reserved for widows. Other towns show comparable patterns.[14]

Reasons for the disproportionate number of females among the poor are not difficult to find. Because of family responsibilities women frequently could only work part time, and they usually worked in the lowest-paid occupations: in the Norwich census, 76 percent of the women were engaged in spinning.[15] The death of the male head of household and the subsequent destruction of the household economy

[10] A. L. Beier, "The Social Problems of an Elizabethan Country Town: Warwick, 1580–90," in *County Towns in Pre-Industrial England*, ed. Peter Clark (New York, 1981), p. 60. Marjorie McIntosh has pointed out to me that the sex distribution of early modern English towns was weighted toward women although not to the degree that women predominated in relief rolls. See Marjorie McIntosh, "Servants and the Household Unit in an Elizabethan Community," *Journal of Family History* 9 (Spring 1984): 9.

[11] Paul Slack, "Poverty and Politics in Salisbury, 1597–1666," in *Crisis and Order in English Towns, 1500–1700*, ed. Peter Clark and Paul Slack (Toronto, 1972), p. 166.

[12] John Pound, *The Norwich Census of the Poor*, Norfolk Record Society (hereafter cited as NRS), 40 (1971): 7ff. In Ipswich in 1597, the census recorded 118 adult female to 68 males. See John Webb, *Poor Relief in Elizabethan Ipswich*, Suffolk Record Society, 9 (1966): 19–22; and Carole Moore, "Poor Relief In Elizabethan England: A New Look at Ipswich," *Proceedings and Papers of the Georgia Association of Historians* 7 (1986): 108–9.

[13] York City Archives (hereafter cited as YCA), B. 25, fol. 134v; E. 66, fols. 138–39; Angelo Raine, ed., *York Civic Records*, Yorkshire Archaeological Society (hereafter cited as YAS), 115 (1949): 93.

[14] YCA, E. 76; G. 36; R. B. Rose, "Charities," and G. C. G. Forster, "York in the Seventeenth Century," in *A History of Yorkshire: The City of York*, ed. P. M. Tillot, *Victoria History of the Counties of England* (London, 1961), pp. 422–24, 170.

[15] Pound, *Norwich Census of the Poor*, NRS, 40: 16, 99. Eighty-five percent of the indigent women were employed, often in more than one occupation, but did not earn enough to escape poverty; only 66 percent of the men were employed.

could thus prove catastrophic to surviving family members.[16] Moreover, indigent males were more likely than their female counterparts to migrate, and the wives, sisters, and daughters they left behind were easily reduced to economic dependency as the resident poor.[17] Finally, surviving surveys of the poor disproportionately represent the elderly, especially the female elderly, and it has been speculated that women may have outlived males in early modern England. In Norwich, women constituted 63 percent of the indigent population over age fifty.[18]

Do the preindustrial towns of England provide early examples of the "feminization of poverty"? The term has usually been applied to industrial societies in which females constitute the majority of clients in social insurance and welfare programs.[19] It is tempting to conclude that the phenomenon also applies to the early modern period, when women's economic vulnerability and dependency meant that they benefited in disproportionate numbers from public poor relief. Yet, having established the large predominance of female paupers, we must qualify the picture.

Social, economic, and demographic trends converged in the sixteenth century to make poverty and the accompanying threat of social disorder a frightening and intractable problem for local authorities. The population grew rapidly, and this increase, coupled with debasement of the coinage and the influx of gold from the New World, stimulated sharp inflation. Both the price of grain and the number of the poor rose dramatically. Concurrently, the Reformation, initiated in the 1530s, undermined traditional methods for dispensing charity because the state secularized hospitals and dissolved the monasteries. As a consequence of such changes, poverty in early modern England was a more general phenomenon than urban authorities could afford to address. Scarcity of resources even more than moral disapprobation enforced a narrow definition that focused on women, the elderly, and children. A broader and no doubt more realistic definition of the poor would have accorded greater recognition to the mass of able-bodied unemployed males, many of whom became vagrants. Indeed, in times of

[16] Tim Wales, "Poverty, Poor Relief and the Life-Cycle: Some Evidence from Seventeenth-Century Norfolk," in *Land, Kinship, and Life Cycle*, ed. Richard M. Smith (Cambridge, Eng., 1984), p. 378.

[17] A. L. Beier, "Social Problems in Elizabethan London," *Journal of Interdisciplinary History* 9 (Autumn, 1978): 209: A. L. Beier, *Masterless Men: The Vagrancy Problem in England, 1560–1640* (London, 1985), p. 52.

[18] Margaret Pelling, "Old People and Poverty in Early Modern Towns," *Society for the Social History of Medicine Bulletin* 34 (June 1984): 43–46.

[19] Barbara J. Nelson, "Women's Poverty and Women's Citizenship: Some Political Consequences of Economic Marginality," *Signs* 10 (Winter 1984): 210. The term has also been applied to colonial America; see Mimi Abramovitz, "The Family Ethic: The Female Pauper and Public Aid, Pre-1900," *Social Service Review* 59 (March 1985): 124.

economic crisis, local authorities admitted the inconsistency of their position by granting temporary ad hoc outdoor relief to able-bodied unemployed males.[20] Male paupers existed but were more mobile than females, less constrained by children, and perhaps less likely to live into old age. The concept of a "deserving poor" therefore created its own gender bias and resulted in gender differentiation in social policy.[21]

Authorities assumed that whenever possible poor relief would serve as a supplement to other income and that even the deserving poor would contribute to their own subsistence.[22] The Norwich census indicates that many indigent children and women, including elderly and lame women, were expected to work. Over a century later, in 1681, Thomas Firmin, a London philanthropist and social reformer, advocated that women and children be taught vocational skills to root out the idleness and vice associated with poverty. The adequate training of children would prevent their poverty in adulthood. Firmin expected women to supervise and teach the children. An "able and honest" woman might instruct forty children in a workhouse to read and to spin in return for the annual salary of £40. For adults, especially women, he preferred work at home over the workhouse: "For suppose a Woman hath a sick Child, or Husband, or some Infirmity upon her self, in all which cases, she may do something at home, but cannot leave her House." Women's participation in a work scheme, then, would reinforce rather than disrupt the family unit. Firmin assured his readers that either a man or woman could easily oversee the project, for little skill would be required to purchase the stock, deliver goods, and keep accounts.[23]

Firmin wrote at the end of the period under study here, but his proposal to employ women to supervise the poor represented no radical departure. For over a century, sometimes on their own initiative, sometimes in response to national legislation, local urban authorities had established various public relief programs to cope with the immigration and concentration of the poor in their towns. Frequently they used female as well as male personnel. Indeed, female participation in the administration of English public relief demonstrates how early

[20] Slack, "Poverty and Politics in Salisbury," pp. 175–77. For ad hoc relief in which males predominated, see YCA, B. 33. fols. 102–47v (1608), fols. 191v–228r (1610), fols. 280v–328v (1612).

[21] For a discussion of gender differentiation in modern social policy, see Virginia Sapiro, "The Gender Basis of American Social Policy," *Political Science Quarterly* 101 (1986): 221–38.

[22] I am grateful to Professor McIntosh for discussing this issue with me. See Marjorie K. McIntosh, "Local Responses to the Poor in Late Medieval and Tudor England," *Continuity and Change* 3 (1988): 211.

[23] T[homas] F[irmin], *Some Proposals for the Imploing of the Poor* ([London], 1681), pp. 9, 11, 17.

women began to provide welfare services and, despite Firmin's concern about the family unit, how women intervened in the public sphere. Many of them came from the ranks of the working poor, earning during the Elizabethan and early Stuart period weekly salaries as low as 10*d.*[24] Their economic status varied, however, and cannot be categorically established. In general, female medical practitioners and hospital keepers enjoyed greater social status and economic compensation than did nurses and those who supervised children. The extent of female participation in public relief can be appreciated by looking first at women's responsibilities in the custody, education, and employment of children, then at their work in nursing, medicine, and hospitals.

Both national legislation and local initiatives demonstrated the intent to train and employ pauper children. Like so much of poor relief, these programs reflected genuine moral concerns as well as inescapable fiscal realities: if children would stop begging and instead learn a productive trade, both individual children and the community at large would benefit.[25] The Elizabethan statutes of 1597 and 1601 stipulated that when parents were unable to maintain their children, parish overseers were either to set such children to work or enroll them in pauper apprenticeships, and throughout the seventeenth century, apprenticeships remained the most common method of disposing of pauper children aged seven or older. Only in a minority of cases did parish authorities entrust women with responsibility for such apprentices, a reflection of the relatively small percentage of women in guilds.[26] Notwithstanding this important qualification, women provided care and training of youths through service in children's hospitals, supervision of child-employment schemes, and foster care in their own homes.

Christ's Hospital in London made the most ambitious attempt to address the problem of poor orphan children. One of the five great royal hospitals founded in the wake of the monastic dissolution, Christ's Hospital opened its doors in 1553 to 380 children, 100 of whom were under the age of four.[27] The latter were put out to nurse in nearby counties for the rate of 10*d.* per week. At first, wet nurses performed their service in their own homes, but eventually the hospital acquired

[24] In the census for Salisbury, the average weekly wage for poor men was 1*s.*2*d.*; in Ipswich, it was 2*s.* The comparable weekly wage for a woman or child was 8*d.* or 9*d.* (Paul Slack, *Poverty and Policy in Tudor and Stuart England* [London, 1988], pp. 82–83).

[25] Ivy Pinchbeck and Margaret Hewitt, *Children in English Society,* 2 vols. (London, 1969), 1:91–92. See also Stephen M. Macfarlane, "Studies in Poverty and Poor Relief in London at the End of the Seventeenth Century" (Ph.D. diss., Oxford University, 1982), pp. 157ff.

[26] 39 Eliz., c. 3, 43 Eliz., c. 2.; Diane Willen, "York Guildswomen, 1560–1700," *Historian* 46 (February 1984): 217 n. 62.

[27] See William Lempriere, *History of the Girls' School of Christ's Hospital, London, Hoddesdon, and Hertford* (Cambridge, Eng., 1924).

separate facilities to house certain of them. Even so, supervision of infant care could not be rigorous.[28] A large staff, including a matron and twenty-five nurses, attended the children at the London facility. The matron was held accountable for the presence of all children, the condition of their clothes and hospital goods, the quality of their food, even their warmth at night to prevent sickness. Beyond the care of children, nurses were enjoined to keep their wards clean and to sew or spin in their free time.[29] The nurses enjoyed little economic security. In 1607 Katherine Barber was dismissed for negligence in caring for the children, yet the governors of the hospital, "considering her great age and poore estate," felt constrained to confer on her a weekly pension of 18*d.* for her diet and an annual 40*s.* for rent, thereby compensating her for the loss of room and board. Barber had exchanged her status from a dispenser to a recipient of aid.[30]

Although London had much larger numbers of poor than any other city, Norwich, the second city of the realm, developed what is usually considered the most advanced relief system in the Elizabethan period. Legislation involved many strategies, including interesting plans for women and pauper children. According to the Norwich Orders for the Poor of 1571, each of the city's four wards was to appoint "so many select women as shal suffyse" to teach and supervise in their homes pauper children and "maydes that lyve ydelye." The city employed these "select women" through the 1580s. Each woman was given responsibility for six to twelve persons, over whom she had disciplinary control; she was to oversee a six- to eight-hour workday for those in her charge in addition to teaching them to "learne letters"; and for these duties she received the small salary of 20*s.* per annum. The city apparently anticipated that some of the select women might be reluctant to serve, for the Orders of 1571 stipulated that any woman who refused to serve "shall suffer inprisonemente by the space of twentie dayes at the leaste."[31] The city also employed a man and his wife to

[28] E. H. Pearce, *Annals of Christ's Hospital* (London, 1901), pp. 37, 163. For a list of nurses, children, and weekly wages in 1659, see GL, Christ's Hospital, MS 12860/1. Nurses' names include those of males.

[29] GL, MS 12878/1, fols. 25–28, 57–61. In 1553, hospital governors hired women to teach "women children" (GL, MS 12819/1, fol. 35r). During the seventeenth century, the hospital developed into a school, predominately for boys. A contingent of about forty girls were educated at London, and from 1675 to 1697, a small separate girls' school was established first at Hoddesdon, briefly at Hertford. The hospital employed a headmistress and other female personnel to teach girls reading and spinning (Lempriere, *History of the Girls' School,* p. 14; GL, MS 12878/1, fols. 81, 96–99).

[30] GL, MS 12806/3, fol. 105r.

[31] William Hudson and John C. Tingey, eds., *The Records of the City of Norwich,* 2 vols. (Norwich, 1910), 2:352–53; see also pp. 356–58. John Pound notes that the city dispensed with the select women by 1588 ("The Elizabethan Corporation of Norwich, 1558–1603" [M.A. thesis, University of Birmingham, 1962], p. 216).

run the free school in the Hospital of St. Giles, where twelve children were to be taught.[32] The education provided in such circumstances was no doubt rudimentary, but, probably for that very reason, such free schools proliferated during the seventeenth century. The city valued them enough to mandate in 1630 "a knittinge Schooledame shalbe provided in every parishe where there is not one already to sett children and other poore on work."[33] Norwich officials also relied on women to help staff the Boys' and Girls' Hospitals, both privately endowed but operated by the city to provide pauper children with some form of industrial education.[34]

Evidence indicates that some other towns also employed women to execute relief measures, especially child-employment schemes, which demanded neither the long-term commitment nor the technical expertise expected in many apprenticeships. In the mid-1620s, the town of Salisbury enacted an ambitious program for poor relief, which included a scheme to employ pauper children and adults. Two-thirds of the "workfolk" were children under fifteen, one hundred in all, whom the city found difficult to place as pauper apprentices. The high percentage of children undoubtedly explains the recruitment of female personnel: thirty of the fifty-eight "masters" were women, most of whom were bonelace makers. The women employed children almost exclusively; only one was charged with an adult over age twenty-one. Unfortunately, the scheme did not survive into the 1630s. Not surprisingly, city officials experienced difficulty in sustaining the cooperation of employers, who themselves practiced economically marginal and vulnerable trades.[35]

Such examples should not imply that all local authorities employed women to teach and train the poor. Records for the city of York, for example, give no indication of "select women," schooldames, or "masters" comparable to those in Norwich and Salisbury. In fact, when weaving schools were established in York at St. Anthony's Hall and St. George's Chapel in 1568 as part of the scheme to employ the poor, the

[32] Hudson and Tingey, eds., *Records of the City of Norwich*, 2:352.

[33] William Sachse, ed., *Minutes of the Norwich Court of Mayoralty, 1630–1631*, Norfolk Record Society, 15 (1942): 92 (hereafter cited as *Minutes*, NRS).

[34] NNRO, D. 16a, no. 15, fol. 298r; G. 25, f.

[35] Paul Slack, *Poverty in Early Stuart Salisbury*, Wiltshire Record Society, 31 (1975): 5, 10, 12–13, 15; the Survey of the Poor, 1625, which reveals details of the employment scheme is printed on pages 65–75. Although several female supervisors were married, only two acted as part of a couple. By the late century, reformers and urban magistrates increasingly turned to workhouses to train or employ poor youths. The London Corporation of the Poor in 1700 admitted one hundred children, and its staff included six nurses, a matron and a schoolmistress. See Macfarlane, "Studies in Poverty and Poor Relief in London," p. 293; Stephen Macfarlane, "Social Policy and the Poor in the Later Seventeenth-century," in *London, 1500–1700: The Making of the Metropolis*, ed. A. L. Beier and Roger Finlay (London, 1986), pp. 262–70.

city relied on male supervisors.[36] In January 1590, the corporation forgave Janet Alderson a debt of 20s. "in consideracion of her panes in teaching viij poore children to knit." But that autumn, when the city embarked on a more ambitious scheme to teach children to spin and knit, authorities hired a male instructor and promised him an annual salary of at least £10, which covered the children's wages and probably included the cost of the stock. No doubt the amount of capital to be invested determined the choice of personnel to supervise such projects.[37]

One service which women performed in their own homes needs special mention: the care and housing they provided for orphaned or abandoned children and others on relief rolls. At the behest of either town, parish, or hospital officials, such "foster mothers" took children, sometimes their neighbors or relatives, into their homes and, in return, received a weekly or yearly payment; on occasion, an individual might care for more than one child at a time. The children were usually but not exclusively under age seven. Authorities could provide neither close supervision nor protection of the children's interests, but recent research indicates that at least some London parishes in the late seventeenth century spent adequate sums (over £5. per annum) for the maintenance of each child.[38] Males also took responsibility for foster children, more frequently in some localities than others; their wives might well have attended such children, even when records name the head of the household as guardian.[39]

Women also contributed significantly to the process of medical poor relief. Historians of medicine have broadened their definition of medical practitioner in early modern England to include all persons who practiced medicine whether or not licensed, university-educated, or active in a guild. As a consequence, they recognize the prevalence of

[36] *York Civic Records*, YAS, 112:129–30.

[37] Ibid., YAS, 138:86, 115, 120, 128. A women in Norwich received a comparably high sum (5s. weekly) when she was appointed in 1630 to employ the poor. No doubt she too was expected to provide necessary materials (*Minutes*, NRS, 15:109). In January 1631, Thomas and Ellen Walknigton petitioned the mayor's court at York "to practice to teach poore children in dressing and knitting Jersey" (YCA, B. 35, fol. 95r). Much later, in 1683, the city employed Robert Newhause and his mother to set up a spinning school for children; YCA, E. 68, fol. 4ff. Salaries are not revealed.

[38] Valerie Pearl, "Social Policy in Early Modern London," in *History and Imagination: Essays in Honor of H. R. Trevor Roper*, ed. Hugh Lloyd Jones, Valerie Pearl, and Blair Worden (New York, 1982), p. 126; Macfarlane, "Studies in Poverty and Poor Relief in London," pp. 160–62. For examples of child custody, see GL, MS 12806/1, fol. 45; MS 12806/3, fol. 114v; Norman Moore, *The History of St. Bartholomew's Hospital*, 2 vols. (London, 1918), 2:319; NNRO, D. 16a, no. 15, fol. 212v.

[39] In exchange for custody of pauper children, the mayoralty court of York at times reduced or canceled assessments for poor relief taxes. Hence records often specify heads of household who paid the tax; see *York Civic Records*, YAS, 138:41–42, 45–47, 51, 54, 82–83, 85, 106, 132.

women healers and surgeons, many of whom offered significant services, especially in the provinces, well into the seventeenth century. Civic authorities, facing a large demand for medical services, willingly employed women practitioners to treat the infirm and disabled poor. The city of Norwich employed seven female practitioners when the Orders for the Poor went into effect in the early 1570s.[40]

Of equal significance, Norwich authorities relied heavily upon women to operate and staff the city's various hospitals, which numbered from seven to nine after the Reformation. As was the case elsewhere, hospitals in Norwich had a mixed clientele among the indigent: inmates included not only patients who were temporarily ill but also persons permanently disabled, the elderly, and the mentally ill. Depending on its size, each hospital was assigned one or more "keepers," an ambiguous term that might mean anything from custodian to medical practitioner. No matter the gender, a keeper served by the authority of the mayor's court and was usually responsible to aldermen who served as auditors. Despite such restrictions, however, when women were in charge as sole keeper of an institution, they inescapably made administrative decisions, sometimes those regarding who would be admitted and receive care.[41]

Records are too incomplete to give specific statistics, but, either in their own right or as co-keepers with their husbands, females appear to have held more than half the positions of keeper in Norwich. They were employed as supervisors and caretakers for both male and female inmates. For example, mayoralty court records of June 1631 indicate that five women keepers were responsible for ninety-two paupers at St. Giles.[42] In some instances the keepers at St. Giles were themselves paupers.[43] Such female personnel were nowhere more significant than at the small lazar houses (public hospitals) in Norwich, where in the early seventeenth century they admitted and assumed responsibility for the cure and care of patients. Even when they were co-keepers with their husbands, they had their own separate patients and charged fees comparable to those of their husbands.[44]

[40] Margaret Pelling and Charles Webster, "Medical Practitioners," in *Health, Medicine, and Mortality in the Sixteenth Century*, ed. Charles Webster (Cambridge, Eng., 1979), pp. 165–235; A. L. Wyman, "The Surgeoness: The Female Practitioner of Surgery, 1400–1800," *Medical History* 28 (January 1984): 28–30, 40–41; Margaret Pelling, "Healing the Sick Poor: Social Policy and Disability in Norwich, 1550–1640," *Medical History* 29 (April 1985): 222–23. Cf. Wiesner, *Working Women in Renaissance Germany*, chap. 2.

[41] See, for example, NNRO, D. 16a, no. 15, fols. 54v, 198v, 210v, 363v; *Minutes*, NRS, 15:95, 211; *Minutes*, NRS, 36 (1967): 67.

[42] *Minutes*, NRS, 15:34, 162.

[43] NNRO, D. 16a, no. 15, fols. 272v, 391v, 397v.

[44] Pelling, "Healing the Sick Poor," pp. 125–28, 136; NNRO, D. 16a, no. 15, passim; *Minutes*, NRS, 15:211.

A somewhat different system prevailed in the city of York. Although York officials relied on women to staff its hospitals and nurse inmates, in general women seem to have played a more menial, caretaking role than in Norwich. The term *keeper* was not used at St. Thomas's Hospital, whose inmates numbered fewer than twenty. Instead, York officials designated a "huswif," chosen from the poor to earn salary beyond the 4*d.* given weekly to all other inmates and to serve upon her "honest" behavior.[45] The housewife acted in part as nurse: when Agnes Egglestone, a poor, "somewhat distrect" person, was committed to St. Thomas's in 1581, the mayor's court ordered her to be "kept in some convenient place by herself; and the husewif to look to her and to have her releif weeklie for keping the said Agnes."[46] The housewife alone, however, could not tend all the ill residents and, both at St. Thomas's and St. Anthony's, additional women were hired. In other cases, the city employed nurses to perform their services in their own homes.[47]

By the mid-seventeenth century, the royal hospitals in London served more than three thousand of the city's poor, sick, and homeless.[48] Although they usually retained male physicians and surgeons on their staffs, hospitals also employed female practitioners, usually on an ad hoc basis, for the treatment of scald head and other skin ailments.[49] Moreover, like Christ's Hospital, others depended on matrons and sisters to perform a variety of necessary services, including both nursing and housekeeping.[50] Male boards of governors administered the hospitals under the authority of the city and in some instances interviewed prospective matrons and sisters before employing them. As employers, they were concerned with personal attributes as well as work skills and, on occasion, dismissed female staff for bad behavior, marriage, and unorthodox religious views.[51] Though some

[45] YCA, E. 66, fol. 21.

[46] *York Civic Records*, YAS, 119:51.

[47] YCA, B. 33, fols. 88, 190r, 117v.

[48] Valerie Pearl, "Puritans and Poor Relief: The London Workhouse, 1649–1680," in *Puritans and Revolutionaries: Essays in Seventeenth-Century History Presented to Christopher Hill*, ed. Donald Pennington and Keith Thomas (Oxford, 1978), p. 211; and Thomas Bowen, *Extracts from the Records and Court Books of Bridewell Hospital . . .* (London, 1798), pp. 32–33.

[49] GL, MS 12819/1, fol. 26r; MS 12806/3, fol. 71v; F. G. Parsons, *The History of St. Thomas's Hospital*, 2 vols. (London, 1932–36), 1:184–85; Moore, *History of St. Bartholomew's Hospital*, 2:230–31. Wyman suggests that scald head may have been ringworm of the scalp ("Surgeoness," p. 30).

[50] See "The Ordre of the Hospital of St. Bartholomewes" in Thomas Vicary, *The Anatomie of the Bodie of Man . . .*, ed. F. J. Furnivall and Percy Furnivall, Early English Text Society, 53 (1888; rpt. Millwood, N.Y., 1975): 309–11.

[51] GL, MS 12806/4, fols. 613–15; Parsons, *History of St. Thomas's Hospital*, 1:232–33; 2:85, 103, 113–15, 231–32; Moore, *History of St. Bartholomew's Hospital*, 2:350–51. At Christ's Hospital, male and female officers were forbidden to marry or "hath any charge

female staff were guilty of scandalous behavior, for others, living quarters in the hospital became a genuine home, perhaps even a surrogate family, and in old age, some became pensioners for life.[52] One matron at St. Bartholomew's, Jane Andrewes, was both affluent and dedicated enough to bequeath a large legacy to the hospital. In another case, when the great epidemic of plague subsided in December 1665, the board of governors expressed their debt and gratitude to Matron Margaret Blague "for her attendance and constant great paynes about the poor . . . wherein she hath adventureed herselfe to the greate peril of her life."[53]

Traditional resources and procedures for medical poor relief were inadequate to cope with outbreaks of plague, and London magistrates, prodded by the Privy Council, reluctantly employed special plague officials. In the Elizabethan period, London Orders for the Plague stipulated that two "sober ancient women" serve as viewers in each parish to inspect the sick for signs of plague; likewise, "two honest and discreet matrons" or searchers were to inspect bodies to determine the cause of death. In at least one instance, women also acted as purveyors to bring food and other necessities into quarantined homes and, by the early seventeenth century, some were employed as nurses by the richer parishes (or private individuals). Males performed comparable tasks for comparable wages as purveyors, watchmen, grave diggers, and warders to enforce the quarantine of stricken homes.[54] Similar procedures prevailed in the provinces during plague epidemics. In 1579 in Ipswich, where no pesthouse yet existed, the assembly recruited "women fytt to be kepers," and the city paid them up to a shilling a day "for attendyng one of the vesettyd howses." Ipswich women also viewed and prepared dead bodies.[55]

Although nurses and hospital sisters provided indispensable services, their work remained menial, their wages low, their reputations sullied by the dishonesty of a few. Unlike female keepers, co-keepers, and medical practitioners, nurses exercised little authority. Their wages rose to respectable levels only during outbreaks of plague, a reflection of the danger and the relatively short duration of epidemics. Their low status was a reflection not only of their social class but also

of children," but the prohibition was not always enforced. See GL, MS 12806/3, fols. 105r, 114v.

[52] Parsons, *History of St. Thomas's Hospital,* 2:78.

[53] Moore, *History of St. Bartholomew's Hospital,* 2:221, 231–32, 325.

[54] F. P. Wilson, *The Plague in Shakespeare's London* (London, 1927), pp. 64–66, 68–69, 179–80.

[55] Webb, *Poor Relief in Elizabethan Ipswich,* pp. 110–15. For Norwich, see *Minutes,* NRS, 15:62, 147, 172, 190. See also Alice Clark, *Working Life of Women in the Seventeenth Century* (1919; rpt. London 1982), pp. 249–50.

of the secularization of hospitals, a legacy of the Reformation. They enjoyed little of the respect given to nurses in religious or lay orders in Catholic societies or to godly matrons in Protestant England, who nursed the poor as an act of charity and virtue. Yet they performed necessary services and frequently made at least primitive medical care accessible to their local community or their own peers.

III

As this survey indicates, in London and in provincial cities where relief entailed far more than outdoor payments to pensioners, authorities frequently turned to female personnel to put programs into practice and extend various types of relief in individual cases of need. Some of these personnel, notably the independent medical practitioners, were in good economic position, but the majority came from the lower economic strata. Their employment in welfare services, especially medical poor relief and supervision of children, could easily be interpreted as an extension of their traditional domestic responsibilities into the public sphere. Indeed, medieval hospitals had relied on sisters to perform similar services. The secularization of hospitals, the intrusion of the state, and the expansion of relief programs involved increased participation of women in the public sphere rather than a new departure in the nature of women's work.[56]

This arrangement explains some of the weaknesses as well as the strengths of English poor relief. Work schemes frequently failed because they lacked knowledgeable, successful employers willing to commit to the projects on a long-term basis. Women could not effectively fill this need. Their own education and their marginal economic position severely limited their value in the areas of industrial education and work supervision. Hence the prevalence of pauper apprenticeships and the ineffectiveness of urban employment schemes. But women did provide a pool of cheap labor which facilitated the development of public relief beyond a mere system of doles. Through their participation, English poor relief gained flexibility and accessibility, a point all the more important given the tendency in recent scholarship to rehabilitate public poor relief and to reassert its effectiveness and continuity.[57] Women successfully participated in areas that demanded

[56] For continuity of women's work in such service occupations on the Continent, see Wiesner, *Working Women in Renaissance Germany*, pp. 187–88. Wiesner sees these occupations as "extensions of women's work in the home." Esther Cope argues that women exercised public functions more easily "when those functions appeared to be domestic in nature." Cope commented on the session "Overlapping Spheres in Early Modern England" at the Berkshire Conference on Women's History, Wellesley College, June 20, 1987.

[57] See Ronald W. Herlan, "Poor Relief in London during the English Revolution," *Journal of British Studies* 18 (Spring 1979): 30–51; Pearl, "Social Policy in Early Modern

relatively little technical knowledge and few financial resources. The case of Norwich with its select women, female hospital keepers, and female medical practitioners suggests that the more developed and comprehensive were public relief measures, the more local officials relied on women for the daily operation of the system.

Evolving within a patriarchal society, the system of poor relief reflected a variety and complexity of gender roles throughout the seventeenth century. In some respects, the system was gender-specific. Males held authority and, as churchwardens, overseers of the poor, justices of the peace, and "city fathers," they directed public relief. They distributed a disproportionate amount of relief to women, who, as a result of economic, demographic, and cultural factors, made up a disproportionate number of the deserving adult poor. The reality of patriarchy, however, should not detract from the interchangeable gender roles in these urban communities. For example, in placing pauper children, authorities relied on males to supervise apprentices and females to care for young children—yet both males and females served as foster parents, hospital keepers, medical practitioners, and work supervisors.

Reformers and officials did not hesitate to employ women in poor relief because women, whether acting within or beyond the household economy, already worked for wages or sought employment. Often they already performed social services like wet nursing or child care, which Michael Roberts calls "only vestigially dignified as work," yet "fundamental to the maintenance of social well-being." Roberts emphasizes the "flexibility of female work," an impression conveyed also by women's employment in poor relief.[58] Examples from the Norwich census make the case: Widow Margaret Usher, age sixty, kept other women and spun; Grace Tooke, age sixty, whose eighty-year-old husband was ill, kept sick persons and spun wool; Agnes Palmer, age forty-one, a laborer's wife, spun and taught children to knit; Margaret Knott, age forty-four, whose husband was an employed weaver, sewed and sold bread and victuals while her seven-year-old child, eldest of three, kept shop.[59] Such economic vulnerability sharply contradicts romanticized notions of the preindustrial household economy in which husband and wife worked productively side by side.

The lives of these women implicitly challenge our modern assumptions and suggest that the dichotomy between domestic and public, like our very definitions of private and public, do not apply in this

London," pp. 116, 122, 130; McIntosh, "Local Responses to the Poor." For additional historiography, see the original version of this essay, p. 574 n. 58.

[58] Michael Roberts, " 'Words they are Women, and Deeds they are Men': Images of Work and Gender in Early Modern England," in *Women and Work in Pre-Industrial England*, ed. Lindsey Charles and Lorna Duffin (London, 1985), pp. 154, 141.

[59] *Norwich Census of the Poor*, NRS, 40:39, 57, 58, 83.

context. Excluded from politics and power, women of the laboring classes were participants in public matters—albeit in ways that did not challenge traditional patriarchy and hierarchy. They routinely worked in the public marketplace to sustain their households; when employed by civic authorities to perform social welfare services, they served a public function, extending welfare services to the general population. Moreover, just as women acted in the public sphere, local authorities did not hesitate to interfere or intrude in what we would see as essentially private matters. Civic authorities accepted the household economy and placed the highest priority on protecting the stability of the family so that no element of the family unit would become economically dependent on the larger community. Hence they protected the employment rights of widows; they sought supervision of single women to minimize the risk of illegitimate children; and they required fathers to support children and wives, even when the father worked in another county. When necessary, through institutionalized relief, city fathers created a sort of surrogate family for the elderly, the very young, and the infirm.[60] In some cases, the surrogate mother figures—the hospital matrons and nurses—were required to be single or widowed, with no competing family ties, and were to demonstrate proper religious and moral attributes, demands which hospital governors found difficult to enforce. This paternalism entangled the public with the private and created the social and economic context for the lives of laboring women in sixteenth- and seventeenth-century England.

[60] Rosemary O'Day, *Education and Society, 1500–1800: The Social Foundations of Education in Early Modern Britain* (London, 1982), pp. 241, 247.

CHAPTER TWELVE

Good and Bad Mothers: Lady Philanthropists and London Housewives before World War I

Ellen Ross

By the 1880s the poor of London, the world's largest city, had replaced those of Britain's northern industrial belt as objects of official scrutiny. For women from the business and professional classes, the slums of the metropolis beckoned with opportunities for adventure, self-discovery, and meaningful work. When Beatrice Potter sought a public identity for herself, she signed on as a rent collector in East London and there formed a part of a group of women who had made similar choices. Jane Harrison remembered that her London lectures on classical history in the 1880s were attended by masses of well-educated and vigorous women for whom involvement with "Friendly Girls and Workhouse Nursing" was a way of life. In the 1890s, settlement worker Clara Grant gave up her lifelong ambition to be a missionary in central Africa to live, work, and teach among the East London poor. Marcella, the female protagonist in Mary Ward's 1894 novel about conflicting models of philanthropy, sought peace and wisdom working as a district nurse among London's chaotic Soho poor, initiating a "Marcella period" among young upper-class women. Katharine Symonds, one of the "Marcella crop" of the late 1890s, yearned to work at Toynbee Hall in Whitechapel but settled for a clerical job at a Charity Organisation Society (COS) office in Whitechapel

The research on which this essay is based was done with support from the Shelby Cullom Davis Center for Historical Studies at Princeton University and from Ramapo College's sabbatical, research, and travel funds. The published essay was revised with the aid of a Fellowship for College Teachers granted by the National Endowment for the Humanities for 1989–90. I am most grateful to all three institutions.

Road. In the early twentieth century, the school charity bureaucracy and borough health visiting programs were supplanting the COS and the district nursing services as places where young ladies could find interesting volunteer or even paid work.[1]

Superintendence of the young, so prominent in the work of the middle-class visitors to the slums of Victorian and Edwardian London, was a pillar of activist women's identity in the worlds of charity and public service. The arguments of both suffragists and nonsuffragists for the local and national franchise were routinely expressed in the language of national motherhood. Wherever they managed to get elected to political office and whatever their political views, women were usually placed, and placed themselves, in situations in which they worked with children. Lady Margaret Sandhurst, one of two women elected to the London County Council (LCC) in 1888, plunged headlong into inspecting twenty-three "baby farms" for the LCC. Tory Susan Lawrence, a longtime leader in child-oriented charities elected to the LCC in 1907, quickly broke with the Conservatives, in good measure over their positions relating to children.[2]

The women activists' claims to be mothering the children of the poor should be taken seriously. Motherhood was, especially in the two decades before 1918, a newly stressed term in public discourses, one with which teachers, social workers, nurses, and health visitors would have to reckon. The state and local initiatives of this period, and those of voluntary agencies, which became known collectively as the infant welfare movement, were an effort to transform the meaning and practice of motherhood throughout Britain.[3] Scrutiny was directed at the newly urgent problem of the ability of the nation's working-class mothers, who reared Britain's foot soldiers, to bring up healthy chil-

[1] Sandra J. Peacock, *Jane Ellen Harrison: The Mask and the Self* (New Haven, 1988), p. 61; Clara Grant, *Farthing Bundles* (London, 1930), p. 72; Mrs. Humphrey Ward, *Marcella* (1894; rpt. New York, 1985); Dame Katharine Furse, *Hearts and Pomegranates: The Story of Fifty-Five Years, 1875 to 1920* (London, 1940), p. 156. On the influence of *Marcella*, see David Rubinstein, *Before the Suffragettes: Women's Emancipation in the 1890s* (New York, 1986), p. 33 and n. 47.

[2] F. K. Prochaska, *Women and Philanthropy in Nineteenth-Century England* (Oxford, 1980); Jo Manton, *Mary Carpenter and the Children of the Streets* (London, 1976). Patricia Hollis, *Ladies Elect: Women in English Local Government, 1865–1914* (Oxford, 1987), tells this story of women in local government in wonderful detail. On Lady Sandhurst's election to the LCC along with Jane Cobden, see ibid., pp. 307–17; on Susan Lawrence, see p. 415.

[3] For recent work on the infant welfare movement see Anna Davin, "Imperialism and Motherhood," *History Workshop* 5 (Spring 1978): 6–66; Carol Dyhouse, "Working-Class Mothers and Infant Mortality in England, 1895–1914," *Journal of Social History* 12 (1978): 248–67; Jane Lewis, *The Politics of Motherhood* (London, 1982); Nikolas Rose, *The Psychological Complex: Psychology, Politics and Society in England, 1869–1939* (London, 1985); and Deborah Dwork, *War Is Good for Babies and Other Young Children: A History of the Infant and Child Welfare Movement in England, 1898–1918* (London, 1987).

dren. Motherhood was no longer a natural attribute of women but a problem. As one of the movement's male activists put it later, in his own history of those years, "The mother was evidently the factor of paramount importance. Evidently, also, the capacity to bring up a baby successfully through the first year of life was not an innate feminine character. . . . It was proved to be a skilled job requiring a technique which, like any other kind of technique, has to be acquired."[4]

The infant welfare movement elevated the social status of mothers while at the same time propagandizing for what has recently been called the "myth of maternal omnipotence."[5] Infant welfare spokespeople emphasized that it was a mother's responsibility—and that it was within her power—to raise healthy and orderly children. These propositions were radical and problematic in general; they were still more doubtful among working-class men and women, who well knew that their poverty prohibited them from supplying their families with healthy foods, clothes, housing, doctors, and medicines. Infant welfare writers made motherhood the fulcrum of adult women's identity; their position reflects a slow redefinition that had begun in the early nineteenth century in several middle-class cultural groups in England but was by no means universal throughout the higher British social orders. [6] The new urgency of motherhood jarred, however, with working women's sense of themselves as household providers and managers first, child caretakers second.

We tend to think of motherhood in dichotomies. The concept of madonna/whore divides women into asexual mothers or barren but eroticized nonmothers; evil stepmothers and fairy godmothers are the substance of fairy tales. In a parallel split—as formulated by Melanie Klein, or, somewhat differently, by Margaret Mahler—"good" and "bad" psychic mothers are created out of more complex and mixed real ones by infants and small children, who project their own good or ugly feelings onto adult intimates. To her child, the same woman might seem alternately good and bad; or the child might project the badness

[4] G. F. McCleary, *The Early History of the Infant Welfare Movement* (London, 1933), p. 35.

[5] Nancy Chodorow and Susan Contratto, "The Fantasy of the Perfect Mother," in *Rethinking the Family*, ed. Barrie Thorne and Marilyn Yalom (New York, 1982), p. 71.

[6] On motherhood in the nineteenth- and twentieth-century middle and upper classes see Christina Hardyment, *Dream Babies* (Oxford, 1984), chaps. 2 and 3; Leonore Davidoff and Catherine Hall, *Family Fortunes: Men and Women of the English Middle Class, 1780–1850* (Chicago, 1987), pp. 335–43; Joan Perkin, *Women and Marriage in Nineteenth-Century England* (London, 1989); Pat Jalland, *Women, Marriage and Politics, 1870–1914* (Oxford, 1986); Judith S. Lewis, *In the Family Way: Childbearing in the British Aristocracy, 1760–1860* (New Brunswick, 1986), chap. 2; John Gillis, "The Feminization of Motherhood," paper presented at the Workshop on the European Fertility Decline, Pembroke College, Cambridge University, July 1989; M. Jeanne Peterson, *Family, Love, and Work in the Lives of Victorian Gentlewomen* (Bloomington, 1989), pp. 103–8.

of her mother—her moments of anger and nastiness—onto another caretaker such as a baby-sitter. As Klein and object relations psychologists outline the childhood psychic processes of splitting and projection, residues are bound to exist in some form in adults of all classes and both sexes as products of the universal, unavoidable experience of having been an infant. Psychoanalysis deals primarily with the child's perception of the parent; mothers' subjectivity is a peripheral concern. In a review of Mary Gordon's novel *Men and Angels,* however, Susan Suleiman considers mothers' consciousness and points to the ways modern American mothers find it impossible to think of themselves outside of these same dichotomies: if a woman does creative work, she is hurting her child and is "bad"; if someone else cares for the children, that person must be either "better" or "worse" at mothering them, a rival who will win or lose the title of good mother.[7]

There are many appropriate ways of analyzing the infant welfare movement, but good mothering was manifestly at its center, which invites a reading through the participants' spoken and unspoken images of motherhood. The good mother/bad mother dichotomy gave shape to the passions of the thousands of middle-class women who chose to work with the babies of the London poor around the turn of the century. For the charity givers of the infant welfare years, especially for the numerous women among them, adventure, professional satisfaction, and the exercise of patriotic duty could be confounded by envy and hatred of the working-class mothers who were central to many of their programs, by love of their children, and by rivalry with them (and sometimes with other charitable women as well) for the label of good mother.

The political and administrative workings of the infant welfare movement were also structured by the good mother/bad mother dichotomy. Among the legislators, medical officers, and journalists who dominated the debates of this era, sheer ignorance of life among the workers invited fantasies of drunken, superstitious crones, images that were the obverse of the policy makers' own sentimentalized mothers. Accordingly, it was morally, politically, and psychologically possible to take the close-fisted stance that dominated the maternal and infant welfare legislation of this era. Far more resources, both public and private, were devoted to regulating, correcting, and policing working-class mothers than toward offering them food, clothing, medical ser-

[7] Melanie Klein, *Envy and Gratitude* (London, 1957); Phyllis Grosskruth, *Melanie Klein: Her World and Her Work* (Cambridge, Mass., 1987), pp. 374, 395, 440. On Klein also see Dorothy Dinnerstein, *The Mermaid and the Minotaur: Sexual Arrangements and Human Malaise* (New York, 1977), pp. 95–100. Susan Rubin Suleiman, "On Maternal Splitting: A Propos of Mary Gordon's *Men and Angels,*" *Signs* 14 (Autumn 1988): 25–41; also Marianne Hirsch, *The Mother/Daughter Plot* (Bloomington, 1989).

vices, housing, or cash.[8] The Children Act of 1908 is, for example, an astonishing omnibus piece of legislation based on the proposition that the workers' parenting was just a step away from neglect.

In Major General Sir Frederick Maurice's famous series of articles in 1902 on the the threat of race degeneration, the main culprit was "ignorance on the part of the mothers of the necessary conditions for the bringing up of healthy children."[9] The figure of the bad mother, the slum mother, was dominant: poor, lazy, ignorant, slovenly, and possibly drunken, she hovered near the surface of all subsequent discussions of infant mortality and "physical deterioration," which were subjects of a series of government Inter-Departmental Committee hearings in 1903 and 1904. Leaders in the infant welfare movement often spoke as children rather than as parents and located the mothers at one pole or another. Former dock worker John Burns, opening the first National Conference on Infantile Mortality in 1906 in his capacity as president of the Local Government Board, "did nothing more than fulminate against modern women while praising his mother," as a recent commentator has put it. The explanation for infant mortality figures, high or low, Burns said, was nothing more than "good or bad motherhood."[10] Even when the practical and more distinctly medical and sanitary problems of tuberculous milk or poorly designed privies were addressed, the bad mother of the slums was not dispensed with. As Anna Davin points out, though the Inter-Departmental Committee made fifty-three different recommendations in its final report in 1904, dealing with such social problems as overcrowding, sanitation, the milk supply, overwork, and food adulteration, policy makers in subsequent years took up only those that involved instructing women and girls in infant and child care.[11]

London's late Victorian and Edwardian working-class culture accorded mothers considerably more dignity than did contemporaneous bourgeois culture. Children's street chants reflected respect and fear of mothers. Music-hall songs, often comic, like "If You Knew My Muvver," rejoiced in the power of mothers in their households and neighborhoods. London mothers had their own definitions of good and bad mothering, which differed profoundly from those of infant welfare workers. The differences were in part over the care babies and young

[8] This argument is made very forcefully in Lewis, *Politics of Motherhood,* and in Davin, "Imperialism and Motherhood."

[9] Quoted in Davin, "Imperialism and Motherhood," p. 15; see also Rose, *Psychological Complex,* chap. 6; Bentley B. Gilbert, *The Evolution of National Insurance in Britain: The Origins of the Welfare State* (London, 1966), pp. 81–101; and Dwork, *War Is Good for Babies,* chaps. 1 and 2.

[10] Dwork, *War Is Good for Babies,* p. 114.

[11] Davin, "Imperialism and Motherhood," p. 27.

children needed—adequate feeding, comfortable dress, sufficient sleep, and so forth. The poor mothers thought babies should be plump and worried that feeding breast milk alone would keep them skinny and vulnerable; they carried their infants constantly, slept with them, and dressed them very warmly in layer after layer—practices the infant welfare workers found tantamount to infanticide. More profoundly disturbing for the welfare workers was the refusal of most working-class women to accept guilt if any of their children died, no matter how much they mourned. If a mother had "done all I could," she did not see blame as relevant, for she knew that her own practices and ministrations were severely constrained by her income and living conditions. More elusively still, the poor mothers defined themselves in ways that their middle-class peers had not yet dreamed of—simultaneously as child caretakers, as workers, and as significant members of neighborhoods and kinship groups.

Health visitors, sanitary inspectors, and clinic workers began their work armed with principles of good mothering that they were taught in early twentieth-century training programs. In her series of 1906 lectures for health visitors, midwife Emilia Kanthack assumed that they would be schooling local mothers in many new and unfamiliar principles: the necessity for unsupplemented breast-feeding in the early months; the vital importance of medical advice as a guide to infant care; the evils of pacifiers; the dangers of letting babies share the parents' bed. Kanthack and her colleagues portrayed the mothers alternately as compliant, grateful for professional help, and "pitiably ignorant and superstitious." The neighbors, the grandmothers, "ignorant old women who have buried 10 out of 14 or 15," as one social worker put it, were the rivals in a duel over children's bodies with the medico-hygienic (to adapt from Jean Donzelot's vocabulary) personnel.[12]

The mothers themselves, when they appear in the human encounters generated by the infant welfare movement, were tight-lipped and skeptical about the new welfare programs. They weighed their obligations toward individual children against the claims of their other children and the demands of child care against the more pressing need for daily household subsistence. When, for instance, the School Care committees, groups of volunteer school-based charity workers, confronted mothers who were charged with carrying out the school doctors' orders for their children, the mothers irritatingly dodged the instructions: "Unable to leave her other children to take [Benjamin] to

[12] Emilia Kanthack, *The Preservation of Infant Life: A Guide for Health Visitors* (London, 1907), p. 4; also see Evelyn Bunting et al., *A School for Mothers* (London, 1907), pp. 38–39, for an account of the operation of a Marylebone clinic; Helen M. Blagg, *Statistical Analysis of Infant Mortality and Its Causes in the U.K.* (London, 1910), p. 15; S.B.A., "A School for Mothers," *Toynbee Record*, January 1908, p. 54; Jean Donzelot, *La Police des familles* (Paris, 1977).

Treatment Centre," or "inconvenient to leave her stall to take the boy to the hospital," the committees recorded regularly in their minutes.[13] Such obligations conflicted squarely with the newer goals of the middle-class volunteers: to improve children's physical comfort with spectacles, impetigo treatments, or tonsil surgery and to cultivate their imaginations by listening to their stories of school experiences and recent adventures.

Working-class children surely had split images of motherhood, though to read the autobiographical legacy of Edwardian children, London mothers were nearly all angelically "good." Most of the autobiographies are posited on the central place in the child's life of the mother's sacrifice; the books are offered as payments, debts of gratitude, acts of reparation, in Melanie Klein's terms. The good mothers, as their children reconstruct them, "worked for" their children rather than ministering to their feelings or becoming their friends. They patched boys' trousers when they might have let them go about in rags, ate bread at their own meals so that their children could have hot stew, told off teachers who had caned their sons or daughters. Yet they were often strict and severe and made enormous demands on their children for work, proper behavior, and self-denial. It is often fathers who are the repositories of badness. Obviously many fathers, violent or greedy, richly earned their children's hostility. But perhaps also, in London's working-class subcultures, where fathers' place in their families was often marginal, mothers could safely direct children to view their husbands as bad "other mothers."

Implementing the new policies of infant preservation generated thousands of new middle-class jobs, some voluntary, some professional, and most of them for women: health visitors, school meals organizers, school doctors and nurses, clinic workers, district nurses, licensed midwives. By 1910, for example, the London Medical Officer of Health reported that only three of the twenty-nine London boroughs had no health visiting program. In ten very populous boroughs, health visitors were actually getting to 60 percent or more of the homes of newborns within a few days of the births. The North Islington School for Mothers, a mothers' and babies' clinic founded in 1913, listed by the end of World War I a staff of three visiting women doctors, five nurses, and thirty-seven volunteers, most of whom did home visiting among the center's clients. The responsibilities of the London School Care

[13] Minutes of Children's Care Committees: St. Matthews (N.) school, January 28, 1916, and Popham-road school, April 22, 1910, both in Greater London Record Office, EO/WEL/2/vols. 17 and 6.

committees also expanded in the "deterioration" era and by the eve of the war involved close to ten thousand men and women members.[14]

From the trickle of ladies doing church visiting in the 1840s and the district nurses and social investigators of the 1880s, middle-class women had, by the 1900s, become a real presence in the lives of poor mothers. They came to their homes with leaflets and instructions when their babies were a few days old, nagged them to get their school-children deloused, questioned them about why Jim or Violet at age twelve or fourteen was being placed in a dead-end job rather than an apprenticeship. The ladies helped the poor women save up for children's winter boots and for summer holidays in the country, provided nursery schools and after-school play programs for (a few of) their children, sat up nights with them caring for the sick. These contacts invited intimacy and generated strong emotions on the middle-class side, some of which were surely filtered through the good mother/bad mother split.

Their right to prescribe for children and their anomalous situation in doing so were burning issues for many of the ladies who worked with poor women and children. Elizabeth Wilson rather unkindly remarks in *Women and the Welfare State* that the story of Victorian social work involves "an army of surplus middle-class spinsters," whose task it was to teach "their impoverished married sisters how to be better wives and mothers."[15] The volunteers and professionals were heavily, though not exclusively, spinsters, and this status could be intensely problematic. Beatrice Potter documented in detail the temptations of a conventional marriage to Joseph Chamberlain, which would have destroyed her career ambitions, and throughout her life she regretted not having children. Martha Vicinus's *Independent Women,* a book about single women's communities in this period, is filled with the doubts and misgivings of stalwart women in hard-earned and rewarding professional positions. Constance Maynard, for example, head of Westfield College, was tormented by a series of relationships with her girl pupils in which her hunger to mother them was surely as disruptive as her unacknowledged sexual passions. Many single women activists, like Mary Carpenter in an earlier generation, eventually adopted children. Bible women, most of whom were working-class residents of the

[14] Janet Campbell, and E. W. Hope *Report on the Physical Welfare of Mothers and Children: England and Wales,* 2 vols. (Liverpool, 1917), 2:86–90. An 1884 survey of London school managers found enormous variations in committees' sexual composition; in the twentieth century higher proportions of women served, according to my reading of School Care Committee minutes (Greater London Record Office, EO/WEL/2/vols. 2, 10, and 15). The survey is described in Peter Gordon's *The Victorian School Manager: A Study in the Management of Education, 1800–1902* (London, 1974), pp. 161–64.

[15] Elizabeth Wilson, *Women and the Welfare State* (London, 1977), p. 43.

neighborhoods to which they were assigned, sometimes adopted local children whose homes were being broken up, and so did the more upper-class members of district nursing services.[16]

The issue of their own childbearing was a live one even for the more favored generation of social workers and activists of the 1900s. Clearly their clients were constantly bringing it up. The *Sanitary Officer*, a journal whose readers included health visitors, editorialized in its first year, 1909, that the view that unmarried inspectors could know nothing of babies was "absolute nonsense." Pointed references to their professional training as nurses, a female sanitary inspector wrote, could help refute the mothers' charges that single women were ignorant of babies: "A reminder that I was a hospital nurse, and have had a great many children under my care, soon puts the matter to right." Nursery pioneer Margaret McMillan, though admitting that "no crèche can take the place of home," defended her Deptford nursery as "a school for home makers."[17]

One solution to the apparent contradiction of spinsters in charge of the children of the nation was to grant them fictive motherhood. At a 1912 conference, Ethel Bentham, then a volunteer doctor at the Women's Labour League babies' clinic in Kensington, somewhat awkwardly assigned her organization a mother's role toward the nation's children and a sisterly one toward its mothers: "Being, many of us mothers, and the rest of us at least 'maiden aunts,' we know that [medical care] is something . . . that could lift a burden of worry and anxiety from many a woman's life." Caleb Williams Saleeby, a militant eugenicist and infant welfare activist, made a case for the maternal superiority of the single women teachers and nurses who were at the center of the infant work. Naming them "foster mothers" and even "Virgin Mothers," Saleeby argued, "Everyone knows maiden aunts who are better, more valuable, completer mothers in every non-physical way than the actual mothers of their nephews and nieces. This is woman's wonderful prerogative, that in virtue of her *psyche*, she can realize herself, and serve others . . . even though she forego physical motherhood."[18]

The life trajectories of upper-class women tended to bring them to the slums when they were young, though the philanthropic agencies

[16] Martha Vicinus, *Independent Women: Work and Community for Single Women, 1850–1920* (Chicago, 1985), pp. 195, 43–44. On the Bible women, see *The Missing Link* and its successor journals, the newsletters of Ellen Ranyard's Bible and Domestic Female Mission. For a description of a group of nurses temporarily adopting two motherless babies in succession, see Edith E. G. May, *True Tales of a District* (London, 1908).

[17] *Sanitary Officer*, August 1909, p. 51, June 1910, p. 253, October 1909, p. 95. Margaret McMillan, *Infant Mortality* (London, n.d. [1907?]), p. 14.

[18] Women's Labour League of Central London, *The Needs of Little Children: Report of a Conference on the Care of Babies and Young Children* (London, 1912), p. 22; C. W. Saleeby, *Woman and Womanhood* (New York, 1911), p. 164, quoted in Davin, "Imperialism and Motherhood," p. 51.

were often grossly insensitive to the incongruity of girls, many of them just out of secondary school, teaching or monitoring mature women with many children. A young settlement worker's first assignment was often as an investigator for the Charity Organisation Society, which meant thoroughly probing a family's affairs through many home visits and lengthy interviews, usually with the woman of the house.[19] Indeed, Mary Brinton's mother, from the prominent and socially active Liberal Rendel family, refused to let her seventeen-year-old daughter do any home visiting for the Saffron Hill Elementary School Care Committee, of which Mary became secretary in 1908. As Mrs. Brinton put it, for a girl so young to make home visits to "mature mothers of families . . . and possibly question them" was simply "impertinent."[20]

For the welfare workers the temptation to be the good mother, a foil to the poor and bad "other mothers" of London, was hard to resist entirely, and, from the COS to the Labour party, they yielded to it. The rhetoric of the infant welfare movement invited this response by defining working-class care of infants as a national problem. A good example is the Notification of Births Act of 1907 (which local governments were permitted but not required to adopt). Enacted in twenty of the twenty-nine boroughs that made up Greater London, its explicit purpose was to enable local health officials to locate newborn babies and to superintend the care they were getting. As one worker representing the St. Pancras Mothers' and Infants' Society gleefully put it in 1908: "Directly a baby was heard of [we] pounced down upon it."[21]

A special object of the welfare workers' solicitude was the "ex-baby," the one- or two-year-old who had just acquired a younger sibling. These infants were casualties of the closely spaced births that still dominated inner London. Sometimes newly weaned, ex-babies were, it was speculated, subject to wasting and other nutritional disorders.[22] Normal working-class mothering in London involved close confinement of infants and toddlers, whose high spirits, curiosity, and mobility were ill-suited to the close quarters, steep stairs, hot grates, kettles of boiling water, and the like that were part of ordinary working-class homes. During much of the day, toddlers were often stuck in high chairs or tied into ordinary seats, waiting in frustration for older sib-

[19] Vicinus, *Independent Women*, p. 226. See also E. Sylvia Pankhurst, *The Home Front: A Mirror to Life in England during the World War* (London, 1932), pp. 25, 46, 252; *Sanitary Officer*, October 1909, p. 97; Margaret Loane, *From Their Point of View* (London, 1908), p. 128.

[20] Mary Stocks, *My Commonplace Book* (London, 1970), p. 58.

[21] *Report of the Proceedings of the National Conference on Infantile Mortality* (London, 1908), p. 69.

[22] Bunting et al., *School for Mothers*, p. 6 and passim; Maud Pember Reeves, *Round about a Pound a Week* (1913; rpt. London, 1979), chap. 13; [Florence] Petty et al., *The Pudding Lady: A New Departure in Social Work* (London, [1910]), p. 2.

lings to return from school to take them out. Middle-class educators, especially progressive women with a knowledge of Montessori principles, were deeply attracted to the friendly, chatty cockney children and obviously thought they were getting bad mothering. Honnor Morten in the 1890s, Muriel Wragge and Margaret McMillan in the 1900s, and many anonymous others asserted that the mothers were far too hard on their toddlers: too ready to punish with force, too demanding of quiet and order.[23] On the public level, though, many of these women were staunch defenders of the mothers' "goodness."

Clearly the presence of toddlers overloaded the frail domestic systems of London mothers. The London board (public) schools were forced to fill this large gap in resources. The schools officially accepted children as young as three, and children five and under made up a tenth of the London elementary school population in 1904.[24] School officials well knew that the child-care gap that flooded schools with babies was in fact a product of compulsory education, which removed the toddlers' normal playmates and baby-sitters from their homes every day.

Nursery schools and crèches made similar efforts to fill the child-care gap. The Women's Freedom League's settlement in Nine Elms south of the Thames addressed the ex-baby directly when it founded a guest house for children from age two in 1916. The workers' description of their program very characteristically mingles reproach with the recognition of a need and the offer of a service:

> The Guest House for children was started by the Settlement to supply a want that seemed to have been hitherto overlooked—a home where mothers could send what have been called the "dowager babies" to be cared for while they themselves were laid up during the advent of a new baby, or in hospital for an operation. The workers here watched the results in our street, where new babies arrive with alarming frequency, and their elders, often only just able to crawl, spend their time on the doorstep, eating frequent unvaried meals of bread-and-margarine, or taking adventurous walks in the gutter.[25]

In the writing of Margaret McMillan, a crusader for municipally funded school meals and clinics, the tension between a political "good mother" position—a powerful commitment to defending the rights

[23] Honnor Morten and H. F. Gethen, *Tales of the Children's Ward* (London, 1894); Muriel Wragge, "News of the Woolwich Mission Kindergarten," *Child Life*, no. 10 (April 1901): 100.

[24] Nanette Whitbread, *The Evolution of the Nursery-Infant School* (London, 1972), p. 66, table 3, p. 68, table 4; David Rubinstein, *School Attendance in London, 1870–1904: A Social History* (Hull, [1969]), p. 11.

[25] *The Vote*, August 4, 1916, p. 1127.

and meeting the needs of working-class mothers and children—is undercut by her identification with the children at her Deptford school in their many clashes with their mothers, clashes she was rather proud of generating. McMillan saw herself as an ally of the imagination and physical freedom of her young charges as they struggled against the confinement their mothers thought natural for them and needed from them. In a moving fictionalized sketch of an encounter between a boy and his harassed, overworked mother, McMillan described the boy's long and painful efforts to get his mother to share his excitement at seeing the stars for the first time after sleeping outdoors at the school. In another account by McMillan, a similar boy, Jack—a six-year-old pupil at the Deptford nursery—had become a problem for his mother, a "delicate" woman who took in sewing for the income. Before Jack started at the school, the child had sat "quiet as a mouse" near his mother all day winding spools or putting pins into a cushion. But after some months under McMillan's care, Jack became so noisy and spirited that his mother threatened to take him away. "He used to sit still for hours but now he has that much life in him that I can't abide him in the room," according to the mother.[26] McMillan clearly imagined herself the nursery children's good mother, who would bring out the spontaneity, joy, and energy stifled by their own. Yet she fully recognized the forces that kept these mothers "bad" and maintained such warm relations with most of them that much of her fund-raising was done among the poor households in the streets surrounding the school.

The regular requirement of most crèches and nursery schools (of which there were only fifty-five in the city in 1904) that children must bathe and put on a special uniform for the day was correctly interpreted by mothers as a vote of no confidence in their standards of dress and cleanliness. Even Sylvia Pankhurst's wartime Norman Road Babies' House followed this convention. The chairman of the National Society of Day Nurseries was aware that "the usual bath upon admission" with its "implied neglect of cleanliness on the part of the parent" told against the crèches with the local mothers.[27]

Clothing the children was a way nursery staffs laid claim to them, muting their working-class identity and their existence as other peoples' daughters and sons. At McMillan's school, the children were given colorful tunic-style smocked uniforms suggesting the garb of rural laborers of an earlier era. The teachers were always saddened, McMillan reported, at the end of each day when the children put on

[26] Margaret McMillan, "Guy and the Stars," in her *Nursery School* (London, 1919), p. 185.

[27] Anna Davin, *Little Women: Nineteenth-Century Girlhood in London,* (London, forthcoming), chap. 8; F. S. Toogood, M.D. "The Role of the Creche or Day Nursery," in *Infancy,* ed. Theophilus N. Kelynack (London, 1910), p. 84.

their own clothes and were transformed from gay woodfolk into grubby slum children. The workers at the Nine Elms guest house felt the same wrenching loss when their children returned to their homes on the streets surrounding the huge West Thames Gas Board Works. "The sad part for the Settlement workers," wrote one of them, "comes at the end, when the neat, pretty clothes are taken off and the babies dressed up again in their poor little Cinderella garments, minus, sometimes so many tapes, buttons, and hooks and eyes, and always either much too warm or not half warm enough." The settlement workers were convinced that their care was superior to what the children got at home: the "open windows day and night, nightly baths, wholesome and regular meals, and a long sleep at night" left the children fitter and healthier, they were certain. One of the young guests was quoted in *The Vote,* the Women's Freedom League newspaper, proclaiming that the guest house, with its attractive toys and plentiful food, was "like Heaven."[28] This Nine Elms child was not the only slum youngster to be seduced by the sweetness of young settlement workers, schoolteachers, or hospital nurses whose offers of friendship were often accompanied by snowy linen, currant buns, soft voices, or gleaming bathrooms.[29]

Many of the women most caught up in the competition for the good mother title—McMillan, Anna Martin, Clara Grant—were, in public, determined and effective political advocates for the poor mothers of the country. Disfranchised, sorely overworked, poorly educated, active in national politics only at widely separated points, the London mothers had almost no public voice during the years when they were constant objects of discussion. For the middle-class feminists who worked among them, women who did have links to major national political parties and organizations, giving the poor a voice with which to defend themselves against the bad mother charges was a solemn obligation and, as Bonnie Smith suggests, a central element in their commitment to various brands of feminism.[30] In the late 1880s, when Annie Besant was an advocate for London working women, the motto of the newspaper she edited, the *Link,* was a quotation from Victor Hugo: "The people are silence. I will be the advocate of this silence. I will speak for the dumb. I will speak of the small to the great and of the feeble to the strong. . . . I will be the Word of the People."[31] Hugo's remarkable

[28] McMillan, *Nursery School,* pp. 286–87; *The Vote,* August 4, 1916, p. 1127.

[29] See, among many such accounts, Alice Linton, whose *Not Expecting Miracles* (London, 1982) includes an account of a long stay at Great Ormond Street Children's Hospital.

[30] Bonnie Smith, "Writing Women's Work," unpublished paper, University of Rochester, June 1987. See also Carol Dyhouse, *Feminism and the Family in England, 1880–1939* (Oxford, 1989), pp. 133–38.

[31] Quoted in Annie Besant, *An Autobiography* (Philadelphia, n.d. [1893]), p. 331.

formulation really does mute the poor, whose silence is axiomatic here, but the late Victorian and Edwardian social workers saw their job differently. As Emmeline Pethick (better known by her hyphenated married name, Pethick-Lawrence, and her later identity as a militant suffragist) rephrased Hugo in an 1898 essay describing her experience as a West London settlement worker: "By an actual knowledge and experience gained in direct contact with the people, we are fitted to become their voice, and to give utterance to their claim upon society, for a life that is worth the living."[32]

The mothers' advocates of early twentieth-century Britain listened and tried to reproduce the words of poor women in strategic political situations. They operated through the lenses of new academic disciplines: anthropologists' interest in matriarchy and family structure; economic historians' concerns with the influence of industry on the family; economists' interest in family budgets.[33] These new disciplines let them see more and tell it more authoritatively.

Though the authorial voice was surely the one that prevailed (the neighborhood women were their informants in the anthropologists' sense), the mixture of voices is quite new in turn-of-the-century and early twentieth-century writings, and so is the mixture of modes—the scientific ideas of the professional women about budgets and nutrition, the shopping and family and street stories of the mothers. As Bonnie Smith demonstrates in a Europe-wide survey, women and ladies were talking together everywhere in these years, often about newly politicized topics: birth control, husbands' violence or drinking, state maternity policies. Some became friends, like Frances Orchard, who first applied to the COS in 1908 and grew old with the organization and friendly and confiding with her successive case workers, remaining in the active file through 1946. In London, settlement workers or health visitors and their clients could be co-workers for women's suffrage; they marched together in the 1905 unemployment demonstrations; they could be found in some of the local Women's Cooperative Guild chapters.[34]

[32] Emmeline Pethick, "Working Girls' Clubs," in *University and Social Settlements*, ed. Will Reason (London, 1898), p. 114.

[33] Dyhouse, *Feminism and the Family*, pp. 66–74; Rosalind Coward, *Patriarchal Precedents: Sexuality and Social Relations* (London, 1983), chaps. 1–3. This point became clearer in a conversation with Judy Walkowitz in New York, September 1989.

[34] Smith, "Writing Women's Work." Frances Orchard is a made-up name for a COS case from St. Pancras North (A/FWA/TH/B2/2, Family Welfare Association Papers, Greater London Record Office; used with kind permission of the association). The unemployment agitation, centered in East London, was directed against the newly passed and extremely ineffectual Unemployed Workmen Act. There were separate women's meetings and marches during the months of October and November 1905. Clara Grant was extremely active in these events, along with Dora Montefiore, Charlotte Despard, and several other settlement house women and women local government officials.

Although many of the writings of the early twentieth-century feminist generation take the stance of witnesses of working-class life, their gaze is warm and sympathetic, in comparison with the cool, critical appraisals of such earlier observers as Beatrice Potter and Helen Dendy. To use one well-known example, in *Round about a Pound a Week*, an account of a 1909–13 Fabian Women's Group project with Lambeth mothers and infants living on subsistence incomes, the view is from the *inside* of the working woman's house. In her account of the project, Maud Pember Reeves makes herself and her ladies at several points the outsiders intruding into the mothers' space: "A weekly caller becomes the abashed object of intense interest on the part of everybody in the street, from the curious glances of the greengrocer's lady at the corner to the appraising stare of the fat little baker who always manages to be on his doorstep across the road. And everywhere along the street is the visitor conscious of eyes which disappear from behind veiled windows."[35]

Pember Reeves's political statement is that the Lambeth women were indeed very good mothers: given their poor cooking facilities, overcrowded and decayed housing, large families, and small cash reserves, they were nothing less than national heroes. When outsiders criticized working-class wives for improvidence, for a penchant for fried or grilled foods over nutritious dishes like oatmeal, or their efforts to get free school dinners for their children, it was simply because they did not know what it was like inside the working-class woman's world. Oatmeal, for example, Pember Reeves spelled out very carefully (for the "oatmeal question" had been a hot issue between social workers and mothers for at least a generation), might be nutritious and cheap, but it is disgusting if you have to climb several flights of stairs to get water to wash the pot for cooking it and so skip that step; if you lack fuel for the long cooking oatmeal required; and, in any case, if you cannot afford the milk and sugar that always appear on the breakfast tables of the rich. The proof that the women were good mothers was to be found in just such concrete investigations.

Other feminist writings of this era show the same determination to speak for—and to let speak—working-class women's goodness as mothers: the Women's Cooperative Guild's three collections of working-class women's voices, two of which were interventions in parliamentary policy debates;[36] Emmeline Pethick-Lawrence's

---

These activities are described in the *East London Observer*, the *Daily News*, *Justice*, and the *Daily Chronicle*.

[35] Pember Reeves, *Round about a Pound*, p. 4; see also, on p. 16, the author's very empathic grasp of the housewives' discomfort in her presence.

[36] Margaret Llewelyn Davies, *Maternity: Letters from Working Women* (1915; rpt.

accounts of her life as a West London settlement worker years before she took up the suffrage cause; Margaret McMillan's pleas for school clinics, meals, and provision of public nurseries; the wartime work of Sylvia Pankhurst, who had perfected the old feminist propaganda technique of introducing delegations of live, speaking working-class women, often in their everyday clothes, to members of the cabinet in Whitehall.[37]

Anna Martin, a suffragist and social worker with the Nonconformist Bermondsey Settlement in Rotherhithe from 1899 until she died in 1937, was a particularly passionate defender of London's working-class mothers: "the staunchest champion that working women ever had," her friend Emmeline Pethick-Lawrence wrote the year after her death. Martin was a prolific writer of articles and pamphlets, each one representing the views and interests of the Rotherhithe married women who were Martin's special charge at the settlement.[38] Martin's political ideas are an amalgam of radical liberalism, feminism, and socialism. Her major rhetorical strategy is to fill her texts with Rotherhithe women speaking on the issues that concerned them: school lunches, drink, husbands' money, education for the handicapped, a rise in the legal school-leaving age.

Martin was enraged, for example, at World War I local laws in scattered English towns making pubs partly off-limits to women. She wrote two articles in a prominent journal, *The Nineteenth Century and After,* "from the point of view of one whose knowledge of the subject [women's drinking] comes from many years' close intercourse with poor working-women living in a London waterside district." Martin gave the women space to defend themselves against constantly reiterated charges that mothers' drinking was a major cause of infant mortality. Within a few paragraphs Martin was quoting at length from "Mrs. G.," who explained in half a page that by 11:00 A.M., after five hours of domestic work, she was ready for lunch and a glass of beer. Martin establishes the neighborhood standard of moderation, a half-

---

New York, 1978); Women's Cooperative Guild, *Working Women and Divorce* (1911; rpt. New York, 1980).

[37] Emmeline Pethick-Lawrence, *My Part in a Changing World* (London, 1938), chaps. 6 and 7. In the agitation around the Mines Regulation Amendment Act of 1887 Louisa, Lady Goldsmid, and Millicent Fawcett sponsored a deputation of Cradley Heath chainmakers to the home secretary. Josephine Butler led another delegation of women pitbrow workers to Parliament in the same year, 1887. See Ray Strachey, *"The Cause": A Short History of the Women's Movement in Great Britain* (1928; rpt. Port Washington, N.Y., 1969), pp. 236–37; Rosemary Feurer, "The Meaning of 'Sisterhood': The British Women's Movement and Protective Labor Legislation, 1870–1900," *Victorian Studies* 31 (Winter 1988): 245–46; Angela John, *By the Sweat of Their Brow: Women Workers at Victorian Coal Mines* (London, 1980), pp. 135–62.

[38] Pethick-Lawrence, *Changing World,* p. 346.

pint or a pint a day, by reproducing a discussion between three local women. Alcoholism, Martin concludes in her own more sociological voice, is overwhelmingly a male, not a female, problem; drink is not what keeps women from rearing healthy children, but the fact that their husbands give them so little of their wages, while the state does nothing to intervene.[39]

As a mothers' advocate, Anna Martin was very critical of most of the policy generated by the infant welfare movement, posited as it was on the assumption that mothers would be better if scrutinized more closely and regulated more tightly. She stressed the legislating role of a male-controlled state, which, with the consent of organized male workers, attempted to solve national problems of health and welfare by heaping ever more burdens on the backs of disfranchised working-class women who had few resources for defending themselves:

> In London and other large towns children are ordered up to the hospitals in droves to have their spectacles fitted, their teeth out, and their tonsils cut. . . . Grave legislators debate the material of which the baby's night-wear should be composed, and endeavour to lay down the principles which should regulate its sleeping arrangements. Local authorities decide the hours at which Annie may earn twopence by cleaning steps or Johnnie add to the family income by lathering chins. School doctors take a hand in the administration of the family finances, and virtually decree that Mrs. Smith shall spend less on bread and boots and more on Adeline's adenoids.[40]

Martin graphically conveys how harassing and irrational most infant welfare legislation looked to the working-class wives who were its main objects. After a decade or so of work with Rotherhithe mothers, Martin had come to fuse her voice and theirs as few of her social work contemporaries could.

The infant welfare movement has often been blandly described as a chapter in the development of the welfare state. More recent commentators, it is true, have pointed to the heavy doses of social control that underlay the movement and to the legislators' disregard of the realities of working-class motherhood. To look at the infant welfare workers' passions and rivalries is to appreciate further the movement's emotional richness and complexity. For the women who carried out the daily work of visiting real mothers in their own homes, attending them at clinics, or caring for their children in crèches and classes, their

[39] Anna Martin, "Working Women and Drink," Part I, *Nineteenth Century and After* 78 (December 1915): 1378–79.

[40] Anna Martin, "The Mother and Social Reform," *Nineteenth Century and After* 73 (May 1913): 1061–62.

own positions between good and bad mother were indeed thorny. Dreams of reconciliation with and reformation of bad mothers; fantasies of finding the perfect mother, a golden thread hidden in the coarse working-class weave; the illusion of supplanting their client mothers and becoming the nation's maternal ideal—all these must have mingled with the more prosaic pleasures of finding decently paid professional jobs and sometimes helping people.

CHAPTER THIRTEEN

Federal Help for Mothers: The Rise and Fall of the Sheppard-Towner Act in the 1920s

Molly Ladd-Taylor

In 1921, an Alabama mother wrote to the U.S. Children's Bureau to inquire if stories that Congress was about to pass a bill to protect mothers were true. "If so I sure am glad," she wrote. "I do hope it will help us Poor Country people who need help. We live on a farm and have very hard work to do. I am 27 yrs. old and have Five Little one's to Care for besides my husband an[d] his Father."[1] Thousands of women wrote similar letters asking the government for help with child rearing. Mostly working-class and farm mothers, they joined middle-class club women and reformers in an unusual alliance which demanded that the government take responsibility for child health, transformed "private" concerns about infant and prenatal care into national policy, and secured the passage of the nation's first social welfare measure.

The first "women's" bill to pass after women won the vote, the 1921 Sheppard-Towner Maternity and Infancy Protection Act was designed by Children's Bureau chief Julia Lathrop in response to requests and demands like those of the Alabama mother. It appropriated $1,480,000 for 1921–22 and $1,240,000 for the next five years to be used as matching funds to the states for information and instruction on nutrition and hygiene, prenatal and child health conferences, and visiting nurses for pregnant women and new mothers. The Sheppard-Towner Act was the culmination of the Progressive Era women's movement for child welfare, and virtually every women's organization supported the bill.

[1] Molly Ladd-Taylor, *Raising a Baby the Government Way: Mothers' Letters to the Children's Bureau, 1915–1932* (New Brunswick, 1986), p. 193.

"Of all the activities in which I have shared during more than forty years of striving," declared National Consumers' League secretary Florence Kelley, "none is, I am convinced, of such fundamental importance as the Sheppard-Towner Act."[2]

Despite women's support, the pioneering experiment in social welfare did not outlive the 1920s. A coalition of conservative organizations and the American Medical Association charged that Sheppard-Towner was a communist-inspired step toward state medicine which threatened the home and violated the principle of states' rights. In 1927, they defeated Children's Bureau efforts to renew appropriations, forcing a compromise that allocated funds for two more years but repealed the law in 1929. Brought into existence by the Progressive Era women's movement, the Sheppard-Towner Act could not survive the absence of a strong women's movement in the 1920s. By 1930, the increasing bureaucracy in government, the professionalization of the child health field, and the declining effectiveness of the women's reform lobby had reduced grass-roots involvement in maternal and child health care. When federal funds for maternal and child health were restored during the New Deal under Title V of the 1935 Social Security Act, they were the product of the lobbying efforts of women in government rather than a broad-based women's movement. They were seen as charity for children who could not afford a private physician rather than an entitlement for all.[3]

The U.S. Children's Bureau, established in 1912, was the driving force behind the child welfare movement. Directed by former Hull House residents Julia Lathrop (from 1912 to 1921) and Grace Abbott (from 1921 to 1934), the Bureau was staffed primarily by women who maintained close ties to women's clubs and social settlements. Limited by law to research and education, the Children's Bureau ran an educational campaign consisting of a birth registration drive, child-rearing bulletins, and studies of infant mortality, which it hoped would lead mothers to demand the health care to which they were entitled. "The importance of prenatal care has not until quite recently been fully realized by the medical profession as well as the general public," wrote Bureau physician Florence Kraker. "That women realize and appreciate the need of prenatal care is a great factor in developing the service rendered."[4]

[2] Quoted in J. Stanley Lemons, *The Woman Citizen: Social Feminism in the 1920s* (Urbana, 1973), pp. 155, 158–59. Also see Sheila Rothman, *Woman's Proper Place: A History of Changing Ideals and Practices, 1870 to the Present* (New York, 1978), pp. 136–53.

[3] On feminism in the 1920s and 1930s, see Nancy F. Cott, *The Grounding of Modern Feminism* (New Haven, 1987); and Susan Ware, *Beyond Suffrage: Women in the New Deal* (Cambridge, Mass., 1981).

[4] Ladd-Taylor, *Raising a Baby*, p. 165. On the Children's Bureau, see Molly Ladd-

The Children's Bureau publicized the fact that the United States had one of the highest infant and maternal mortality rates in the Western world. In 1915, approximately 6 women and 100 infants in the U.S. birth registration area died for every 1,000 live births. Deaths were even greater outside the registration area, and mortality was twice as high among people of color. Nationally, 11 black women and 181 black infants died for every 1,000 live births. In some areas one-quarter of all babies failed to reach their fifth birthday.[5] By investigating and quantifying infant mortality, the Bureau turned the private grief shared among friends and family into a public—and political—issue.

Women were responsible for the health and well-being of their children, but before women's organizations and the Children's Bureau began publishing child-rearing bulletins and organizing baby clinics, many mothers cared for sick children and coped with difficult pregnancies virtually unaided. Traditionally, female friends and family members gave women assistance and emotional support during childbirth and child rearing. Yet in the early twentieth century, migration and the decline in family size, combined with the persistence of Victorian attitudes about sex and reproduction, left many young wives without traditional support systems, experience in child care, or vital information about reproduction and their bodies.[6]

Many of these women turned to the Children's Bureau for help and received personal replies from Julia Lathrop and other staff members. The correspondence benefited both groups: mothers received needed

Taylor, "Hull House Goes to Washington: Woman and the Children's Bureau,"in *Gender, Class, Race, and Reform in the Progressive Era*, ed. Nancy Schrom Dye and Noralee Frankel (Lexington, Ky., 1991); Robyn Muncy, *Creating a Female Dominion in American Reform, 1890–1935* (New York, 1990); Jacqueline K. Parker and Edward M. Carpenter, "Julia Lathrop and the Children's Bureau: The Emergence of an Institution," *Social Service Review* 55 (March 1981): 60–76; Nancy Pottishman Weiss, "Save the Children: A History of the Children's Bureau, 1903–1918" (Ph.D. diss., University of California at Los Angeles, 1974); Louis J. Covotsos, "Child Welfare and Social Progress: A History of the United States Children's Bureau, 1912–1935" (Ph.D. diss., University of Chicago, 1976).

[5] U.S. Bureau of the Census, *Historical Statistics of the United States, Colonial Times to 1970*, pt. 1 (Washington, D.C. 1975), p. 57; U.S. Children's Bureau, *Maternal Mortality* (Washington, D.C., 1926), p. 37. See Richard A. Meckel, *Save The Babies: American Public Health Reform and The Prevention of Infant Mortality, 1850–1929* (Baltimore, 1990).

[6] On childbirth in the eighteenth and nineteenth centuries, see Richard W. Wertz and Dorothy C. Wertz, *Lying-In: A History of Childbirth in America* (New York, 1979); Judith Walzer Leavitt, *Brought to Bed: Childbearing in America* (New York, 1986); Carroll Smith-Rosenberg, "The Female World of Love and Ritual," *Signs* 1 (Fall 1975): 1–29. For examples of women's isolation, see Ladd-Taylor, *Raising a Baby*; and Elizabeth Hampsten, *Read This Only to Yourself: The Private Writings of Midwestern Women* (Bloomington, 1982). See also Nancy Schrom Dye and Daniel Blake Smith, "Mother Love and Infant Death, 1750–1920," *Journal of American History* 73 (September 1986): 329–53.

information and, occasionally, money and health care donated by Children's Bureau contacts, while the Bureau staff learned about the poverty, ill health, and determination of most American mothers. For example, Lathrop was deeply moved by the strength of a Wyoming mother, expecting her third child, who lived sixty-five miles from a doctor and was "filled with perfect horror at the prospects ahead." She was also impressed by the courage of an Idaho mother of four, with another on the way, who was burdened by overwork and poverty and feared she would die. "Talk about better babys," the Idaho woman wrote bitterly, "when a mother must be like some cow or mare when a babys come. If she lives, all wright, and if not, Just the same." These letters made Lathrop and her colleagues aware how "very urgent [was] the great question of protecting motherhood" and played an important part in the creation of the Sheppard-Towner Act.[7]

In making maternal and child health a public issue, the Children's Bureau undermined traditional fatalism about maternal suffering and generated a broad-based movement demanding that the government take responsibility for women's and children's health. The Wyoming woman had often assisted neighbors during childbirth, even adopting the baby of a woman who died, but it was not until the Children's Bureau campaign that she realized that those deaths were not inevitable. "It seems strange that conditions . . . year after year . . . have been perfectly needless," she wrote. "It is only necessary to make the people realize that their conditions are not normal." Like thousands of others, she volunteered to help the Children's Bureau "in any way." By 1918, 11 million women had joined the federal baby-saving campaign. In the 1920s, the General Federation of Women's Clubs, the National Congress of Parents and Teachers, the League of Women Voters, the Red Cross, the State Federation of Colored Women's Clubs, and American Legion auxiliaries helped the Children's Bureau publicize and administer the Sheppard-Towner Act.[8]

Yet women's enthusiasm for the Sheppard-Towner Act could not guarantee its continuation. A chief reason for the bill's defeat, as J. Stanley Lemons has argued, was that most politicians initially backed it more out of fear of women voters than out of commitment to the program. "On a secret ballot I don't think it would have got 50 votes," remarked Alice Robertson, the only woman in Congress and a staunch opponent of Sheppard-Towner. "Nineteen men who voted for it—so one of them told me—were cursing it and themselves at once in the

[7] Ladd-Taylor, *Raising a Baby*, pp. 49–51, 134.

[8] Ibid., p. 51; Grace Abbott, "Ten Years' Work for Children," *North American Review* 218 (August 1923): 189–200; U.S. Children's Bureau, *Promotion of the Welfare and Hygiene of Maternity and Infancy for the Fiscal Year Ending June 30, 1929* (Washington, D.C., 1931), pp. 24, 27.

cloak room."[9] Politicians afraid of the female vote in 1921 knew by 1926 that they had nothing to fear. In an increasingly conservative political climate, the knowledge that women did not vote as a bloc significantly reduced the effectiveness of the women's reform lobby.

A second factor in the defeat of the Sheppard-Towner Act was the opposition of the male medical establishment. The American Medical Association was afraid that public health services would threaten physicians' incomes and control over the health care system, and it opposed Sheppard-Towner as a step toward "state medicine." When the bill was first enacted, however, its female supporters successfully resisted efforts to transfer its administration from the female-run Children's Bureau to the medically run Public Health Service by distinguishing the preventive public health education they provided from private medical care. Physicians treated sick children, they argued, but infant welfare clinics were educational and were geared toward the healthy child. Yet despite the Children's Bureau's efforts to placate physicians (in some states Sheppard-Towner nurses refused to examine children who did not have permission from their doctors), medical societies objected to "lay" people administering child health programs. Over the course of the 1920s, they managed to replace many of the women in top positions in the state bureaus of child hygiene with male physicians and to convince private doctors to incorporate preventive health examinations into their medical practices. Sheppard-Towner services and the improvements in private medical practice both contributed to the decline in mortality among white infants, making federally funded health care appear less urgent to the middle class.[10]

A third factor in the defeat of the maternity bill was the weakness of the child health movement in the states. Although most of the Children's Bureau staff believed that universally available medical and nursing care was a "minimum standard" of child welfare, to secure passage of some form of maternity aid, they supported a weak bill that gave no outright financial aid or medical care and established a decentralized administration giving the federal Children's Bureau little control over local programs. After the passage of the very moderate Sheppard-Towner Act, the Bureau's position changed from that of leader of a political campaign for child welfare into that of administrator and defender of an existing—and inadequate—program. The

[9] Lemons, *Woman Citizen*, p. 157; Alice Robertson to Elizabeth Lowell Putnam, November 21, 1921, Folder 300, Elizabeth Lowell Putnam Papers, Arthur and Elizabeth Schlesinger Library on the History of Women in America, Radcliffe College, Cambridge, Mass.

[10] Rothman, *Woman's Proper Place*, pp. 144, 150–52. See Muncy, *Creating a Female Dominion*, pp. 135–50; and Paul Starr, *The Social Transformation of American Medicine* (New York, 1982), pp. 189–97.

Bureau staff, who had never had much authority within the government, were caught between their roles as reform-minded "outsiders," who had little power in government, and as pragmatic "insiders," who had to maintain the status quo to defend their own positions in government and protect the welfare programs for which they had fought so hard.[11]

Most histories of the Sheppard-Towner Act focus on debates over federal legislation and on the Children's Bureau's relations with the American Medical Association, but evaluation of the bill must rest ultimately on an analysis of the actual work that Sheppard-Towner funded in the states. The terms of the bill ensured that state politics would play a crucial role in the success or failure of the act. Before a state was eligible to receive funds, it had to pass special qualifying legislation, vote matching funds, provide a plan for implementation, and create a special bureau for administering the program. Still, forty-one states joined the program in 1922; eventually only Massachusetts, Connecticut, and Illinois refused aid. The decentralized administration of the Sheppard-Towner Act allowed communities to devise programs that suited their needs, but it also made maternity work vulnerable to political opposition and incompetent administration. The achievements of Sheppard-Towner varied depending on state and local politics, the personnel in the state bureaus of child health, the attitudes of local physicians and civic leaders, and climate and geography (such as snow, mountains, floods, and poor roads). The program had a tremendous impact in states where the federal Children's Bureau worked effectively with local women's groups and doctors, but it never got off the ground in others.[12]

The most successful states used Sheppard-Towner funds both to provide services and to build a strong grass-roots campaign for maternal and child welfare. Distribution of literature is a case in point; when women shared government publications on child rearing and prenatal care with friends and relatives, they both passed on much-needed information and created a wider demand for health care. In 1929, the last year of Sheppard-Towner's operation, the Children's Bureau estimated that the care of almost one-half of all babies born in that year had been influenced by its advice.[13]

Child health conferences also functioned as a helpful service and one of the most effective tools for building community support for ma-

[11] See Judith Sealander, *As Minority Becomes Majority: Federal Reaction to the Phenomenon of Women in the Work Force, 1920–1963* (Westport, Conn., 1983), pp. 3–11, for a similar phenomenon in the Women's Bureau.

[12] U.S. Children's Bureau, *Promotion of the Welfare*, p. 27.

[13] Ibid., p. 21.

ternal and infant health care. They were social as well as educational events in rural areas: some communities closed schools, businesses, and stores so that everyone could attend the festivities. Families came for the movies, refreshments, prizes, and carnival atmosphere of the clinics, as well as for physical examinations and child-rearing advice. Although attendance could be small at a poorly organized clinic, conferences actively supported by local club women, civic leaders, and physicians were generally well attended. More than two hundred women attended a meeting in a remote county in Mississippi. Some mothers rode horseback or walked several miles carrying small children to attend the conferences in one-room schoolhouses or local churches.[14]

Many women welcomed the Children's Bureau's baby-saving campaign, but some were offended by the agency's efforts to make health care a public issue and resisted government intervention into their "private" concerns. For example, prenatal examinations challenged religious beliefs about feminine modesty and maternal suffering. In Florida, six white women left a meeting attended by twenty women after the nurse began to talk about prenatal care. "The Lord gives and the Lord takes and we have no business talking of such things," they reportedly said. Yet many expectant mothers did want to be examined, even when their families considered prenatal care to be indecent or indulgent. According to a North Dakota nurse, some women too embarrassed to seek help for themselves borrowed neighbors' children so that they could go to the conferences. Others fought with their families for their right to prenatal care, slowly changing social attitudes.[15]

Distribution of literature and health conferences were effective in most states, but they had little impact in very isolated areas where few people could read. When difficult terrain, inclement weather, lack of roads, or a busy harvest season made it difficult to get a crowd to clinics, nurses spent most of their time on home visits. They helped with childbirth, treated sick children, and showed mothers how to prepare modified milk or get the house ready for childbirth using materials available in their homes. In New Mexico, a fourteen-month-old baby weighing less than nine pounds gained weight after the nurse taught

[14] See, for example, [Mississippi], "Narrative and Statistical Report," March 1924, File 11-26-1, Central Files, 1914–40. Children's Bureau Records, National Archives (hereafter cited as CB).

[15] Division of Maternity and Infancy Hygiene, Bureau of Child Welfare, Florida State Board of Health, "Biennial Report," July 1, 1922, to December 31, 1922, File 11-11-8, Correspondence and Reports, Children's Bureau Records (hereafter cited as C&R, CB); "Conference of Directors of State Divisions Administering the Federal Maternity and Infancy Act Held under the Auspices of the Children's Bureau," September 19–21, 1923, p. 39, File 11-0, C&R, CB.

his mother how to prepare milk formula and keep it cool, clean, and free from flies.[16]

The work of Sheppard-Towner nurses was not confined to education and medicine. They met with local doctors, civic leaders, and club women to build community support and lay the groundwork for health conferences, and they lectured on child hygiene before a wide range of groups, including missionary societies and the Girl Scouts. In 1927, nurses in Mississippi were forced to abandon their maternity work and midwife classes temporarily because a flood had destroyed the homes—and the "black bags"—of most of the midwives. Instead, they helped with flood relief, vaccinated refugees, and cooked breakfast for rescue workers. In the process, they built local support for their campaign.[17]

Despite the good intentions of most Sheppard-Towner nurses, their middle-class standards of hygiene and faith in science and medicine could put a wedge between them and their patients, reducing the effectiveness of the child health campaign. Poor women were often grateful for health care, but they rarely abandoned traditional practices such as employing midwives and having female friends and relatives present during childbirth. Although they frequently combined old and new methods of child care and delivery, women rejected the efforts of Sheppard-Towner agents to replace traditional healing with modern medicine. For example, the family of a New Mexico woman who had been in labor for six days refused to relinquish the midwife's services even after the doctor refused to help if the midwife were there. Similarly, a Sheppard-Towner nurse in Montana reported with annoyance that a Native American family refused to allow whites to intervene in a case they considered the domain of the traditional healer.[18]

Although Sheppard-Towner programs were based on white middle-class notions of proper hygiene and child-rearing methods, most of the women who came into contact with Sheppard-Towner agents were not coerced by the power of the state. With the exception of midwives, women were free to accept or refuse government assistance, and, for the most part, they were enthusiastic about Sheppard-Towner services. In contrast, efforts to license and regulate birth attendants depended on state authority. In some states, Sheppard-Towner agents who lacked sensitivity to local customs and were offended by what

[16] Dorothy Anderson to G. S. Luckett, October 6, 1926, File 11-33-8, CB.

[17] Mississippi Department of Health Bureau of Child Welfare, "Narrative and Statistical Report," March 1924, File 11-26-1; "[Mississippi] Narrative and Statistical Report," April–August 1927," File 11-26-8, CB. See the 1926 reports of Dorothy Anderson, R.N., Sheppard-Towner Special Agent in New Mexico, File 11-33-8, CB.

[18] Dorothy Anderson to G. S. Luckett, October 6, 1926, File 11-33-8, CB; Child Welfare Division, Montana State Board of Health, "Narrative Report of Activities," July 1 to December 31, 1924, File 11-28-8, C&R, CB.

they saw as midwives' "very ignorant and superstitious ways" had the power to withhold licenses and to threaten the livelihood of local midwives. For their part, midwives were understandably distrustful of the nurses and resented the government's intrusion into their practices. Sheppard-Towner agents in New Mexico reported difficulty locating Mexican midwives, who were afraid of anyone who represented the law and often hid out in the hills until the nurse left the county.[19]

Although many midwives resisted government efforts at instruction, there is evidence that others enjoyed the attention they received. Perhaps they saw midwife classes as recognition of their work or a way to facilitate the nearly impossible task of collecting fees. Or perhaps they wanted the opportunity to have their pictures taken, watch movies, and drink Coca Cola. Like expectant mothers, midwives turned government programs to their advantage and incorporated modern innovations into traditional practices; they readily adopted suggestions they found useful, such as substituting newspaper pads for old quilts during childbirth, but held on to other traditional practices. Midwives followed nurses' instructions because they wanted to win the money offered for the best-stocked black bags, because they were afraid of losing the right to practice, and because they were used to obeying white women—at least to their faces. Much to the dismay of their instructors, even midwives who won prizes for their black bags rarely took them on actual cases.[20]

That the delivery of Sheppard-Towner services and, therefore, the success of the act depended on support from local physicians, politicians, and women's groups is evident in Nevada, one of two or three states which Grace Abbott felt was "not making some real headway." The poor administrative skills of the Nevada director were compounded by physicians' objections because the agency that administered the bill was not directed by a doctor. As a result, Sheppard-Towner programs languished. A nurse in one of the richest counties in the state had no supplies except for scales; a nurse in another county had only three cases in one year. Frustrated by the lack of progress in Sheppard-Towner work, some women reformers withdrew their active support for the program. "I am so thoroughly disgusted with the situation that I feel that I cannot waste any more time in trying to do something . . . so long as the present people are in charge," complained the president of the Nevada League of Women Voters.[21]

[19] "Report of Work Done under the Maternity and Infancy Act in the State of New Mexico," July 1, 1925, to June 30, 1926, File 11-33-8, C&R, CB.

[20] For more detailed discussion, see Molly Ladd-Taylor, " 'Grannies' and 'Spinsters:' Midwife Training under the Sheppard-Towner Act," *Journal of Social History* 22 (December 1988): 255–75.

[21] Grace Abbott to Lillie M. Barbour, July 13, 1925, File 11-30-1; Marie Phelan to Florence Kraker, October 30, 1924, File 11-30-1; Marie Phelan to Blanche Haines, June 15–

The inability and unwillingness of the Children's Bureau staff to intervene in political disputes and personnel decisions in the states meant that discriminatory practices went unchallenged. Although Native American infants in Montana were 2.7 times more likely to die than whites, Sheppard-Towner did not have a full-time nurse on the reservations. Despite higher death rates among blacks, the Georgia State Board of Health tried to save money by providing inferior services to African Americans. It hired an inexperienced black nurse to work with black midwives because it considered the salary demanded by an experienced nurse "too much for any negro." Unwilling to jeopardize support for the Sheppard-Towner Act among white public health officials, the Children's Bureau did not comment.[22]

The Sheppard-Towner Act was clearly not, as its supporters initially hoped, a stepping-stone to federally funded infant and maternity care for women of every region and class. But for a brief time it transformed women's and children's health from a "personal matter only to be discussed 'en famille' " into a national priority and contributed to the decline in infant mortality.[23] In seven years, Sheppard-Towner agents held 183,252 health conferences, established 2,978 permanent prenatal centers, made 3,131,996 home visits, and distributed 22,030,489 pieces of literature. Nationally, infant deaths dropped from 76 to 69 per 1,000 live births between 1921 and 1928. Deaths from gastrointestinal disease, most easily prevented by educational programs, declined by 47 percent. The Bureau attributed a slight rise in maternal mortality—from 68 per 10,000 live births in 1921 to 69 in 1929—to the inclusion of predominantly black counties with high maternal death rates into the birth registration area for the first time. In all, the Children's Bureau estimated that Sheppard-Towner funds saved the lives of 60,000 babies.[24]

The federal and state Children's Bureaus received hundreds of letters showing women's support for Sheppard-Towner. "I trust you'll find by many letters that your work is doing much and will continue it," wrote a West Virginia mother of twins. "There are many who do not

---

20, 1925, File 11-30-1; Lillie Barbour to Grace Abbott, July 2, 1925, File 11-30-1; Mrs. J. B. Clinedinst to Grace Abbott, January 2, 1928, File 11-30-8, all in CB.

[22] "Report of Work Done under Federal Maternity and Infancy Act in the State of Montana," July 1, 1926, to June 30, 1927, File 11-28-8, C&R, CB; [Georgia] Division of Child Hygiene, "Annual Report," 1925, File 11-12-8, C&R, CB; Clark Goreman, Georgia Committee on Interracial Cooperation, to Blanche Haines, July 8, 1926, File 11-12-2, CB.

[23] "Semi-Annual Report of Maternity and Infancy Work [Mississippi]," July 1, 1922, to December 31, 1922, File 11-26-8, C&R, CB.

[24] Although the white infant mortality rate declined from 72 to 64, the death rate among babies of color showed only a slight decline, from 108 to 106 (U.S. Children's Bureau, *Promotion of the Welfare*, pp. 28–34).

Pay attention But It Is a great Benefit to those that do." A Georgia woman agreed: "I don't see how we poor mothers could do without them [prenatal clinics]. . . . I am the mother of 14 children, and I never was cared for till I begin going to the good will center clinic. . . . We are so glad the day has come when we have someone to care for our babies when they get sick."[25] Sheppard-Towner convinced many mothers that infant deaths were not inevitable, helped them find better ways to care for their babies within the constraints of poverty and isolation, and forced the medical profession to take infant and prenatal care seriously.

Ironically, the success of the Sheppard-Towner Act contributed to its defeat. Sheppard-Towner was an important factor in the declining death rate of white infants and in the incorporation of preventive health services into private medical practice, both of which made publicly funded maternity and infancy programs appear less urgent to the middle class. It also furthered the professionalization of public health and heightened the tension inherent in the Children's Bureau's dual role as service provider and leader of a political campaign for child welfare, rendering it more difficult to sustain grass-roots involvement in child health reform. By the 1930s, the medicalization of maternal and infant care had reduced the control even middle-class women had over childbirth and their children's health care.[26]

The repeal of the Sheppard-Towner Act in 1929 was a reassertion of the principle that children's welfare was the responsibility of individual mothers, not society. Although the 1935 Social Security Act restored federal funds for maternal and infant health care, services were restricted to those who could not afford private physicians. In contrast to "entitlement" programs like Social Security, which mainly benefit middle-class men, public maternal and child health services were (and are) stigmatized as charity and largely cut off from mainstream political support.[27] The two-tier health care system in place today helps keep the death rate of African-American babies almost twice that of whites and is in part an unintended legacy of the Sheppard-Towner Act.[28]

[25] West Virginia Division of Child Hygiene and Public Health Nursing, "Extracts from Statements of Mothers Who Took Motherhood Correspondence Course," enclosed in Katharine Lenroot to Julia Lathrop, September 23, 1926, File 11-0, CB; "Letters from Georgia Women Attending Prenatal Clinic," enclosed in Joe Bowdoin to Dorothy Kirchwey Brown, April 30, 1929, Dorothy Kirchwey Brown Papers, Schlesinger Library.

[26] See Leavitt, *Brought to Bed*; and Wertz and Wertz, *Lying-In*.

[27] See Barbara Nelson, "The Origins of the Two-Channel Welfare State: Workmen's Compensation and Mothers' Aid," in *Women, the State, and Welfare*, ed. Linda Gordon (Madison, 1990).

[28] Children's Defense Fund, *A Call for Action to Make Our Nation Safe for Children* (Washington, D.C., 1988), p. 3.

CHAPTER FOURTEEN

A Right Not to Be Beaten: The Agency of Battered Women, 1880–1960

Linda Gordon

The fact that a great majority of Americans today condemn wife beating represents progress, because several centuries ago it was widely accepted. This transformation was not a gradual, epiphenomenal result of "modernization" or individualism but was produced in large part by political activity, to which both waves of feminism contributed. In addition to organized feminists, victims of wife beating, including some of the very poorest and most wretched of women, also contributed to the delegitimation of a once common patriarchal privilege.

The efforts of these victims are important for several reasons. These women, often seen mainly as victimized and defeated, deserve credit for their bravery, ingenuity, and perseverance. Their activism has implications for several important issues in feminist scholarship: the meanings of patriarchy and social control, the relation between feminists and nonfeminists, and how "rights" talk as a particular way of making claims emerges out of social change. I will return to these themes at the end of this essay.

That wife beating is an important contemporary problem has in some ways made it harder to put into an accurate historical perspective. The legacy of victim blaming is so strong that much of the contemporary feminist discourse about wife beating still concentrates on disproving sexist mystifications, such as that women provoke it or that it is mutual marital conflict. Some premises that I take as already demonstrated are that the basic condition of wife beating is male dominance—not superior physical strength but social, economic, political, and psychological power; that wife beating is a social problem, not only a personal one; and that stopping it requires social action.

My evidence comes from a history of family violence, a study of the case records of child protection agencies in Boston from 1880 to 1960. These agencies originated with the discovery of child abuse in the 1870s and tried to limit their jurisdiction to mistreatment of children. Their clients, mainly mothers, virtually dragged the child protectors into wife-beating problems, with the result that 34 percent of all the cases in this study involved incidents of marital violence.[1]

The Nineteenth-Century Feminist Campaign against Wife Beating

I do not suggest that wife-beating victims would have behaved as they did had there been no feminist movement. Both clients and case workers were influenced by a substantial campaign against wife beating, a campaign which has been underestimated because it produced no separate organizations and operated largely from within the temperance, child-saving, and social purity movements.[2]

The image of the beaten wife, the indirect victim of drink, was prominent in temperance rhetoric since the 1830s. In the latter half of the century, particularly in the work of the Women's Christian Temperance Union, drinking was a veritable code word for male violence.[3] The child protectors were usually temperance advocates who considered family violence the inevitable result of drink. Putting a temperance frame around criticisms of male behavior allowed feminists to score points obliquely, without attacking marriage or men in general. Male brutality, not male tyranny, was the target. The problem came from exceptional, "depraved" men, not the male gender as a norm. Nevertheless, temperance agitation made drunkenness a gendered vice—male—and its victims quintessentially female. Considered as a veil thrown over challenges to male supremacy, temperance was a thin cloth indeed.

[1] Evidence and sources for these and following generalizations are spelled out in detail in my *Heroes of Their Own Lives: The Politics and History of Family Violence, Boston, 1880–1960* (New York, 1988).

[2] Historian Elizabeth Pleck has unearthed records of a Chicago group for the protection of both women and children, but it was exceptional. See her "Feminist Responses to Crimes against Women, 1868–1896," *Signs* 8 (Spring 1983): 465–69.

[3] Jerome Nadelhaft, "Domestic Violence in the Literature of the Temperance Movement," unpublished paper, quoted by Elizabeth Pleck, *Domestic Tyranny: The Making of American Social Policy against Family Violence from Colonial Times to the Present,* (New York, 1987), chap. 5, esp. pp. 98–101; Ruth Bordin, *Woman and Temperance: The Quest for Power and Liberty, 1873–1900* (Philadelphia, 1981), p. 162; Barbara Leslie Epstein, *The Politics of Domesticity: Women, Evangelism, and Temperance in Nineteenth-Century America* (Middletown, Conn., 1981), p. 114.

The feminist campaign for divorce provided another frame in which to tell shocking narratives about wife beating.[4] Women's rights leaders publicized particular cases, usually those involving victims of substantial social standing or popular appeal. Feminists sheltered runaway wives, agitated in divorce and child-custody cases, and held a few public meetings on egregious cases.[5]

Moreover, these campaigns had had substantial success by the 1870s. Elizabeth Pleck has shown that, contrary to some common misconceptions, wife beating was not generally accepted as a head of household's right at this time but was considered a disreputable practice.[6] By the 1870s courts commonly denied men the right to chastise their wives, particularly through physical punishment.[7]

Hostility to wife beating was integrated into the child protection movement as well. Elizabeth Cady Stanton, arguing for women's rights, believed that "the condition of the child always follows that of the mother."[8] Mothers in any properly operating family were not thought to have interests separate from, let alone antithetical to, those of children. A damage to one was a damage to both.

Clients' Views of Their Victimization

But if wife beating was not widely considered legitimate, neither was public discussion of it. Most feminist as well as conservative moralists preferred that it remain a hidden or at least whispered subject, and this preference characterized the child protectors as well. Thus it is not surprising that child protection clients adapted to this indirect approach.

Most preindustrial communities had tolerated a male privilege to hit ("punish") wives. This does not mean that before modern feminism women never objected to or resisted beating. A better if rough paradigm with which to understand "tolerance" of wife beating is as a tense compromise between male supremacy and female resistance in a

[4] For an early example of this propaganda, see *Una* 1, no. 6 (1853): 84. That the divorce advocates harped more on marital rape (although rather than using this term they discussed brutality and "excessive demands") than on wife beating suggests that they considered the latter to have criminal remedies, while the former had none. See "Debates on Marriage and Divorce, 10th National Women's Rights Convention, 1960," in *The Concise History of Woman Suffrage*, ed. Mari Jo Buhle and Paul Buhle (Urbana, 1978), pp. 170–89.

[5] Ellen Carol DuBois, ed., *Elizabeth Cady Stanton, Susan B. Anthony: Correspondence, Writings, Speeches* (New York, 1981), p. 95; Pleck, "Feminist Responses."

[6] Elizabeth Pleck, "Wife Beating in Nineteenth-Century America," *Victimology* 4 (1979): 60–74.

[7] Gordon, *Heroes*, pp. 255 and 364n.

[8] "Address to the Legislature of New York on Women's Rights," 1854, in DuBois, ed., *Stanton, Anthony, Correspondence*, p. 49.

system that also rested on a great deal of mutual interest in cooperation between men and women. Communities had standards as to what constituted excessive violence. Recently such notions as the "rule of thumb"—that a man might not use a stick thicker than his thumb to beat his wife—have been cited as evidence of women's total humiliation and powerlessness. On the contrary, such regulation was evidence of a degree of women's power, albeit enforceable mainly through the willingness of others to defend it. But women often did have allies within a patriarchal community. If that much abused word *patriarchy* is to have any usefulness, it must describe a system larger than any individual family, which required regulation even of its privileged members. Patriarchal fathers could control their households, but they in turn were subject to sanctions—social control—by the community, whose power brokers included not only fellow patriarchs but also women, particularly senior women. The agency clients were accustomed to appealing to fathers as well as mothers, brothers as well as sisters and friends, for support against abusive husbands.

Nevertheless, in the nineteenth and early twentieth centuries, many women clients did not seem to believe they had a right to freedom from physical violence. When social workers expressed disgust at the way they were treated, the clients sometimes considered that reaction naive. They spoke of the inevitability of male violence. Their refusal to condemn marital violence in moral terms must be interpreted carefully. It did not mean that they were fatalistic about beatings. They often resisted assault by fighting back, running away, attempting to embarrass the men before others, or calling in the police or other authorities. And they did express moral outrage if their men crossed some border of tolerability. There is no contradiction here. The language of "rights" is only one approach to self-defense. In a patriarchal system there were neither institutions nor concepts defending absolute rights, but rather custom and bargaining. Because the client women did not conduct a head-on challenge to their husbands' right to hit them does not mean that they liked being hit or believed that their virtue required them to accept it. Failure to make this distinction is the result of flat and ahistorical conceptions of patriarchy and female subordination. There was no society in which women so "internalized" their inferiority, to use a modern way of explanation, that they did not struggle to improve their situation. All systems of domination—gender, class, race, wage labor, slave—are systems of conflict.

The fullest discourse about what counted as abusive was, of course, that of the social workers, who wrote the case notes and who determined what constituted a case. But the clients' views were also discernible. In their complaints against husbands there emerged, over time, an idea of a "right," meaning, in the context of this study, that is, in dealings with social work agencies, an entitlement to help in leaving their marriages on the grounds of abuse. It was a claim women began to make only when they had some reasonable expectation that they could win; until then, strategies other than head-on confrontation with a husband's prerogatives were more effective. Furthermore, this rights claim reflected, I will argue, the erosion of certain other forms of protection that had been characteristic of more patriarchal societies.

Women's invention of a right not to be beaten came from a dialectic between changing social possibilities and aspirations. When women's best hope was husbands' kindness, because they were economically dependent on marriage, they did not protest violations of their individual rights but rested their case on their importance as mothers. As women's possibilities expanded to include wage earning, remarriage after divorce, birth limitation, and aid to single mothers, their best hopes escalated to include escape from marital violence altogether.

In the earlier decades of this study, for example, several women clients complained bitterly about their husbands' obscene language and its effect on children. In 1916 a wife who had left her husband agreed that she would "keep his house if he would treat her respectfully and use decent language before the chn."[9] In 1920 a mother thought her husband's "dirty mouth" was "the hardest thing we have to bear in this house, harder even than [his] not working."[10]

By far the most striking and consistent women's complaint, however, until the 1930s, focused on husbands' nonsupport rather than abuse. Nonsupport cases involved married women whose husbands did not adequately provide, for reasons that might include unemployment, illness, drunkenness, hostility, or negligence. In 1910 a mother who was permanently crippled by her husband's beatings, who had appeared to the police and her priest so badly bruised that they advised her to have him arrested, complained to the Massachusetts Society for the Prevention of Cruelty to Children (MSPCC) only about his failure to provide.[11] In 1901 a young mother complained only about nonsupport, yet the abuse discovered was so severe that an MSPCC agent began making secret plans to sneak the mother and two children out of the house after the father had gone off to work.[12]

In approaching child-saving agencies, the mothers had to present evidence of mistreatment of children. Some women apparently calculated that foul language was a violation of norms of respectability that

[9] Case #3646. These are code numbers developed by the author to preserve confidentiality; they do not refer to agency case numbers. Abbreviations such as "chn." for "children," are used in the original caseworkers' notes.

[10] Case #3240.

[11] Case #2027.

[12] Case #3363.

social control agents could be expected to defend. The emphasis of so many on nonsupport does not necessarily mean that they considered it more unbearable than beating. Rather, it may have meant that they knew that social workers considered it criminal and actionable. These women believed that they had a claim on the community, as represented by the social work agencies, for their support by husbands but not to protection from physical violence in marriage. Nineteenth-century women also brought wife-beating charges in court but with little success; despite anti-wife-beating precedents, conviction was likely only in egregious cases or those including nonsupport, intemperance, or both.

Women tried to get support for their autonomy from social control agencies without directly challenging male authority. In 1893 a wife complained that she had left her husband "with his permission," but that he broke his word.[13] In 1917, a wife and children were beaten for not fulfilling the father's work demands; but the woman complained only about his demands, not about the beatings. She asked the case workers to persuade him to take in fewer boarders because the work was too much for her. Her logic differed from that of the agency, which was willing to investigate the violence but told her that the "agency was not in [the] business" of regulating his labor demands.[14]

Surprisingly, women's complaints about wife beating escalated just as feminism was at its nadir. The 1930s formed a divide in this study, after which the majority of women clients complained directly rather than indirectly about wife beating. In 1934, for example, a young mother of three, married through a matchmaker at age sixteen to an Italian-born man, repeatedly made assault and battery complaints against him. He was also a nonsupporter, but her logic differed from that of earlier clients, and it was the beating that she considered actionable. Perhaps this client, because she was an American-born woman, much younger than her immigrant husband, may have had less-patriarchal expectations than average among the largely immigrant family violence clients. Her husband's probation officer described her as a "high-type Italian," and the case worker thought she expected "people to do things for her."[15] Women continued to allege child abuse to get agency help, but in the ensuing investigations they protested about their own abuse more strenuously than they previously had. One MSPCC agent complained in 1940 that the mother was not very interested in her son's problem but wanted only to talk about herself.[16]

[13] Case #1040.
[14] Case #2523.
[15] Case #4007A.
[16] Case #4584.

In other cases in that year, women rationalized their battering in new ways: not as an inevitable part of the female condition or the male nature but as something they individually deserved. One woman said, "This is my punishment for marrying against my mo.'s wishes."[17] Thus even in blaming themselves they expressed a new sensibility that wife beating should not be the inevitable lot of women.

Accusations of wife beating stood out even more because of the virtual disappearance of nonsupport complaints, even in the midst of the Depression. This striking inverse correlation between nonsupport and wife-beating complaints stimulates an economistic hypothesis: economic dependence prevented women from formulating a sense of entitlement to protection against marital violence, but it also gave them a sense of entitlement to support; by contrast, the growth of a wage labor economy, bringing unemployment, transience, and dispersal of kinfolk, deprived women of the certainty that they could get support from their husbands but allowed them to insist on their physical integrity. It is a reasonable hypothesis that the Depression, by the leveling effect of its widespread unemployment, actually encouraged women regarding the possibilities of independence and therefore of individual rights claims.[18]

Clients' Actions against Wife Beating

Rights-talk is only one way of struggling against wife beating, and its development from the 1930s does not mean that battered women's overall resistance escalated at that time. In fact, an attempt to identify and quantify women's efforts to escape beatings showed continuous and relatively steady levels of resistance from the beginning to the end of this study.

The barrage of complaints to the agencies continued even though they produced little help for most women. The complainants' difficulties were essentially those faced by single mothers. The biggest obstacle for most women dealing with abusive men was that they did not wish to lose their children; indeed, their motherhood was for most of them (including, it must be emphasized, many who were categorized as abusive or neglectful parents) their greatest source of pleasure, self-esteem, and social status. In escaping they had to find a way simulta-

[17] Case #4284.

[18] That wife-beating complaints to social workers increased in the 1930s does not, of course, constitute evidence against the influence of organized feminism. This was (and remains) a complex influence, continuing to work even as feminist organizational forms diminished and always combining, as I have argued, with a sense of the possible largely determined by economic and social opportunity for independence.

neously to earn money and raise children in an economy that offered limited jobs for women, little child care, and almost no reliable aid to single mothers. They often had the low confidence characteristic of women trying to take unconventional action. Moreover, these women had the added burden of defying a social norm condemning marital separation and encouraging submission as a womanly virtue.

Mrs. O'Brien, for example—not her real name—whose story began in Charlestown in 1910, changed her mind repeatedly about how she wanted to deal with her abuse, and one might imagine her condemned as masochistic or at least passive, not really wanting to escape her victimization. Scrutinized more closely, her seeming ambivalence reflects the lack of options open to her and so many others. Both she and Mr. O'Brien were born in Ireland; he worked as a freight handler for the Boston and Maine Railroad; they had three surviving children in 1910 and four more were to be born while the case continued, three of them surviving. The beatings she suffered were so apparent that several outside authorities—police, her priest, the MSPCC—all took her side. The police advised her to have him arrested; but she responded, speaking for thousands, "She does not want to lose her chn. however and the little money which she does receive from fa. enables her to keep her home together." Instead, she tried to get the MSPCC agent to "scare" him into treating her and her children "right," even though previous jail terms had not "reformed" him. She agreed to another prosecution at one peak of rage—"would rather starve than endure the treatment"—then changed her mind and agreed to let him return to live with her if he would give her all his wages. The MSPCC got her to agree that it would collect $10 per week from him and give it to her. When he agreed to this, she raised her demand to $11, evidently dreading taking him back. But he agreed to this, too. Three months later he was sentenced to six months for assaulting her; she was pregnant and soon began campaigning to get him out of jail. This pattern continued for years; in 1914 and again in 1920 she was threatening to murder him, describing herself as in a "desperate state of mind."[19]

Mrs. O'Brien's ambivalence was a rational response to her situation. The presence of her children, numbering six by 1920, literally forced her into submission to her husband. Her problems illustrate the limited usefulness of prosecution as a remedy in the absence of economic provisions for single mothers. (It also suggests why prosecution might have different meanings today, when greater employment opportunities, Aid to Dependent Children, and shelters offer women a better chance of survival alone with their children.) But Mrs. O'Brien, like many victims, believed in the potential benefit of prosecution as a

[19] Case #2027.

deterrent; this was not an option forced on her by social control agents. And her contradictory behavior was typical. Many women who successfully prosecuted their husbands for abuse then quickly petitioned for pardons for them, and the numbers of those who withdrew their complaints before trial or whose husbands were not convicted must have been even greater but were untraceable. To cite but one of scores of examples: Arnold W., a second offender, whose wife had testified that she feared for her life, was sentenced to five months in 1870 by a judge who considered him "incorrigible." But Mrs. W. returned within two months to say she had testified against him "while angry" but now needed his release on grounds of poverty; the district attorney, supporting her petition, wrote that "certainly she is right, if the starved appearance of her children is any indication."[20]

Batterers knew women could not seek prosecution for fear of losing economic support. One husband threatened that "if she ever sues for divorce or separation or if she ever has him brought into court . . . he will throw up his job and then she will be without support."[21] Others derided their wives' chance for independence: "If you want to come back, all right, if not all right, we will see who wins out in this deal. . . . I work for W. C. Hill, when you want me arrested," one wife beater wrote in 1911 to his wife who had left.[22]

Short of prosecution and more commonly, women sought to use the police to threaten prosecution, hoping to frighten the men. Police were called in 49 percent of these wife-beating cases (there was very little change over time in the rate of police involvement). Women had no other agency to call for emergency help, but what they got was almost always unsatisfactory. Their stories sound familiar. The police implicitly (and sometimes explicitly) identified with the husband and, while urging him to moderate his violence and to sober up, sympathized with his frustration and trivialized his assaults. They did often remove the angry men from their homes for a while, calming them, and this service was of some limited value to women. Sometimes the police threatened men with arrest and jail. Often, too, the police knew that little they could do would be useful to the women, who could not survive without these men. At times the police were worse than useless: in one 1910 case a woman who went to the station to complain about her husband was arrested herself instead for drunkenness.[23] Often the police refused to respond to domestic disturbance calls. In 1930 one officer told a social worker, "She is always calling on the Police for the

[20] Commonwealth of Massachusetts, States Archives, Executive Council, Pardon, Commutation and Parole Files, unnumbered box 12-1-69 to 3-1-70.

[21] Case #6040.

[22] Case #2024.

[23] Case #3040.

slightest things and the Police will no longer go to the home when [she] requests them to."[24] Or, as another woman reported in 1960, the police pacified her husband in another room and did not talk with her at all.[25]

Mrs. O'Brien's ultimate desire was for a "separation and maintenance" agreement, as such provisions were then known: she wanted the state to guarantee her the right to a separate household and require her husband to pay support. Such a solution was the most common desire of the beaten wives in this study. As another woman explained, "She did not wish him to be put away as he is a steady worker but wd. like the case arranged so that he wd. live apart and support her and the chn."[26] Mrs. O'Brien managed to get aid from the new Massachusetts mothers' pension program in 1920, but only after she had been struggling against her husband's abuse for at least ten years, during which he built up a record of convictions and jail terms for assault and nonsupport.

Failing to get separation and maintenance agreements and unable to collect support even when it was promised, only the most depressed, disheartened, and desperate women took the remaining option—called desertion. A moralistic nomenclature no longer common, desertion meant a woman leaving a husband *and* children. Female desertion was extremely uncommon in these cases, especially in contrast with the prevalence of male desertion. The low female desertion rate revealed the strength of women's attachments to their children. Moreover, the guilt and stigma attached to such action usually meant that women "deserters" simultaneously cut themselves off from friends or kin. All in all, it was unlikely that ridding themselves of the burdens of children would lead to better futures for wife-beating victims.

Another response to beatings was to fight. The incidence of mutual combat and female aggression in marital violence has been obscured by the legacy of victim blaming in the interpretation of the problem. For differing reasons, feminists and antifeminists were reluctant to recognize or acknowledge women's physical aggression. Moreover, poor women of the past may have been more comfortable with fighting than "respectable" women and contemporary women.[27] Fourteen percent of the marital violence cases I studied contained some female violence—8 percent mutual violence and 8 percent husband beating.

[24] Case #3560A.
[25] Case #6041.
[26] Case #3040.
[27] These case records contain, for example, instances of fights among women, particularly among neighbors but also family members.

Most of the women's violence was responsive or reactive, as distinguished from men's violence, which grew out of mutual conflict, to be sure, but was more often a regular tactic in an ongoing power struggle. Some examples may help to illuminate this distinction. Women's violence toward husbands in these records fell into three typical patterns. The most common pattern was women's active, ongoing participation in mutual violence. In the 1934 case of an Irish Catholic woman married to a Danish fisherman, who was gone at sea all but thirty days a year, violence occurred whenever he returned. One target of his rage was Catholicism: he beat his sons, she claimed, to prevent them from going to church with her and loudly cursed the Irish and the Catholics (he was an atheist). The neighbors took her side and would hide her three sons when their father was in a rage. The downstairs tenants took his side. They reported that she swore, yelled, hit him, and chased him with a butcher knife and that she threw herself down the stairs to make it look as though he had beaten her. Despite these conflicting charges, it was certain that she wanted to leave her husband, but he refused to let her have custody of the children; after a year of attempted mediation, the MSPCC ultimately lent its support for a separation.[28] In this case the woman responded with violence to a situation she was eager to leave, and her husband used violence to hold her in the marriage. Her violence, as well as her maintenance of neighborhood support, worked relatively effectively to give her some leverage and ultimately to get her out of the situation. An analogous pattern with the sexes reversed could not be found and, indeed, probably could not occur. Women's violence in these situations was a matter of holding their own or hurting a hated partner whom they were not free to leave. The case records contain many plaintive letters from wife beaters begging for their wives' return: "The suspense is awfull at times especially at night, when I arrive Home, I call it Home yet, when I do not hear those gentle voices and innocent souls whisper and speak my name."[29]

A second pattern consisted of extremely frightened, usually fatalistic, wives who occasionally defended themselves with a weapon. In 1960, for example, the MSPCC took on a case of such a woman, underweight and malnourished, very frightened of her husband, who had a record for drunkenness as well as a diagnosis of mental illness. Profane and abusive, he was hospitalized as a result of a powerful blow on the head she had given him.[30] (This is the pattern that most commonly led, and leads, to murder.)

[28] Case #4060. See also cases 2008, 2561, 3541, 3546, and 5085.
[29] Case #2024.
[30] Case #6024. See also cases 3363, 5543.

In a third pattern, the least common, women were the primary aggressors. In 1932 one mother, an obese, unhealthy woman, described as slovenly, kicked and slammed her six children around, locked them out of the house, knocked them down the stairs, and scratched them, as well as beating her husband and forcing him and the oldest daughter to do all the housework. His employer described him as "weak and spineless, but very good-hearted." Ultimately this woman was committed to a state mental hospital, at her own request, as a psychotic.[31]

Of the three patterns of female violence, the latter two usually involved extremely distressed, depressed, even disoriented women. The fighting women in mutual violence cases were not depressed and may have been better off than more peaceful ones. They were often struggling, albeit sometimes ambivalently, for separations; defending rights their husbands were challenging (for example, an outside job); or battling over resources and labor.

Over the period of this study there appeared to be a decline in mutual violence and women's aggression.[32] Particularly noticeable was the disappearance of women attacking other women. In the first decades of this study there were several cases like that of an Irish-American woman who in 1910 had "drinking parties" with other women, not infrequently ending in name-calling and fights; she and her daughter fought physically in front of an MSPCC agent; and her daughter was arrested for a fight with another girl.[33] This decline was offset by an increase in the number of women leaving marriages. A likely hypothesis is that there is a trade-off between women's physical violence and their ability to get separations or divorces.

Although women usually lost in fights, the decline in women's violence was not a clear gain for women and their families.[34] Condemnation of female violence went along with the romanticization of female passivity which contributed to women's participation in their

[31] Case #3024. See also cases 4261, 4501, and 6086. I cannot resist the only partly humorous observation that if there is a pattern of "masochism" in violent marriages, it describes male better than female behavior because it is mainly the men who appear to want to continue the violent relationships.

[32] I do not have enough data on women's violence to support this impression statistically. Several experts on contemporary marital violence have found, contrary to my impression, continuing high rates of mutual violence and women's violence—according to Murray Straus, in 49.5 percent of couples reporting any violence, although women remain the more severely victimized. See, for example, Murray Straus, "Victims and Aggressors in Marital Violence," *American Behavioral Scientist* 23 (May–June 1980): 681–704. The studies reporting female-to-male violence have been sharply criticized for producing misleading data; see, for example, Elizabeth Pleck, Joseph H. Pleck, Marilyn Grossman, and Pauline Bart, "The Battered Data Syndrome: A Reply to Steinmetz," *Victimology* 2, nos. 3–4 (1977–78): 680–84.

[33] Case #2047.

[34] It is possible that there was no decline in women's violence but only in the reporting of it.

own victimization. Historian Nancy Tomes found that a decline in women's violence in England between 1850 and 1890 corresponded to an increase in women's sense of shame about being beaten and reluctance to report or discuss it.[35] In this area the impact of feminism on women in violent families was mixed. The delegitimization of wife beating increased battered women's guilt about their inability to escape; they increasingly thought themselves exceptional, adding to their shame. First-wave feminism, expressing its relatively elite class base, helped construct a femininity that was oppressive to battered women: by emphasizing the superiority of women's peacefulness, feminist influence made women loathe, and attempt to suppress, their own aggressiveness and anger.

Few battered women attempted to resolve their problems exclusively diadically, whether violently or otherwise. Neighbors, kinfolk, and friends were of limited help, but not because the victims failed to ask. Beaten women often asked for places to stay, the minimum condition for escape. One 1910 incest and wife-beating case developed in part because of a woman's lack of a place to live. She had previously left her abusive husband to stay with her mother but was left homeless when her mother died; she returned to her husband in 1911; in 1914 he was convicted of assault and battery on her and in 1916 of incest with their oldest daughter.[36]

Or women might ask for money to help maintain their own households. Close neighbors, landladies, and relatives might be asked for child care, for credit, or for food. One very young wife, at age twenty-one already a four-year veteran of extreme abuse, had at first displayed the typical ambivalent pattern, leaving several times to stay with her relatives and always returning. Taking a firm decision when she discovered that her husband had infected her and her young daughter with venereal disease, she left for good, able to return to a household that still contained a mother, sister, and brother who supplied child care as well as a home. This support was her ticket to success: four years later, in 1914, she was managing on her own, her daughter cared for by her sister while she worked as a stenographer.[37] But kinship support was no guarantee of safety. In Charlestown in 1917 a beaten wife stayed with her parents and took a job. But whenever her payday came, the estranged husband would arrive to demand her money; her father refused to let him in, but the wife would meet him secretly and give

[35] Nancy Tomes, "A Torrent of Abuse: Crimes of Violence between Working Class Men and Women in London, 1840–1875," *Journal of Social History* 2 (Spring 1978): 328–45.

[36] Case #2054A.

[37] Case #2058A.

him money.[38] In a 1940 case, a battered wife had already left her husband and gone to live with her mother, but he threatened and attacked his mother-in-law until she became frightened to have her daughter with her; he also terrorized the welfare workers who were, in his view, supporting his wife's defiance.[39]

There were occasional cases of more direct intervention by relatives, more frequent in the first half of this study. One extremely patriarchal Italian father tried to stop his son from assaulting his wife in 1910.[40] In 1893 a woman's brother came to another part of Boston to stay with her at night to protect her from her husband, "who would lie in wait for her with a club."[41] But relatives also set clear limits on their involvement. In 1917 an Italian-born husband had battered his wife for years, ending their relationship by forcibly committing her to a mental hospital (despite the attempts of a thirteen-year-old daughter to convince an MSPCC agent that abuse was her mother's main mental problem). Her parents lived close by and had been very involved with the family; the wife had fled to them on several occasions, and they vociferously condemned her husband in speaking to a social worker; when the wife's mother died they blamed it on her anguish at her daughter's abuse. But they were unwilling to interfere with his authority to the extent of sheltering her when he demanded her return. Moreover, having committed his wife, he retained his right to be accepted by her relatives as a member of the family.[42]

More important than the material help offered by neighbors, friends, and relatives was their influence on how victims defined the standards of treatment they would tolerate. The reactions of confidants, or even of neighbors who heard the fights, affected the responses of victims and assailants. Some counseled resignation and passivity, while others, by their outrage or partisanship, suggested that battering need not be accepted. Parents like those above who expressed their commitment by their willingness to take their daughter in, but nevertheless deferred to her abusive husband's ultimate authority, were telling their daughter that beatings should be tolerated. By contrast, in another Italian-American family, the mother and sister of a battered woman not only took in her and her six children but brought her to complain to the MSPCC.[43]

Battered women sometimes turned to child welfare agencies because their informal networks could not protect them, but often they added these agencies to a reservoir of resistance strategies, just as they had

[38] Case #2520.
[39] Case #4502.
[40] Case #2042.
[41] Case #1040.
[42] Case #2800A.
[43] Case #6300.

added rights claims to other strategies. Sometimes they benefited from the agencies, mainly when they were able to get legitimation and financial support for leaving their marriages. Such benefits were owing sometimes to the skill and insight of social workers, but more to the ingenuity of the victims.[44]

Indeed, sometimes the victims taught the social workers the best helping techniques, chipping away at their hostility to separation, divorce, and female-headed households, just as the victims learned from social workers what aspirations might be within their reach. I do not mean to suggest that clients were equals in their contacts with the child protectors; on the contrary, cumulatively the agencies were more successful in imposing their standards. Rather, I am emphasizing the importance of seeing these battered women as agents, not merely victims, in creating the history of wife beating and its solutions.

A narrative that includes battered women simultaneously as victims and as agents, not only in helping themselves but in formally defining their entitlements, has several implications. First, it challenges the dominant use of the term *patriarchy*, referring to undifferentiated and absolute male domination. By contrast, the male power evident in these family violence stories involved in its very essence sharp conflict between men and women, children and adults, and the outcome of individual cases was by no means determined.

Second, it similarly challenges a history of social work—and a parallel history of social control more broadly—told as a static, determined domination. When one scrutinizes the actual records of a set of social control agents, the child protectors, the "clients" or subjects appear far more active and more efficacious than has previously been imagined in influencing social control agencies in their own interests.

Third, this reading of the evidence suggests that battered women's claim to rights, to a claim on the state to protect them from violence, arose precisely because of the weakening of patriarchy and the contradictions, imperfections, and dysfunctionality of the social control system. The battered women's stories speak against functionalist and structuralist analyses of social control.

Finally, this work on wife beating raises questions about the relation between (identified and organized) feminists and nonfeminist women. The victims I studied did not consider themselves part of women's movements, but they were exquisitely sensitive to new opportunities and to new rhetoric that they could manipulate in their interest. Moreover, with social workers as an important conduit, some of the most wretched women were able to influence the solutions that reformers proposed for the problems of poor women. They did so before they

[44] Linda Gordon, "The Frustrations of Family Violence Social Work: An Historical Critique," *Journal of Sociology and Social Welfare* 15 (December 1988): 139–60.

spoke the language of rights, and their more traditional claims to community help against abusive husbands deserve further attention and analysis. Certainly the model that has feminist ideas flowing downward to less privileged groups of women is not the whole story of the development of women's "rights."

CHAPTER FIFTEEN

The Black Community and the Birth Control Movement

Jessie M. Rodrique

The decline in black fertility rates from the late nineteenth century to World War II has been well documented. In these years the growth rate of the black population was more than cut in half. By 1945 the average number of children per woman was 2.5, and childlessness, especially among urban blacks, had reached unprecedented proportions. Researchers who explain this phenomenon insist that contraception played a minimal role; they believe that blacks had no interest in the control of their own fertility. This belief also affects the interpretation of blacks' involvement in the birth control movement, which has been understood as having been thrust upon an unwilling black population.

This essay seeks to understand these two related issues differently. First, I maintain that black women were, in fact, interested in controlling their fertility and that the low birth rates reflect in part a conscious use of birth control. Second, by exploring the birth control movement among blacks at the grass-roots level, I show that despite the racist ideology that operated at the national level, blacks were active and effective participants in the establishment of local clinics and in the birth control debate, as they related birth control to issues of race and gender. Third, I show that despite black cooperation with white birth control groups, blacks maintained a degree of independence that allowed the organization for birth control in their communities to take a qualitatively different form.

Demographers in the post–World War I years accounted for the remarkable decline in black fertility in terms of biological factors. Fears of "dysgenic" population trends coupled with low birth rates among native white Americans underlay their investigations of black fertility. Population scholars ignored contraception as a factor in the birth decline even as late as 1938. Instead, they focused on the "health hypothesis," arguing that the drop in fertility resulted from general poor health, especially sterility caused by venereal disease. Although health conditions seem likely to have had some effect, there is no reason to exclude contraceptive use as an additional cause, especially when evidence of contraceptive knowledge and practice is abundant.[1]

In drawing their conclusions, researchers also made many questionable and unfounded assumptions about the sexuality of blacks. In one large study of family limitation, for example, black women's lower contraceptive use was attributed to the belief that "the negro generally exercises less prudence and foresight than white people do in all sexual matters."[2] Nor is the entire black population represented in many of these studies. Typically their sample consists of women whose economic status is defined as either poor or very poor and who are either illiterate or have had very little education. Population experts' ideological bias and research design have tended to foreclose the possibility of Afro-American agency and thus conscious use of contraception.[3]

Historians who have chronicled the birth control movement have focused largely on the activities and evolution of the major birth control organizations and leading birth control figures, usually at the national level. None have interpreted the interests of the movement as particularly beneficial to blacks. Linda Gordon, in her pathbreaking book *Woman's Body, Woman's Right,* focused on the 1939 "Negro Project," established by the Birth Control Federation of America (BCFA) as a conservative, elitist effort designed "to stabilize existing social relations." Gordon claims that the birth control movement in the South was removed from socially progressive politics and unconnected to any analysis of women's rights, civil rights, or poverty, exemplifying the movement's male domination and professionalization over the course of the twentieth century. Other historians concur,

[1] Reynolds Farley, *Growth of the Black Population* (Chicago, 1970), pp. 3, 75; Stanley Engerman, "Changes in Black Fertility, 1880–1940," in *Family and Population in Nineteenth-Century America,* ed. Tamara K. Hareven and Maris A. Vinovskis (Princeton, 1978), pp. 126–53. For an excellent review of the demographic literature, see Joseph McFalls and George Masnick, "Birth Control and the Fertility of the U.S. Black Population, 1880 to 1980," *Journal of Family History* 6 (1981): 89–106; Peter Uhlenberg, "Negro Fertility Patterns in the United States," *Berkeley Journal of Sociology* 11 (1966): 56; James Reed, *From Private Vice to Public Virtue* (New York, 1978), pp. 197–210.

[2] Raymond Pearl, "Contraception and Fertility in 2,000 Women," *Human Biology* 4 (1932): 395.

[3] McFalls and Masnick, "Birth Control," p. 90.

asserting that birth control was "genocidal" and "anathema" to black women's interests and that the movement degenerated into a campaign to "keep the unfit from reproducing themselves." Those who note its presence within the black community in a slightly more positive light qualify their statements by adding the disclaimer that support and information for its dissemination came only from the black elite and were not part of a grass-roots movement.[4]

There is, however, an ample body of evidence that suggests the importance of birth control use among blacks. Contraceptive methods and customs among Africans as well as nineteenth-century slaves have been well documented. For example, folklorists and others have discovered "alum water" as one of many birth control measures in early twentieth-century southern rural communities. The author of a study of two rural Georgia counties noted the use of birth control practices there and linked it to a growing race pride. In urban areas a "very common" and distinctive practice among blacks was to place Vaseline and quinine over the mouth of the uterus. It was widely available and could be purchased very cheaply in drugstores.[5]

The black press was also an abundant source of birth control information. The *Pittsburgh Courier*, for example, carried numerous mail order advertisements for douche powder, suppositories, preventive antiseptics, and vaginal jellies that "destroyed foreign germs."[6] A partic-

[4] Linda Gordon, *Woman's Body, Woman's Right* (New York, 1976), pp. 332–35; Paula Gidding, *When and Where I Enter: The Impact of Black Women on Race and Sex in America* (New York, 1984), p. 183; Robert G. Weisbord, *Genocide? Birth Control and the Black American* (Westport, Conn., 1975); William G. Harris, "Family Planning, Socio-Political Ideology and Black Americans: A Comparative Study of Leaders and a General Population Sample" (Ph.D. diss., University of Massachusetts, 1980), p. 69.

A brief chronology of early birth control organizations is as follows: the American Birth Control League was founded in 1921 and operated by Margaret Sanger until 1927. In 1923 Sanger had organized the Clinical Research Bureau and after 1927 controlled only that facility. In 1939 the Clinical Research Bureau and the American Birth Control League merged to form the Birth Control Federation of America. In 1942 the name was changed to the Planned Parenthood Federation of America (hereafter cited as ABCL, BCFA, and PPFA).

[5] For contraceptive use among Africans, see Norman E. Himes, *Medical History of Contraception* (New York, 1936). For statements concerning birth control use among black Americans, see W. E. B. Du Bois, "Black Folks and Birth Control," *Birth Control Review* 16 (June 1932): 166–67 (hereafter cited as *BCR*); Herbert Gutman, *The Black Family in Slavery and Freedom, 1750–1925* (New York, 1976). Du Bois had first observed the trend toward a steadily decreasing birth rate in *The Philadelphia Negro: A Social Study* (Philadelphia, 1899). For folk methods see Elizabeth Rauh Bethel, *Promiseland: A Century of Life in a Negro Community* (Philadelphia, 1981), pp. 156–57; Newbell Niles Puckett, *Folk Beliefs of the Southern Negro* (New York, 1926); Arthur Raper, *Preface to Peasantry: A Tale of Two Black Belt Counties* (Chapel Hill, 1936), p. 71; "Report of the Special Evening Medical Session of the First American Birth Control Conference" (1921), Box 99, Folder 1017, Margaret Sanger Papers, Sophia Smith Collection, Smith College, Northhampton, Mass.

[6] *Pittsburgh Courier*, April 25, 1931, n.p. (hereafter cited as *Courier*).

ularly interesting mail order ad was for a product called "Puf," a medicated douche powder and applicator that claimed to be a "new guaranteed method of administering marriage hygiene." It had a sketch of a calendar with the words "End Calendar Worries Now!" written across it and a similar sketch that read "Tear-Up Your Calendar, Do Not Worry, Use Puf." The instructions for its use indicate euphemistically that Puf should be used "first," meaning before intercourse, and that it was good for hours, leaving little doubt that this product was fully intended to be used as a birth control device.[7]

Advertisements for mail order douches are significant because they appear to reflect a practice that was widespread and well documented among black women. Studies conducted in the mid-1930s overwhelmingly concluded that douching was the preferred method of contraception used by black couples. Yet contemporary researchers neglected to integrate this observation into their understanding of the decline in fertility because they insisted that douching was an "ineffective contraceptive." However ineffective the means, the desire for birth control in the black community was readily apparent, as George Schuyler, editor of the *National Negro News,* explained: "If anyone should doubt the desire on the part of Negro women and men to limit their families it is only necessary to note the large sale of preventive devices sold in every drug store in various Black Belts."[8]

Within the black community the practice of abortion was commonly cited by black leaders and professionals as contributing to the low birth rates. Throughout the 1920s and 1930s the black press reported many cases of abortions that had ended in women's deaths or the arrest of doctors who had performed them. Abortion was discussed in the *Pittsburgh Courier* in 1930 in a fictionalized series entitled "Bad Girl," which dealt with a range of attitudes toward childbearing among Harlem blacks. When Dot, the main character, discovers she is pregnant, she goes to a friend who works in a drugstore. The author writes: "Pat's wonderful remedy didn't help. Religiously Dot took it and each night when Eddie came home she sadly admitted that success had not crowned her efforts. 'All that rotten tasting stuff just to keep a little crib out of the bedroom.' After a week she was tired of medicine and of baths so hot that they burned her skin."[9] Next, she sought the advice of a friend who told her that she would have to have "an operation" and knew of a doctor who would do it for fifty dollars.

[7] *Courier,* December 1, 1934, p. 7.

[8] McFalls and Masnick, "Birth Control," p. 103; George Schuyler, "Quantity or Quality," *BCR* 16 (June 1932): 165–66.

[9] See, for example, *Courier,* March 9, 1935, p. 2; and *San Francisco Spokesman,* March 1, 1934, p. 1 (hereafter cited as *Spokesman*); Vina Delmar, "Bad Girl," *Courier,* January 3, 1931, p. 2.

The *Baltimore Afro-American* observed that pencils, nails, and hat pins were the instruments commonly used for self-induced abortions, and the *Birth Control Review* wrote in 1936 that rural black women in Georgia drank turpentine for the same purpose. The use of turpentine as an abortifacient is significant because it is derived from evergreens, a source similar to rue and camphor, both of which were reported by a medical authority in 1860 to have been used with some success by southern slaves. Although statistics for abortions among black women are scarce, a 1938 medical study reported that 28 percent or 211 of 730 black women interviewed said that they had had one or more abortions. A black doctor from Nashville in 1940 asserted in the *Baltimore Afro-American* that abortions among black women were deliberate, not only the result of syphilis and other diseases: "In the majority of cases it is used as a means of getting rid of unwanted children."[10]

These data, though somewhat impressionistic, indicate that a variety of contraceptive methods were available to blacks. Many were, and still are, discounted as ineffective "folk methods."[11] There was, however, a discernible consciousness that guided the decline in fertility. A discourse on birth control emerged in the years from 1915 to 1945. As blacks migrated within and out of the South to northern cities, they began to articulate the reasons for limiting fertility, and one begins to see how interconnected the issue of birth control was to many facets of black life. For women, it was linked to changes in their status, gender roles within the family, attitudes toward motherhood and sexuality, and, at times, feminism. Birth control was also integral to issues of economics, health, race relations, and racial progress.

In these years blacks contributed to the "official" nationwide debate concerning birth control while also voicing their particular concerns. Frequent coverage was given to birth control in the black press. Newspapers championed the cause of birth control when doctors were arrested for performing abortions. They also carried editorials in favor of birth control, speeches of noted personalities who favored its use, and occasionally sensationalized stories on the desperate need for birth control. Often, the topic of birth control as well as explicit birth control information was transmitted orally through public lectures and debates. It was also explored in fiction, black periodicals, and several issues of the *Birth Control Review* dedicated to blacks.[12]

[10] *Baltimore Afro-American*, August 3, 1940, n.p. (hereafter cited as *Afro-American*); "A Clinic for Tobacco Road," *BCR* 3 (New Series) (January 1936): 6; Gutman, *Black Family*, pp. 80–85; John Gaston, "A Review of 2,422 Cases of Contraception," *Texas State Journal of Medicine* 35 (September 1938): 365–68; *Afro-American*, August 3, 1940, n.p. On abortion see also "Birth Control: The Case for the State," *Reader's Digest*, November 1939, pp. 26–29.

[11] McFalls and Masnick, "Birth Control," p. 103.

[12] "Magazine Publishes Negro Number on Birth Control," *Spokesman*, June 11, 1932, p. 3; "Birth Control Slayer Held without Bail," *Courier*, January 11, 1936, p. 4.

Economic themes emerged in the birth control discourse as it related to issues of black family survival. Contraceptive use was one of a few economic strategies available to blacks, providing a degree of control within the context of the family economy. Migrating families who left behind the economy of the rural South used birth control to "preserve their new economic independence," as did poor families who were "compelled" to limit their numbers of children. A 1935 study of Harlem reiterated this same point, adding that the low birth rates of urban blacks reflected a "deliberate limitation of families." Another strategy used by black couples for the same purpose was postponing marriage. Especially in the years of the Depression, birth control was seen as a way to improve general living conditions by allowing more opportunities for economic gain.[13]

Birth control was also linked to the changing status of black women and the role they were expected to play in the survival of the race. On this issue a degree of opposition to birth control surfaced. Some, most notably black nationalist leader Marcus Garvey, believed that the future of the black race was contingent upon increasing numbers and warned that birth control would lead to racial extinction. Both Garveyites and Catholic church officials insisted that birth control interfered with the "course of nature" and God's will.[14]

These issues were evident in an exchange between the journalist J. A. Rogers and Dean Kelly Miller of Howard University in 1925. Writing in *The Messenger*, Rogers took Miller to task for his statements concerning the emancipation of black women. Miller is quoted as saying that black women had strayed too far from children, kitchen, clothes, and the church. Miller, very aware that black women had been having fewer children, cautioned against race suicide. Using the "nature" argument of Garvey and the Catholic church, he argued that the biological function of women was to bear and rear children. He stated, "The liberalization of women must always be kept within the boundary fixed by nature." Rogers strongly disagreed with Miller, saying that the move of black women away from domesticity and childbearing was a positive sign. Rogers wrote, "I give the Negro woman credit if she endeavors to be something other than a mere breeding machine. Having children is by no means the sole reason for being."[15]

Other black leaders supported this progressive viewpoint. In his 1919 essay "The Damnation of Women," W. E. B. Du Bois wrote that "the future woman must have a life work and future independence. . . .

[13] Alice Dunbar Nelson, "Woman's Most Serious Problem," *Messenger* (March 1927): 73; Clyde Kiser, "Fertility of Harlem Negroes," *Milbank Memorial Fund Quarterly* 13 (1935): 273–85; Caroline Robinson, *Seventy Birth Control Clinics* (Baltimore, 1930), pp. 246–51.

[14] Weisbord, *Genocide?* 43.

[15] J. A. Rogers, "The Critic," *Messenger* 7 (April 1925): 164–65.

She must have knowledge . . . and she must have the right of motherhood at her own discretion."[16] In a later essay he described those who would confine women to childbearing as "reactionary barbarians."[17] Dr. Charles Garvin, writing in 1932, believed that it was the "inalienable right of every married woman to use any physiologically sound precaution against reproduction she deems justifiable."[18]

Black women also expressed the need for contraception when they articulated their feelings about motherhood and sexuality. Black women's fiction and poetry in the years from 1916 to the early 1930s frequently depicted women who refused to bring children into a racist world and expressed their outrage at laws that prevented access to birth control information. Nella Larsen, for example, in her 1928 novella *Quicksand,* explored the debilitating physical and emotional problems resulting from excessive childbearing in a society that demanded that women's sexual expression be inextricably linked to marriage and procreation.[19]

Others spoke of the right not to have children in terms that were distinctly feminist. For example, a character in the *Courier* serial "Bad Girl" put it this way: "The hospitals are wide open to the woman who wants to have a baby, but to the woman who doesn't want one—that's a different thing. High prices, fresh doctors. It's a man's world, Dot. The woman who wants to keep her body from pain and her mind from worry is an object of contempt."[20] The changing status of women and its relation to childbearing were also addressed in Jessie Fauset's 1931 novel *The Chinaberry Tree.* Fauset's male characters asserted the need for large families and a "definite place" for women in the home. The female character, however, remained unconvinced by this opinion. She had "the modern girl's own clear ideas on birth control."[21]

Other writers stressed the need for birth control in terms of racial issues and its use to alleviate the oppressive circumstances of the black community. For example, Chandler Owen, editor of *The Messenger,* wrote a piece for the 1919 edition of the *Birth Control Review* en-

[16] W. E. B. Du Bois, "The Damnation of Women," in *Darkwater: Voices from within the Veil,* ed. Herbert Aptheker (1921: rpt. Millwood, N.Y., 1975), pp. 164–65.

[17] W. E. B. Du Bois, "Birth," *Crisis* 24 (October 1922): 248–50.

[18] Charles H. Garvin. "The Negro's Doctor's Task," *BCR* 16 (November 1932): 269–70.

[19] For an excellent discussion of the theme of sexuality in black women's fiction, see the introduction to Nella Larsen, *Quicksand and Passing,* ed. Deborah E. McDowell (New Brunswick, 1986). See also Mary Burrill, "They That Sit in Darkness," and Angelina Grimké, "The Closing Door," *BCR* 3 (September 1919): 5–8, 10–14; Jessie Fauset, *The Chinaberry Tree* (New York, 1931); Angelina Grimké, *Rachel: A Play in Three Acts* (1920; rpt. College Park, Md., 1969); Georgia Douglas Johnson, *Bronze: A Book of Verse* (1922; rpt. Freeport, N.Y., 1971).

[20] Delmar, "Bad Girl," *Courier,* January 3, 1931, p. 2.

[21] Fauset, *Chinaberry Tree,* pp. 131–32, 187.

titled "Women and Children of the South." He advocated birth control because he believed that having fewer children would result in general improvements in material conditions. Observing that young black women in peonage camps were frequently raped and impregnated by their white overseers, Owen also linked involuntary maternity to racial crimes.[22]

Birth control for racial progress was advocated most frequently during the Depression, and it helped to mobilize community support for clinics. Newell L. Sims of Oberlin College, for example, urged in his 1931 essay "A New Technique in Race Relations" that birth control for blacks would be a "step toward independence and greater power." In his opinion, a controlled birth rate would free more resources for advancement. The black press hailed the essay as "revolutionary."[23] Other advocates insisted that all blacks, but especially poor blacks, become involved in the legislative process to legalize birth control. It was imperative that the poor be included in the movement because they were the ones most injured by its prohibition. One black newspaper, the *San Francisco Spokesman*, promoted a very direct and activist role for blacks on this issue. "To legalize birth control, you and I should make expressed attitudes on this question a test of every candidate's fitness for legislative office," it argued in 1934. "And those who refuse or express a reactionary opinion should be flatly and uncompromisingly rejected."[24]

For many blacks birth control was not a panacea but one aspect of a larger political agenda. Unlike some members of the white community who myopically looked to birth control as a cure-all for the problems of blacks, most blacks instead described it as a program that would "modify one cause of their unfavorable situation."[25] They stressed that true improvement could come only through the "equalization of economic and social opportunities."[26] Sims summed up this position most eloquently in his 1932 essay "Hostages to the White Man." It was a viewpoint stressed well into the 1940s by numerous and leading members of the black community. He wrote:

> The negro in America is a suppressed class and as such must struggle for existence under every disadvantage and handicap. Although in three gen-

[22] Chandler Owen, "Women and Children of the South," *BCR* 3 (September 1919): 9, 20.

[23] Quoted in *Courier*, March 28, 1931, p. 3, and *Norfolk Journal and Guide*, March 28, 1931, p. 1.

[24] J. A. Ghent, "Urges Legalization of Birth Control: Law against Contraception Unjust to the Poor," *Spokesman*, July 9, 1932, p. 3; "The Case of Dr. Devaughn, or Anti-Birth Control on Trial," ibid., February 22, 1934, p. 6.

[25] W. G. Alexander, "Birth Control for the Negro: Fad or Necessity?" *Journal of the National Medical Association* 24 (August 1932): 39.

[26] Charles S. Johnson, "A Question of Negro Health," *BCR* 16 (June 1932): 167–69.

> erations since slavery he has in many ways greatly improved his condition, his economic, social and political status still remain that of a dominated exploited minority. His problem is, therefore, just what it has been for three quarters of a century, i.e., how to better his position in the social order. Naturally in all his strivings he has found no panacea for his difficulties, for there is none. The remedies must be as numerous and varied as the problem is complex. Obviously he needs to employ every device that will advance his cause. I wish briefly to urge the merits of birth control as one means.[27]

Many also insisted that birth control be integrated into other health care provisions and not be treated as a separate problem. E. S. Jamison, for example, writing in the *Birth Control Review* in 1938, exhorted blacks to "present an organized front" so that birth control and other needed health services could be made available to them. Yet he, too, like Sims, emphasized independence from the white community. He wrote that "the Negro must do for himself. Charity will not better his condition in the long run."[28]

Blacks also took an important stand against sterilization, especially in the 1930s. Scholars have not sufficiently recognized that blacks could endorse a program of birth control but reject the extreme views of eugenicists, whose programs for birth control and sterilization often did not distinguish between the two. The *Pittsburgh Courier,* for example, whose editorial policy clearly favored birth control, was also active in the antisterilization movement. It asserted in several editorials that blacks should oppose the sterilization programs being advanced by eugenicists and so-called scientists because they were being waged against the weak, the oppressed, and the disfranchised. Candidates for sterilization were likely to be those on relief, the unemployed, and the homeless, all victims of a vicious system of economic exploitation. Du Bois shared this viewpoint. In his column in the *Courier* in 1936 he wrote, "The thing we want to watch is the so-called eugenic sterilization." He added that the burden of such programs would "fall upon colored people and it behooves us to watch the law and the courts and stop the spread of the habit." The *San Francisco Spokesman* in 1934 called upon black club women to become active in the antisterilization movement.[29]

Participation in the birth control debate was only one aspect of the black community's involvement; black women and men also were ac-

[27] Newell L. Sims, "Hostages to the White Man," *BCR* 16 (July–August 1932): 214–15.

[28] E. S. Jamison, "The Future of Negro Health," *BCR* 22 (May 1938): 94–95.

[29] "Sterilization," *Courier,* March 30, 1935, p. 10; "The Sterilization Menace," ibid., January 18, 1936, p. 10; W. E. B. Du Bois, "Sterilization," ibid., June 27, 1936, p. 1; "Are

tive in the establishment of birth control clinics. From 1925 to 1945 clinics for blacks appeared nationwide, many of them at least partly directed and sponsored by local black community organizations. Many of the organizations had a prior concern with health matters, creating an established network of social welfare centers, health councils, and agencies. Thus birth control services were often integrated into a community through familiar channels.[30]

In Harlem the black community showed an early and sustained interest in the debate over birth control, taking a vanguard role in agitation for birth control clinics. In 1918 the Women's Political Association of Harlem, calling upon black women to "assume the reins of leadership in the political, social and economic life of their people," announced that its lecture series would include birth control among the topics for discussion.[31] In March 1923 the Harlem Community Forum invited Margaret Sanger to speak at the Library Building in the Bronx, and in 1925 the Urban League asked the American Birth Control League to establish a clinic in the Columbus Hill section of the city.

Although this clinic proved unsuccessful, another, supported by the Urban League and the Birth Control Clinical Research Bureau, opened a Harlem branch in 1929. This particular clinic, affiliated with Margaret Sanger, had an advisory board of approximately fifteen members, including Harlem-based journalists, physicians, social workers, and ministers. There was apparently very little opposition to the work of this clinic, even among the clergy. One minister on the advisory board, William Lloyd Imes of the St. James Presbyterian Church, reported that he had held discussions on birth control at his church; at another meeting he announced that if a birth control pamphlet were printed, he would place it in the church vestibule. Another clergyman, the Reverend Shelton Hale Bishop, wrote to Sanger in 1931 that he believed birth control to be "one of the boons of the age to human welfare."[32]

Women Interested Only in Meet and Eat Kind of Club?" *Spokesman*, March 29, 1934, p. 4.

[30] For examples of black social welfare organizations see William L. Pollard, *A Study of Black Self-Help* (San Francisco, 1978); Edyth L. Ross, *Black Heritage in Social Welfare, 1860–1930* (London, 1978); Lenwood G. Davis, "The Politics of Black Self-Help in the United States: A Historical Overview," in *Black Organizations: Issues on Survival Techniques*, ed. Lennox S. Yearwood (Lanham, Md., 1980). This statement is also based on extensive reading of the *Pittsburgh Courier, Norfolk Journal and Guide, Baltimore Afro-American, San Francisco Spokesman*, and *New York Age* for the 1920s and 1930s.

[31] Messenger 7 (July 1918): 26.

[32] "Report of Executive Secretary," March 1923, Ser. I, Box 4, Planned Parenthood Federation of America Papers, American Birth Control League Records, Sophia Smith

The Reverend Adam Clayton Powell of the Abyssinian Baptist Church both endorsed birth control and spoke at public meetings denouncing the "false modesty" surrounding questions of sex. Ignorance, he believed, led to unwanted pregnancies among young girls.[33]

Support for birth control clinics by black community organizations was also apparent in other locations throughout the country. Their activism took various forms. In Baltimore, for example, a white birth control clinic had begun to see blacks in 1928. In 1935 the black community began organizing, and by 1938 the Northwest Health Center was established, sponsored and staffed by blacks. The Baltimore Urban League played a key role in its initial organization, and the sponsoring committee of the clinic was composed of numerous members of Baltimore's black community, including ministers, physicians, nurses, social workers, teachers, housewives, and labor leaders.[34]

In Richmond, Fredericksburg, and Lynchburg, Virginia, local maternal welfare groups raised funds to pay for expenses and supplies for the birth control clinics at the Virginia Medical College and the Hampton Institute and publicized birth control services at city health departments. And in West Virginia, the Maternal and Child Health Council, formed in 1938, was the first statewide birth control organization sponsored by blacks.[35]

Local clubs and women's organizations often took part in either sponsoring birth control clinics or bringing the topic to the attention of the local community. In New York these included the Inter-Racial Forum of Brooklyn, the Women's Business and Professional Club of Harlem, the Social Workers Club of Harlem, the Harlem branch of the National Organization of Colored Graduate Nurses, the Harlem YWCA, and the Harlem Economic Forum. In Oklahoma City fourteen black women's clubs sponsored a birth control clinic for black women, directed by two black physicians and one black club woman. The

---

Collection, Smith College, Northampton, Mass. (hereafter cited as PPFA Papers); Hannah Stone, "Report of the Clinical Research Department of the ABCL" (1925), Ser. I, Box 4, ibid.; "Urban League Real Asset, Clinic an Example of How It Assists," *Courier*, November 2, 1935, p. 1; William Lloyd Imes to Margaret Sanger, May 16, 1931, and November 23, 1932, Box 122b, Folders 1333 and 1336, Sanger Papers; Shelton Hale Bishop to Margaret Sanger, May 18, 1931, Box 122b, Folder 1333, ibid.,

[33] "Minutes of the First Meeting of 1932, Board of Managers, Harlem Branch," March 25, 1932, Box 122b, Folder 1336, Sanger Papers; "Companionate Marriage Discussed at Forum," *New York Age*, May 12, 1928, n.p.

[34] E. S. Lewis and N. Louise Young, "Baltimore's Negro Maternal Health Center: How It Was Organized," *BCR* 22 (May 1938): 93–94.

[35] "West Virginia," *BCR* 23 (October 1938): 121; "Birth Control for the Negro," Report of Hazel Moore (1937), Box 22, Folder 10, Florence Rose Papers, Sophia Smith Collection, Smith College; "Negro Demonstration Project Possibilities," December 1, 1939, Box 121, Folder 1309, Sanger Papers.

Mother's Health Association of the District of Columbia reported to the *Birth Control Review* in 1938 that it was cooperating with black organizations that wanted to start a clinic of their own.[36]

Clinics in other cities were located in black community centers and churches. For example, the Kentucky Birth Control League in 1936 reported that one of the clinics in Louisville was located in the Episcopal Church for Colored People and was operated by a black staff. The Cincinnati Committee on Maternal Health reported in 1939 the opening of a second black clinic that would employ a black physician and nurse.[37]

Community centers and settlement houses were also part of the referral network directing blacks to birth control services. The Mother's Health Office in Boston received clients from the Urban League, the Robert Gould Shaw House, and the Harriet Tubman House. The Henry Street Settlement sent women to the Harlem clinic, and the Booker T. Washington Community Center in San Francisco directed black women to the birth control clinic in that city. In 1935 the Indiana Birth Control League reported that black clients were referred from the Flanner House Settlement for Colored People.[38]

In 1939 the Birth Control Federation of America (BCFA) established a Division of Negro Service and sponsored pilot clinics in Nashville, Tennessee, and Berkeley County, South Carolina. The division consisted of a national advisory council of thirty-five black leaders, a national sponsoring committee of five hundred members who coordinated state and local efforts, and administrative and field personnel. The project in Nashville was integrated into the public health services and located in the Bethlehem center, a black social service settlement, and the Fisk University Settlement House. Both clinics were under the direction of black doctors and nurses. The program was

[36] For information on black organizations, see Box 122b, Sanger Papers, esp. March 25, 1932; "Minutes of the Regular Meeting of the Board of Directors of the ABCL," December 1922, Ser. I, Box 1, "Report of the Executive Secretary," November 11, 1930, Ser. I, Box 4, "ABCL Treasurer's Annual Reports for the Year 1936," Ser. I, Box 4, PPFA Papers; "Harlem Economic Forum Plans Fine Lecture Series," *Courier*, November 14, 1936, p. 9; "Birth Control Clinic Set Up for Negroes; Sponsored by Clubs," *Oklahoma City Times*, February 28, March 4, 1938; "Illinois Birth Control League," *BCR* 22 (March 1938): 64. By 1931 many black organizations in Pittsburgh supported the use of birth control; see "Pittsburgh Joins Nation-Wide League for Birth Control," *Courier*, February 21, 1931, p. 1.

[37] "Annual Reports of the State Member Leagues for 1936, the Kentucky Birth Control League," Ser. I, Box 4, PPFA Papers; "Annual Report 1938–39, Cincinnati Committee on Maternal Health," Box 119A, Folder 1256, Sanger Papers.

[38] "Mother's Health Office Referrals," January 5, 1933, Massachusetts Mother's Health Office, Central Administrative Records, Box 35 and 36, Planned Parenthood League of Massachusetts, Sophia Smith Collection, Smith College; "PPFA Field Report for California, 1944," Box 119, Folder 1215, Sanger Papers; "Annual Meeting of the BCFA, Indiana Birth Control League, 1935," Ser. I, Box 4, PPFA Papers.

supplemented by nine black public health nurses who made home visits and performed general health services, including the distribution of birth control devices and information. The home visits served the large numbers of women who worked as domestics and could not attend the clinics during the day; five thousand home visits were made in Nashville in a two-year period. In South Carolina, clinic sessions providing both medical care and birth control services were held eleven times each month at different locations in the county for rural women, 70 percent of whom were black.[39]

Simultaneously with the development of these two projects, the BCFA launched an educational campaign to inform and enlist the services of black health professionals, civic groups, and women's clubs. Although professional groups are often credited with being the sole source of birth control agitation, the minutes and newsletters of the Division of Negro Service reveal an enthusiastic desire among a broad cross section of the black community to lend its support to birth control. In fact, black professional groups often worked closely with community groups and other "nonprofessionals" to make birth control information widely available. For example, the National Medical Association, an organization of black physicians, held public lectures on birth control in conjunction with local groups beginning in 1929, and when birth control was discussed at annual meetings the otherwise private sessions were opened up to social workers, nurses, and teachers. The National Association of Colored Graduate Nurses, under the direction of Mabel Staupers, was especially active in birth control work. Cooperation was offered by several state and local nursing, hospital, and dental associations. One nurse responded to Staupers's request for help with the distribution of birth control information by writing, "I shall pass the material out, we will discuss it in our meetings and I will distribute exhibits at pre-natal clinics at four health centers and through Negro Home Demonstration Clubs."[40]

The participation of Negro Home Demonstration clubs in birth control work is significant because it is an entirely overlooked and potentially rich source for the grass-roots spread of birth control information in the rural South. Home Demonstration clubs grew out of the provisions of the Smith-Lever Cooperative Extension Act of 1914 and had,

[39] "Chart of the Special Negro Project Demonstration Project," Box 22, Folders 8 and 2, Rose Papers; John Overton and Ivah Uffelman, "A Birth Control Service among Urban Negroes," *Human Fertility* 7 (August 1942): 97–101; E. Mae McCarroll, "A Condensed Report on the Two Year Negro Demonstration Health Program of PPFA, Inc.," paper presented at the Annual Convention of the National Medical Association, Cleveland, August 17, 1942, Box 22, Folder 11, Rose Papers; Mabel K. Staupers, "Family Planning and Negro Health," *National News Bulletin of the National Association of Colored Graduate Nurses* 14 (May 1941): 1–10.

[40] "Preliminary Annual Report, Division of Negro Service," January 7, 1942, Box 121,

by the early 1920s, evolved into clubs whose programs stressed health and sanitation. The newsletter of the Division of Negro Service in 1941 reported that five rural state Negro agricultural and home demonstration agents offered full cooperation with the division. The newsletter included the response of H. C. Ray of Little Rock, Arkansas. He wrote, "We have more than 13,000 rural women working in home demonstration clubs . . . it is in this connection that I feel our organization might work hand in hand with you in bringing about some very definite and desirable results in your phase of community improvement work. We will be glad to distribute any literature." Also involved with rural birth control education were several tuberculosis associations and the Jeanes Teachers, educators funded by the Anna T. Jeanes Foundation for improving rural black schools.[41]

Other groups showed interest in the programs of the Division of Negro Service either by requesting speakers on birth control for their conventions or by distributing literature to their members. Similar activities were conducted by the Virginia Federation of Colored Women's Clubs, which represented four hundred women's clubs, the Negro Organization Society of Virginia, the National Negro Business League, the National Negro Housewives League, the Pullman Porters, the Elks, the Harlem Citizens City-Wide Committee, and the Social Action Committee of Boston's South End. In 1944, for example, the National Association for the Advancement of Colored People and a black boilermakers' union distributed Planned Parenthood clinic cards in their mailings to their California members. Twenty-one Urban Leagues in sixteen states as of 1943 actively cooperated with the BCFA in the display of exhibits, distribution of literature, promotion of local clinical service, and adult community education programs. These national and local black organizations advocated birth control as one aspect of a general program of health, education, and economic development in the late 1930s and early 1940s.[42]

Folder 1309, Sanger Papers; "Doctors' Annual Meeting Marked by Fine Program; Local Committee Involved in Planning Meeting," *New York Age*, September 7, 1929, p. 8; "National Medical Association Meeting Held in Washington," ibid., August 27, 1932, p. 4.

[41] For information on the Smith-Lever Extension Act, see Alfred True, *A History of Agricultural Extension Work in the United States, 1785–1923* (Washington, D.C., 1928). Information on home demonstration clubs also appears in T. J. Woofter, Jr., "Organization of Rural Negroes for Public Health Work," *Proceedings of the National Conference of Social Work* (Chicago, 1923), pp. 72–75; "Activities Report, Birth Control Negro Service," June 21–July 21, 1941, and "Progress Outline 1940–42," Box 22, Rose Papers. For information on Jeanes Teachers see, for example, Ross, *Black Heritage*, p. 211.

[42] Information on organizations is based on numerous reports and newsletters from the years 1940–42 in Box 22, Rose Papers; see also "Newsletter from Division of Negro Service, December, 1941," Box 121, Folder 1309, and "PPFA Field Report for California, 1944," Box 119, Folder 1215, Sanger Papers.

Even in their cooperation with the BCFA, leading members of the black community stressed their own concerns and disagreements with the overall structure of the birth control movement. Their comments reveal important differences in orientation. At a meeting of the National Advisory Council of the Division of Negro Service in 1942, members of the council made it clear that birth control services and information must be distributed to the community *as* a community. Their goal was inclusion; members stated that they were disturbed at the emphasis on doctors, and that teachers, ministers, and other community members must be employed in birth control work. Even the black physicians on the council stressed the need for keeping midwives, volunteers, and especially women practitioners involved in the movement and suggested that mobile clinics traveling throughout the rural South distribute birth control information and other needed health services. This approach to birth control diverged significantly from the conservative strategy of the white BCFA leadership, which insisted that birth control services be dispensed by individual private physicians. Black physicians, it seems, were more sensitive to the general health needs of their population and more willing to experiment with the delivery of birth control services. They favored the integration of birth control into public health services, which many white physicians opposed.[43]

Others on the council state that black women could be reached only through community organizations that they trusted, and they stressed again the necessity of not isolating birth control as a special interest to the neglect of other important health needs. Still others pointed to the need for birth control representatives who recognized social differences among urban blacks.

Clinicians also observed a difference in clinic attendance between white and black patrons. Black women, they noted, were much more likely to spread the word about birth control services and bring their relatives and friends to the clinics. Some rural women even thought of "joining" the clinic as they might join a community organization. A white woman, however, was more likely to keep the information to herself and attend the clinic alone. A statistician from the Census Bureau supported this observation when he speculated in 1931 that

[43] "Activities Report, January 1, 1942–February 6, 1942" and "Progress Outline 1940–42," Box 22, Folder 4, Rose Papers; *Family Guardian* (Massachusetts Mother's Health Council) 5 (December 1939): 3, and 10 (July 1940): 3; "Minutes of the National Advisory Council Meeting, Division of Negro Service," December 11, 1942, Box 121, Folder 1310, Sanger Papers; Peter Murray, *BCR* 16 (July–August 1932): 216; M. O. Bousefield, *BCR* 22 (May 1938): 92. James Reed notes the opposition of the American Medical Association to alternative forms of health care systems in *From Private Vice to Public Virtue*, Part IV and p. 254.

"grapevine dissemination" of birth control information contributed to low black birth rates. These reports are a testimony to the effectiveness of working-class black women's networks.[44]

Moreover, many local birth control groups were often able to maintain independence from the Planned Parenthood Federation of America (PPFA) even though they accepted and used PPFA's display and educational materials. This situation was evident at the Booker T. Washington community center in San Francisco. A representative from PPFA had sent this center matrials and then did not hear from anyone for some time. Almost one year later, the director of the Washington center wrote back to PPFA, informing the staff that birth control programs were flourishing in the center's area and that the group had used the federation's materials extensively at community centers and civic clubs and the local black sorority, Alpha Kappa Alpha, had accepted sponsorship of a mothers' health clinic. The PPFA representative described this situation as typical of many black groups. They would not respond to PPFA communications but would use PPFA materials and engage actively in their own form of community birth control work.[45]

In a speech delivered to PPFA in 1942 Dr. Dorothy Ferebee, a black physician and leader, said, "It is well for this organization to realize that the Negro at his present advanced stage of development is increasingly interested more in programs that are worked out with and by him than in those worked out for him."[46] This statement reveals a fundamental difference in the goals and strategies of the black and white communities. In the past scholars have interpreted the birth control movement as a racist and elitist set of programs imposed on the black population. Although this characterization may describe the intentions of the national white leadership, it is important to recognize that the black community had its own agenda in the creation of programs to include and reach wide segments of the black population.

As this essay demonstrates, black women used their knowledge of "folk" and other available methods to limit their childbearing. The dramatic fertility decline from 1880 to 1945 is evidence of their success. Moreover, the use of birth control was pivotal to many pressing issues within the black community. The right to control one's fertility

[44] "Notes on the Mother's Clinic, Tucson, Arizona," Box 119, Folder 1212, Sanger Papers; "A Clinic for Tobacco Road," *BCR* 3 (New Series) (January 1936): 6–7; Leonore G. Guttmacher, "Securing Patients for a Rural Center," *BCR* 23 (November 1938): 130–31; "Chas. E. Hall [sic] Census Bureau Expert, Gives Figures for Ten States in Which Number of Children under Five Shows Decrease," *New York Age*, November 7, 1931, p. 1.

[45] "Activities Report, Birth Control Negro Service," November 21, 1942, Box 22, Rose Papers.

[46] "Project Reports," *Aframerican* (Summer and Fall 1942): 9–24.

emerged simultaneously with changing attitudes toward women in both the black and white communities that recognized their rights as individuals and not only their roles as mothers. And these changing attitudes contributed to the dialogue within the black community about the future of the family and strategies for black survival. Birth control also emerged as part of a growing race consciousness, as blacks saw it as one means of freeing themselves from the oppression and exploitation of white society through the improvement of their health and economic and social status. Birth control was also part of a growing process of politicization. Blacks sought to make it a legislative issue, they opposed the sterilization movement, and they took an active and often independent role in supporting their clinics, educating their communities, and tailoring programs to fit their needs. In their ideology and practice blacks were indeed a vital and assertive part of the larger birth control movement. What appears to some scholars of the birth control movement as the waning of the movement's original purposes during the 1920s and 1930s was within the black community a period of growing ferment and support for birth control. The history of the birth control movement, and the participation of black Americans in it, must be reexamined in this light.

PART IV

LINKED LIVES: THE WORLDS OF GENDER, WORK, AND FAMILY

CHAPTER SIXTEEN

The Just Price, the Free Market, and the Value of Women

Alice Kessler-Harris

Feminist historians might have described the 1980s in the words with which Charles Dickens introduced his famous story *A Tale of Two Cities:* as the best of times and the worst of times. On one hand, the creative outpouring of historical scholarship on women became a source of energy and of continuing pressure for change. In the absence of a mass political movement, the enormous extension of historical knowledge (of which women's history remains the center) should, if it does nothing else, ensure that women's orientations are permanently imprinted in the vocabulary of the past. But there is another hand: our sense of purpose seems to have wavered, our direction to be unclear. The feminist community no longer looks to history as the leading edge of scholarly research. Postmodern forms of literary criticism seem to have moved into that exalted rank. And even within the profession, women's history seems to have lost some of its shine as accusations of partisanship and fears of politicization limit our courage and restrict our vision.

And yet the voices of historians of women are needed now more than ever. Some of the most significant social issues on the political agenda—family life, abortion, reproduction, and a range of issues having to do with economic equality—have a special meaning for women. As these issues become grist for legislative committees and judicial decisions, lawyers and policy makers increasingly invoke the past. In their hands, the history of women emerges as something other than

The essay, originally delivered as the keynote address at the 1987 Berkshire Conference, is reprinted from *Feminist Studies* 14 (Summer 1988): 235–50, by permission of the publisher, Feminist Studies, Inc., c/o Women's Studies Program, University of Maryland, College Park, MD 20742.

the product of historians. Women appear historically as well as philosophically "other," as a single unified whole, instead of an amalgam of diverse experiences."

A few examples will illuminate the issue. Feminist lawyers have disagreed sharply about whether to struggle for special treatment for women in the work force or to opt for equal treatment with men. In 1986 and 1987, the argument focused on pregnancy disability leaves. In the case of the *California Federal Savings and Loan Association* v. *Mark Guerra et al.* (commonly known as the *CalFed* case), the U.S. Supreme Court upheld a state law that provided such leaves for women but did not provide comparable time off for disabled men. Feminists, who supported both sides, agreed in repudiating protective labor legislation that "classified men and women based on stereotypical notions of their sex roles." But they differed dramatically on the message of the past. One side drew a parallel between pregnancy disability legislation and the discredited protective laws, arguing that special treatment for women had distorted the contours of the labor force, encouraging employers to discriminate against them and contributing to occupational segregation in the labor market. Opposing lawyers insisted that a law that provided pregnancy leaves differed from earlier legislation in that it focused on "how women's unique reproductive role affects them in the work place." Pregnancy disability laws would not repeat the history of discrimination, this group suggested, but would, instead, enhance the possibility of achieving equality for women.[1]

In a second 1987 decision, the Supreme Court sustained the affirmative action plan of Santa Clara County, California. The plan included gender among the qualifications an employer could consider in assessing candidates for promotion and hiring. The majority affirmation of this moderate plan evoked a blistering dissent from Justice Antonin Scalia, who called attention to the central issue underlying such cases: "It is a traditionally segregated job category," he noted of the road dispatcher's job in question, "*not* in the Weber sense, but in the sense that, because of longstanding social attitudes, it has not been regarded *by women themselves* as desirable work."[2] Scalia then gave his own historical commentary: "There are, of course those who believe that the social attitudes which cause women themselves to avoid certain

[1] *Brief of the American Civil Liberties Union et al., amici curiae, in California Federal Savings and Loan Association v. Mark Guerra,* #85-494, U.S. Supreme Court, pp. 12–14; and *Brief of Equal Rights Advocates et al., amici curiae in California Federal Savings and Loan Association v. Mark Guerra,* ibid., pp. 7–9.

[2] In *U.S. Steelworkers* v. *Weber,* 443 U.S. 193 (1979), the Court sustained a voluntary and temporary affirmative action plan to redress past grievances suffered by a specific group. Quotations are from the decision as it appeared in the *Daily Labor Report,* March 20, 1987, p. D16.

jobs and to favor others are as nefarious as conscious, exclusionary discrimination. Whether or not that is so . . . the two phenomena are certainly distinct." With all due respect to Justice Scalia, his description of these "two phenomena" reflects a historical consciousness to which many of us might object. Are conscious discrimination and social attitudes so easily separated? We once called this the difference between long-range and immediate causes.

A third example comes from an interview on comparable worth that appeared in the magazine *New Perspectives*, published by the U.S. Civil Rights Commission. The commission has in the last several years been an outspoken opponent of most forms of affirmative action and of all forms of comparable worth. "We do not have massive evidence that there was wage discrimination against women over the past one hundred years," commented the interviewer, an editor of the magazine. "So why should we now pass legislation or have a court make a ruling that assumes that the difference between men and women is due to discrimination?"[3] Does anyone dispute that invidious distinctions between men and women are deeply rooted in the history of women's work? What "massive evidence" would satisfy this interviewer?

These examples illustrate how public or popular conceptions of the past can construct the future. They remind us that we have a responsibility as scholars to speak to public issues—to shape the visible perception of a past whose contours we have fundamentally altered. They suggest that history, as a way of thinking, speaks to these issues whether we, as individuals, will it or not, and therefore plays a crucial role in forming consciousness. A concern with contemporary issues enhances our capacity to think about the theoretical implications of the concrete empirical data in which we are immersed. Attention to historical reality encourages public policy makers to consider context, particularity, and diversity in the formulation of issues. A reciprocal relationship between history and public policy thus strengthens both areas, each on its own terms. And it offers historians of women a way of enhancing women's understanding of womanly traditions.

I want to illustrate how this dialogue might work by looking at one of the burning issues of the day: pay equity or comparable worth. A major tenet of the feminist demand for equality is equity, or fairness, or justice. The demand underlines affirmative action programs and equal pay slogans. But what is equity in the job market? Like surrogate motherhood, homework, and pregnancy disability leaves, the pay equity strategy evokes contrary responses among feminists as well as antifeminists. Antifeminists suggest that it could increase labor conflict, worsen America's international competitive posture, and encourage a

[3] "Comparable Worth: An Interview with Heidi Hartmann and June O'Neill," *New Perspectives* 17 (September 1985): 29.

destructive female independence that will finally destroy the patriarchal family. Feminists who dismiss these arguments worry that it might produce a host of evils including ghettoization in segrated occupations, economic inflation, expanded female unemployment, and increased female welfare dependency.

But comparable worth is clearly on the nation's political agenda. More than twenty states have legislation that favors it; the 1984 Democratic party platform supported it; the AFL-CIO and several of its constituent unions have made it a priority issue. Minnesota has implemented it for state jobs. The state of Washington is well on the way to doing so. Yet proponents and opponents of comparable worth differ sharply as to its justice or fairness.

Proponents suggest that the need for equity is self-evident. As one study observed, "The work women do is paid less, and the more an occupation is dominated by women, the less it pays."[4] That, they say, is manifestly unfair. But they disagree about the basis for paying women more. Some argue that "jobs that are equal in value to the organization ought to be equally compensated whether or not the work content is similar."[5] Others suggest that the inequity resides in the market's failure to pay women a fair return on the human capital they have invested in the job.[6] Each calls on a different perception of history to solve two seemingly intractable historical problems facing women who earn wages: persistent occupational segregation and the stubborn wage gap between female and male workers. On the theory that low wages inhere in the job, which is itself sex-typed, advocates of comparable worth posit two central assumptions: first, that the free market has not worked for women, and second, that every job has an inherent value that can be compared with that of other jobs. Value, according to proponents of comparable worth, can be measured by such factors as the skill, effort, responsibility, training, and working conditions that are its requisites.

Critics ridicule the notion that value inheres in jobs. The market, they suggest—the demand for labor and the available supply—determines the wage paid. If women are not paid well, it is because they have made bad choices. And if these choices are historically conditioned, why should employers be held responsible? The language they use indicates something of the fear the idea evokes. Phrases like "the

[4] *Women, Work, and Wages: Equal Pay for Jobs of Equal Value,* ed. Donald J. Treiman and Heidi Hartman (Washington, D.C., 1981), p. 28.

[5] Ibid., p. ix.

[6] Barbara R. Bergmann, "Pay Equity—Surprising Answers to Hard Questions," *Challenge* 30 (May–June 1987): 47. See also *Comparable Worth and Wage Discrimination: Technical Possibilities and Political Realities,* ed. Helen Remick (Philadelphia, 1984), for essays that are generally favorable to comparable worth.

looniest idea since loony tunes" and "the feminist road to socialism" are the catchwords of the day.[7]

The historian hears these arguments impatiently, for whatever the abstract models proferred by economists, the historical record introduces the balm of experience. The market, as it functions in the daily lives of people, is not independent of the values and customs of those who participate in it. Justice, equity, and fairness have not been its natural outcomes. Rather, market outcomes have been tempered by customary notions of justice or fairness. The specific forms these take have been the object of struggle. And just as ideas of fairness influence our response to the market so, too, do they infuence how the market works.

Such notions go back to the earliest days of commerce. In the eleventh century, churchmen developed widely accepted notions of "just price" to resist an incipient market. Trying to avoid the inevitable disruption of traditional relationships that would occur if scarce labor were able, by restricting supply, to raise wages above those appropriate for its station, the church and the schoolmen who interpreted doctrine argued for an objective assessment of value. Measured by fair exchange or an equivalence or labor, value and therefore price inhered in every article of commerce and in the wage of every worker. Trade, in the minds of Thomas Aquinas and Albertus Magnus, might be a necessary evil, but it should be engaged in within the "customary estimate." Departure from that norm infringed on both religious and moral codes.

From the beginning the notion of just price embodied a subjective judgment. Since an important component of the wage and the price of the commodity to be sold was determined by the extent of the laborer's needs, just price rested on medieval conceptions of social hierarchy. "It corresponded," in the words of one economic historian, "to a reasonable charge that would enable the producer to support his family on a scale suitable to his station in life."[8] Economic historians still debate the extent to which that correspondence emerged from the "common estimate" or market value of an object, but everyone agrees that a complex array of exchange factors mingled with a sense of propriety to form the final price. Thus, in one sense, just price was a subterfuge that enabled public authority to regulate an emerging market.

[7] Michael Levin, "Comparable Worth: The Feminist Road to Socialism," *Commentary* 79 (September 1984): 13–19. See also *Comparable Worth: Issues and Alternatives*, E. Robert Livernash (Washington, D.C., 1984), for essays that are generally opposed to comparable worth.

[8] Raymond de Roover, "The Concept of the Just Price: Theory and Economic Policy," in *Economic Thought: A Historical Anthology*, ed. James Gherity (New York, 1969), p. 23.

Whatever the weaknesses of just price theory and its rootedness in the moral concerns of the church, it passed down a continuing notion that nonmarket factors have a place in the valuation of objects or wage rates. In a period of labor shortages, notions of just price restricted the wages of labor and prevented skilled workers from banding together in what were labeled "conspiracies." When labor shortages gave way to surpluses and the consensual wage that had been used to keep wages down began to decline, craftsmen and laborers (sometimes organized in guilds) resorted to just price theory to maintain a floor under wages. And as just price began to break down in the fifteenth century when the market expanded, notions that the wage ought to reflect some sense of need, rather than merely supply, lingered on. Its components are visible in the market system that emerged in the fifteenth century and reached full flower by the nineteenth. The customary wage, the wage demanded by the craftsperson or laborer, reflected a social sense of how a worker should live, as well as the amount of labor used to create the product for sale. These notions remain. Changing ideas of fairness are implicit in evaluations of the market and influence the way taxes are imposed and market outcomes are regulated.

In the free market, theoretically, demand and supply determine price. But in practice, wage theorists recognize a variety of what Harvard professor and former secretary of labor John Dunlop has called "exterior" factors in determining the wage.[9] These exterior factors are influences on the labor market that emerge from such nonmarket factors as union contracts, seniority systems, and a sense of equity. Contemporary wage theorists have elaborate ways of describing how the market is restricted by these historical tendencies. Arthur M. Ross argues that wages move in what he calls "orbits of coercive comparison," which is another way of saying that traditional market forces do not have "compelling significance" in the determination of wages.[10] Rather, wages are influenced by the force of ideas about justice and equity and the power of organizations and individuals to sustain them. In this widely accepted model, workers compare their wages to those of other workers; pride and dignity prevent them from settling for less than their peers are getting. Other economists talk about "job clusters": firefighters insist on parity with police; steelworkers strike to maintain equivalent wages nationwide, though the market could eas-

[9] John Dunlop, "Wage Contours," in *Unemployment and Inflation: Institutional and Structural Views,* ed. Michael Piore (White Plains, N.Y., 1979), p. 66. Elaine Sorenson, "Equal Pay for Comparable Worth: A Policy for Eliminating the Undervaluation of Women's Work," *Journal of Economic Issues* 18 (June 1984): 465–72, provides a convenient summary of some of these arguments.

[10] Arthur M. Ross, *Trade Union Wage Policy* (Berkeley, 1948), p. 49. See also Robert Solow, "Theories of Unemployment," *American Economic Review* 70 (March 1980): 1–11.

ily pay less in some areas of the country. All these ideas and the social sensibilities that sustain them limit or modify market wages.

According to Ross, workers use comparisons to establish the dividing line between a "square deal, and a raw deal." In a competitive market in which most workers do not leave jobs for wages but are promoted from within and rely on their jobs for security, a worker might not earn what he would like, but as Ross put it, "He wants what is coming to him . . . [it is] . . . an affront to his dignity, and a threat to his prestige when he receives less than another worker with whom he can *legitimately* be compared."[11] I leave hanging for the moment the gendered content of "legitimately."

If wages reflect the relationship between some workers and others, they also tell us something about the relation between the craftsperson and the object produced, between the laborer and the employer, and among employers as well. Autoworkers, for example, agree that productivity and profits shuld be considered when determining the wage. They demand a share in the distribution of profits in good years and may reluctantly accept cutbacks in bad ones. Similarly, employers refuse wage increases that would raise the standard of an industry even when their own profits make such raises possible. "Wage rates," economist Michael Piore sugests, "perform certain basic social and institutional functions. They define relationships between labor and management, between one group of workers and another. . . . [They define] the place of individuals relative to one another in the work community, in the neighborhood, and in the family."[12]

Because wages, like the labor market, function to structure relationships, comparable worth provides a parallel rather than a substitute strategy for achieving equity. Some feminists criticize comparable worth on the grounds that it will ghettoize women. The wage, they suggest, is a function of jobs held, and the proper remedy for women who want equal wages is to seek access to traditionally male jobs that pay better. After all, the argument goes, affirmative action legislation, now in place, will open up the market to women's labor and eliminate the main cause of the wage gap: occupational segregation. The Equal Pay Act of 1963 will then ensure that women are treated equally. Fighting for affirmative action increases women's admission to male bastions and, by encouraging them to act on male conceptions of the market, will secure for them permanent access to the best jobs.

But like the wage, the labor market is a regulating device, the product of a long history of social relationships heavily influenced by

[11] Ibid., pp. 50–51, emphasis added.

[12] Michael J. Piore, "Unemployment and Inflation: An Alternative View," in *Unemployment and Inflation*, ed. Piore, 6. And see Peter Doeringer and Michael Piore, *Internal Labor Markets and Manpower Analysis* (Lexington, Mass., 1971).

traditional conceptions of gender roles. Although abstract market models indicate that people choose jobs, the historical record suggests that occupational segregation has been the product of deeply ingrained attitudes. What appears to be a "natural" consequence of women's social roles has to be measured against the specific shape of occupational segregation at a given historical moment. Ideas about women "following" jobs into the marketplace, or choosing jobs that fill nurturing roles, or preferring to satisfy some abstract social ethic rather than to make money are all ways of rationalizing nonmarket behavior by means of some other notion of equity. These and other specific social customs help legitimize the continuing and changing shape of the labor market. But they are and have been the frequent subject of negotiation and challenge by women. The historian who explores the workings of the labor market and reads complaints about its rigidities in particular times and places learns how segmentation functioned at certain moments and contributes to understanding the way gender roles have helped to construct the market as well.

Notions of craft and brotherhood, of masculinity and femininity, are embedded in and confirmed by the labor market, raising questions about the definition of justice embodied in a "free labor market" in which inclusion and exclusion are a function of many things—including sex. Even a cursory glance at the rationalizations employers and managers have used to regulate women's participation leaves no doubt that the labor market has been socially not abstractly constructed. Thus particular notions of equity are expressed by the London guilds that declared in the fourteenth century that "no man of the trade should set any woman to work other than his wife and daughter."[13] Medieval injunctions are echoed by those of many trade unions and male workplaces in our own time. As late as the 1960s and 1970s, employers explained why they had no women in certain jobs by calling upon customary ideas. "The nature of the work. . . . [did] not lend itself to employment in production of either women or the handicapped," said a wire manufacturer in 1973. And a pharmaceutical manufacturer told an interviewer in 1968 that the company would hire women in clerical occupations and elsewhere "where the physical requirements of the task involved do not preclude it."[14] Such social attitudes continue down to this moment to serve as guides to what is equitable in the labor market. A 1987 cover story in *Business Week* notes that women "are being promoted because they bring new management styles to the corporation." According to the article, experts report

[13] Eileen Power, *Medieval Women* (London, 1975), p. 60.

[14] William Bielby and James Baron, "Undoing Discrimination: Job Integration and Comparable Worth," in *Ingredients for Women's Employment Policy*, ed. Christine Bose and Glenna Spitz (Albany, 1987), p. 218.

"that female personality traits such as an ability to build consensus and encourage participation are in demand today. . . . Women typically show more warmth and concern about human relationships and human sensitivities."[15] And when such qualities go out of fashion, will women be demoted?

We begin now to see why the idea of comparable worth is so threatening. Just price theory imbued the market with a sense of equity that serves as a compelling (if sometimes unpredictable) influence on it. But whose sense of equity? An important element of equity, itself historically rooted, is a subjective evaluation of gender roles. A customary wage—a wage that reflects a social sense of how men and women should and do live—is partially an effort to preserve the status quo. Because the customary wage was built on a sense of the family as an economic unit, it incorporated and passed down prevailing conceptions of gender. Because it was tied to continuing social hierarchy and women's restricted place, it affirmed women's secondary positions. Thus "a woman's wage" has long been a term of opprobrium among men. A male worker could not legitimately be compared with a female worker without violating his sense of dignity and justice. Nor did the sense of justice of most female workers historically require such comparisons.

But times have changed, and our conceptions of justice are altering. As E. H. Carr put it, abstractions "are indispensable categories of thought but they are devoid of meaning or application till specific content is put into them." Like checks drawn on a bank, "the printed part consists of abstract words like liberty and equality, justice and democracy . . . valueless until we fill in the other part, which states how much liberty we propose to allocate to whom, whom we recognize as our equals and up to what amount. The way we fill in the cheque from time to time is a matter of history."[16] Many (but never all) women in the past accepted a model of equity in the labor market based on the ideology of the patriarchal family. Most arguments for female equality derived from male conceptions of justice and were debates about access, not about new rules. New material conditions have shifted the content of equity from a demand for equality with men to a challenge to male structures. The altered terms of the debate no longer ask how women can achieve equality in a predominantly male work world so much as how to revalue the world of work and workers in a way that incorporates female self-interest. Rooted not in the moral economy of the male but in the traditions, customs, and practices of women, the

[15] "Corporate Women: They're About to Break Through to the Top," *Business Week*, June 22, 1987, p. 74.

[16] Edward Hallett Carr, *What Is History?* (New York, 1962), pp. 105–6.

idea of comparable worth evokes history that assesses the changing sense of right or dignity on which people will act.

That sense emerges from a historical context that alters definitions of what people are willing to accept. Disruptive conditions of early industrialization framed nineteenth-century arguments for a male wage sufficient to keep wives out of the work force. Early twentieth-century battles for a wage adequate to sustain women who were not secondary earners reflected a mature industrial economy in which women had essential but apparently temporary roles as wage laborers. The U.S. Women's Bureau fought bitterly to defend protective labor legislation in the 1920s—a battle rooted in historically conditioned understandings of women's primary task as bearers and rearers of children. By the mid-twentieth century, campaigns for equal pay for equal work reflected a shift in notions of equity rooted in the job to be performed rather than in an abstract conception of women's roles. Within the last ten years, the increasing pauperization of women and children in the United States has become a major incentive to redistribute income and thus an important argument for comparable worth. The campaign for pay equity reflects this new historical stage: because both men and women are recognized providers, the search for equity now includes a demand that jobs be evaluated on their own terms. Changing family structures have clearly played a political part in encouraging a revaluation of women's economic roles. The emergence of the argument is itself an indication that the conception of justice that underlined the legitimacy of a woman's wage is now called into question.

Like other redefinitions of equity, the consequences of this one are not self-evident. Thus we argue over whether struggles for the family wage in the nineteenth century reflected women's interests in stable family life or men's desire to keep women out of the labor market; over whether the capacity of women to earn wages yielded independence and autonomy or served to extend family obligations. Each stage reflects a social transformation that delegitimized certain customary roles and replaced them with others and from which some women benefited while others did not. So with the struggle for pay equity for women. We can and must debate the way it will affect particular groups of women within a context that observes the social transformation of which the demand is a part.

Comparable worth now appears as part of a long political process within which women have tried to achieve some sense of equity and justice as it is defined in their historical period. Why, then, is it so strongly resisted? I suggest that in part it is because a large and potentially powerful group of wage earners, in challenging the conception of the free market, challenges its ideological roots as well. Because it raises to consciousness the issue of equity on which the market rests, comparable worth challenges the legitimacy of gender lines. It purports to delegitimize one element of the market pattern—sex. The end result would be to equate male and female workers, to threaten a male worker's sense of self, pride, and masculinity, and to challenge the legitimacy of basic institutions that touch all aspects of social and political life. The federal district court that rejected the request of Denver nurses that they be paid as much as the city's tree trimmers caught the problem exactly. Such a change, the court commented, in a much-quoted decision, "was pregnant with the possibility of disrupting the entire economic system of the United States."[17]

The point is that it might be true. In refusing to acknowledge the legitimacy of gender distinctions, comparable worth raises a long line of earlier challenges to a new level. The historical context reveals pay equity to be both an issue of the gendered definition of justice and of the way justice manifests itself in the market. Seen from that perspective, comparable worth calls for nothing less than the revaluation of women. Its strength lies in its potential for acting upon female traditions, for it assumes that women have a right to pursue traditional roles and to achieve equity in that pursuit. Thus it sustains those qualities of womanhood—nurture, community, and relational abilities—that are likely to have been products of women's cultural and social roles and have, as a result, been traditionally devalued in the job market.

But comparable worth poses one other crucial challenge to historians. Because it rests on a redefinition of equity, which is historically specific, it confronts us with definitions of difference that are rooted in historical experience. The debate over comparable worth thus opens the question of what difference has meant to various groups of women and how it has manifested itself. The task is crucial to understanding changing forms of justice. If we allow abstract descriptions of "woman" and abstract notions of "woman's culture" to govern our interpretations of the past we provide what Carr called a "blank cheque." We offer empty categories that invite ideological uses of the past. We have seen (in *E.E.O.C* v. *Sears Roebuck and Co.*) the consequences that this "blank cheque" can have in arguments that the nurturing and biological roles of all women preclude working women and needy women from seeking rewards in the work force, discourage them from investing in human capital, and lead them to devote more time and attention to their families.[18] These arguments, which are

[17] Quoted in Mary Heen, "A Review of Federal Court Decisions under Title VII of the Civil Rights Act of 1964," in *Comparable Worth and Wage Discrimination*, ed. Remick, p. 217.

[18] See Ruth Milkman, "Women's History Goes to Trial," *Feminist Studies* 12 (Summer 1986): 375–400; Alice Kessler-Harris, "*Equal Employment Opportunity Commis-*

partly sustained by appeals to recent philosophy and psychology of sex differences and rest on conceptions of the universal female, are negated by historical experience. Not that most women have not performed traditional tasks, but the history of women's actual roles in the work force demonstrates a far more complex set of struggles by which different women at different times and places have tried to find their own directions in their own ways. In the United States, immigrant women, educated women, black women, poor women, married and unmarried women have each in their own ways come to locate their places within the shifting bounds of historical possibility.

Notions of universal womanhood blind us to the reciprocally confirming relationship of the work force and gendered ideas of social role. Judith Long Laws says the labor market provides information that conditions aspiration and channels people's expectations along realistic paths.[19] The historical record reveals how readily information changes in wars and depressions, how selectively it is presented to poor women as opposed to those who are well off, how much more limited it is for women of color than for white women. It demonstrates that difference is not a universal category but a social specific. And it reveals that the way women handle differences can vary dramatically with historical circumstance. Carole Turbin and Mary Blewett, among other scholars, offer evidence of "nondichotomous" differences.[20] They suggest that women can be different in their life patterns and family commitments and yet struggle in the work force like men and with them.

We are led to two conclusions. First, although social and cultural differences between men and women surely exist, their abstract expression is less instructive than is clear-eyed analysis in historical context. Second, such analysis should not be allowed to obscure differences among women and the historically specific ways in which they manifest themselves and serve as sources of tension and change. Poet Audre Lorde argued that difference "must be not merely tolerated, but seen as a fund of necessary polarities between which our creativity can spark like a dialectic."[21]

---

sion v. *Sears Roebuck and Company:* A Personal Account," *Radical History Review* 35 (April 1986): 57–79.

[19] Judith Long Laws, "Work Aspirations of Women: False Leads and New Starts," in *Women and the Workplace: The Implications of Occupational Segregation*, ed. Martha Blaxall and Barbara Reagan (Chicago, 1976), pp. 33–49.

[20] Carole Turbin, "Reconceptualizing Family, Work and Labor Organizing: Working Women in Troy, 1860–90," *Review of Radical Political Economy* 16 (Spring 1984): 1–16; Mary Blewett, *Men, Women, Work, and Gender* (Urbana, 1988).

[21] Audre Lorde, "The Master's Tools Will Never Dismantle the Master's House," in *This Bridge Called My Back: Writings by Radical Women of Color*, ed. Cherríe Moraga and Gloria Anzaldúa (New York, 1983), p. 99.

In the labor market, difference provides the core of the struggle. It is entrenched in the cultural symbolism of jobs. Outdoor, heavy, and skilled jobs are associated with high-paying/provider roles, while dexterity and compassion are tied to poor pay and secondary jobs. Difference is reflected as well in the struggle of men and women to maintain dependent as well as independent relationships. The working-class husband who tells an interviewer that his wife "doesn't know how to be a real wife, you know, feminine and really womanly. . . . She doesn't know how to give respect because she's too independent. She feels that she's a working woman and she puts in almost as many hours as I do and brings home a pay check, so there's no one person above the other. She doesn't want there to be a king in this household,"[22] is saying something about his expectations of traditional roles that we need to hear. The women who opposed the Equal Rights Amendment because they feared giving up alimony are reluctant to abandon their conceptions of equity for new and unknown forms. But these are not universal statements. They are pieces of a historical struggle. They tell us something about the distribution of rewards in a society and about the role sexual constraints play in it, about the structure of power, and about gendered meanings. They therefore tell us something about the reciprocal relationship between sexuality and social power.

In negating individual and particular experience, abstract arguments from difference ride roughshod over the aspirations and motivations of most women. The undifferentiated "woman" becomes a reified object instead of a social category subject to analysis, an abstraction rather than an actor in the historical enterprise. This is not an argument against theory or against conceptualizing. Rather, it is a plea that our theories be conditioned by the experiences of real actors: an expression of concern that the "universal female" not become a device to negate the possibility of equity and inadvertently open the door to perpetual inequality.

We are brought full circle. History offers a picture of wage relations that are not systemic but constructed and processual—a picture from which most women were once excluded and into which they are now drawn. Like the labor market, the wage relation is constructed out of subjective experience and rests ultimately on the legitimacy of historically specific notions of gender "difference." The historical record puts teeth into arguments for pay equity. As part of a changing battle for a changing definition of justice, its political parameters become comprehensible and the meaning of the argument becomes more apparent.

Comparable worth illustrates how we construct consciousness out of historical experience, and it illustrates as well how the historian

[22] Lillian Breslow Rubin, *Worlds of Pain: Life in the Working Class Family* (New York, 1976), p. 176.

who explores the past in dialogue with the present can develop a richer understanding of the past. The struggle of women to redefine concepts like justice, liberty, and power, which reflect a vision of the future, pushes us to explore the past from which such ideas emerged. Because ideas do not come from thin air, our attempts to discover how they took shape, how diverse groups appropriated, shaped, and rejected them, enriches our understanding of the historical process and places content into what is otherwise a blank cheque or an empty box.

The reverse is also true. Without a history, public policy follows the paths of social myth. By entering the debate, historians of women have the possibility of shaping the future. Without a history the argument that women have a right to paid work can be turned into an excuse to push women with small children to take poorly paid, meaningless jobs. Without a history, the search for safe and accessible methods of birth control can be (and has been) translated into forced sterilization for the most vulnerable. Without a history, it is plausible for policy makers, legislatures, New Right groups, and ordinary women to interpret the problems women encounter in doing paid jobs as products of personal "choices" rather than as social issues. Without a history, employed women are asked to find solutions to what are called their own personal problems in their own ways.

An influential pair of sociologists demonstrated the consequences of an obligingly absent historical consciousness: when "family obligations come to be perceived as obstacles to self-realization in [women's] careers, individual women will have to decide on their priorities. Our own hope is that many will come to understand that life is more than a career and that this 'more' is above all to be found in the family. But, however individual women decide, they should not expect public policy to underwrite and subsidize their life plans."[23] The historian of women, politely eschewing the temptation to tackle the false historical assumptions contained in the statement, responds that as long as policy makers can invent a history that ignores the rich diversity of women's experiences, our task will not be completed.

[23] Brigitte Berger and Peter L. Berger, *The War over the Family: Capturing the Middle Ground* (Garden City, N.Y., 1983), p. 205.

CHAPTER SEVENTEEN

The Masculinization of Production: The Gendering of Work and Skill in U.S. Newspaper Printing, 1850–1920

Ava Baron

Despite numerous studies of women's work, a satisfactory explanation of the persistence of women's inequality in the labor market has not yet emerged. This essay is based on the view that the masculinization of work, not just its feminization, requires examination and explanation to understand fully occupational sex segregation. To this end, I studied the social constructions of gender and skill definitions of work in newspaper composing rooms before and after the introduction of typesetting machines in the late nineteenth century.

The study of gender has been oversimplified. Gender is not a simple or static dichotomy but a complex and dynamic social process. Exploring the historical conditions that heighten expressions of sexual difference in the discourse of working men and their employers helps to move the debate on the causes of occupational sex segregation forward by seeing it as more than conspiracies of men to dominate women or means to increase capitalists' profit.[1]

Newspaper printing is ideal for the study of gender and work because it was a focus of nineteenth- and early twentieth-century debates over

This essay is based on material from my book manuscript "Men's Work and the Woman Question: The Masculinization of Printing, 1830–1920." An earlier version was published as "Contested Terrain Revisited: Technology and Gender Definitions of Work in the Printing Industry, 1850–1920," in Barbara Wright et al., *Women, Work, and Technology: Transformations* (Ann Arbor, 1987) pp. 58–83. I thank Robert Asher, Mary Blewett, Richard Butsch, Patricia Cooper, Roslyn Feldberg, Myra Marx Ferree, Maurine Greenwald, Susan Klepp, David Noble, Joan Scott, Carole Turbin, and Lise Vogel for comments and criticisms on earlier versions of this essay.

[1] On the value of studying gender discourses see Joan W. Scott, *Gender and the Politics of History* (New York, 1989).

occupations that were appropriate for women. Different answers to this so-called woman question were put forth by employers and workers, middle-class reformers, and machine manufacturers. Although women were a minority in the printing industry, the intense debates throughout the nineteenth and twentieth centuries over whether printing was appropriate woman's work highlight the significance of gender for the development of class relations and the organization of work.[2]

Since Harry Braverman's analysis of the transformation of the capitalist labor process numerous studies have examined the deskilling of work in blue-collar and white-collar occupations. But Braverman's approach has been justifiably criticized for underestimating workers' responses; in his text, capitalists seem unopposed. Research has increasingly shown, however, that workers actively resist transformations of production that reduce their control over work.[3]

Researchers, however, have applied a gender-blind analysis to the transformation of work, technological change, and conflicts in the workplace. As a result, research on the labor process has reinforced the view that the feminization of jobs is synonymous with their deskilling and that the displacement of women by men means upgrading of jobs. Men's work experience has been the starting point of most investigations. From this vantage point, women are seen as the tools used by capitalists to deskill work. Skill has been conceptualized as something men have and women lack.

Gender affects the labor market not just at the point of recruitment but before and after, that is, in the organization of the labor process itself. The job structure is created out of relationships between capital and labor, but these actors are also gendered, and this profoundly affects what happens. As this study of printing reveals, deskilling created a crisis of masculinity, a crisis for men workers simultaneously as men and as workers.

In the old "hand set" days, before the introduction of typesetting machines in the 1890s, the printer, often called the compositor or typesetter, read the manuscript, selected the typefaces, justified the lines, set up the page, distributed the type, proofread, and prepared the type

[2] For a discussion of the contemporary feminization of printing in the United States, see Patricia A. Roos, "Hot-Metal to Electronic Composition: Gender, Technology, and Social Change," in *Job Queues, Gender Queues, Explaining Women's Inroads into Male Occupations*, ed. Patricia A. Roos and Barbara F. Reskin (Philadelphia, 1990), pp. 275–98.

[3] Harry Braverman, *Labor and Monopoly Capital: The Degradation of Work in the Twentieth Century* (New York, 1974). For case studies of deskilling see Andrew Zimbalist, ed., *Case Studies on the Labor Process* (New York, 1979). On workers' resistance to deskilling see David Montgomery, *Workers' Control in America: Studies in the History of Work, Technology, and Labor Struggles* (Cambridge, Eng., 1979).

for the press. The men of the typographical union considered themselves skilled craft workers, proud of their work and its traditions.[4]

To these printers wage work was a measure of manliness, essential to men's role as family providers. Further, the particular nature of the work involved in printing was considered masculine. In the nineteenth century men gained masculine stature as family breadwinners. A measure of manliness was not only winning the wage in the public sphere but the amount of the wage. A man's degree of manliness could be gauged by the size of his wage. The "woman question"—whether it was appropriate for women to work in the printing industry—therefore provoked extensive discussion and debate among union printers.[5] By jeopardizing men's wages and thereby their role as family providers, the employment of women printers threatened men with a loss of manliness. Men claimed that women printers increased the available labor supply and reduced men's bargaining position so they were "impotent" in their warfare against capital.[6]

Employers, by contrast, insisted that typesetting was distinctly "woman's work." During the second half of the nineteenth century, publishers increasingly employed women to do the relatively simple typesetting of columns of text known as straight matter, which constituted over two-thirds of the work for newspapers. In the 1850s and 1860s publishers recruited thousands of women from the textile and clothing industries, gave them a six-week training program, and set them to work as typesetters.[7]

Employers and middle-class women reformers during the mid-nineteenth century claimed that the work was gendered as feminine. They emphasized its intellectual aspects as particularly feminine because it was light, clean, and easy, whereas manual work was masculine.[8]

A second contradictory claim put forth by employers and reformers was that the work required particular aptitudes or characteristics that only women had. Printing itself was not gendered, but it required

[4] Presswork and typesetting became distinct operations by the 1850s. For discussion of printers' occupational culture see Ava Baron, "Women and the Making of the American Working Class: A Study of the Proletarianization of Printers," *Review of Radical Political Economics* 14 (Fall 1982): 23–42.

[5] George A. Stevens, *New York Typographical Union #6: Study of a Modern Trade Union and Its Predecessors,* in New York State, Department of Labor, Bureau of Labor Statistics, *Annual Report,* 1911 (Albany, 1913), pp. 421–40.

[6] "Address to Printers of the U.S.," 1850, in James M. Lynch, *Epochal History of the International Typographical Union* (Indianapolis, 1925), p. 24; *New York Tribune,* July 17, 1854; Stevens, *New York Typographical Union,* pp. 423, 427.

[7] See Baron, "Women and the Making of the American Working Class."

[8] Virginia Penny, *The Employments of Women: A Cyclopedia of Woman's Work* (Boston, 1863); *Harper's* 37 (June-November 1868): 530.

workers with particular traits and was "peculiarly adapted" to the inherent aptitudes of women. Publishers viewed women as "admirably suited for the work, having a nicety of touch which would enable them to manipulate type with greater facility than men."[9]

Men printers, however, thought printing conferred masculinity on its practitioners. It was a "manly art" because it combined intellectual and manual labor.[10] Though conceding that women could do typesetting and citing examples of women who could compose with rapidity and exactness, men still argued that women should not be printers because typesetting would "unsex" them. Reading the material being typeset might endanger women's morals. Further, they would lose their femininity by working alongside men, hearing men's foul language on the shop floor, and being in contact with the aggressive, masculine nature of shop-floor culture.[11]

Men printers described the "awful consequences" that would result for women and society if women worked in newspaper composing rooms. As they put it: "For our part we should be loth to see a daughter or sister of ours confined to the atmosphere of a morning paper office, . . . We should be loth, too," they stated, for her to be in a workroom, "where she is apt to associate, or come in contact with, men and youth of every grade of morals." Contact with the world "in the same method that man finds necessary would have a pernicious effect upon her morals."[12] Thus gender was an issue for printers even before the Linotype heightened the salience of the "woman question."

The speed and output of printing presses increased dramatically during the nineteenth century. Many typesetting machines were invented, but none were widely adopted, despite their speed.[13] Employers had to

[9] *Inland Printer* 3 (May 1886): 470.

[10] *Printers' Circular* 1 (February 1, 1867): 161, and 2 (November 1867): 328. Clean, intellectual work, not involving physical labor, was considered feminine. See Sara Eisenstein, *Give Us Bread, but Give Us Roses: Working Women's Consciousness in the United States, 1890 to the First World War* (Boston, 1983), p. 79. Paul Willis found that working-class boys in England in the 1970s defined manual work as masculine and desirable and mental work as effeminate. See Willis, *Learning to Labour: How Working Class Kids Get Working Class Jobs* (Westmead, Eng., 1977). Cynthia Cockburn found that contemporary British printers believe white-collar work makes a boy's masculinity suspect (*Brothers: Male Dominance and Technological Change* [London, 1983], p. 139).

[11] *Printers' Circular* 3 (December 1868): 293; *Finchers' Trades Review* (October 1, 1864); Stevens, *New York Typographical Union*, p. 423; *Inland Printer* 2 (October 1884-September 1885): 109–10. On printers' shop-floor culture see Baron, "Women and the Making of the American Working Class."

[12] "Women in Printing Offices," Letter to the Editor, *Sunday Dispatch*, ca. 1853, in Joel Munsell, comp., *Printers' Scraps*, 9 (Albany 1860), p. 96; *Finchers'* (October 1, 1864); and "Printers' Manifesto," 1854, in Stevens, *New York Typographical Union*, p. 427.

[13] John S. Thompson lists over seventy different typesetting machines developed before 1904 (*History of Composing Machines* [1904; rpt. New York, 1972]).

weigh the potential for expanded productivity against enormously increased capital investment. The tremendous growth of the newspaper industry in the 1880s changed this picture. Publishers of the large newspapers weighed the capabilities of typesetting machines and had sufficient capital to afford them.[14]

The Linotype, patented in 1885, became the standard mechanical typesetting system for newspaper composition by the early twentieth century.[15] Like other machines, the Linotype used a keyboard resembling that of a typewriter. But instead of the key releasing a type character, it released a small brass matrix, which was a mold for casting the type character.

The success of the Linotype was not assured from the outset. Many options were available to publishers in the 1880s, and even in the 1890s they were debating the merits of different typesetting machines. When the American Newspaper Publishers' Association studied the various machines available in 1891, it concluded that other models were either cheaper or faster than the Linotype.[16]

To promote the machine in the 1890s, the Mergenthaler Company, the Linotype manufacturer, set up schools to train operators. These trainees were sent as strikebreakers to help publishers during strikes and lockouts. Eventually the International Typographical Union (ITU) and the Mergenthaler Company negotiated an agreement by which the company would refrain from training operators to be used as strikebreakers and the ITU would encourage its members to learn to use the machine and not to interfere with its introduction. When affiliated locals struck to oppose the use of the Linotype, the ITU interceded, and in at least one case the ITU sent in union men from other locals to break the strike.[17]

The union's acceptance of the Linotype set in motion conflicts with employers regarding the machine's implications. The ITU sought to secure Linotype operation for union members, to obtain wages equivalent to those paid for hand composition, and to retain control over

[14] George E. Barnett, *Chapters on Machinery and Labor* (Cambridge, Mass., 1926).

[15] Most typesetting machines were used in newspaper offices, and most of these were Linotypes. In 1904 there were 5,491 machines in newspaper offices and 1,638 in book and job offices (Barnett, *Chapters on Machinery and Labor;* U.S. Bureau of Labor Statistics Bulletin 13, no. 67 [Washington, D.C., 1906], p. 743n).

[16] *Newspaperdom* 1 (1892–93): 16–21; and American Newspaper Publishers' Association *Bulletin,* 1892.

[17] Charles J. Dumas, "When the Linotype Came: How the Craft Was Stirred by the Appearance of the First Successful Composing Machine Forty Years Ago," *Typographical Journal* 79 (September 1931): 247; Jacob Loft, *The Printing Trades* (New York, 1944), p. 49; U.S. Bureau of Labor, *Eleventh Special Report of the Commissioner of Labor, Regulation and Restriction of Output,* 58th Cong. 2d sess., House Document 734 (1904), pp. 35–36.

hiring and firing, setting the production norm, and certifying workers' competence.[18]

Central to the union's strategies was its effort to define the Linotype as a skilled masculine process, but they met significant resistance from employers. Both employers and men printers made claims about the specific inherent characteristics of men and women and the work they were capable of, but they articulated different versions of masculinity and femininity. The union claimed that the work was intrinsically masculine and that women did not have the necessary capabilities to do the job. Employers, however, claimed that women were ideal Linotypists because the work required typically feminine characteristics such as steadiness and dexterity. For more than thirty years following the introduction of the Linotype the typographical union and employers battled over the gender and skill definitions of the new occupation.

Even before mechanical typesetting technology was developed, employers viewed such machines as a logical extension of women's work as hand compositors. To the publishers, all typesetting machines, regardless of specific design, were suitable for female use.

Use of the keyboard appeared to open up the work of printing to educated women. Unlike publishers' recruitment efforts of the 1860s, which focused on uneducated foreign-born women from the clothing and textile industries, publishers in the 1890s sought to recruit literate native-born women skilled in stenography and typewriting.[19]

Many of the typesetting machines were marketed as suitable for women and requiring little training. Linotype advertisements showed women operating the machines; to emphasize the ease with which the machines could be operated, ads and articles in the *Linotype Bulletin* portrayed monkeys, blind people, deaf-mutes, and one-handed workers as expert and efficient on the machine. Employers and the machine manufacturer claimed that women typists and stenographers could efficiently operate the machine with little or no training on the Linotype itself. As testimony before an arbitration board, a publisher exhibited a Linotype keyboard. He then showed an uncorrected galley proof, claiming that his stenographer had produced it on the Linotype after less than ten days' experience.[20]

Employers built on their earlier claims that typesetting was work that was respectable for women because it was intellectual. Middle-class women's claims that typesetting was "one of the most pleasant,

[18] Dumas, "When the Linotype Came," p. 244; Loft, *Printing Trades*, p. 48.

[19] Barnett, *Chapters on Machinery and Labor*, p. 26. On recruitment of women in the 1850s and 1860s see Baron, "Women and the Making of the American Working Class."

[20] *The Printer* 6 (July 1865): 88; *Inland Printer* 6 (April 1889): 580, and 5 (March 1888): 442; 3 *Newspaperdom* 3 (September 1894): 122, and (March 1894): 425; *Linotype Bulletin* 6 (September 1910): 66, 9 (November 1913): 183, 13 (July 1917): 179.

respectable, and profitable occupations" for women were bolstered in the 1890s by contemporary changes in clerical work, particularly the introduction of the typewriter and the increasing feminization of office work.[21]

Publishers claimed that keyboard work on the Linotype was essentially the same as on the typewriter and that both required the same abilities and characteristics from workers. They then tried to establish that Linotype work was unskilled because the typists who were recruited required no extensive special training on the keyboard. Typing, publishers claimed, was not a skill but a "natural" feminine ability that women brought to the work.[22]

Linotype work heightened the dilemmas male printers faced. The bases of their definition of masculinity in their work were progressively disintegrating. The physical strength requirements of printing eroded during the nineteenth century because of the division of labor and the introduction of steam-powered machinery. The mental aspects of their work were either threatened by increased supervision and management control or defined as analogous to clerical work and therefore effeminate.

Men may have accepted the Linotype in part because it diminished rather than increased opportunities for women printers. The percentage of women working on machines was lower than on hand composition. In 1884, just a few years before introduction of the Linotype, one-quarter of Boston's compositors were women. Yet nationwide, by 1900 women made up only 15 percent of printers and compositors, and by 1904 only 520 women operated typesetting machines, about 5 percent of the total in the United States and Canada. The typesetter who specialized in straight matter, not the all-around craft printer, was displaced by typesetting technology; 95 percent of the unemployed printers in 1899 had specialized in straight composition.[23]

Men printers supported the Linotype over other machines because it posed less of a threat to their class and gender positions. While other machines separated the setting of type from justifying lines and distributing type, the Linotype made typesetting a single integrated operation. The Linotype appeared to enhance craft respectability because it did not subdivide the work and because it made typesetting a more masculine process by adding typecasting to the typesetter's job. At the same time, unlike machines that used type characters or kept

[21] See "Woman's Work and Wages," *Harper's* 37 (June-November *1868*): 550.

[22] *Fourth Estate*, no. 361 (January 26, 1901): 7; *Newspaperdom* 2 (1893–94): 241.

[23] *Inland Printer* 2 (October 1884): 43; Edith Abbott, *Women in Industry: A Study in American Economic History* (New York, 1910), p. 258; Barnett, *Chapters on Machinery and Labor*, p. 28; *Annual Report*, ITU Convention, 1899, in George A. Tracy, *History of the Typographical Union: Its Beginnings, Progress and Development* (Indianapolis, 1913), p. 577.

typecasting as a separate mechanism, and so kept the operator free from heat, dust, and discomfort created by the typecasting, the Linotype required the operator to contend with the heat and gas fumes produced by the pot of molten metal located near the operator's seat. Men embraced the Linotype because its dirty aspects made it less respectable for women.[24]

Printers disagreed with employers' and machine manufacturers' claims about the skills and characteristics needed to be proficient as a Linotype operator. According to Lee Reilly, a printer-operator, "to be rapid and competent requires training as a printer." The assumption that typists made efficient machine operators he called "a delusion."[25]

In an effort to deal with the crisis of masculinity posed by the new job process, men began to redefine the source of masculinity. In contrast to earlier years, when men claimed the work itself was masculine, after the Linotype they claimed there was "no sex in labor." Work did not embody gender, workers did, and some workers could do work that others could not. "In some varieties of work strength of a man is required, or endurance which is too exacting for the female frame. In others, the greater delicacy of manipulation which women can give is demanded." Further, men held on to the belief that they had skill and masculinity, even if the job did not.[26] Inherent masculine characteristics, not just acquired skills, were needed for proficiency on the machine, therefore men made better operators than women.

Sexual difference between men and women as workers was heightened and redefined in biological terms. Women, men printers argued, could not do the work because women were physically inferior and lacked the necessary mental abilities and the natural temperament. Men pointed to their ability to lift heavy forms and to change the machine magazines as evidence that physical strength was needed for the work. Although the operators rarely actually did these tasks, they claimed it was important to be able to do them. But most significantly, men printers claimed that the work required endurance that women lacked.

For the men, endurance was important because it symbolized their superiority over women, and that argument was used to distinguish hand composition, which they had formerly acknowledged women could do, from machine composition, which they claimed women were not capable of doing. They argued that the higher speed attained

[24] New York State Bureau of Labor Statistics, *Twenty-fourth Annual Report* (Albany, 1906), p. xciii.
[25] *Newspaperdom* 2 (March 1894): 425.
[26] *Unionist* 24 (February 14, 1901): 26.

on machines made the work more exhausting than hand composition, and therefore both mental retention and physical endurance were required.[27]

Men printers were forced to emphasize the physical attributes necessary for the job because keyboard work, which was defined as intellectual, was increasingly associated with natural female attributes. As a New York City printer described the work in composing rooms in 1903: "Typesetting is exhaustive work. Standing hour by hour brings on backache and in some men varicose veins and swollen feet. Sitting on the high printing office stool doubles the typesetter up, constraining his arm motions and interfering with his digestion."[28]

In the conflicts over the gender and skill definitions of the new job created by the introduction of the Linotype, a new standard of competence and measurement of performance developed. Previously, a completed apprenticeship certified competence and was a prerequisite for union membership. Following the introduction of the Linotype, publishers required workers to prove their competence on a daily basis—to work up to the production standard—in order to obtain and maintain their jobs. The replacement of piece rates with time wages, initially supported by the union, ironically further exacerbated conflicts over the pace of work and the production norm.[29] Employers increasingly sought to control and measure the output of each individual employee. In the early days of the machine, employers encouraged speed contests, adopted bonus systems, and some even measured each employee's output and speed with a linometer attached to the machine.[30]

Men's efforts to resolve the crisis of masculinity led them to redefine competence in terms that heightened the demands on them both as men and as workers. In earlier decades they stressed the difference between men and women printers in terms of morality and training. By contrast, in the 1890s men viewed competence as derived from their particular biological traits as men, which women lacked, enabling men to work faster and for longer periods.

Men's desire to prevent their work from being defined as analogous to that of typists enmeshed them in speed contests for greater productivity. As a U.S. government report explained:

[27] U.S. Bureau of Labor Statistics, *Bulletin 13*, p. 742.

[28] New York State Bureau of Labor Statistics, *Twenty-fourth Annual Report*, p. xciii.

[29] Loft, *The Printing Trades*, p. 45; Barnett, *Chapters on Machinery and Labor*, p. 10.

[30] *Editor and Publisher* 1 (November 2, 1901): 8; *Fourth Estate* 4 (March 22, 1894): 9; U.S. Congress, *House Regulation and Restriction of Output*, Eleventh Special Report of the Commissioner of Labor, 58th cong., 2d sess., House doc. 734 (Washington, D.C., 1904), pp. 38, 43; *Report of the 25th Annual Meeting of the American Newspapers Publishers' Association* (New York, 1911): 25–26.

> The high average speed maintained by linotype operators is the foremost factor in preventing the displacement of men by women in this line of work. When the machines first came into use there was a great fear among the printers that female stenographers would work the machines, a fear arising from the close resemblance of the keyboard of the Linotype to that of the typewriter. While it is true that women learn to operate the machine readily they have not the endurance to maintain continually the speed which men maintain.[31]

Defining masculinity in terms of speed and endurance, however, meant that men workers continually had to prove themselves as men. By cooperating in publishers' view that the new technology required endurance and speed, men printers locked themselves into the new standards of masculinity that allowed for work speedup.

While men printers articulated the requirements of the machine based on endurance, publishers sought to establish other criteria for defining the "ideal" worker. For publishers, traditional notions of craft manliness interfered with production and with management's control. The work process and work culture of the pre-Linotype years had enhanced printers' control over their work.

In the 1850s and 1860s, men's work culture had been consistent with the characteristics of hand composition. There was little presssure to be a steady worker and to work consistently because extra workers were taken on during the busy periods. This work schedule was compatible not only with drinking and gambling but also with tramping from city to city in search of work and with relatively undisciplined attitude toward work time and dependability. Newspaper publishers complained of problems disciplining printers who were "incompetent, insubordinate, and intoxicated." Employers found men printers to be "supremely offensive in their manners; uncleanly in their personal habits; filthy in their language."[32]

Publishers sought to enhance their managerial authority by seeking out and rewarding workers with the "proper" behavior traits and personality characteristics along with technical skills needed to operate the machines. By redesigning work, publishers hoped to redefine the equation of masculinity with printing work and thereby to transform authority relations. Publishers used the Linotype as leverage to make this transformation. They emphasized that the machine required work styles and worker characteristics that were distinctly different from those needed for hand composition. Because the Linotype lessened the rush before press time, employers argued that work required more consistent rates of speed over longer periods of time. The Linotype reduced

[31] U.S. Bureau of Labor Statistics, *Bulletin 13*, p. 721.

[32] *ANPA Labor Bulletin*, no. 358 (July 1, 1911); *Inland Printer* 2 (September 1885): 439.

the need for temporary substitutes, and the "tramping system" in which workers traveled from town to town searching for short-term work ceased to exist. Optimal production on the machines, publishers claimed, required sobriety, which they made a condition of employment. Typesetting with the machine, according to management at the *New York Herald,* changed the nature and pace of work, and as a result, "the great magician Progress has summoned the printer to the helm, and the old printer in consequence passes from the scene of his former usefulness, perhaps to death, surely to oblivion."[33]

Publishers increasingly sought workers "of steady, moderate speed," who could be relied on rather than "record breakers," who were "too nervous, irriatable, and prone to 'lay off.' " A "good operator" was not one who could "set a word, or two or three words, very rapidly," but one who could "maintain an evenness of speed."[34]

Women, publishers claimed, had the right work habits and proper characteristics for work on the Linotype: women were dexterous, sober, and dependable. Employers preferred women clerical workers as Linotypists because they considered them neater, quicker, more industrious, more loyal, and more trustworthy than men printers.[35] Women received lower wages than men because publishers claimed that the characteristics that made them ideal workers were part of women's natural temperment and aptitudes rather than acquired skills.

Publishers' efforts to transform printing into women's work following introduction of the Linotype ultimately failed. According to a New York State Department of Labor survey in 1926, only fifty-three out of seventy-seven newspapers in the state replying to the survey employed women workers. Of the total of 150 women employed, only 69 were Linotype operators, a few worked on other typesetting machines, and the bulk worked as proofreaders.[36] By the early twentieth century publishers publicly accepted the union's claims that women were too delicate for the physically and mentally demanding work on the Linotype.[37]

There were many reasons for publishers' failure and particularly for their inability successfully to recruit female typesetters. The demand for clerical workers, in particular typists, expanded rapidly in this

[33] Joseph W. McCann, "Linotypes of Newspaper Offices: Comment on Changed Conditions," in Columbia Typographical Union, *Yearbook* (1901), p. 81; *Fourth Estate* 3 (May 16, 1895): 9.

[34] U.S. Congress, *Eleventh Special Report,* p. 76; *Linotype Bulletin* (June-July 1905): 123.

[35] Massachusetts Bureau of Statistics of Labor, *Twenty-fourth Annual Report,* "Compensation in Certain Occupations of Graduates of Colleges for Women," Part I (1895), pp. 29, 41–45; *Inland Printer* 2 (October 1884): 33; U.S. Department of Labor, *Bulletin* 2 (1897): 255.

[36] New York Department of Labor, *Industrial Bulletin* (November 1926), p. 37.

[37] *Editor and Publisher* 13 (July 19, 1913): 97.

period.[38] The relatively higher wages women received in clerical work combined with perceptions of office work as more respectable for women made typesetting less attractive to educated women.[39]

Nevertheless, publishers were successful in transforming the social relations of printing into forms they found more acceptable through a complex process that included redefinitions of masculinity and shifts in the relationship between gender and work. Men printers, for their part, could successfully maintain their craft and manly respectability only by redefining the meaning of masculinity and its relationship to work.

In sum, the new technology set into motion a struggle over the gender and skill definitions of the occupation of Linotypist. Changes in the work process and the strategies used by employers made the existing foundations for men printers' class and gender identities increasingly precarious. Men printers began to legitimate their control by making explicit claims to the innate superiority of men over women, premising workers' control and male privilege on their status as men rather than their ability as workers. Union men and publishers reached a "negotiated settlement," wherein publishers accepted definitions of the new work as masculine and the meaning of masculinity and its relation to work were significantly revised in ways that established new terms of authority between publishers and union men. Workingmen maintained their positions as privileged craft workers, but the new definitions of masculinity required them continually to prove themselves at work. In class terms this meant their acceptance of work speedup; in gender terms it meant the formulation of their gender identities in ways that left them insecure.

[38] The clerical workforce increased 38-fold between 1870 and 1920. In the job category of steno/typist, for example, the number of workers increased from 154 in 1870 to over 600,000 in 1920 (Ileen A. DeVault, *Sons and Daughters of Labor: Class and Clerical Work in Turn-of-the Century Pittsburgh* [Ithaca, 1990], pp. 12, 16; Margery Davies, *Woman's Place Is at the Typewriter: Office Work and Office Workers, 1870–1930* [Philadelphia, 1982], pp. 178–79).

[39] Before the introduction of the Linotype, women hand compositors earned less than copyists; in 1884 women copyists in Boston earned an average weekly wage of $7.00, while women in printing and publishing earned an average of $6.61 (Carroll D. Wright, *The Working Girls of Boston* [Boston, 1889], p. 83). If a woman printer worked fifty weeks in 1884, she would earn $330 per year. The average wage of women printers in 1900 was $310 per year. Men printers in 1900, however, earned $610.97, considerably more than women. DeVault found that at the turn of the century clerical workers in Pittsburgh were frequently the children of skilled workers (*Sons and Daughters of Labor,* pp. 90, 94–95). On working-class women's views of respectability, see Eisenstein, *Give Us Bread, but Give Us Roses.*

CHAPTER EIGHTEEN

Between Taylorism and *Dénatalité*: Women Welfare Supervisors and the Boundaries of Difference in French Metalworking Factories, 1917–1930

Laura Lee Downs

Studying women's labor history often means looking for women in places they are not meant to be, for instance, on the metalworking shop floor. The middle-class "lady welfare superintendent" (*surintendante d'usine*) was an especially unlikely traveler in the notionally all-male and distinctly proletarian world of the metals factory. Yet her presence in this world was no accident. Employers brought the *surintendante* into their factories during World War I for the sole purpose of attending to the health and welfare of the new female work force. Ultimately, however, the *surintendante*'s work went far beyond assuring the physical and moral well-being of France's working mothers. Ever mindful of the connection between the individual worker's health and her productivity on the shop floor, metals employers were quick to call their welfare supervisors into more directly productive service. The "welfare lady's" expert and intimate knowledge of the woman worker's capacities and character made her a valuable ally in management's wartime and postwar struggle to raise productivity in French industry.

World War I simultaneously disrupted the two systems on which the prewar metalworking industry had rested, namely, a sexually segregated labor market from which employers recruited their overwhelmingly (94.5 percent) male work forces, and a labor process organized

I thank Kathleen Canning, Young Sun Hong, Pieter Judson, Sue Juster, and Susan Thorne for their helpful comments on earlier drafts of this essay. I owe a special debt of gratitude to Robert Paxton, who has met the *surintendante d'usine* on more than one occasion—in this essay and in the dissertation from which it is drawn. Each time, his careful reading and close criticism have helped me strengthen the argument without losing the sense of novelty which surrounds this peculiarly French institution.

around the skilled male production worker.[1] The shifting boundaries in gender segregation and the division of labor converged in the work of the *surintendantes d'usine.* Employers first introduced these women to oversee the welfare and "moral discipline" of women metalworkers. Their arrival thus signaled a new managerial concern with the health of workers, male and female, and its impact on productivity. Ultimately, the *surintendantes* came to embody management's renewed effort to tighten control over the redivided labor process and over the new, largely female work force employed within that process.

These managerial ambitions were not incompatible with a broader public concern over the health of working mothers, a concern shared by employers, state officials, and middle-class feminists, who collaborated in instituting welfare supervision in the metals factories. In the eyes of the wartime state and an anxiously pronatalist public, welfare management promised to reverse France's perilously low birth rate[2] through careful attention to the health and maternal condition of France's working women. From the employers' perspective, welfare supervision could also assist in the struggle to raise productivity by maintaining the workers in good fighting trim: "The workers give a higher output than before; production rises in proportion to their well being."[3]

[1] In the Belle Epoque, French metalworking stood poised between a craft-based labor process and a subdivided, mass-production organization of work. Under the former system, skilled men organized the labor process and performed most production work, with the assistance of unskilled laborers and boy apprentices. Under the latter regime, skilled processes were broken down into their component elements, and each fragmented task became the particular province of a single semi- or unskilled worker. Skilled men were withdrawn from production work and concentrated on the supervision of production workers, or the repair and regulation of machine tools. In 1914, the French metalworking industry formed a patchwork of small shops, organized more or less along craft lines, and enormous factories, such as Renault and Citroen, in which employers were experimenting with several production techniques. Accordingly, the labor force was segregated primarily along lines of skill, with a new semiskilled class of men (and some women) forming around the new, deskilled forms of work spawned by experiments in mass production.

[2] Pronatalist sentiment won a permanent place in public discourse with the formation of the national "alliance for the increase of the French population" (1896), under the guiding influence of natalist advocate Jacques Bertillon. Natalist influence waxed and waned from that date until the outbreak of war at which point unfavorable comparisons between the stable French birth rate and an ever-increasing German natality made the issue a matter of broad patriotic concern. See Laura Lee Downs, "Women in Industry, 1914–1939: The Employers' Perspective" (Ph.D. diss., Columbia University, 1987), pp. 195–201; Monique-Marie Huss and Philip Ogden, "Demography and Pro-Natalism in France in the 19th and 20th Centuries," *Journal of Historical Geography* 8 (1982): 283–98; and Angus MacLaren, *Sexuality and Social Order* (New York, 1983).

[3] All translations are my own. Pierre Magnier de Maisonneuve, *Les institutions socialies en faveur des ouvrières d'usine* (Paris, 1923), pp. 57–58. Of course, employers generally evaluated the worker's health in terms of her productivity, neatly evading the individual's own assessment of her needs.

By linking maternal health to productivity, welfare management effectively erased the line between public and private, as far as the woman metalworker was concerned, opening her sexuality, personal health, and domestic arrangements to the sharp scrutiny of the employer's newest intermediary. Thus *surintendantes* were hired to monitor workers' health, maintain shop-floor discipline, and raise output, three distinct functions which the *surintendante* wove into a single, comprehensive managerial practice in the course of her daily activity on the shop floor. In part, these women were elements in a new style of management that was being developed to organize and control a redivided labor process. But they were also special managerial personnel brought in to address what employers understood as the "distinctive needs" of women workers for moral control and for particular attention to their health, especially their maternal well-being. Welfare supervision thus stands as an innovative and gender-specific managerial strategy, intended to reach a new and undisciplined labor force which employers perceived as qualitatively different from the traditional, male work force.

The *surintendante* had breached a notionally impermeable class divide, crossing from a world of bourgeois ease and privilege into the harshly proletarian realm of the factory. Yet her function in the factory demanded that she reconstitute the class boundary within the factory walls as the basis for her authority over her female charges. But the metals factory was not only divided by distinction of class. In the war and interwar periods, metalworking formed a locus of gender division as well, with women workers defined as the intruding "other." Gender identity thus formed a potential ground of solidarity between the woman welfare supervisor and her proletarian sisters, if only she could reach across the same class divide on which her authority rested and establish the intimate bonds of sisterly contact. For the *surintendante d'usine*, then, daily life on the shop floor involved a delicate balancing act, simultaneously negotiating boundaries of difference and those of a notional identity to manage her workers more effectively.

The war, which juxtaposed an abrupt shift in labor supply with dramatic changes in the organization of production, created a conjuncture of circumstance without which the *surintendante* might never have been called into existence. The sudden mobilization disrupted sexually stratified labor markets, draining men from the traditionally male metalworking factories. Munitions employers were left with the option of shutting down altogether (which many of them did during the first six weeks of the war) or seeking to supplement their depleted work forces with women drawn from other industries and trades. By the second year of the war, nearly a quarter of all metalworkers were women, and the work forces in many factories were 30 to 50 percent women.[4]

This abrupt shift in the sexual composition of the work force coincided with General Joseph Joffre's urgent plea for more weapons. The order to raise production pushed industrialists to experiment with mass-production methods, redividing labor by fragmenting and simplifying individual tasks within the work process. In redrawing the horizontal boundaries that divided the labor process, employers defined new, deskilled forms of work constituted by a series of rapid, repetitive gestures. Initially compelled by the shortage of skilled men to place women on many of these new jobs, employers quickly forged a positive connection between women and fragmented task work, grounding this connection in the notional identity between women's distinctive work attributes (swift, dexterous, and patient) and the character of subdivided labor.

In the effort to classify women as a source of labor power, employers consulted the sociobiological "facts" of women's essential nature, which formed a lens of belief through which they observed and specified women's particular qualities as workers. Thus employers observed that women "work more carefully and more regularly [than men] . . . for women's precision of movement and visual acuity are superior."[5] Moreover, they were ideally suited to repetitive labor, for "a woman, no matter how skilled, brings a constant level of attention to her work."[6] Their wartime observations are peppered with domestic analogies that purport to capture women's difference from men on the factory floor: "The machines which the women operate function similarly to the men's but seem to run more continuously, at a more reg-

[4] Metals employers were munitions employers, supplying artillery, shells, planes, bombs, and, later, tanks to the army. Although some women munitions workers had been in the metals industries before the war (the Ministry of Labor found that in twenty-two metals and electronics factories surveyed, anywhere from 13 to 29 percent of the women had worked in the industry before the war), women war workers came overwhelmingly from "women's occupations"—textiles, garment making, and the small luxury trades of Paris such as flower making. These trades contracted sharply after August 4, 1914, and had expelled most of their work forces in the first weeks of war. Unemployed women thus formed an abundant and ready source of labor for the munitions industries. See Downs, "Women in Industry," pp. 195–201. The Ministry of Labor survey, which dates from 1918, can be found in the Archives Nationales (hereafter cited as AN), F 22 534.

[5] Commandant E. Hourst, *Le problème de la main-d'oeuvre: La taylorisation et son application aux conditions industrielles de l'après-guerre* (Paris, 1917), p. 55.

[6] AN 94 AP 348 (Fonds Thomas), M. Pavin, director of the Loire Works, cited in "Note on the Recruitment of Female Labor" (undated), pp. 2–3. The employer goes on to explain women's greater regularity at work: "Undoubtedly, this is due to her education, which teaches her to perform monotonous work and, perhaps, to let her mind travel while her fingers fly. . . . I would gladly replace all the men with women. [They are] more conscientious, more assiduous at their work and more eager to earn."

ular rhythm, because of the gentleness of women's movements and because of their vigilance. There remains a housewife in every woman turning shells at the lathe, and women produce metal parts as they do sweaters."[7]

Yet even as they drew on cultural presumptions about male-female differences to establish appropriate gender divisions on the shop floor, employers altered those same notions by importing them into a previously male realm of production. The domestic analogies were, after all, merely analogies, and women metalworkers were producing shells and metal parts, not sweaters. Nonetheless, the recurrent language of domesticity in employers' assessments of women's work attributes suggests that these ideas played a crucial role in redrawing the boundaries that defined the shop floor. This idea emerged even more strikingly when employers turned to the question of initiative and authority on the factory floor.

Job fragmentation entailed the extension of work processes across the factory floor; the production process that had been spatially contained under a craft-based organization now extended outward in long chains of repetitive task work as skilled jobs were broken down into their component elements. Skilled craftsmen no longer coordinated these individual elements. Under a mass-production organization of work, management had to intervene directly to reintegrate an increasingly far-flung production process. In this context, women's distinctiveness as a source of labor power lay not only in their "inherent" capacity for rapid, repetitive task work but also in their "natural" lack of initiative: "Women are able to examine pieces as long as they're always the same, where all that's called for is a repetitive action, and not some initiative or understanding. It's like the stitches in their crocheting and lace-making. But one must never demand an impromptu or unexpected vigilance from them; women draw parallels, they compare, but they are incapable of inventive thought."[8] For employers, the prominence of women in the ranks of unskilled process workers reinforced the demand for a more intensive managerial surveillance independent of the technical need to intervene and reintegrate a fragmented labor process.

Finally, beyond their technical dependence on male expertise and initiative lay women's peculiar moral condition: outside their "natural" setting of home and family, women demanded special tutelage that would recreate and reinforce that domestic setting, providing a context within which they could be managed and their unique

[7] Gaston Ragéot, *La française dans la guerre* (Paris, 1918), p. 4.

[8] Pierre Hamp, factory inspector, reporting on employers' opinions of women metalworkers, in *L'Information Ouvrière et Sociale*, April 1918.

productive potential tapped. The boundaries of female difference as defined by metals employers thus dovetailed neatly with the requirements of a redivided labor process. Employers, however, could not fully exploit the productive potential of newly deskilled labor processes, and of the women employed within those processes, until they found some means of disciplining and directing workers whom they believed to be technically and morally dependent by nature. The answer to this problem slowly materialized over the course of 1917, though not in a form most employers would have expected.

The institution of welfare supervision gradually took shape at the confluence of private and public, springing from the state's concern with the health of women munitions workers and from the broader moral anxieties of private philanthropists. Outside the factory gates, the French public was acutely aware that women workers were abandoning their traditionally feminine pursuits (textiles, garment making, and domestic service) and entering the harsh male world of metalworking. Wartime conditions and the horrific slaughter in the trenches heightened long-standing fears about the health of French women, especially their reproductive health and moral capacity for motherhood. The discourse on women's work thus entangled pronatalist anxieties with an uncomfortable awareness of the rapidly shifting sexual division of labor. Women doing "men's" work threatened an already faltering birth rate: "the child, that annoying impediment, remains for some less scrupulous women an obstacle to their freedom, a barrier between them and the maximum profit to be drawn from exceptionally well-paid work."[9]

This constellation of concerns had already impelled several employers' wives and daughters to organize canteens and infirmaries in the war factories.[10] By May 1917, republican feminist Cécile Brunschvicg had decided it was time to move beyond this sporadic voluntarism and professionalize what had begun as informal charity work. Inspired by the development of welfare supervision in British munitions factories, Brunschvicg and four other like-minded women founded the Association des Surintendantes d'Usines, an organization whose avowed purpose was to train women to "create, oversee or direct the social organization of working women in factories, from the point of view of material well-being and of moral preservation."[11]

[9] Académie de Médécine, Debate on the protection of women and infants in factories, 1917, in AN F22 444.

[10] Françoise Thébaud, Catherine Vincent, and M. Dubesset, *When Women Enter the Factories . . . (Master's thesis, University of Paris VII, 1974), p. 223.*

[11] de Maisonneuve, *Institutions sociales,* p. 268. Although the institution of welfare supervision first arose in Great Britain in 1915, it never took permanent hold among British employers, perhaps because paternalistic labor management strategies had never been popular in Britain. The last welfare supervisors disappeared from British factories within months of the Armistice. See Downs, "Women in Industry," chap. 5.

Brunschvicg and her associates were deeply concerned with the fate of working women, their material condition and their exhausting double burden of work in the factory and the home. But they were equally animated by the prospect of carving out a new and distinctly feminine profession, one that demanded the uniquely feminine (and bourgeois) qualities of "empathy, tact and discretion."[12] The association promptly opened the Ecole des Surintendantes d'Usines to train the daughters of the bourgeoisie in factory-based social work. By August, the school had placed twelve *surintendantes* in the state artilleries alone. By the end of the war, about fifty women had been placed, largely in the metalworking trades, and the school was poised for expansion.[13]

Minister of Munitions Albert Thomas had strongly endorsed Brunschvicg's initiative and consistently supported the notion of welfare for women, especially for mothers and mothers-to-be, who had been "torn from their homes" to labor on behalf of the national defense.[14] Yet beyond such hortatory statements the state played no direct role in underwriting the school, structuring its curriculum,[15] or placing graduate *surintendantes* in the factories. The enterprise remained a private one from the outset, and *surintendantes* were directly responsible to the industrialists who hired and paid them.

Initially, the *surintendante*'s work was shaped by national concern over the flagging birth rate. The wartime state had passed several

[12] Twenty years later, Brunschvicg outlined her feminist philosophy before a meeting of the Association des Surintendantes d'Usines, stressing the uniquely "feminine" mission of welfare work among factory women: "True feminism does not consist of doing exactly the same things men do, but in complementing their work. One can affirm that, if they do certain jobs better than we do, on our side, we can fulfill better than they certain natural jobs which are essentially feminine or familial." (Allocution de Cécile Brunschvicg," *Bulletin de l'Association des Surintendantes* [1937]: 30). Brunschvicg was married to the radical solidarist politician Léon Brunschvicg and was a political figure in her own right. She later went on to become the first woman member of a French cabinet, serving as minister of education under Léon Blum. For a detailed analysis of the shape and structure of France's tiny but vigorous bourgeois feminist movement, see Anne Kenney and Steven Hause, *Women's Suffrage and Social Politics in the French Third Republic* (Princeton, 1984).

[13] The number of *surintendantes* employed in French industry rose rapidly after the war, doubling in the first postwar decade (from about 50 in 1919 to 101 in 1928), then doubling again in the 1930s (191 in 1935 and 218 in 1937) (Annie Fourcaut, *Femmes à l'usine en France dans l'entre-deux-guerres* [Paris, 1982], p. 20).

[14] Thomas's many circulars reminded munitions employers that welfare supervision was no "mere luxury"; on the contrary, *surintendantes* could "relieve upper management of many difficulties of detail; they raise the factory's productivity even as they guard over the health, capacities and happiness of the women workers" (AN, Fonds Albert Thomas, 94 AP 348, "Devoirs de l'Inspectrice de Bien-Etre," p. 4). The welfare policies of this right-wing socialist thus dovetailed neatly with those of the bourgeois feminists who made up Brunschvicg's association.

[15] The curriculum stressed health and matters of "industrial organization" such as Taylorist schemes for raising output. See Downs, "Women in Industry," pp. 218–19.

measures intended to preserve the health of worker-mothers and their children in the war factories, and the *surintendante*'s first task centered on administering those services—creches, infirmaries, nursing rooms, and the like.[16] The connection between workers' health and their efficiency on the job, however, first made by a state concerned to raise the output of both bombs and babies, established the basis for *surintendantes* gradually to assume the role of welfarist labor managers vis-à-vis their women workers. Thus *surintendantes* hired women whom they considered physically and morally suited to the work, participated in organizing the labor process by assigning jobs according to individual women's capacities, and kept output high by monitoring individual performance and disciplining idle or slow workers.

These clearly managerial functions were embedded in a broader framework of personal, "woman-to-woman" interventions in the everyday lives of the *surintendante*'s proletarian charges, both on the shop floor and in their homes: "Who better than the *surintendante* to intervene and alert management to the abilities of a woman worker? Who better than she to look into their little weaknesses, their problems? [Who better than she] knows how to give them joy in their work, which is necessary for a good output."[17]

In the *surintendante,* employers believed they had found an answer to the problem of reconciling women's work in metals factories with their maternal function. Equally important, the *surintendante* could create an appropriately "domestic" context for labor discipline because she stood in a motherly relationship to her women workers: "This intermediary between the women workers, the employers and the foremen [has] a considerable moral influence over the worker-mother: a kind of familiarity springs up between them, a familiarity engendered only by [one of] the same sex."[18] The language of motherly concern and face-to-face intimacy pervaded employers' characterizations of the *surintendate*'s work, in part because such images construct a model of factory relations which denies the inevitability of class conflict without abandoning the central fact of hierarchically structured authority relationships: "We expect a great deal of the *surintendente*—neither nun nor worker nor woman of the world, or perhaps all three things together, she stands as the strongest link between the working class and our class: the godmother-elect of social peace."[19] As far as the Al-

[16] Ibid, chaps. 2 and 4, pp. 201–14.

[17] Général Appert, Director at Alsthom Electrical Factory, Paris, quoted in "Allocution de Général Appert," *Bulletin de l'Association des Surintendantes* (1929): 24.

[18] G.-A. Doléris and J. Bouscatel, *Hygiène et morales sociales: Néomalthusianisme, maternité et féminisme; education sexuelle* (Paris, 1918), p. 255.

[19] Réné Doumic, speaking at the Académie Française when it awarded its Prix de Vertu to the Association des Surintendantes, 1921, quoted in de Maisonneuve, *Institutions sociales,* p. 291. Welfare management theorists sought to replace an unnecessarily

sthom Electrical Works was concerned, this harmonious matriarchal order had stifled any mutinous murmuring among the women during the massive (and largely female) strike wave of May-June 1917. By monitoring workers' discontent and "gently rebuking" the more rebellious souls, Alsthom's *surintendante* ensured that "order and calm reigned . . . despite the excitement and the threats [from women already out on strike]."[20]

The *surintendantes,* too, saw themselves in a familial and essentially maternal relation to women workers and to the "male" (technical) side of management. Thus they spoke of themselves as "mistress of the house, nurse, and teacher" and "agent of liaison between employers and workers,"[21] blending the technical with the social in a single web of welfare relations.

Productivist intentions, pronatalist anxieties, and a general concern with the structure of working-class family life all shaped the *surintendante*'s work, proclaiming employers' hope that output and work discipline could be enhanced by adding this new figure to the managerial hierarchy, one who could give industrial capitalism a human and female face.

In stressing the link between women's physical condition and their efficiency within a deskilled work process, state and employers alike conflated women's health with their reproductive capacity. As one metals employer declared: "it is clearly in the employer's interest to provide maternity leave, infant and child care, and to encourage mixed nursing, all issues which are closely linked to the question of Taylorized work."[22] This conflation profoundly influenced the way metals employers approached the problem of managing women workers and hence defined the work of *surintendantes* throughout the war and interwar periods. Nascent strategies for a "scientific management" of the redivided labor process focused on measuring the pace and content

---

polarized labor-capital relation with the "natural" harmony of familial structures writ large across the factory floor: "Where men and women are employed at the same operation foremen and forewomen are essential. This is no more dual control than that of father and mother. It is a combined, more intimate and broader control. . . . The foreman's chief responsibility is production and the quality and quantity of the work. The forewoman's just care is for the producers. She must keep her squad up to the requisite strength and each individual of it happy and fit. This is a natural division of responsibility and makes for sweeter working and greater efficiency" (Cecil Walton [manager of the Cardonald National Projectile Factory], *Welfare Study—What It Is* [Glasgow, 1918], p. 10).

[20] Général Appert, Director at Alsthom, "Allocution," *Bulletin de l'Assocation des Surintendantes* (1925).

[21] Report by Mlle Geoffroy, *Bulletin de l'Association des Surintendantes* (1928): 29–34.

[22] Hourst, *Problème de la main-d'ouevre,* p. 57.

of workers' gestures within that fragmented process. In postwar years, employers were to place the connection between health and efficiency at the heart of schemes intended to raise individual output by intensifying the pace of work. Because women's health invariably translated as their maternal condition, the scientific management of women's labor was intimately connected to the welfarist management of their maternity, actual or potential, and the regulation of their domestic lives. Both spheres of management fell within the expert domain of the *surintendante d'usine.*

Despite the rapid spread of welfarist managerial strategies in the war industries, many employers remained cautious about the *surintendante.* Uncertain as to where her loyalties truly lay and concerned therefore that she might undermine their authority, several industrialists expressed considerable ambivalence about the idea of welfare supervision and, perhaps more important, the presence of educated, middle-class women on the shop floor: "in daily contact with the woman worker, they might worry too frequently about the exhaustion women workers feel; ultimately, they would implant notions of fatigue in the worker's spirit by autosuggestion."[23]

This initial circumspection comes across especially clearly in the rules industrialist Louis Loucheur (Thomas's successor at the Ministry of Munitions) recommended to his fellow employers, defining the role and working conditions of *surintendantes.* On one hand, he secured her position in the shop floor hierarchy by specifying that she be placed "under the employer's direction, or that of his designated officer," and that she wear a special khaki uniform with the initials "S.U." embroidered on the shoulder. On the other hand, her salary (300 to 400 francs per month) barely exceeded the average earnings of a semiskilled woman metalworker, and Loucheur's careful specification of her rank (reporting directly to her employer) was probably designed to guard against that which he feared most: that the *surintendante,* roaming freely across the factory floor, speaking with individual women at will, might become "a danger to his [the employer's] authority and that of the foreman."[24]

When they began hiring *surintendantes,* most industrialists adopted Loucheur's method and contained the potentially subversive effect of a roving workers' advocate by having her report directly to her employer. The *surintendante* thus formed a nascent new line of command, directly linking top management to the shop floor. The old chain of com-

[23] Interview with André Citroën, June 1, 1918, *La Vie Féminine.* He must have changed his mind rather quickly, for twelve months later, the Ecole des Surintendantes had sent at least one trainee to the Citroën works.

[24] Louis Loucheur, "Dispositions générales régissant les surintendantes," *Bulletin des Usines de Guerre,* November 25, 1918, pp. 245–46.

mand, running through foremen, charge hands, and other technical staff, continued to function alongside this new line, though not without some friction between skilled male supervisors and the middle-class "welfare ladies." And because welfare management connects health and productivity, the sexual division of authority over women production workers remained a murky and contested terrain; there was no single point at which the foreman's technical authority left off and the *surintendante*'s welfare authority began. Thus the *surintendante* had power to shift workers around on the line or even remove them altogether.

Although she was generally expected to consult with the foreman before taking such steps, her right to intervene in the deployment of labor represented a real encroachment on the foreman's territory. Indeed, the *surintendante* sometimes pitted her authority against the foreman's and on behalf of the women, transferring them from impossible jobs or helping them bypass a difficult foreman and carry grievances directly to the boss. In these instances she was impelled to act by her sense of the workers' vulnerability, as women, to male authority in its proletarian incarnation—a brutal form of authority to the bourgeois eye of the lady welfare supervisor. Her power to intervene in the organization of labor, though consonant with the employer's wish to exert a more "scientific" control of labor, radically disrupted traditional authority structures.

In postwar years, employers gradually discarded several of their more narrowly natalist wartime installations such as factory nursing rooms. Costly to maintain and under used by women workers, the nursing rooms were a form of welfare that did little to advance productivity on the shop floor. But the disappearance of these rooms did not signal the abandonment of welfare management as a labor strategy in France. On the contrary, in these years of demographic crisis and rapid industrial growth, metals employers took up a more direct regulation of proletarian family life through an intensified supervision of the female work force. Through new initiatives on the shop floor—offering home economics classes for the women and sending the *surintendante* directly into workers' homes to help order proletarian domesticity—employers sought to extend their influence beyond the factory walls and into the notionally private realm of the working-class household. Antonio Gramsci characterized this shift in managerial strategy as nothing less than a campaign to redefine the worker: "It is worth drawing attention to the way in which industrialists (Ford in particular) have been concerned with the sexual affairs of their employees and with the family arrangements in general. One should not be misled by this concern. The truth is that the new type of man demanded by the rationalisation of production and work cannot be developed until the sexual instinct has been suitably regulated and until it too has been rationalised."[25]

Welfare management thus continued to blur distinctions between the worker's private, domestic existence and her public function in the world of work, although the emphasis had shifted away from pure natalism and toward controlling the structure of family life. Practitioners of this "modern paternalism" saw the relationship between home and work as clearly reciprocal, especially in the case of women workers. Their strategies for control thus centered on the regulation of women's values and behavior not only on the shop floor but in the private domestic sphere as well. By linking an increasingly intrusive paternalism with the techniques of scientific management, French metals employers hoped to gain access to workers' motivational core. The invasion of workers' privacy sprang logically from the fundamental principle of welfare management that productivity and labor discipline are grounded in supervising the worker's mental, moral, and bodily condition. Similarly, welfarist ideology deemed women especially appropriate targets of control, not merely because of their reproductive capacity and domestic function but also because they were presumed to require a more comprehensive tutelage and to be more receptive to such overtures than their husbands or brothers.

At the heart of this new strategy stood management's emissary to the proletarian home, preaching order, cleanliness, and thrift in the household as a means of promoting those same values on the shop floor. Like their employers, *surintendantes* rarely saw any incompatibility between productivist goals and seeking to improve the workers' physical and mental state. Indeed, most believed that raising output and tending to the workers' welfare were complementary elements in modern factory management; the former could not help but flow from the latter. Nonetheless, the welfarist aspect of her role demanded that she be alive to the actual effect of intensified labor on the women and men she managed, even as she sought to reconcile their well-being with the increased pace of work. On occasion, she could not escape from the contradictions her dual function entailed:

> One is overcome when one imagines that for years, throughout their entire lives, women will perform the same gestures. . . . Nailed down to one place, with no power to move for eight hours, performing movements which are utterly devoid of all interest but on which one must nonethe-

[25] Antonio Gramsci, "Americanism and Fordism," in *The Prison Notebooks*, ed. Q. Hoare (New York, 1971), p. 297.

> less concentrate, for fear of doing it badly. . . . It seems completely unjust that women are paid less because they work quickly. . . . [26]

But she was ill-placed to draw anything but reformist conclusions; even the angry young student quoted above did not set her bleak vision above the reformist hopes instilled by her education at the Ecole des Surintendantes. For instance, it would never have occurred to her to leave her post and organize the women to agitate for shorter hours, higher wages, and better conditions. Instead, the "almost overcome" author of the report stayed on at Renault, convinced by her education—and by her position, at the foot of the employer's table—that the contradictions she had observed were mere appearance. Beyond them she could discern a deeper reality of mutual interest and eventual harmony, and she concluded her report with the notion that a profit-sharing scheme might eventually resolve "this terrible struggle between . . . capital and labor whose fates are now not so different."[27]

The *surintendante* occupied a pivotal position in the "true" factory, a community of reciprocally ordered relations which, in her own mind, underlay the false and unnecessarily polarized relations of modern industry. Because she was a human link binding workers to their employer (and vice versa), her mission had a strongly maternal overtone. By exercising her "disinterested" influence—softening the strictures and discipline of the employer's rule when warranted or explaining the "just" demands of individual workers—the *surintendante* could reunite an alienated labor force with its stern yet benevolently paternal employer.

The man who had hired her viewed the matter somewhat differently. Though he agreed that the working class, and working women in particular, had much to gain from contact with the *surintendante,* he had not hired this woman to instruct him on labor relations. Throughout the interwar period, employers happily allowed the *surintendante* to function as "an instrument of social policy," domesticating the work force and pressing "the Taylorization of factories."[28] But their autocratic rule of factory relations continued, undisturbed by any moderating influence from the women they had employed to monitor productivity and welfare.

The *surintendante*'s ability to assist her proletarian sisters was thus severely circumscribed by her employer's conception of her responsibilities and by the relentlessly reformist vision she brought to her

[26] Report from a *surintendante-in-training* at Renault, 1920, found in a bundle of old student papers kept in the library at the Ecole des Surintendantes in Paris.

[27] Ibid.

[28] Fourcaut, *Femmes à l'usine,* p. 31..

work. In the end, her viewpoint could not be meaningfully distinguished from that of her boss. Thus she believed in the importance of a hierarchical authority in the factory, agreed that working-class women were peculiarly vulnerable and in need of special care and moral tutelage, accepted the "natural" authority of middle class over working class, and embraced the notion that industry had to raise its productivity at all costs. Employers therefore had little difficulty in containing the reformist impulses of the *surintendante.* Although she saw herself as a mediator between labor and capital, she remained in reality an employee of one side, hired to manage and discipline the other.

CHAPTER NINETEEN

Family, Work, and Community: Southern and Eastern European Immigrant Women Speak from the Connecticut Federal Writers' Project

Laura Anker

In the last years of the Great Depression, before political repression and World War II put an end to their ambitious efforts, Federal Writers' Project fieldworkers walked the streets of Connecticut's immigrant neighborhoods, their own communities, knocking on doors and talking to people.[1] Most of the interviewers for what became known as the Works Progress Administration (WPA) Connecticut Ethnic Survey spoke Italian, Yiddish, Russian, Polish, or Hungarian and could question their neighbors in their native tongues. They talked to immigrants in their kitchens and on their doorsteps as well as in small shops, factories, and ethnic halls. Consequently, project workers, many of whom were women, collected close to two hundred oral histories, almost half of which were the narratives of women. "We interviewed women," recalled Pearl Russo in a recent discussion of the Bridgeport Project, "because we wanted to and because they were at home." "Most people wanted to talk," she explained. "We were part of a whole culture of storytelling. . . . When we were growing up the city was vibrant . . . it had all these nationalities . . . and we knew each other. . . . Today we could live together and be strangers."[2]

[1] In addition to more than two hundred life histories of immigrant women and men, the WPA Connecticut Ethnic Survey contains over ninety boxes of demographic, institutional, and statistical data on all aspects of immigrant life. These documents are housed in the library archives room of the University of Connecticut, Storrs, Conn. A handlist of the Storrs collection is provided in Appendix I of my Ph.D. dissertation: Laura Anker Schwartz, "Immigrant Voices from Home, Work, and Community: Women and Family in the Migration Process, 1890–1938" (State University of New York at Stony Brook, 1983), pp. 780–819.

[2] Author's Interview with Pearl K. Russo, February 16, 1983. I also interviewed

By recounting the stories of Hungarian, Slovak, Polish, southern Italian, and Jewish families in Europe and in the industrial centers of Bridgeport, New Haven, Hartford, and New Britain, the WPA oral histories provide a detailed description of the overlapping worlds of family, community, and work and of the confrontation between ethnic familial cultures and the exigencies of American urban life. They are rare first-person accounts that reflect the immediacy of experience still fresh in the subject's mind, articulated and interpreted within the cultural context in which the events took place and recollected from the special vantage of ongoing ethnic community life. They reveal women as active agents, not passive victims, of the transformation from preindustrial to industrial culture, engaged in every aspect of the migration process from decisions about whether to emigrate and where to go, to considerations of who should work and in what jobs, how to accommodate, when, where, and how to resist. In response to changing conditions in the Old World and the New, immigrant women forged strategies of adaptation and resistance which stressed the goals of family advancement and community welfare over entirely individual needs and which defined success through the prism of household responsibility rather than purely personal gain. These strategies, in turn, mediated the trans-Atlantic renegotiation of gender roles and family relationships.

The WPA narratives offer more than nuggets of new information; they create a comparative framework for analysis that raises new questions and suggests fresh interpretations from the neglected standpoint of ordinary immigrant women about what they believed mattered in their lives. Whereas studies that focus on one ethnic group in isolation from others have tended to emphasize inter-group differences and intra-group similarities, the Connecticut Ethnic Survey highlights commonalities in the experiences of immigrants from diverse cultural backgrounds as well as variations in the responses of individuals of the same ethnicity. It redirects the locus of historical investigation away from the abstract measurement of mobility, ranking of success, or preoccupation with values as the main determinants of behavior to the concrete processes by which women fabricated life strategies in response to specific conditions.[3]

Vincent Frazzetta, another prolific fieldworker on the Bridgeport staff. I am indebted to them both not only for their wonderful oral histories but for their memories and analyses of the Connecticut Ethnic Survey. For a detailed discussion of the history, politics, and methodology of the Connecticut WPA Ethnic Survey, see Schwartz, "Immigrant Voices," esp. chap. 3.

[3] Louise Lamphere makes a similar point in *From Working Daughters to Working Mothers: Immigrant Women in a New England Industrial Community* (Ithaca, 1987), pp. 15–91. See also Elizabeth Ewen, *Immigrant Women in the Land of Dollars: Life and Culture on the Lower East Side, 1890–1925* (New York, 1985), and Judith Smith, *Family*

The perspective of women reveals the collective and familial context of immigrant life, focusing attention on the ways individual experience is embedded in complex fabrics of social organization.[4] The women interviewed by the Connecticut Federal Writers' Project spoke of the people around them and of their relationships to those people, contextualizing social processes in a way that men did not. From women's narratives emerged the outlines of biographies of husbands, children, sisters, brothers, neighbors, and more distant kin and the relational networks that tied them together.

Men more frequently spoke about their actions and decisions as solely their own. For example, Morris Shapiro, a Jewish immigrant to Hartford in 1923, described his migration as a series of self-induced events. Asserting his individualistic self-reliance, he explained: "For the first time in my life, I was actually on my own. . . . No family, no relations and very few friends."[5] Yet he made the journey from Russia to the United States with money from his father and the help of his sisters, who had preceded him. Upon his arrival in New York, he was met by an aunt who directed him to Hartford, where he went to live with his sister and brother-in-law. They, in turn, settled him in a place to live and helped him find a job.

Immigration was a familial, not an individual, act, one of many steps taken by impoverished European households to make survival possible. By the late nineteenth century the spread of capitalism drew peasants and artisans in southern Italy and eastern Europe into an entangling web of market relationships. Competition from commercial agriculture and factory production, compounded by soaring population growth and escalating taxes, undermined the traditional basis for household subsistence. Access to money became imperative to meet the exigencies of daily existence.[6] Helen Doneski described the changes that led to her emigration:

Connections: A History of Italian and Jewish Immigrant Lives in Providence, Rhode Island, 1900–1940 (Albany, 1985). For a focus on one group see Virginia Yans-McLaughlin, *Family and Community: Italian Immigrants to Buffalo, 1890–1930* (Ithaca, 1978); and Sidney Weinberg, *The World of Our Mothers: The Lives of Jewish American Women* (Chapel Hill, 1988), and Susan A. Glenn, *Daughters of the Shtetl: Life and Labor in the Immigrant Generation* (Ithaca, 1990).

[4] Carol Gilligan, *In a Different Voice: Psychological Theory and Women's Development* (Cambridge, Mass., 1982), p. 28. See also Paul Thompson, *The Voice of the Past: Oral History* (New York, 1978); Daniel Bertaux, ed., *Biography and Society* (Beverly Hills, Calif., 1981).

[5] Morris Shapiro, interviewed by Morris Tonkin (box 61, 157:1e; 25 pp.). References are to names of subject, name of interviewer, box, folder number, and number of pages in the life history. Since many of the subjects are referred to by initials, I have assigned them fictional names to facilitate references to them in the text. These names are provided after their initials. See Schwartz, "Immigrant Voices," Bibliography, pp. 726–37 for the complete cross-reference of pseudonyms and full life histories in the archives.

[6] Josef Barton, *Peasants and Strangers: Italians, Rumanians, and Slovaks in an American City, 1880–1950* (Cambridge, Mass., 1975), pp. 27–47; John Bodnar, *The Trans-*

> Besides my mother and father, there were four sisters and two brothers in my family. Our home was small and so was our acreage. Once there were over sixty acres to our little estate, but . . . these areas were divided into smaller ones and given to those of the family who were married. . . . On this little farm of ours there was also little food to be had at times. . . . There was no income whatever in terms of money. We were all there, and what subsistence we received was done so through the toil of the earth. Out of this . . . we had to pay Russian taxes. . . . Nothing happened of great significance that made me desirous of leaving my little home in Poland. Nothing except the fact that we were growing up and were become poorer. Economic conditions, you might call them here. . . . No money and little land.[7]

In response to these conditions, families organized new and intensified modes of cooperation, which included sending daughters, as well as fathers and sons, out of village economies into the world of wage labor. As local sources of employment became saturated or pogroms forced permanent departure, the scope of migration increased to include the United States. Emigration thus became a rational familial response to the economic and political dilemmas of individual households.

With the exception of Jews, who fled the combined oppression of economic strangulation and religious persecution harboring no aspirations to return, male emigrants from southern and eastern Europe significantly outnumbered females.[8] Yet migration was never the exclusive preserve of men, nor was the migration of women restricted to those coming to American cities to join husbands, fiancés, or fathers. Indeed, like Helen Doneski, daughters were sometimes the first to leave, becoming emissaries of family survival in Connecticut cities.

Contradictory realities engulfed the migration process. Confronted by restricted opportunities for wage labor in peasant villages and nearby towns, many young women, often without dowries, journeyed across the Atlantic to earn the money necessary not only for their own support but also for that of their families in Europe. Paradoxically, the

---

planted: A History of Immigrants in Urban America (Bloomington, 1985), pp. 1–56; John W. Briggs, *An Italian Passage: Immigrants to Three American Cities, 1890–1930* (New Haven, 1978), pp. 1–14; Ezra Mendelsohn, *Class Struggle in the Pale: The Formative Years of the Jewish Workers' Movement in Tsarist Russia* (Cambridge, Eng., 1979), chap. 1, pp. 1–26.

[7] "Personal History of a First Generation Pole" (Mrs. Helen Gadomska Doneski, pseud.), interviewed by Stanley Dabkowski (box 87, 187:7b; 28 pp.), pp. 2–3, 12.

[8] Imre Ferenczi and Walter F. Wilcox, *International Migrations*, 2 vols. (1929–31; rpt. New York, 1969), vol. 1, *Statistics*, pp. 401–43, 476–82; Thomas Kessner, *The Golden Door: Italian and Jewish Immigrant Mobility in New York City, 1880–1915* (New York, 1977), p. 28.

very bonds that united families in a common battle for subsistence led mothers to send daughters to America, often resulting in their permanent separation. Forty years after leaving her village in Poland, Julia Karbowski still struggled to comprehend the forces that led to her departure and the conflicting familial and individual contexts of love that separated her girlhood in Europe from her adulthood in the United States: "Then one day we talked about America. My parents thought it would be a good idea if I went there to make some money and then eventually to return. You mustn't get the wrong impression about my mother wishing me to go. You mustn't think that just because your parents wanted you to do that they didn't love you. Oh no! Underneath, they were thinking of me, and of the entire family's welfare. It is something you have to contend with when you grow older."[9]

Wives who remained in Europe while their husbands traveled near and far in search of work ran their households under conditions of increasing scarcity. Often years passed before men returned or sent for their families. After her husband left for America to earn money in the mines, Frank Kovalauskas's mother bought and ran a farm . For sixteen years she headed her household in Lithuania, supporting four children.[10] Agnes Bonsza, a Hungarian woman who ultimately emigrated to Bridgeport, recalled: "My father . . . was coming back and forth, back and forth. He'd come home, leave a child, then go back to America. Every two, three years he was doing that. And my mother was taking care of the farm. My father never made money . . . he was all the time spending what he saved for the passage."[11]

Although husbands usually sent money home, many families relied on the wage labor and the artisanal, entrepreneurial, and management skills of women for survival. Mary Kycinski supported her newborn infant by opening a grocery store when her plans to join her husband in America were temporarily shattered by World War I. She remembered, "I used the money my husband sent me with some of my own to start. . . . I was interested in business."[12] While her husband worked at "pick-and-shovel" jobs in Connecticut, Antoinetta Scavono labored tirelessly on their small garden patch in Sicily, refusing to "leave even ten square meters fallow."[13]

[9] "Polish Woman #1" (Julia Karbowski, pseud.), interviewed by Stanley Dabkowski (box 87, 187:7b; 6 pp.), pp. 1–3.

[10] Frank Kovalauskas (Lithuanian), interviewed by Albert S. Kayeski (box 64, 158:1; 7 pp.), pp. 1–2.

[11] Mrs. B. (Hungarian; Agnes Bonsza, pseud.), interviewed by P. K. Russo (box 21, 109:11; 21 pp.), p. 3.

[12] Mary Kyc (Polish; Mary Kycinski, pseud.), interviewed by Bishop (box 85, 187:3; 10 pp.), p. 5.

[13] Antoinetta Scavono, quoted in Vincent Frazzetta, "Italians in Bridgeport" (box 22, 109:1e; 99 pp.), p. 62.

After her older brothers and sisters left for America, Mildred Hecht worked as a tailor in a small factory to support her aging mother, father, and younger siblings. Her work introduced her to new ideas of labor organization and socialism that undermined her father's patriarchal authority: "My father was a very Orthodox Jew. He used to get mad at me because I didn't believe in those things. He used to say when I come home, 'Nu, here's the revolutionerka.' He was the head of the house and bossed everybody . . . a regular Kahan. . . . When I was small, I used to be afraid of my father . . . but when I went to work and supported the family, I wasn't so afraid."[14]

The incorporation of wage labor and migration into preindustrial household strategies altered women's roles and began a process that would subtly transform values and relationships. The confidence and skills they acquired not only allowed women to negotiate the migration process but enabled them to muster the resources and create the ties necessary to deal with more years of hardship and struggle in a new land. At the same time, differing demographic patterns of migration interacted with the specific employment opportunities available in American cities to influence the particular work patterns and choices of immigrant women from varying ethnic groups.

Carrie Lesiaski left Poland alone but went directly to her brother in Terryville, New York. The day after her arrival, "I went to a factory with another girl and got a job. It was easy, just like that." Within a year, a visit to distant relatives in New Britain resulted in a better-paying job at the Stanley Works. Her story illustrates the process by which single women immigrants were transformed into permanent residents of Connecticut's cities. Lesiaski came to New Britain to earn wages to help her family and then return to her "little village in Russian Poland." But working at various factory jobs from the moment of her arrival, she quickly became integrated into New Britain's growing "Polonia" and, like many of her friends, found a man she wished to marry.[15]

The migration process began and ended in the family. For this reason women with children were most often permanent immigrants from the outset. The migration of women enabled the completion of family units and the creation of household economies that depended on their labor at home and in factories. The existence of extensive wage-earning opportunities for women in Connecticut's cities encouraged permanent settlement and the persistence of ethnic communities.

[14] M. H. (Jewish; Mildred Hecht, pseud.), interviewed by Rahel Mittelstein (box 61; 157:1e; 7 pp.), p. 1.

[15] "Polish Woman #3" (Mrs. Carrie Lesiaski, pseud.), interviewed by Stanley Dabrowski (box 85, 187:4 5 pp.), p. 3.

Immigrants brought with them European patterns of family and communal organization that had already been partially transformed to cope with the very forces that engendered emigration. This process of adaptation continued in Connecticut's cities as kin and ethnic ties became the basis for complex ethnic communities that developed within the interstices of city life. Between households flowed relatives, boarders, and mutual assistance, all lending substance to a dense collective life. The daily demands of existence, of finding and keeping a job and a place to live, were mediated through overlapping networks of family, kinship, and ethnicity. These ties provided the structural foundation for the preservation of European ethics of mutual support and reciprocal obligation and for their expansion into new methods of adjustment and resistance.

Tabulations from the WPA oral histories indicate that 78 percent of immigrants entered the American job market through kin and village networks: 84 percent of new arrivals lodged with relatives or friends from Europe. Whereas households in eastern Europe and southern Italy customarily had been limited to nuclear families and an occasional aging parent, Connecticut households included married siblings, cousins, nephews, nieces, aunts, uncles, and friends. The possibility of sharing wages, services, and other income sources was enhanced by this tendency of Connecticut immigrants to live in extended households or in close proximity to relatives. It also eased the problem of child care for many immigrant women who, like Barbara Orosz, left her mother behind in Hungary but could depend on her sister-in-law to watch her infant.[16]

Women did most of the small acts of mutual aid that solidified kinship and neighborhood ties and extended bonds of reciprocity outward. "Gossip" told where jobs were available, what stores to avoid, how to act, and what to learn if one was to avoid being a "greenhorn."[17] The neighborhood activities of women sometimes bridged ethnic differences or hostilities in Connecticut's medium-sized cities, where various groups lived in closer proximity to each other than they did in great metropolises like New York or Chicago.

The realities of low wages and irregular employment patterns required immigrant families to rely on the work of more than one household member in the United States, as they had in Europe.[18] The main

[16] M. G. Sayers and P. K. Russo, "Survey of Remington City with Interviews" (box 27, 109:23b; 8 pp.), p. 3.

[17] See, for example, Morris Tonken, Jewish Autobiography (box 61, 157:1e; 18 pp.), pp. 9–10; Vincent Frazzetta, "Italians in Bridgeport" (box 22, 109:13a, 99 pp.), pp. 30, 39; Jeremy Brecher, Jerry Lombardi, Jan Stackhouse, and the Brass Worker History Project, *Brass Valley: The Story of Working People's Lives and Struggles in an American Industrial Region* (Philadelphia, 1982), p. 30.

[18] See, for example, Paul H. Douglas, *Real Wages in the United States, 1890–1926*

issue confronting immigrant mothers was how to maintain an economically viable family life. The elimination of home agricultural and craft production, available at least as a limited resource in Europe, made money the key to survival. But the conditions of paid female labor in the United States made it harder for mothers to combine domestic responsibilities and work tasks. Furthermore, women found that the hand skills they had learned and applied in Europe to earn income at home had lost their value in competition with machine-made products. In America their crafts became self-consumed luxuries. Lucia Salanto explained: "In Italy . . . if the girl . . . learns to embroidery and to sew dresses . . . then she could do this work for money. That's all I was doing in Italy. I still do that, but I can't get no work like this, because in this country you could buy all these things in the store."[19]

Despite these constraints, wives in Connecticut found ways to work, as they had in southern and eastern Europe. The WPA oral histories reveal the varying strategies women organized, integrating and alternating their own labor (paid and unpaid, inside and outside the household) with their husbands' and childrens' wage contributions. Different employment patterns emerged from the complex interplay of inherited cultural traditions, new relationships of production, and changing social roles. Many historians have stressed the importance of ethnic values in determining work choices, yet for women job preferences often resulted from their stage in the life cycle at the time of migration. Polish women, who were more likely to be single and alone when they arrived in the United States, were also more likely to work as domestics than were Jewish or Italian women, who came with their families or to join husbands or fathers who had emigrated earlier.[20] Furthermore, economic necessity, combined with the opportunities for paid labor in American cities, altered southern and eastern European work preferences. Mary Huda, like many Slovak women, followed European traditions and networks into domestic service when she first came to Bridgeport, but subsequently she took factory jobs because they paid higher wages and offered predetermined hours. She explained:

> When I would get home [from her job as a cleaning woman], I used to have my lady friend in the next house come to my house and we would talk

(1930; rpt. New York, 1966), p. 584; Winifred D. Wandersee, *Womens' Work and Family Values, 1920–1940* (Cambridge, Mass., 1981), pp. 9–14.

[19] Mrs. L. Salanto (Italian, Lucia, pseud.), interviewed by Vincent Frazzetta (box 23, 109:13b; 3 pp.), p. 2.

[20] For example, see Virginia Yans-McLaughlin, *Family and Community: Italian Immigrants to Buffalo, 1890–1930* (Ithaca, 1978). Yans-McLaughlin stresses patriarchal values as the determining factors in the work choices of southern Italian women, especially their absence from domestic service.

about her work and my work. She used to tell me that she worked in the Corset Co. on bench work . . . that it would be better if I worked in the factory instead of housework. She said that the work wasn't hard and that in the night time you were like free. I told her that in Europe our people all worked on the farms and when there was a chance for a young girl to work in the house of some rich people, it was like being in the family, and that everybody used to like to do housework on the other side. I said that the Slovak people think that there is more respect to work in the house instead to work in the factory. She said that the old country was the old country, and in this country the people think it is better for the woman to work in the factory.[21]

Mothers tended to work when their income was most critical to family survival, not when they had the most time on their hands. These were usually the years when their children were young and unable to contribute to the family economy, which were also years when they had the greatest child-care responsibilities.[22] Immigrant communities provided unique opportunities for first-generation mothers to integrate domestic chores and wage-earning activities just as they had, under different circumstances in Europe. More than 40 percent of southern and eastern European wives and mothers interviewed by the Connecticut Ethnic Survey performed income-generating work at home—tending boarders and lodgers, washing clothes, doing piecework, or working alongside other household members in small artisanal and retail stores.[23] Hermina Lovasz ran a grocery business with her mother and brother. Marie Esposito's mother cooked much of the food sold in the family's small delicatessen and also assisted her husband with customers in the store. One Jewish daughter recalled that it was her mother who had the real "head" for business and was the central figure in the family butcher shop.[24] Julia Satmory found that the working day was too long in the factories, restaurants, and hospitals where she had been employed and the distance from home too great to

[21] Mrs. Mary Huda (Slovak), interviewed by Vincent Frazzetta (obtained by author from Frazzetta, 10 pp.), pp. 2–3. During World War I, Slovak women left domestic work in droves for better-paying jobs in shops like Bridgeport Brass, Acme Shear, Singer Manufacturing Company, Holmes and Edwards Silver, United Metallic Cartridge, and other factories in and around the Eastside Slovak community.

[22] Joan W. Scott and Louise Tilly, *Women, Work, and Family* (New York, 1978), make a similar point about differing conditions of women's work in Europe.

[23] The figure of 40 percent is an underestimate because women were counted as not working if no such work was mentioned.

[24] Ms. A. (Hungarian; Miss Hermina Lovasz, pseud.), interviewed by P. K. Russo (box 21, 109:11; 19 pp.); Marie Esposito (Jewish), interviewed by William A. Becker (box 22, 109:13a, 11 pp.). Author's interview with Pearl Russo, February 16, 1983. See also among others, N Family (Polish; Novakowski, pseud.), interviewed by Stanley Dabkowski (box 87, 187:7b; 28 pp.).

accommodate her domestic responsibilities. She therefore opened a small Hungarian restaurant in the West End of Bridgeport. Her family lived in two rooms behind the tiny establishment.[25]

Industrial homework also provided Connecticut immigrant women with cash-producing employment that could be integrated into their domestic routines. Michealangelo Russo recalled his whole family sitting at their kitchen table in Bridgeport helping his mother sew garters, work brought home from Warner Corset and smaller shops.[26] Other factories provided jobs for women at home finishing garments, stringing beads, linking chains, and filling cards with pins or buttons. In the brass manufacturing center of New Britain, the most common production work done in immigrant households was attaching brass snap fasteners to the cards on which they were sold. Women also took in washing, ironing, and sewing. Kalya Greenberg had learned to be a skilled dressmaker in Russia. She then "started working at home as a dressmaker when I came [to New Haven], and I am still working."[27]

More commonly, however, Connecticut immigrant mothers earned money at home by cooking and cleaning for boarders and lodgers. An Italian woman recalled: "I had to take care of the house and we had four boarders and I had to cook for them. When I first came here I didn't want to do this because everybody wants to have their own house. Well, I change my mind because everybody was doing this thing."[28]

Boarding and lodging provided a familial atmosphere in which immigrants from the same country, region, village, or family, speaking the same language and often sharing the same skills and occupations, could collectively face their first encounters with American society.[29] Joint residence served to provide mutual aid, extending the bonds of assistance to new arrivals. A Polish woman explained: "I paid my sister out of my earnings. She also had about five other boarders in her home. A lot of Polish people also had many boarders at that time. Most of them were single, without much money, and since they only paid four or five dollars a month for board, outside of food, of course, they

[25] Mrs. Julia Satmory (Hungarian), interviewed by P. K. Russo (box 21, 109:11; 10 pp.), pp. 2–3.

[26] Author's interview with Pearl Kosby and Michaelangelo Russo, February 26, 1983. See also Brecher et al., *Brass Valley*, p. 64.

[27] K. G. (Jewish; Kalya Greenberg, pseud.), interviewed by Rahel Mittelstein (box 61, 157:1e; 14 pp.), p. 13.

[28] Sixty-seven-year-old woman, quoted in Vincent Frazzetta, "Italians in Bridgeport" (box 22, 109:13a, 49 pp.), pp. 18–19.

[29] See, for example, John Modell and Tamara K. Hareven, "Urbanization and the Malleable Household: An Examination of Boarding and Lodging in American Families," in *Family and Kin in Urban Communities, 1700–1930*, ed. Tamara Hareven (New York, 1977), pp. 167–68.

could save money that way. They didn't want to go anywhere else because they could only speak in Polish and they wanted to be with their own people."[30]

Such collective living arrangements were rational economic choices for both lodgers and the women who housed them. Women who worked outside the home were seldom paid more than five or six dollars a week by Connecticut shops before 1915. If each of five boarders paid four to five dollars a month, married women could earn as much or more working at home as in factories. Women who had worked before marriage took in boarders while their children were young and then returned to factory work when their children grew older.[31] Boarding and lodging also provided needed income when older children no longer contributed their paychecks to the family economy.

Economic necessity forced many mothers to seek employment in the factories, textile mills, and machine shops that skirted Connecticut's immigrant neighborhoods. By the late 1930s the declining availability of home-based sources of income and male unemployment pushed even more women out of their homes into factories, retail stores, and personal service industries. Connecticut's diversified industrial cities provided opportunities for women to work which were unavailable in one-industry towns. Women were employed in machine and tool manufactories, brass and metal factories, electronics and munitions plants, and other "male" industries. Their employment was not limited to traditional areas such as textiles, garment manufacture, and domestic service that could be seen as an extension of their household roles or encapsulated them in a distinct "feminine" mentality.

By providing a glimpse of the entire life cycle, oral histories reveal the integration of the spheres of unpaid family labor and wage work in women's lives. Cross-sectional tabulations of the percentages of women who worked at any given time hide the importance of paid labor outside the home for immigrant women, but an analysis of the Connecticut WPA life histories demonstrates its enormous significance. Among the southern and eastern European women interviewed, 92 percent who were single when they arrived in the United States worked outside the home before they were married. A majority continued to work until the birth of their first child. Although most labored at home while their children were young (often for money at piecework or taking in boarders and lodgers), their domestic routines

[30] Mary Gadomska (Polish), interviewed by Stanley Dabkowski (box 87, 187:7b; 5 pp.), p. 4.

[31] See, for example, the N Family (Polish, Novakowski, pseud.), p. 18; Joseph Julianelle (Italian), interviewed by Frank Nolan (box 23, 109:13b; 8 pp.), p. 5.

were attuned to the rhythms and demands of wage labor. Moreover, 65 percent of the women, including those who were married in Europe, returned to jobs outside the household for substantial periods in their later lives.[32] When immigrant women left the work force they usually expected to return. They lived and perceived the trajectories of their lives as part of an immigrant working-class world in which the arenas of family, work, and community could not be separated.

Although work outside the home was a necessary alternative for first-generation mothers, old dogmas prevailed, proclaimed by men and sometimes echoed by women. We hear: "The husband is the boss of the house and . . . everything that he says is to be obeyed." "The man in the family should be the only worker." "The woman is not made for work."[33] But actions more frequently contradicted articulated attitudes, and the exigencies of material existence gradually altered the values themselves. A case in point was the joint interview of Mr. and Mrs. Carpati, an impoverished Hungarian couple with six children. Although Mr. Carpati assured the interviewer that his wife had stopped factory work immediately after their marriage because he believed married women should stay at home, Mrs. Carpati corrected him, explaining that she had not quit but was laid off. Thereafter, she continued to work intermittently.[34]

The traditional European division of labor required women to work hard indoors and alongside husbands in fields and shops, but the place of men at the head of the preindustrial family was firmly grounded in their control over the land and skills that provided subsistence. Once landownership and artisanal status were undermined, wages became both the major means of family support and the main foundation for male superiority. But women's work outside the home implicitly threatened traditional role relationships. The angry illogic of a Slovak man's testimony reveals how employers' practices, which pitted male against female workers, could cause this contradiction to erupt into overt hostility. As the following passage indicates, the sexist stereotypes this worker embraced blinded him to his own manipulation, subverting the possibility of effective resistance.

[32] Schwartz, "Immigrant Voices," pp. 636–86. Statistical sources indicate that 26 percent of all Connecticut women were working in 1929, and immigrant women were always more likely to be in the work force than their native-born sisters. See Harold Bingham, *History of Connecticut*, 4 vols. (New York, 1962), 2:850; Joseph Hill, *Women in Gainful Occupations, 1870–1920*, Census Monograph 9 (Washington, D.C., 1929), pp. 13, 19, 67, 105, 123.

[33] Pasquale Gruci (Italian), interviewed by Vincent Frazzetta (box 2, 109:13b; 18 pp.), p. 8.

[34] Mr. and Mrs. C. (Hungarian; Carpati, pseud.), interviewed by Tanna Sayers and P. K. Russo (box 25, 109:19; 13 pp.), p. 6.

> The shop started to transfer women . . . to our department. This burned up a lot of the old-timers like myself. . . . After a couple of weeks, we found out that some of the men in our department were getting knocked off and they were putting the broads in their places. The men were sent home a little at a time, and the press jobs were done by the women after that. A couple of old-timers like myself stayed there on the job, and the whole thing dragged on like that for a couple of years. . . . A while after the women came . . . prices on all the piece work jobs went down. The few men that were left in this department started to see that it was the fault of the women were starting to do more work than the men ever did when they were working on the same jobs. And they got less money for it. . . . When the women started to come on they put in newer machines that could go faster. . . . I don't mind that a broad has to work in a shop, but why the Christ does a married woman have to work. Their business is to take care of the house.[35]

When the income of husbands and children was sufficient, married women often preferred to labor at home rather than take the low-paid, exhausting, and often dangerous jobs available to them. But many women did not have this choice; they worked outside the home because their wages were crucial to family survival.[36] Moreover, married women's entry into the industrial work force could be rationalized as an extension of European traditions of women's work. Lucia Salanto insisted on working in a laundry after marriage. To her husband's objections, she responded that such work was simply a continuation of Italian practices: "In Italy, when the husband don't make enough money, the wife she have to work too . . . they have to pick fruits and everything . . . that's hard." Although she stopped working when her first baby was born, Mrs. Salanto returned to work when the child was only three years old. She claimed that "Italian girls they are always knowing that they have 'responsibilita' of the house and they want to help." Ironically, Mrs. Salanto portrayed the refusal of some non-Italian women to work outside their homes as the real break with traditional culture.[37]

If the "responsibilita" of women in traditional Italian culture provided a belief system within which Mrs. Salanto could adapt to and actively influence her new industrial environment, the experience of work itself transformed these values. She refused to stop working when her husband got a better job, claiming that she would stay on to

[35] Slovak man, quoted by Vincent Frazzetta, "Slovak Community in Bridgeport" (box 18, 109:4; 80 pp.), pp. 57–59.

[36] See, for example, Slovak woman, foreperson at Frisbie Pie Company, quoted by Frazzetta, ibid., pp. 51–52.

[37] Mrs. L. Salanto (Italian; Lucia, pseud.), pp. 2–3.

ease paying bills. Mrs. Salanto had grown used to working. She began her employment at the laundry to make possible the family's subsistence, but by the late 1930s she was working to improve their standard of living.[38]

Mildred Hecht bitterly complained of her dual exploitation as a working wife, and yet she did not want to stop working. She described the independence and power that contributing wages to the family gave women within the home. Work entered into within the familial values of traditional patriarchal culture had the potential to subvert that culture: "Still there is advantage of working. It makes me independent. You see, I am a hot communist and my husband isn't and is against communists. . . . He reads the *Forward*, that's the trouble. I read the *Freiheit*. . . . I got angry and told him he can't stop me from going where I want to go. I couldn't talk like that if I wasn't working."[39]

Housekeeping in immigrant apartments that had none of the legendary "American conveniences" was a continuous battle.[40] But since women's domestic labor was unpaid, it often went unnoted. One mother complained: "The only time a woman is the center of attention is when she gets married and when she has a baby, then everything goes the same old way."[41] Nevertheless, women expressed pride in their mastery of the skills necessary for efficient household management. "I'm the carpenter, I'm the electrician, I'm the painter, plumber, everything around here," Bella Chornoy explained. "I fix cords, change sockets, fix lamps, put in curtain rods. Sure I'm good. I'm the jack of all trades."[42]

Women's unpaid labor in the home permitted working-class immigrants to tolerate low wages, unsatisfactory housing, frequent unemployment, and the complex logistics of managing many workers in a single family, but it also provided an indirect support to an oppressive industrial order, enabling families to endure below-subsistence incomes and unemployment by sweating women's labor in the household. Agnes Bonza, a Hungarian CIO activist, recalled repeated arguments with a friend who, in times of distress, increased her own work load and never complained. "I always tell her, 'If all the people

[38] Ibid., p. 3.

[39] M. H. (Jewish; Mildred Hecht, pseud.), p. 3.

[40] See among others, Mary Gadomska (Polish), interviewed by Stanley Dabkowski (box 87; 187:7b), p. 5; Mrs. Blizman, quoted in Robert C. Goulden, "Growth of Hell's Kitchen" (box 28, 109:23e; 12 pp.), pp. 1–2; Mrs. Donato Verilli (Italian), interviewed by Emil Napolitano (box 23; 109:13; 11 pp.), p. 3.

[41] "#10" (Jewish), unsigned interview (box 61, 157:1e; 20 pp.), p. 15.

[42] Mrs. C. (Hungarian; Bella Chornoy, pseud.), interviewed by Pearl K. Russo (box 21, 109:11; 41 pp.), p. 28.

was like you, the capitalists give the people hay.' Then they never have to give the people anything."[43]

If men took money from their pay envelopes for entertainment, smoking, or alcohol, the family still had to be fed, clothed, and lodged. When corners had to be cut, women's own comfort was frequently the only resource over which they had control. In many families there were two levels of subsistence, one for wives and one for husbands and children. An immigrant mother of seven described the tragic consequences of her desperate self-sacrifice in an attempt to stretch her husband's meager earnings: "[My youngest child] is a year old now, and doesn't make any attempt to get up. I wasn't getting the proper nourishment when I was carrying her. What I had, I gave to my husband and the children, and didn't take it for myself. I cheated her to feed the others. Somehow you don't think of the one that isn't there yet."[44]

Mothers attempted to enforce traditional codes of mutual support and responsibility on all family members. Husbands were valued for diligent labor and for the delivery of the pay envelope undepleted by a costly stopover at the neighborhood saloon. Nevertheless, patriarchal prerogatives allowed fathers and sons to retain substantial portions of their pay for themselves. One son explained: "My parents felt that the family was an economic unit. I felt the family was a group of individuals. . . . I was expected to turn in what money I earned [but] I felt that I should be allowed to keep part of it."[45]

Under such circumstances, mothers came to depend heavily for family assistance on their daughters, who could be called upon as dedicated and loyal lieutenants even when loyalty meant active self-deprivation. One daughter recalled: "Whenever I got some money, I useta' give it to my mother, I useta' make some money helpin' the neighbors. Anything over two penny, I'd always give it to my mother. When I was workin' in Harvey and Hubbell's I useta' give my mother my whole pay. . . . I never kept any of it for myself."[46]

It was not the size of the daughter's contribution so much as its reliability that created her mother's dependence on her earnings. Daughters brought home only half the wages their fathers and brothers earned. But the very insufficiency of women's earnings caused by sexist wage differentials meant that mothers could count on their daughters' commitment to the family economy. Young women, unlike their

[43] Mrs. B. (Hungarian; Agnes Bonsza, pseud.), pp. 3–4. See also Susan Kleinberg, "Technology and Women's Work: The Lives of Working Class Women in Pittsburgh, 1870–1900," *Labor History* 17 (Winter 1976): 58–72.

[44] Mrs. B. (French-Canadian; Marie Bretagne, pseud.), interviewed by P. K. Russo and M. G. Sayers (box 19, 109:7; 16 pp.), p. 2.

[45] Paul Kubisek (Slovak), autobiography (box 18, 109:4; 8 pp.), p. 7.

[46] Mrs. C. (Hungarian; Bella Chornoy, pseud.), p. 39.

brothers, could not afford to live separately from their parents; they did not earn enough.[47] Whereas mothers were afraid to enforce familial obligations too stringently on sons, who might be pushed into leaving altogether, daughters were as dependent on their families as their mothers were on them.

Immigrant daughters' work outside the home was seldom an expression of independence from family obligation; its primary purpose was to augment inadequate family income. But for unmarried women who entered factories within the ideological framework of the home, the factory opened up new possibilities for comradeship and self-sufficiency. "Americanization" and rebellion by these young women were contradictory consequences of the innovative application of traditional values of mutual obligation. As in migration, mothers sent their daughters out of the family to preserve the family; and, like migration, this process created both new bonds and tensions.

Women frequently suffered under the yoke of the very traditions they upheld. Girls were sent to work to provide money so that their brothers could continue their educations; working daughters were denied the autonomy in spending money and leisure time that was granted to husbands and sons. Whereas men could socialize in saloons and clubs or on street corners, married women were kept home by chores, child care, homework, jealousy, and traditional values that barred them from public places without their husbands. Bella Chornoy's husband was frequently away from Friday to Monday night "among his Polacks, Russians, Slavs. Do you wonder why I don't like them?"[48] Yet he resented her going out on her own, even to pray, and certainly did not want her to dance in a tavern.

Although urban conditions and wage labor exacerbated the contradictions between male dominance and the familial values of reciprocity, they also provided a context within which women resisted the constraints of patriarchal traditions, taking advantage of the new chances for self-sufficiency created by job opportunities and the broadened support provided by extended kinship and neighborhood ties. Annie Burkowski, for example, was able to leave her morose and stingy husband because she found a job and could put her young children in a nursery. Later her married daughter contributed to her support.[49] Mrs. Michalowski endured years of beatings from an alcoholic husband while she worked to maintain her family of seven children. But when she finally separated from her husband, she acknowledged the

[47] Louise C. Odencrantz, *Italian Women in Industry* (New York, 1919), pp. 176, 179. See also Amy Hewes, "Bridgeport on the Rebound," *Survey*, October 14, 1916, p. 65.

[48] Mrs. C. (Hungarian; Bella Chornoy, pseud.), p. 7.

[49] Mrs. B. (Polish; Annie Burkowski, pseud.), quoted in Vincent Frazzetta, "Polish Community in Bridgeport" (box 25, 109:19, 117 pp.), p. 77.

satisfaction she felt in being independent: "For me, I be like this all the time. I don't want nobody supportin' me so long that I have health and I could work all myself."[50]

The values of mutual support and communal responsibility that women upheld in their households provided a powerful moral stance from which to challenge the low pay and high prices that undermined the family wage economy. In 1915, for example, mothers in Hartford mobilized the community for a strike by bakers that linked wage demands to calls for stable or lower prices. Their support enabled the strikers to hold out until they had not only won their wage demands but had exacted a promise from employers that bread prices would remain the same.[51]

Immigrant working-class organizations were embedded in household economies that depended upon women's labor at home and in factories. Family solidarity, kinship ties, and community cohesion sustained consumer movements, as well as ethnic and labor associations, creating an intense social and ethical basis for militant resistance rooted in the defense of an entire way of life. Their perception of the individual worker as part of a greater collectivity could be translated into women's fierce and steadfast defense against employers' practices that threatened not just their own livelihood but also that of the family and community. Matilda Broca lived at home under her parents' strict supervision. Although the Brocas carefully monitored the propriety of their daughter's social relationships, her family's dependence on Matilda's wages led them to champion her very "unladylike" trade union activities. Expectations of support from the ethnic community further contributed to the militancy Matilda depicts in her description of Italian working girls on strike at the Flossie dress shop in Stamford:

> We grabbed the foreman. . . . We pulled his pants down and made him stay that way in his undies. We laughed like hell. He got pushed back and forth along the picket line, in his underwear. . . . He begged us to let him go, and said he would join the union the next day. We told him never mind tomorrow, but to come down to the union hall right then and there in his underwear. . . . The next day he came down to the union with the forelady. She was Italian too. They both joined the union and everything was settled. We were like one big happy family together.[52]

[50] Mrs. Michalowski, quoted ibid., p. 7.

[51] *Hartford Daily Courant,* May 5, 1916, p. 21, May 6, 1915, p. 13, clippings in WPA Connecticut Ethnic Survey, box 52.

[52] Matilda B. (Italian; Broca, pseud.), unsigned interview (box 89, 195; 9 pp.), pp. 1–6. See also Sayers and Russo, "Survey of Remington City"; "Charter of the Ladies Brass Workers of Waterbury," in Brecher et al., *Brass Valley,* p. 77.

Like many women, Mary Rauci Young took a factory job to support her children. But once there, she participated in one of Bridgeport's first sit-down strikes at Casco's and subsequently joined the CIO. "Since I'm in the CIO I haven't much time for recreation," she explained. "I give a couple of nights a week for that. I don't like the sound in the West End theatre anyway." The community orientation of early CIO strategies and demands in cities like Bridgeport and New Britain were, at least in part, a legacy of the integration of the spheres of work, family, and neighborhood that immigrant women embodied and sought to defend. At the same time, industrial unionism built multiethnic networks that enabled women to forge a new consciousness of their worlds and their lives. Mrs. Young explained: "I'm glad I'm in the union, though. Through the union I've met a lot of wonderful people I wouldn't have met otherwise. . . . People that know what they're talking about. As I said, I never belonged to any organizations before. The people I've been meeting have a much wider variety of knowledge than I do."[53]

In Connecticut cities, southern and eastern European women achieved a means of survival and even betterment under conditions they did not create and could not entirely control. Their actions were conditioned both by the defense of a familial culture of mutual obligation and the transformation of that culture by the migration process and their own strategies for adaptation and resistance. The differing work patterns of immigrant women from diverse ethnic backgrounds were created by the complex interaction of many factors: male income, available employment opportunities, inherited skills and traditions, stage in the life cycle, and the existence of familial, friendship, or ethnic ties to specific jobs. Premigration patterns were not rigidly preserved; they persisted and evolved because they were useful in Connecticut cities. New strategies arose from the interaction of customary practices and new economic realities. Family needs sent women into the paid work force in immigrant households not yet affected by the possibilities of single-income support or Victorian domesticity. Their jobs, in turn, altered family relationships, introducing new arenas of oppression and new possibilities for liberation.

The strength and resourcefulness of immigrant women who sustained their households under harsh and unpredictable circumstances should not blind us to the constraints under which they labored. Persistent patriarchal values and American industrial practices imposed stultifying limitations on immigrant mothers and their daughters. WPA interviewer Pearl Russo cautioned against substituting for the

[53] Mrs. Z. (Hungarian; Mary Rauci Young, pseud.), interviewed by P. K. Russo (box 21, 109:13b; 9 pp.), p. 6. See also "Labor in New Britain" (box 49) and "Strikes and Labor Relations" (box 52).

ideology of success through Americanization a new tradition of happy endings that reifies and romanticizes preindustrial values. In contrast, she recalled her own perspectives in recording the life histories of her immigrant neighbors and friends: "We could not be nostalgic about the lives of our neighbors. Why would we, when we lived them. In your generation you see this sort of roseate picture. . . . It's not true at all. These [actions] were the exigencies that the situation demanded; they came naturally to you because you came from poor people."[54]

[54] Author's interview with Pearl K. Russo, February 16, 1983.

CHAPTER TWENTY

Sexism by a Subtler Name?: Postindustrial Conditions and Postfeminist Consciousness in the Silicon Valley

Judith Stacey

During the past three decades profound changes in the organization of family, work, and gender have occurred in the United States, coincident with the rise of second-wave feminism.[1] Feminist scholars have demonstrated that an important historical relationship existed between the development of the earlier feminist movement and capitalist industrialization in the West. In the United States, for example, the disintegration of the agrarian family economy and the reorganization of family, work, and gender relationships that took place during the nineteenth century provided the major impetus for the birth of American feminism.[2] Although the more recent history of feminism and social change is also intertwined, it has received far less attention.

This essay explores connections between the recent transition to an emergent "postindustrial" stage of capitalist development and the

I wish to thank the Center for Social Research and Education, Berkeley, California, for permission to republish this essay, which first appeared in *Socialist Review*, no. 96 (November–December 1987): pp. 7–28. I thank Linda Gordon, Carole Joffe, David Plotke, Rayna Rapp, and Barrie Thorne for their challenging and supportive responses to earlier drafts of this article.

[1] By "second-wave" feminism I refer to the resurgence of feminist politics and ideology that began in the mid-1960s, peaked in the early 1970s, and has been a major focus of social and political struggle since the late 1970s.

[2] Historians have argued that the establishment of separate spheres for the sexes had, as one of its paradoxical consequences, the development of feminist consciousness and activity. See, for example, Nancy Cott, *The Bonds of Womanhood: "Woman's Sphere" in New England, 1750–1835* (New Haven, 1976); Mary Ryan, *Womanhood in America: From Colonial Times to the Present*, 3d ed. (New York, 1983). There were similar de-

simultaneous rise and decline of a militant and radical phase of feminism in the United States.[3] First, I reflect on the ironic role second-wave feminism played as an unwitting midwife to the massive social transformations of work and family life that occurred in the post–World War II era. Second, I will draw from my field research on family life in California's Silicon Valley—a veritable postindustrial hothouse—to illustrate some of the effects of this ironic collaboration in fostering emergent forms of "postfeminist" consciousness.

Let me begin, however, by explaining my use of the troubling term *postfeminist*, a concept offensive to many feminists, who believe that the media coined it simply "to give sexism a subtler name."[4] Whatever the media's motives, I find the concept useful in describing the gender consciousness and the family and work strategies of many contemporary women. I view the term as analogous to *postrevolutionary* and use it not to indicate the death of the women's movement but to describe the simultaneous incorporation, revision, and depoliticization of many of the central goals of second-wave feminism.[5] I believe postfeminism is distinct from antifeminism and sexism, for it aptly describes the consciousness and strategies increasing numbers of women have developed in response to the new difficulties and opportunities of postindustrial society. In this sense the diffusion of postfeminist consciousness signifies both the achievements of, and challenges for, contemporary feminist politics.

---

velopments in Europe and, by contrast, feminism has been weak in most preindustrial and "underdeveloped" societies, including even revolutionary societies with explicit commitments to gender equality. Feminist literature on socialist societies is growing rapidly. For analyses of feminist developments in postrevolutionary societies see Maxine Molyneux, "Socialist Societies Old and New: Progress towards Women's Emancipation?" *Feminist Review* 8 (Summer 1981): 1–34; Molyneux, "Mobilization without Emancipation? Women's Interests, the State, and Revolution in Nicaragua," *Feminist Studies* 11 (Summer 1985): 227–54; Judith Stacey, *Patriarchy and Socialist Revolution in China* (Berkeley and Los Angeles, 1983); Stacey, "State Socialism, the 'Woman Question,' and Socialist-Feminist Theory," *Insurgent Sociologist* 12 (Winter 1986): 20–29; Elisabeth Croll, "Women in Rural Production and Reproduction in the Soviet Union, China, Cuba, and Tanzania: Socialist Development Experiences," and Croll, "Women in Rural Production and Reproduction in the Soviet Union, China, Cuba, and Tanzania: Case Studies," *Signs* 7 (Winter 1981): 361–99.

[3] I use the term *postindustrial* with some trepidation because it carries a great deal of ideological and polemical charge. I use it here exclusively in a descriptive sense to designate a form and period of capitalist social organization in which traditional industrial occupations supply a small minority of jobs to the labor force and the vast majority of workers labor in varieties of clerical, sales, and service positions. Daniel Bell claims to have formulated the theme of postindustrial society in 1962. See his *The Coming of Post-Industrial Society: A Venture in Social Forecasting* (New York, 1973), p. 145.

[4] Thus Geneva Overholser concludes a *New York Times* editorial opinion titled "What 'Post-Feminism' Really Means," September 19, 1986, p. 30.

[5] My appreciation to Steven Buechler for first suggesting this analogy to me.

Feminism as Midwife to Postindustrial Society

Hindsight allows us to see how feminist ideology helped legitimate the massive structural changes in American work and family patterns that invisibly accompanied the transition to postindustrial society in the 1960s and early 1970s. I believe this period of postindustrialization should be read as the unmaking of a gender order rooted in the modern nuclear family system, the family of male breadwinner, female homemaker, and dependent children, that was grounded in the male family wage and stable marriage, at least for the majority of white families. Family and work relations in the emergent postindustrial order, by contrast, have been transformed by the staggering escalation of divorce rates and women's participation in paid work. As the United States changed from an industrial to a service-dominated occupational structure, unprecedented percentages of women entered the labor force and the halls of academe and unprecedented percentages of marriages entered the divorce courts. Unstable and often incompatible work and family conditions have become the postindustrial norm as working-class occupations become increasingly "feminized." This process generated an extreme disjuncture between the dominant cultural ideology of domesticity that became particularly strident in the 1950s and the simultaneous decline in marriage and motherhood and the rise of employment in the lives of American women.[6]

The gap between the ideology of domesticity and the increasingly nondomestic character of women's lives helped generate feminist consciousness in the 1960s and resulted in an assault on traditional domesticity—an assault on a declining institution and culture.[7]

[6] Labor force participation rates for women increased steadily but slowly between 1900 and 1940, climbing from 20.5 percent to 25.4 percent. This pattern accelerated rapidly in the post-1940 period. In 1950 29 percent of women fourteen years and older were in the labor force; in 1960 this percentage had grown to 34.5; in 1984 63 percent of all women ages eighteen to sixty-four were in the labor force. See Valerie Kincade Oppenheimer, *The Female Labor Force in the United States*, Population Monograph Series No. 5, Institute of International Studies, University of California (Berkeley, 1970); and *Women's Work, Men's Work: Sex Segregation on the Job*, ed. Barbara F. Reskin and Heidi I. Hartmann (Washington, D.C., 1986). The dramatic increase in female enrollment in colleges occurred in the 1960s and 1970s, rising from 38 to 48 percent of enrollees between 1960 and 1979 (Rosalind Petchesky, *Abortion and Woman's Choice* [Boston, 1984], p. 109). Divorce outstripped death as a source of marital dissolution in the mid-1970s, and fertility and marriage rates declined. By 1989, demographers were projecting that two-thirds of first marriages would dissolve before death (Larry Bumpass and Teresa Castro, "Recent Trends and Differentials in Marital Disruption," Center for Demography and Ecology Working Paper 87–20, University of Wisconsin, Madison). In 1960, 17.3 percent of women and 23.2 percent of men over the age of fifteen had never married; by 1983, these figures rose to 22.9 percent of women and 30 percent of men (Suzanne Bianchi and Daphne Spain, *American Women in Transition* [New York, 1986], p. 12). See also Susan Van Horn, *Women, Work and Fertility, 1900–1986* (New York, 1988).

[7] Betty Friedan's *Feminine Mystique* (New York, 1963) was one of the earliest, most

Therefore, this feminist movement was backward-looking in its critique and unwittingly forward-looking (but not to the future of our fantasies) in its effects. Feminists developed a devastating critique of the stultifying, infantilizing, and exploitative effects on women of female domesticity, especially of the sort available to classes that could afford an economically dependent housewife. Although the institutions of domesticity and their male beneficiaries were the intended targets of that critique, many housewives felt themselves to be on the defensive. Feminist criticism helped to undermine and delegitimize the flagging but still celebrated model of the male breadwinner and promote the newly normative double-income (with shifting personnel) white family. It also provided ideological support for the sharp rise of single-mother families generated by the soaring divorce rates.[8]

Millions of women have derived enormous tangible and psychological benefits from these changes in occupational and family patterns and from the ways in which feminist ideology encouraged them to initiate and to cope with these changes. Yet it is also true that since the mid-1970s, when the contours of the new postindustrial society began to be clear, economic and personal conditions have worsened for many groups of women, perhaps for the majority. The emerging shape of postindustrial society seems to have several rather disturbing characteristics. As unionized occupations and real wages decline throughout the economy, women are becoming the postindustrial "proletariat," performing the majority of "working-class" low-skilled, low-paying jobs. Because the overall percentage of jobs that are secure and well-paid has declined rapidly, increasing numbers of men are unemployed or underemployed. Yet the majority of white male workers still labor at jobs that are highly skilled and comparatively well paid.[9] Family instability is endemic and has devastating economic effects on women, as the "feminization of poverty" literature has made clear. Increasing

---

successful polemical examples of this assault.

[8] In 1984, 14.7 percent of white families with children under age eighteen and 48.8 percent of black families were headed by single women (Heidi Hartman, "Changes in Women's Economic and Family Roles in Post–World War II United States," in *Women, Households and the Economy,* ed. Lourdes Beneria and Catharine Stimpson [New Brunswick, 1987], p. 41).

[9] These are among the findings of a study that attempted to operationalize Marxist criteria for assigning class categories to workers in the United States. Even though the study excluded housewives from its sample, it found "that the majority of the working class in the United States consists of women (53.6%)." See Erik Olin Wright et al., "The American Class Structure," *American Sociological Review* 47 (December 1982): 22. For additional data on female occupational patterns and earnings and an astute analysis of the paradoxical relationship between female employment and poverty, see Joan Smith, "The Paradox of Women's Poverty: Wage-Earning Women and Economic Transformation," *Signs* 10 (Winter 1984): 291–310.

percentages of women are rearing children by themselves, generally with minimal economic contributions from fathers and former husbands.[10] Yet rising numbers of those single mothers who work full time, year-round, do not earn wages sufficient to lift their families above the official poverty level.[11]

In the emerging class structure, marriage is becoming a major axis of stratification. The married female "secondary" wage earner lifts a former working-class or middle-class family into comparative affluence, while the loss or lack of access to a male income plunges women and their children into poverty.[12] In short, the drastic increase in female employment during the past several decades has meant lots more work for mother but with very unevenly distributed economic benefits and only modest improvements in relative income differentials between women and men.[13]

The massive rise in female employment also produces a scarcely visible but portentous social effect. Its flip side is a drastic decline in the potential pool of female volunteers, typically from the middle class, who have sustained much of family and community life in the United States since the nineteenth century. The result may be a general dete-

[10] As the much-publicized findings from Lenore Weitzman's study of no-fault divorce in California underscores, in the first year after divorce divorced women and minor children in their care suffer a 73 percent decline in their standard of living while former husbands enjoy a 42 percent gain (*The Divorce Revolution: The Unexpected Social and Economic Consequences for Women and Children in America* [New York, 1985]).

[11] In 1980 households headed by fully employed women had a poverty rate almost three times greater than husband-wife households and twice that of households headed by unmarried men. The number of female-headed families doubled between 1970 and 1980. By 1981, women headed almost one-fifth of all families with minor children (Smith, "Paradox of Women's Poverty," p. 291).

[12] Households with working wives accounted for 60 percent of all family income in 1985, which made it possible for 65 percent of all families to earn more than $25,000 per year, compared with only 28 percent of families who achieved comparable incomes twenty years ago. In 1981, the median earnings of full-time year-round women workers were $12,001, 59 percent of the $20,260 that men earned. That year married women contributed a median of 26.7 percent of family income. The lower the family's annual income, however, the higher the proportion contributed by women. But paradoxically, there is an inverse relationship between family income and the percentage of wives working. See The Conference Board, *The Working Woman: A Progress Report* (Washington, D.C., 1985), and *Women's Work, Men's Work*, ed. Reskin and Hartmann, p. 4. The combined effects of these trends is acute for Black women, for whom astronomical divorce rates have overwhelmed the effects of their gains in earnings relative to Black men and white women, leaving Black women increasingly poor. For data see U.S. Department of Labor, *Time of Change: 1983 Handbook on Women Workers* (Washington, D.C., 1983), p. 29; Paula Giddings, *When and Where I Enter: The Impact of Black Women on Race and Sex in America* (1984; rpt. Toronto, 1985), p. 353.

[13] Very recent data suggest that women's median earnings have risen to nearly 70 percent of men's (Alison Cowan, "Poll Finds Women's Gains Have Taken Personal Toll," *New York Times*, August 21, 1989, p. A8). For a more optimistic evaluation of postindustrial changes on women, see Hartman, "Changes in Women's Economic and Family Roles."

rioration of domesticity and social housekeeping that is fueling reactionary nostalgia for traditional family life among leftists and feminists as well as among right-wing forces.[14]

In light of these developments, many women (and men) have been susceptible to the appeals of the antifeminist backlash, and especially to profamily ideologies. Because of its powerful and highly visible critique of traditional domesticity and the sensationalized way the media disseminated this critique, feminism has been charged with responsibility for family and social crises that have attended the transition from an industrial to a postindustrial order in the United States. Despite efforts by such feminists as Barbara Ehrenreich to portray men as the real deserters of the family,[15] feminism continues to be blamed for a general decline of domesticity and nurturance within families and communities. Feminism serves as a symbolic lightning rod for the widespread nostalgia and longing for "lost" intimacy and security that presently pervades social and political culture in the United States.[16]

It is in this context, I believe, that we can best understand why during the late 1970s and the 1980s even many feminists began to retreat from the radical critique of conventional family life of the early second wave.[17] During the decade when postindustrial social patterns became firmly established, various forms of postfeminist consciousness and family strategies emerged.

[14] A concomitant decline in political activism as well seems plausible, for example, the stark contrast in the amount of time available for politics for women active on opposing sides of the abortion controversy. In a recent study of this conflict, most of the antiabortion activists were housewives who spent at least thirty hours per week on antichoice politics, whereas most of the pro-choice activists were career women, few of whom spent more than five hours per week on this issue. See Kristin Luker, *Abortion and the Politics of Motherhood* (Berkeley and Los Angeles, 1984). Although there are problems with Luker's pro-choice sample that may exaggerate its career and income levels, it seems unlikely that the contrast is spurious.

[15] Barbara Ehrenreich, *The Hearts of Men: American Dreams and the Flight from Commitment* (Garden City, N.Y., 1983).

[16] Christopher Lasch has made a sideline industry out of this sort of attack on feminists. For some of his polemics on this subject, see "What's Wrong with the Right?" *Tikkun* 1, no. 1 (January/February 1986): 23–29; and "Why the Left Has No Future," *Tikkun* 1, no. 2 (March/April 1986): 92–97. The latter was his response to critics of the former, including Lillian Rubin's "A Feminist Response to Lasch," *Tikkun* 1, no. 2 (1986): 89–91. The most comprehensive and popular recent book to use feminism as a scapegoat in this way is probably Sylvia Ann Hewlett, *A Lesser Life: The Myth of Women's Liberation in America* (New York, 1986). For a critical discussion of this book that does not deny the power of its approach, see Deborah Rosenfelt and Judith Stacey, "Second Thoughts on the Second Wave," *Feminist Studies* 13 (Summer 1987): 341–61.

[17] The most conspicuous representatives of this backlash within feminist thought are Betty Friedan, Jean Bethke Elshtain, and Germaine Greer. For critical discussions of their writings see my "Are Feminists Afraid to Leave Home? The Challenge of Conservative Pro-Family Feminism," in *What Is Feminism?* ed. Juliet Mitchell and Ann Oakley (London, 1986), pp. 219–48, and Zillah Eisenstein, *Feminism and Sexual Equality: Crisis in Liberal America* (New York, 1984).

Family and Work in the Silicon Valley

Material from my study of family and work experience in California's Silicon Valley highlights some of the features of postindustrial society and the diverse postfeminist strategies that contemporary women have devised to cope with them. After briefly describing the major postindustrial contours of the region, I draw from my fieldwork to illustrate them.

As the birthplace and international headquarters of the electronics industry, the Silicon Valley, Santa Clara County, California, is popularly perceived as representing the vanguard of postindustrialism. Until the early 1950s the region was a sparsely populated agricultural area, one of the major fruitbaskets in the United States. But in the three decades since the electronics industry developed there, its population grew by 350 percent and its economy, ecology, and social structure were dramatically transformed.[18]

During this period, electronics, the vanguard postindustrial industry, feminized (and "minoritized") its production work force. In the 1950s and 1960s, when the industry was young, most of its production workers were men, who found significant opportunities for advancement into technical and, at times, engineering ranks even if they had very limited schooling. But as the industry aged, it turned increasingly to female, ethnic minority, and recent migrant workers to fill production positions that offered fewer and fewer advancement opportunities.[19] By the late 1970s, the industry's occupational structure was crudely stratified by gender, as well as by race and ethnicity. At the top was an unusually high proportion (25 percent) of the most highly educated and highly paid salaried employees in any industry—the engineers and professionals employed in research and design. As in traditional industries, the vast majority were white males (89 percent males, 89 percent non-Hispanic whites). At the bottom, however, were the women, who constituted three-fourths of the very poorly paid assembly workers and operatives who performed the tedious, often health-threatening work assigned to 45 percent of employees. In between were the moderately well-paid technicians and craft workers,

[18] The county population grew from 290,547 in 1950 to 1,295,071 in 1980 (U.S. Bureau of the Census, *Census of Population: 1950*, vol. 2, *Characteristics of the Population*, pt. 5, California, 1952; and *Census of Population: 1980*, vol. 1, *Characteristics of the Population, General Population Characteristics*, pt. 6, California, 1982).

[19] For data and a superb ethnographic and analytical account of this transition, see John Frederick Keller, "The Production Worker in Electronics: Industrialization and Labor Development in California's Santa Clara Valley" (Ph.D. diss. University of Michigan, 1981).

also primarily Anglo males, but into whose ranks women and Asians were making gradual inroads.[20]

In the heady days of technological triumph and economic expansion, when the Silicon Valley was widely portrayed as the mecca of the new intellectual entrepreneurs and as a land where factories resembled campuses, its public officials also liked to describe it as a feminist capital. Indeed, San Jose, the county seat, had a feminist mayor in the late 1970s and was one of the first public employers in the nation to implement a comparable worth standard of pay for city employees.

What is less widely known is that the area is also the site of a significant degree of family turbulence. Much of the data on local family change represent an exaggeration of national and even California trends. For example, whereas the national divorce rate has doubled since 1960, in Santa Clara County it nearly tripled so that by 1977 the number of divorces exceeded that of marriages. Likewise, the percentage of "nonfamily households" grew faster than in the nation, and abortion rates were almost double the national figures. And although the percentage of single-parent households was not as high as in the United States as a whole, the rate of increase was more rapid.[21] The coincidence of pathbreaking changes in economic and family patterns makes the Silicon Valley an ideal site for examining women's responses to these transformations.

Paths to Postfeminism

Let me first introduce Pam, currently a staff analyst in a municipal agency.[22] We became friendly in 1984, when I was interviewing clients at a feminist-inspired social service program in which Pam was then an administrator. From various informal conversations, lunches, and observations of her work goals and relations, I had pegged Pam as a slightly cynical divorcee who came to feminist consciousness through divorce and a women's reentry program at a local community college.

[20] Marcie Axelrad, *Profile of the Electronics Workforce in the Santa Clara Valley* (San Jose, 1979); Lennie Siegel and Herb Borock, "Background Report on Silicon Valley," prepared for the U.S. Commission on Civil Rights (Mountain View, Calif., 1982).

[21] For data on divorce rates and household composition for Santa Clara County in comparison with California and the United States as a whole, see Bureau of the Census, *Census of Population,* 1960, 1970, and 1980. During the 1970s, Santa Clara County recorded 660 abortions for every 1,000 births, compared with a statewide average of 489.5 and a ratio of less than 400 for the nation. See Bureau of the Census, *Statistical Abstract of the United States,* 1981.

[22] I have given pseudonyms to all the individuals described in this essay.

I had learned that Pam's first husband, Don, to whom she was married for twelve years and with whom she had three children, was a white Anglo male electronics industry success story. A telephone repair worker with an interest in drafting when they married, Don entered the electronics industry in the early 1960s and proceeded to work and job-hop his way up to a career as a packaging engineer, a position that by the mid 1980s earned him $50,000 annually.

I had heard, too, that Don's route to success had been arduous and stormy, entailing numerous setbacks, failures, and layoffs, and requiring such extraordinary work hours that Don totally neglected Pam and their children. This and other problems led to Pam's divorce more than fifteen years ago, resulting in the normative female impoverishment. Pam became a single mother on welfare, continued her schooling (eventually through the master's level) got feminist consciousness, experimented with sexual freedom, cohabited with a couple of lovers, and began to develop an administrative career in social services. Before the 1984 election she made many scornful remarks about Reagan, Reaganomics, and the military buildup. I was surprised, therefore, when, four months after meeting Pam, I learned that she was now married to Al, a construction worker with whom she earlier had cohabited, and that they both were recent converts to evangelical Christianity and were participating in Christian marriage counseling to improve their relationship. Pam had been separated from, but was on a friendly basis with, Al, when he had an automobile accident followed by a dramatic conversion experience. Al "accepted Jesus into his life," and Pam suddenly accepted Al and Jesus back into hers.

Pam acknowledges the paradoxes and contradictions of her participation in "Christian marriage"[23] and Christian marriage counseling, based, as they are, on patriarchal doctrines, but she credits the conversion experience and the counseling with helping her achieve a more intimate, positive marriage relationship than she had experienced before. The conversion, she claims, changed Al from a defensive, uncommunicative, withholding male into a less guarded, more trusting, loving, and committed mate.[24] Although Pam and Al's marriage is not as communicative, nurturant, and intimate as Pam would like, she believes their shared faith is leading them in this direction. And she believes that "if you can work out that kind of relationship, then who would care who's in charge, because it's such a total wonderful relationship?" Moreover, Pam cedes Al dominance only in the "spiritual realm"; financially, occupationally, interpersonally, and politically, she retains strong independence, or even control.

[23] Pam, like many fundamentalists, uses the term *Christian* to designate only fundamentalist Christians.

[24] Both Al and Pam's children agree with this description.

Pam's selective adaptation and blending of feminist and fundamentalist ideologies first struck me as unique as well as extremely contradictory. I later learned, however, that a significant tendency in contemporary fundamentalist thought incorporates many feminist criticisms of patriarchal men and marriage into its activist approach to profamilialism. Many evangelical ministers urge Christian wives to make strong emotional demands on their husbands for communication, commitment, and nurturance within the framework of patriarchal marriage, and they actively counsel Christian husbands to meet these demands.[25]

Feminism served Pam well as an aid for exiting her unsatisfactory first marriage and for building a career and sense of individual identity. But Pam failed to form successful, satisfying, intimate relationships to replace her marriage. Pam describes herself as desperately unhappy much of the time that she struggled alone with the emotional and social crises to which two of her three children were prone. Although Pam received support from several intense friendships with women, neither they nor feminism seemed to offer her sufficient solace or direction. Her retreat from feminism and her construction of an extreme form of postfeminist consciousness took place in this context.

Dotty Lewison, one of the key subjects in the other kinship network I studied, has a more complex story. I first sought out Dotty because of her early experience in electronics assembly work and because of her intact thirty-year marriage to Lou Lewison, another white male electronics industry success story. Dotty had been a teenager in 1954 when she met and married Lou, a sailor who had dropped out of school in the ninth grade. Although Dotty primarily had been a homemaker for Lou and the five children she bore at two-year intervals during her first decade of marriage, she also had made occasional forays into the world of paid work, including one two-year stint in the late 1950s assembling semiconductors. But Dotty neither perceived nor desired significant opportunities for personal advancement within electronics or any other occupation at that time. Instead, several years later she pushed Lou to enter the industry. This proved to be successful strategy for family economic mobility, although it was to have contradictory effects on their marital and family relationships as well as on Dotty's personal achievement goals. With his mechanical aptitude and naval background, Lou was able to receive on-the-job training and advance to the position of line maintenance engineer. Then, as Lou told me, "The companies didn't have many choices. No one even knew what a circuit

[25] For a discussion of feminist influence on contemporary evangelicalism, see Judith Stacey and Susan Elizabeth Gerard, " 'We Are Not Doormats': The Influence of Feminism on Contemporary Christian Evangelical Gender Ideology," in *Negotiating Gender in American Culture*, ed. Faye Ginsburg and Anna Tsing (Boston, 1990).

looked like. [But] you can't find many engineers starting out now who don't enter with degrees . . . because the companies have a lot more choices now."

When I first arrived at the Lewison's modest, cluttered tract home, Dotty was opening a delivery from a local gadgets sale. A self-described "knickknack junkie," Dot unpacked various porcelain figures and a new, gilded Bible. My social prejudices cued me to expect her to hold somewhat conservative and antifeminist views, but I was wrong again. She reported a long history of community and feminist activism, including work in the movement to help battered women. And she still expressed support for feminism, "depending," she said, "on what you mean by feminism."

Later I learned that Dotty's intact marriage had been broken by numerous short-term separations and one that lasted two years and almost became permanent. During that time, she was a welfare mother who hated being on welfare and had a serious live-in love affair. Dot does not repudiate very many of her former feminist ideas, but she has not been active since the late 1970s, and she takes care to distance herself from the "militant man-hating types."

Dotty is a feisty, assertive woman, who had protofeminist views long before she (or most of us) had heard of the women's liberation movement. Yet for twenty years, she tolerated a marriage in which she and her husband fought violently. Her children were battered, sometimes seriously, most often by Lou but occasionally by Dotty as well. Before I learned about the battering, Dotty and Lou led me to believe that their near-divorce in the mid-1970s was caused by Lou's workaholism as an upwardly mobile employee in electronics. They spoke of the twelve- to fourteen-hour workdays and the frequent three-day shifts that led Lou to neglect his family completely. Later I came to understand the dynamic relationships between that workaholism and their marital hostilities. Dotty had become a feminist and community activist by then, involved in antibattering and many other community issues. Partly because of her involvement with feminism (again, some of it encountered in a college women's reentry program), Dotty was beginning to shift the balance of power in her marriage. In this situation, I suspect that Lou's escape into work was experienced more as relief than neglect on all sides. Although now Dotty blames the work demands of the electronics industry for Lou's heart disease and his early death in 1986, at the time, Lou's absence from the family gave Dotty the "space" to develop her strength and the willingness to assume the serious economic and emotional risks of divorce and impoverishment as a single parent.

Dotty kicked Lou out, although she did not file for divorce. Two years later, she took him back, but only after his nearly fatal, and permanently disabling, heart attack, and after her live-in lover left her. Even then she took him back on her own rather harsh terms. She insisted on total independence with her time and relationships. Despite the economic inequality between them, Dotty now held the undeniable emotional balance of power in the relationship, but only because she had proved she could survive impoverishment and live without Lou. And, of course, Lou's disability contributed to the restructuring of the division of labor and power in their household. Lou did most of the housework and gardening, while Dotty participated in the paid labor force. Nonetheless, Dotty remained economically dependent on Lou, and she regrets her limited career options. Indeed, this was one crucial factor in her decision to resume her marriage with Lou.

By the late 1970s, Dotty was no longer active in feminist or community causes. She says she "got burned out" and "turned off by the 'all men are evil' kind of thinking." More important, I believe, Dotty's life stage and circumstances had changed so that she felt she no longer needed or benefited from feminism. In the mid-1970s, she "needed to have my stamp validated," to be reassured that her rebellious and assertive feelings and her struggles to reform her marriage were legitimate. But partly because of the feminist-assisted success of those struggles, Dotty came to feel less need for reassurance from feminists. Dotty also finds she has less time for feminism today. She is "too tired, there's too much other shit to deal with." She has been trying to maintain her precarious hold on her underpaid service sector job while struggling heroically to cope with the truly staggering series of family tragedies that befell the Lewisons during the late 1980s. Lou and two of the adult Lewison children died and one was imprisoned. Under these circumstances, Dotty found more comfort from organized religion than from feminism. After the death of their first son, Dotty and Lou left a spirtualist church they had been attending and returned to the neighborhood church in which Dotty once had been active. After Lou's death, Dotty's oldest daughter, Lyn, and Dotty's mother began attending the church with her regularly.

Parallels and idiosyncrasies in the life histories just described illustrate some of the complex, reciprocal effects of the family and work dynamics and gender consciousness that I observed in the Silicon Valley. Pam and Dotty both were young when they married. They both entered their marriages with conventional "Parsonsian" gender expectations about family and work responsibilities and roles. For a significant period of time, they and their husbands conformed to the then culturally prescribed pattern of "instrumental" male breadwinner and "expressive" female housewife/mother. Assuming primary responsibility for rearing the children they began to bear immediately after marriage, Pam and Dotty supported their husbands' successful efforts to develop middle- to upper-middle-class careers as electronics engineers. In the process, both men became workaholics, increasingly uninvolved with their families.

As their marriages deteriorated, both Pam and Dotty enrolled in women's reentry programs where they were affected profoundly by feminist courses. Eventually both women left their husbands and became welfare mothers, which each found to be both liberating and debilitating. Each experienced an initial "feminist high," a sense of enormous exhilaration and strength in her new independent circumstances. One divorced her husband, developed a viable career, experimented with the single life, and gradually became desperately unhappy. The other did not develop a career, lost her lover, and only then decided to take back her newly disabled husband (with his pension). Their different experiences with failed intimacy and their different occupational resources, I believe, help explain their diverse postfeminist strategies.

Postfeminist Daughters

Between them, Pam and Dotty have five daughters in their midtwenties to early thirties, members of the quintessential postfeminist generation.[26] (One died recently at the age of twenty-six; the surviving four range in age from twenty-three to thirty-one.) To varying degrees, all of the daughters distanced themselves from feminist identity and ideology, in some cases in conscious reaction against what they regard as the excesses of their mothers' earlier feminist views. At the same time, however, most of the daughters semiconsciously incorporated feminist principles into their expectations and strategies for family and work. A brief description of the family and work histories and gender consciousness of Dotty's and Pam's oldest, and most professionally successful, daughters illustrates this depoliticized incorporation of feminist thought.

Pam's oldest daughter, Lanny, is twenty-three. Like Dotty's oldest daughter, Lyn, she is a designer-drafter, who received her initial training in a feminist-inspired skills program. She is now in her second marriage and has one child from each marriage. Lanny dropped out of high school and at seventeen married a truck driver who moves electronics equipment and whom she describes as totally uncommunica-

[26] Indeed, the first media use of the term *postfeminist* to catch my attention was in the title of an essay about women in their late twenties: Susan Bolotin, "Voices from the Post-Feminist Generation," *New York Times Magazine*, October 17, 1982.

tive and addicted to drugs. Staying home with their baby, she found herself isolated and unbearably lonely. Pam encouraged Lanny's entry into a drafting course given by a county agency, and Lanny soon found ready employment in electronics via various temporary agencies.[27] After she discovered her husband's narcotics addiction and convinced him to enter a residential detox program, Lanny spent a brief period as a welfare mother. Although she hated drafting, she "job-shopped" frequently to raise her income sufficiently to support herself and her daughter. She was earning fourteen dollars an hour, without benefits, in 1985, when she met her present husband, Ken, at one of her workplaces, where, until a layoff, he was an expediter in the purchasing department for eight dollars an hour.

Lanny does not consider herself a feminist and has never been active or interested in politics. She hates her work but has no desire to be a homemaker and is perfectly willing to support her husband if he wants to stay home and take care of the children, or if, as they hope, she can afford to send him to engineering school. She would like to become an interior designer.

Although Lanny started out in a rather traditional working-class marriage, she is an authentic postfeminist. She was not able to tolerate the isolation, boredom, and emotional deprivation of that traditional marriage. Lanny's goals are to combine marriage to a nurturant, communicative, co-parenting man (as she perceives Ken) with full-time work at a job she truly enjoys. There is an ease to Lanny's attitudes about the gender division of labor at home and at work, and about gender norms more generally, that is decidedly postfeminist. These are not political issues to Lanny or even conscious points of personal struggle. She did actively reject her traditionally gendered first marriage but did not conceptualize it that way. Lanny takes for granted her right to be flexible about family and work priorities. Remarkably, Ken appears to be equally flexible and equally oblivious to feminist influences on his notably enlightened attitudes.

The postfeminism of Dotty's oldest daughter, Lyn, however, represents a somewhat more conscious and ambivalent response to feminism. Like Lanny, Lyn was a high school dropout who took a variety of low-wage service sector jobs. But unlike Lanny, the father of her child, with whom she cohabited, left during her pregnancy, making Lyn an unwed welfare mother. Lyn got off welfare by moonlighting at an electronics security job while developing her successful career in drafting.

[27] The very concept of "temporary" employment is being reshaped by postindustrial labor practices. High-tech industries in the Silicon Valley make increasing use of temporary agencies to provide "flexible staffing" and to cut employee benefits. In 1985 one of every two hundred workers in the United States but one of sixty workers in the Silicon Valley held a "temporary" job. See David Beers, " 'Temps'—High-Tech's Ace in the Hole," *San Bernardino Sun*, May 28, 1985.

She became a hybrid designer at one of the world's major semiconductor companies. Unlike Lanny, Lyn loves her work in drafting, although she is constantly anxious, exhausted, and deeply frustrated by the extreme demands, stress, and unpredictability of her working conditions and by their incompatibility with her needs as a single mother. There have been long periods when Lyn hardly ever saw her son and depended on her parents and friends to fill in for baby-sitters.

Lyn's desire to find a father for her son was a major motive for her brief marriage to a man who soon abused her. She has lived alone with her son since she divorced her husband six years ago. Although Lyn is proud and fiercely independent, during the period of my fieldwork she somewhat ambivalently pursued a marital commitment from her somewhat resistant boyfriend, Tom. Tom, like Lanny's husband, Ken, appeared unthreatened by Lyn's greater career drive and income as well as flexible about gender norms generally. But, he was much less willing or able than Ken to commit himself to the long-term responsibilities of marriage and parenthood.

Lyn is aware of sex discrimination at work and of issues of gender injustice generally and will occasionally challenge these by herself. Yet more explicitly than Lanny, Lyn distances herself from a feminist identity which she regards as unnecessarily hostile and occasionally petty: "I do not feel like a feminist, because to me my mother is a perfect feminist. . . . If someone asks her to make coffee, she first has to determine if it is because she is a woman." Upon reflection, Lyn acknowledges that it is the word *feminist* that she does not like "because of the way I was brought up with it. It meant slapping people in the face with it. . . . I do what I think is right, and if I am asked, I tell them why. . . . Honestly I guess I am a very strong feminist, but I don't have to beat people with it."

I consider Lyn a stronger postfeminist than feminist because of her thoroughly individual and depoliticized relationship to feminist issues. She cannot imagine being active politically on any issue, not even one like battering, which she experienced: "I leave them for people like my mother who can make issues out of that, because I don't see it that way. I'll help the neighbor next door whose husband is beating her to death . . . but I do it my way. My way is not in a public form. I am very different from my mother." Equally postfeminist are the ways Lyn fails both to credit feminist struggles for the career opportunities for women she takes for granted or to blame sexism or corporations for the male-oriented work schedules and demands that jeopardize her family needs. She would like, for example, to have a second child but accepts the "fact" that a second child does not fit with a successful career. Lyn shares Lanny's postfeminist expectations for family and work, that is, combining marriage to a communicative, egalitarian man with motherhood and a successful, engaging career. While Lanny has achieved more of the former, Lyn has more of the latter.

The relationships between postindustrialism, family turbulence, and postfeminism are nuanced and dialectical. Family crisis, as manifested in escalating rates of divorce and single-mother households, contributes both to the peculiar gender stratification of this postindustrial workforce and to a limited potential for feminist consciousness. Marital instability continually refuels a large, cheap female labor pool that underwrites the feminization of the postindustrial proletariat and of poverty.[28] But this crudely gender-stratified occupational structure further destabilizes gender relationships and family life. Moreover, the skewed wages and salaries available to white men help to inflate housing costs for everyone, contributing thereby to the rapid erosion of the male breadwinner family wage.[29]

One consequence of family instability in such an environment seems to have been an initial openness on the part of many women, like Dotty and Pam, to feminist ideas. Feminism served many mothers of the postfeminist generation well as an ideology to ease the transition from an unhappy 1950s-style marriage and for providing support for efforts to develop independent career goals. Neither feminism nor other progressive movements have been as successful, however, in addressing the structural inequalities of postindustrial occupational structure or the individualist, fast-track culture that makes all too difficult the formation of successful, intimate relations on an egalitarian or any other basis. Organized religion, particularly evangelical varieties, may offer more effective support to troubled family relationships in these circumstances.

I believe this explains the attractiveness of various postfeminist ideologies and strategies for achieving intimacy, or just for surviving in a profoundly insecure milieu. Postfeminist strategies correspond to

[28] The effects of the relationship between marital instability, female production work, and poverty are not confined to the United States. As many have noted, in the postindustrial economy, women work on a "global assembly line." Maria Patricia Fernandez-Kelly discusses the effects of these international processes on Mexican women who work in electronics and garment factories on the Mexican-U.S. border in "Mexican Border Industrialization, Female Labor Force Participation, and Migration," in *Women, Men, and the International Division of Labor,* ed. June Nash and Maria Patricia Fernandez-Kelly (Albany, 1983), pp. 205–23.

[29] More work needs to be done on how the practice of one pattern of family life by some constrains options for others. For a sensitive analysis of other unanticipated feedback effects of the electronics industry on the social ecology of the Silicon Valley, see AnnaLee Saxenian, "Silicon Chips and Spatial Structure: The Industrial Basis of Urbanization in Santa Clara County, California" (Master's thesis, University of California, Berkeley, 1980).

different generational and individual experiences with feminism and with postindustrial family and work conditions. For many women of the "mother" generation, feminism has become as much a burden as a means of support. Although once it helped them to reform or exit from unsatisfactory relationships, now it can intensify the pain and difficulty of the compromises most women must make to mediate the destructive effects of postindustrial society on family and personal relationships. Too seldom today can women find committed mates, let alone ones who also would pass feminist muster.

Perhaps this helps to account for Pam's simultaneous turn to religion and her subtle adaptation of patriarchal, evangelical Christian forms to feminist ends and for Dotty's return to, but also reform of, a previously unsatisfactory marriage coupled with her shift from political engagement to paid work and organized religion. In a climate and stage of their lives characterized by diminished expectations, both seek support for the compromises with, and commitments to, family and work they have chosen to make rather than for greater achievement or independence. Without repudiating feminism, both Dotty and Pam have distanced themselves from feminist identity or activism. By contrast, their postfeminist oldest daughters take for granted the gains in female career opportunities and male participation in child rearing and domestic work for which feminists of their mothers' generation struggled. Lanny and Lyn do not conceptualize their troubling postindustrial work and family problems in political terms. To them feminism and politics appear irrelevant or threatening.

These diverse forms of postfeminism, I believe, are semiconscious responses to feminism's unwitting role as midwife to the new family and work conditions in postindustrial America. Some versions are more reactionary, some more progressive, but all, I believe, differ from antifeminism. They represent women's attempts both to retain and to depoliticize the egalitarian family and work ideals of the second wave. This is an inherently contradictory project and one that presents feminists with an enigmatic dilemma. Is it possible to devise a personal politics that respects the political and personal anxieties and exhaustion of women contending with the destabilized family and work conditions of the postindustrial era? To do so without succumbing to conservative nostalgia for patriarchal familial and religious forms is a central challenge for contemporary feminism.

Contributors

LAURA ANKER is an Associate Professor in the American Studies Program at the State University of New York, College at Old Westbury. She has published articles on intelligence testing, business and government ties, and women and immigration. She is currently completing a book entitled "In Their Own Voices: Southern and Eastern European Immigrant Women and Families in Industrial Connecticut, 1890–1940."

BARBARA BAIR is an associate of the James B. Coleman African Studies Center, University of California at Los Angeles. A recent Rockefeller Humanist-in-Residence at the Institute for Research on Women, Rutgers University, she is the author of critical essays on Willa Cather and May Sarton, the coeditor of a forthcoming multidisciplinary anthology on minority women and health, and the associate editor of *Marcus Garvey: Life and Lessons* and *The Marcus Garvey and UNIA Papers*, vols. 6 and 7.

AVA BARON is Professor of Sociology at Rider College. She is editor of *Work Engendered: Toward a New History of Men, Women, and Work* (1991) and is currently completing her book "Men's Work and the Woman Question: The Masculinization of Printing, 1830–1920."

PATRICIA CLINE COHEN is Associate Professor of History at the University of California at Santa Barbara. She is the author of *A Calculating People: The Spread of Numeracy in Early America* (1982) and is currently working on two projects, a book on the Helen Jewett murder case of 1836 and another on gender and travel in the early republic.

LAURA LEE DOWNS is an Assistant Professor of History at the University of Michigan, Ann Arbor. She has published essays in *Social History* and *Comparative Studies in Society and History* and is currently at work on a comparative study of employers' attitudes toward women metalworkers entitled "Manufacturing Inequality."

LINDA GORDON is the Florence Kelly Professor of History at the University of Wisconsin/Madison. Her books include *Heroes of Their Own Lives: The Politics and History of Family Violence* (1988) and *Women, the State, and Welfare* (1990). Her first book, *Women's Body, Women's Right: The History of Birth Control in America,* was reissued in 1990 in a revised edition with two new chapters on contemporary reproductive-rights politics. Her *America's Working Women,* coedited with Rosalyn Baxandall and Susan Reverby, will be revised and reissued in 1993.

PATRICIA A. GOZEMBA is an activist, teacher, researcher, and gardener. Her most recently published work focuses on union organizing in higher education, the anti–Ku Klux Klan movement, and activist lesbians. She is a professor of English and Women's Studies at Salem State College, Salem, Massachusetts.

GAY L. GULLICKSON is Associate Professor of History at the University of Maryland, College Park. She is the author of *The Spinners and Weavers of Auffay* and is currently working on a book on the women of the Paris Commune.

DOROTHY O. HELLY is Professor of History and Women's Studies at Hunter College, City University of New York. She is the author of *Livingstone's Legacy: Horace Waller and Victorian Mythmaking* (1987); a coauthor of *Women's Realities, Women's Choices: An Introduction to Women's Studies* (1983), now under revision, and currently working on a biography of journalist and imperialist Flora Shaw/Lady Lugard (1852–1929), in collaboration with Helen Callaway.

DOLORES JANIEWSKI lectures in U.S. History at Victoria University at Wellington, New Zealand. She is the author of *Sisterhood Denied: Race, Gender, and Class in a New South Community* (1985) and a contributor to essays in three forthcoming volumes: *Work Engendered: Toward a New History of Men, Women, and Work; Historians of the American South;* and *Visible Women: Essays in Honor of Anne Scott.* She is currently working on a study of gender and race in North Carolina politics, 1865–1930.

PENELOPE D. JOHNSON is Professor of History at New York University. She is the author of *Prayer, Patronage, and Power: the Abbey of la Trinité, Vendôme, 1032–1187* (1981) and has just finished a work on medieval nuns, *Equal in Monastic Profession: Religious Women in Medieval France,* published by the University of Chicago Press (1991).

JANET KAHN is a sociologist who teaches at Tufts University and the Sunray School. She works in the Community Health Program and conducts research in the areas of sexuality, medical sociology, feminist ethics, "deep ecology," Native American wisdom, and the sociology of consciousness. She is also a massage therapist working with incest survivors and people with AIDS. The oral histories upon which her chapter is based were conducted as part of her work with the Boston Area Lesbian and Gay History Project.

NANNERL O. KEOHANE has been President and Professor of Political Science at Wellesley College since 1981. She has taught at Stanford University and Swarthmore College and is the author of *Philosophy and the State in France* (1980) and coeditor of *Feminist Theory: A Critique of Ideology* (1982). Her next project is a study of the social theory of Virginia Woolf.

ALICE KESSLER-HARRIS is Professor of History and Director of the Women's Studies Program at Rutgers University. She is the author of *Women Have Always Worked: A Historical Overview* (1981); *Out to Work: A History of Wage-Earning Women in the United States* (1982); and *A Women's Wage: Historical Meanings and Social Consequences* (1990). She is now working on a book on the uses of gender in the construction of social policy in the twentieth-century United States.

MOLLY LADD-TAYLOR is Assistant Professor of History at Carleton College and editor of *Raising a Baby the Government Way: Mothers' Letters to the Children's Bureau, 1915–1932* (1986). She is completing a book entitled "Mother-Work: Mothers, Child Welfare, and the State, 1890–1930."

LESLIE P. PEIRCE is Assistant Professor of Near Eastern Studies at Cornell University. Her book on the imperial harem and Ottoman politics will soon be published by Oxford University Press. She is currently studying family/neighborhood interaction using court records and the responsa of Muslim jurisconsults and is also preparing a translation of correspondence between a seventeenth-century Ottoman regent queen mother and her grand viziers.

SUSAN M. REVERBY is the Whitehead Associate Professor in Critical Thought and Director of Women's Studies at Wellesley College. She is the author of *Ordered to Care: The Dilemma of American Nursing* (1987); coeditor of *America's Working Women* (1976) and *Health Care in America: Essays in Social History* (1979); and editor of a multivolume reprint series, *The History of American Nursing* (1984–85). She is now working on a study of Eunice Rivers, the nurse in the Tuskegee Syphilis "Experiment" and a revised coedited edition of *America's Working Women.*

JESSIE M. RODRIQUE received her Ph.D. in American History at the University of Massachusetts at Amherst. She is currently working at the National Museum of American History in Washington, D.C.

ELLEN ROSS teaches history and women's studies at Ramapo College of New Jersey. Her book, *Love and Labor in Outcast London: Motherhood, 1870–1918,* will be published by Oxford University Press in 1992.

LONDA SCHIEBINGER is Associate Professor of History and Women's Studies at Pennsylvania State University. She is the author of *The Mind Has No Sex? Women in the Origins of Modern Science* (1989) and is currently a Guggenheim Fellow, working on a book, "Sex Among the Kingdoms of Nature: The Politics of Eighteenth-Century Natural Science."

ANN-LOUISE SHAPIRO is Associate Professor of History at Wesleyan University, where she teaches in the History Department and in the Women's Studies Program. She is the author of *Housing the Poor of Paris, 1850–1902* (1985) and has published several articles on the meaning of female criminality that are part of a forthcoming book, "Breaking the Codes: Interpretations of Female Criminality in Fin-de-Siècle Paris."

BARBARA SICHERMAN is William R. Kenan, Jr., Professor of American Institutions and Values at Trinity College. She is the author of *Alice Hamilton: A Life in Letters* (1984) and *The Quest for Mental Health in America, 1880–1917* (1980) and coeditor of *Notable American Women: The Modern Period* (1980). She is currently working on a book, "Gender and the Culture of Reading in Late-Victorian America."

JUDITH STACEY is Professor of Sociology and Women's Studies at the University of California at Davis. She is the author of *Patriarchy and*

Socialist Revolution in China (1983) and of an enthnographic study of family change in the Silicon Valley, which the essay in this collection foreshadowed, *Brave New Families: Stories of Domestic Upheaval in Late Twentieth-Century America* (1990).

DIANE WILLEN is Associate Professor of History at Georgia State University. She is the author of *John Russell, First Earl of Bedford* (1981) and articles on women's history. She is now working on a book, "Godly Women in Early Modern England: Puritanism and Gender."

Index

Library of Congress Cataloging-in-Publication Data

Berkshire Conference on the History of Women (7th : 1987 : Wellesley
College)
Gendered domains : rethinking public and private in women's history : essays from the 7th Berkshire Conference on the History of Women / edited by Dorothy O. Helly, Susan M. Reverby.
p. cm.
Includes bibliographical references and index.
ISBN 0-8014-2444-5 (cloth : alk. paper). — ISBN 0-8014-9702-7 (paper : alk. paper)
1. Women—History—Congresses. 2. Women in public life—History—Congresses.
I. Helly, Dorothy O. II. Reverby. Susan. III. Title.
HQ1121.B43 1987
305.4'09—dc20 91-55561